Multinational Enterprise, Political Risk and Organisational Change

Hitherto, the organisation of international business has been studied mostly from a managerial point of view or by examining the relationship between firms and the economy. Yet the development of the modern, multinational firm—the most important type of business organisation—has been strongly influenced by the conflicts that bedevilled the 20th century. The volatile macroeconomic and political environments experienced by international business point to how important it is to study political risk. Consequently, *Multinational Enterprise, Political Risk and Organisational Change: From Total War to Cold War* breaks new ground: it argues that non-market elements and historical context are key to understanding the way international business has been organised. This edited volume offers an historical approach to analysing how multinational enterprise has developed over time and around the world, through a series of well-crafted chapters, on important topics in international economic and business history, written by authorities in their respective fields of study and research. The study is based on the underlying premise that the coming of the two world wars, the devastating and long-term consequences of such total wars, and the ideological challenge of the Cold War acted as a pivot points in shaping the nature and character of multinational firms. By examining such phenomena, this study offers insights to anyone who has an interest in business, economic or political history, management and business studies, or international relations.

Neil Forbes is Professor of International History and Associate Dean Research, Faculty of Arts and Humanities, Coventry University, UK.

Takafumi Kurosawa is Professor of Economic Policy at the Graduate School of Economics, Kyoto University, where he received his PhD in 2001.

Ben Wubs is Professor of International Business History at ESHCC, Erasmus University Rotterdam, and Appointed Project Professor at the Graduate School of Economics, Kyoto University.

Routledge International Studies in Business History

Series editors: Jeffrey Fear and Christina Lubinski

World Market Transformation
Inside the German Fur Capital Leipzig 1870–1939
Robrecht Declercq

Industries and Global Competition
A History of Business Beyond Borders
Bram Bouwens, Pierre-Yves Donzé, and Takafumi Kurosawa

Commodity Trading, Globalization and the Colonial Word
Spinning the Web of the Global Market
Christof Dejung

Family Dynasties
The Evolution of Global Business in Scandinavia
Hans Sjögren

Multinational Business and Transnational Regions
A transnational business history of energy transition in the Rhine region, 1945–1973
Marten Boon

Making Managers in Canada, 1945–1995
Companies, Community Colleges, and Universities
Jason Russell

The Evolution of Business
Interpretative Theory, History and Firm growth
Ellen Mølgaard Korsager

Multinational Enterprise, Political Risk and Organisational Change
From Total War to Cold War
Edited by Neil Forbes, Takafumi Kurosawa and Ben Wubs

For a full list of titles in this series, please visit www.routledge.com

Multinational Enterprise, Political Risk and Organisational Change
From Total War to Cold War

Edited by Neil Forbes,
Takafumi Kurosawa and Ben Wubs

Routledge
Taylor & Francis Group
NEW YORK AND LONDON

First published 2019
by Routledge
605 Third Avenue, New York, NY 10017

and by Routledge
2 Park Square, Milton Park, Abingdon, Oxon, OX14 4RN

First issued in paperback 2020

Routledge is an imprint of the Taylor & Francis Group, an informa business

Library of Congress Cataloging-in-Publication Data
A catalog record for this book has been requested

ISBN 13: 978-0-367-73220-2 (pbk)
ISBN 13: 978-1-138-04782-2 (hbk)

Typeset in Sabon
by Apex CoVantage, LLC

The editors would like to dedicate this work to Chris Kobrak, dear friend and esteemed colleague, who was drafting his contribution to the volume before his untimely death.

Contents

Acknowledgements

We gratefully acknowledge the support provided by the Japanese Society for the Promotion of Science for sponsoring, in 2012, a short-term stay in Japan by means of the JSPS Invitation Fellowship for Research, and also for awarding Grants-in-Aid for Scientific Research (KAKEN), (Project code 15KK0087, 16K13377 and 17H02550). This assistance enabled the ideas that frame this volume to be first adumbrated and then developed, not least during the World Economic History Congress, 2015, held in Kyoto, which provided an excellent forum for discussion; we would like to extend our thanks to all those who participated in our panel session—several of the contributors to the panel are represented in this volume—and to the local organising committee for hosting such a successful Congress. We would also like to acknowledge the opportunity which the European Business History Association Annual Congress, held in Bergen in 2016, afforded us to present a conceptual framework for this study. The supportive and insightful comments we gratefully received from colleagues at that point encouraged us to invite authorial contributions from further, leading scholars. Finally, we would like to express our thanks to Coventry University, Kyoto University and Erasmus University, Rotterdam, for extending the resources, of one kind or another, that have facilitated the work involved in preparing and editing this study.

Contributors

Prof. Dr. Ralf Banken is Economic and Business Historian at Goethe-University Frankfurt am Main. He is currently working on West German-Dutch trade relations in the 18th century. His research focusses on topics of German and European industrialisation, the international corporate history of the 18th to 20th centuries, the economic history of the Third Reich and the history of consumption in Germany. His significant publications include: *Hitlers Steuerstaat. Die Steuerpolitik im Dritten Reich*. Berlin (2018); (together with Ray Stokes) *Building on air: The international industrial gases industry, 1886–2006*. Cambridge (2016); *Edelmetallmangel und Großraubwirtschaft. Die Entwicklung des deutschen Edelmetallsektors und die Degussa AG 1933–1945*. Berlin (2009); (together with Johannes Bähr and Thomas Fleming) *MAN. The History of a German Industrial Enterprise*. München (2009); *Die Industrialisierung der Saarregion*. 2 Vols. Stuttgart (2000 and 2003).

Marten Boon is a researcher at the University of Oslo and an affiliated researcher at the Norwegian University of Science and Technology in Trondheim. He received his PhD from Erasmus University, Rotterdam, in 2014. His thesis won the dissertation prize of the European Business History Association in 2016. Boon has published in *Business History* and *Business History Review* and is the author of *Multinational Enterprise and Transnational Regions: A Transnational Business History of Energy Transition in the Rhine Region, 1945–1973*, Abingdon, UK (2018).

Marcelo Bucheli is Associate Professor at Gies College of Business, University of Illinois at Urbana-Champaign, USA. He is the author of *Bananas and Business: The United Fruit Company in Colombia, 1899–2000*, New York University Press (2005), and co-editor (with R. Daniel Wadhwani) of *Organizations in Time: History, Theory, Methods*, Oxford University Press (2014). Other publications include articles and essays on the political strategies of multinational corporations in a historical perspective and on the integration of historical methods in management and organisation studies. He was a John H. Dunning Visiting Fellow in International Business at the Henley Business School, University of Reading, and a Newcomen Fellow in Business History at Harvard Business School. He earned his PhD in history at Stanford University and has a BSc and MA in Economics from Universidad de los Andes (Colombia).

Neil Forbes is Professor of International History and Associate Dean Research, Faculty of Arts and Humanities, Coventry University, UK. His research interests focus on the interaction of foreign policy formulation with the practices of multinational enterprise during the interwar years, Anglo-American relations and the rise of the Third Reich, and cultural heritage (especially in relation to conflict, contested landscapes and the memorialisation of war). Recent publications include: 'The Foreign Office, Foreign Policy and Commerce: Anglo-German Relations in the 1930s', in *The Foreign Office, Commerce and British Foreign Policy in the Twentieth Century* edited by John Fisher, Effie G. H. Pedaliu, and Richard Smith (2016); and 'The Flows of International Finance after the First World War: the Bank of England and Hungary, 1920–1939', in *The Impact of the First World War on International Business* edited by Andrew Smith, Kevin D. Tennent, and Simon Mollan (2017). As Principal Investigator or Co-ordinator, he has played a leading role in several UK and European research projects. He is a member of several advisory bodies and acts in a strategic capacity for UK Research Councils.

Ryo Izawa is Associate Professor in the Faculty of Economics of Shiga University, Japan. His research fields are business history, international taxation history and international business. He is the author of 'The Formation of Companies for Tax Avoidance: The Relationship between UK Multinationals and International Double Taxation in the Interwar Period' (*Business and Economic History On-Line,* Vol. 13, 2015), and 'International Double Taxation and British Investment in the United States from the First World War to the 1945 UK-US Tax Treaty' (*Japanese Research in Business History*, Vol. 35, 2019, *forthcoming*).

Takeo Kikkawa is Professor of Management, Graduate School of Management, Tokyo University of Science. He is also Professor Emeritus at the University of Tokyo and at Hitotsubashi University. He was an Associate Professor at Aoyama Gakuin University and has been a Visiting Scholar at Harvard Business School and a Visiting Professor at St. Gallen University, at Yonsei University, and at Berlin Free University. He is a Past President of the Business History Society of Japan (2013–2016). His research focusses on Japanese business history, especially the history of the energy industry. His publications include, as co-editor, *Policies for Competitiveness: Comparing Business-Government*

Relationships in the 'Golden Age of Capitalism', Oxford University Press, Oxford, UK and New York, USA (1999), and also *Ethical Capitalism: Shibusawa Eiichi and Business Leadership in Global Perspective*, University of Toronto Press, Toronto, Canada, Buffalo, USA and London, UK (2017).

Judit Klement PhD, Dr. habil, is Associate Professor at Eötvös Loránd University, Budapest, and Research Fellow at the Institute of History in the Research Centre for the Humanities, Hungarian Academy of Sciences. She received her PhD in economic and social history from Eötvös Loránd University, Budapest; her study focussed on the entrepreneurs of the Budapest flour-milling industry, in the second half of the 19th century. She has published two books and a number of papers about the flour-milling industry, companies and entrepreneurs of 19th-century Budapest and their connection to the global economy. Her main research interests are in business history and Hungarian capitalism in the 19th and 20th centuries and in the global economy. Since 2003, she has taught at Eötvös Loránd University, specialising in history, cultural heritage studies and archival science. She has been a member of the editorial boards of two historical journals since their foundations—the *Hungarian Historical Review* (since 2012) and the *Korall Journal for Social History* (since 2000).

Takafumi Kurosawa is Professor of Economic Policy at the Graduate School of Economics, Kyoto University, where he received his PhD in 2001. His dissertation analysed the Swiss economy and the formation of cross-border economic regions in the 19th century. His English publications deal with multinational enterprises and political risks, industrial clusters, the paper and pulp industry, industrial policy, and historiography of business history, examining European and Japanese cases. In 2010, he published the Japanese translation of the final report of the so-called Bergier Commission (*Switzerland, National Socialism and the Second World War*, edited by the Independent Commission of Experts Switzerland- Second World War, 2001), adding findings of original research by Japanese scholars as a second section of the volume. Other recent publications include (with co-editors Bram Bouwens and Pierre-Yves Donzé), *Industries and Global Competition: A History of Business Beyond Borders* Abingdon, UK (2018). He is Programme Director of the International Dual Award Doctoral Programme in the field of business history, set up in conjunction with the University of Glasgow.

Luciano Segreto is Full Professor of International Economic History at the School of Political Sciences of the University of Florence, a permanent Visiting Professor of Corporate Governance Models at Gdansk University of Technology since 2015, and Adjunct Professor of Comparative

Business History and Corporate Governance at Bocconi University in Milan since 2011. His main interests are in the history of family capitalism, international business, banking history, and corporate governance. He is involved in many international research programmes dealing with international timber trade, commodities and the European model of capitalism. Among his recent works are: L'economia internazionale dopo la fine della Guerra Fredda, Bologna: il Mulino (2018); 'I protagonisti della grande distribuzione in Europa', in *Dalle marche al marchio. La Rinascente 1970–2017*, edited by Franco Amatori, Milan: Egea (2017); 'La degenerazione dello Stato imprenditore', in *L'approdo mancato. Economia, politica e società in Italia dopo il miracolo economico*, edited by Franco Amatori, *Annali*, LI, Milan, Feltrinelli (2017); (with Miguel Lopez-Morell) 'Did Price Really Matter? The International Mercury Cartel (1928–1957)', in *Business History Review* (June 2015); (with Ben Wubs) 'Resistance of the Defeated. German and Italian Big Business and the American Anti-trust Policy, 1945–57', in *Enterprise and Society* (February 2014).

Mark Spoerer is Professor of Economic and Social History at the University of Regensburg, Germany. He has published on several topics of German and European economic, social and business history, among which are public finances in 19th-century Germany, economic and business history in Weimar and Nazi Germany, forced labour in the Second World War, and the post-war, European Union's Common Agricultural Policy. He is the author of *C&A: A Family Firm in Germany, the Netherlands and the United Kingdom, 1911–1961*, C. H. Beck, Munich (2016).

Ray Stokes holds Chair of Business History at the University of Glasgow, where he is director of the Centre for Business History in Scotland and Head of Subject in Economic and Social History. His research has focussed on a range of themes at the intersection of business history, history of technology and environmental history. He is the author or co-author of nine monographs, including, most recently (with Martin Johnson and Tobias Arndt), *The Thalidomide Catastrophe: How It Happened, Who Was Responsible and Why the Search for Justice Continues after More Than Six Decades*, Exeter (2018); and (with Ralf Banken), *Building on Air: The international industrial gases industry*, Cambridge, (2016). Stokes is a Fellow of the Academy of Social Sciences and Past President of the European Business History Association.

Ben Wubs is Professor of International Business History at ESHCC, Erasmus University Rotterdam, and Appointed Project Professor at the Graduate School of Economics, Kyoto University. He is engaged in various research projects related to multinationals, business systems, transnational economic regions, Dutch-German economic relations and the transnational fashion industry. His publications include: *International Business and National War Interests. Unilever between Reich and Empire* Abingdon (2008); (with Keetie Sluyterman) *Over Grenzen. Multinationals en de Nederlandse Markteconomie* Amsterdam (2009); (with Ralf Banken), *The Rhine Economy. A Transnational Economic History* Baden-Baden (2017); and (with Regina Lee Blaszczyk), *The Fashion Forecasters: The Hidden History of Color and Trend Prediction* London (2018). He is a council member of the European Business History Association. From 2013 to 2016, he was a Principal Investigator on a HERA II research project into the transnational connections of the fashion industry since 1945. He is Programme Director of an Erasmus Mundus project GLOCAL (Global Markets and Local Creativities), an International Master's set up by the Universities of Glasgow, Göttingen, Barcelona and Erasmus University Rotterdam.

Introduction

Multinational Enterprise in the Century of Total War and Cold War: Political Risk and Organisational Change

Neil Forbes, Takafumi Kurosawa and Ben Wubs

In 1989, after the fall of the Berlin Wall, Francis Fukuyama predicted 'The End of History' and the victory of liberal market institutions all of over the world.[1] His predictions in the seminal article and his renowned book, which was published three year later, show, however, at least one thing: making predictions of such magnitude is impossible. The world has changed since his publications, but in the opposite direction of what was predicted. Rather than liberal institutions conquering the world, authoritarian-style governments and economic nationalism appeared to be gaining the upper hand, and clearly history did not come to an end either. Furthermore, a separation of the economic and political dimension has not taken place, and in the last decade we are actually observing a return to a political economy in which the political dimensions have become inseparable from the economic and business ones. The hand did not 'vanish' or become 'invisible'; on the contrary, it has become obvious again how powerful and formative political action can be.[2] Social scientists have discussed the role of institutions in order to understand better the role of markets; but the impact of non-market elements, such as protectionism, nationalism and war, have been largely ignored, particularly in the last 30 years. Nevertheless, relatively recent developments have shown how volatile international business can be and how important it is to assess political risks. In recent years, expressions of populist 'revolt' and nationalist sentiment on both sides of the Atlantic have seriously challenged the post-war order built on Western, liberal values. It has become crystal clear that studying international business and the organisational structures of multinational enterprises (MNEs) is well nigh impossible without taking the state of international relations into account. This book aims, therefore, to demonstrate that non-market conditions have played a role in the global organisation of international business in the course of the 19th and 20th centuries.

What impact did political risk and nationalism have on global business? Have wars and other conflicts caused by national interests and identities retarded or even reversed the trend towards globalisation? When faced with political and geopolitical threats such as war, occupation, expropriation, economic blockade and sanctions, requisition, persecution, or boycott, how did MNEs and other international economic actors manage (or fail) to overcome the situation they found themselves in? Also, how did the response of economic entities like MNEs transform global business, or act to change political risks and the sovereign state system? Furthermore, what insight does the examination of such phenomena present to management history and international business research?

In this book, risks arising from political phenomena including nationalism, are regarded as a part of various 'non-market risks'. Non-market risks include political as well as natural disasters and other risks.[3] One cannot always draw a clear boundary between political and other non-market risks, and market and economic risks. In many cases, political risk works indirectly to influence MNEs and international economic activities through changes in economic conditions (such as price, volume of transactions and transaction conditions) in the market, rather than directly. Nonetheless, there are good reasons to regard political risk as a subject in its own right.

First, political and geopolitical phenomena may directly inhibit or promote business activities without waiting for market mediation, and therefore specific analysis is required. Secondly, political risk not only affects the profitability and competitiveness of the firm, but may also become an existential threat to the corporate assets, life and property of managers, employees and shareholders. Thirdly, the dominant theoretical frameworks in management history and international business base themselves on economic logic, and the problem of political risk tends to be treated as an accidental, exogenous variable and as such has not been considered sufficiently. Although risks will not hurt companies unless they materialise, once an awareness of such risks is developed, it triggers a response by economic entities. Risk is also an economic opportunity. If one entity can avoid risks more skilfully than the others, it puts this entity in a relatively advantageous position in market competition. In this book, therefore, we focus on actual threats, the risks of those threats, and the actors' perceptions and expectations of those risks and responses.

Nationalism is a polysemous concept, but this chapter uses it in its broadest sense. In addition to perceptions and acts based on patriotism, nationalism also more widely encompasses action, including war, taken by a state to advance its own interests. It is not enough to discuss the relationship between 'business and state' and 'business and government' by focussing on a single state. Rather, the main focus of analysis should be on the fact that the international state-system comprises sovereign states who compete with each and whose relationships at times fluctuate between amicable and hostile. Based on this perspective, this study considers the risks caused by conflict, especially between sovereign states, and between sovereign states and national and transnational companies, while keeping in mind general political risk.

The First World War was a turning point in the development of the global economy: international trade declined dramatically and nation states began to intervene directly in the economy. Non-domestic firms were seen (and defined) more and more as foreign. National economics and gross domestic product became watchwords for economists and policy-makers during the interwar period.[4] Simultaneously, trade protectionism, served to stimulate multinational manufacturing as well, because companies opened factories in protected, and sometimes even autarkic, markets. However, after the Second World War, the role of the state did not diminish. In the Soviet Union and its satellites, the state was everywhere, but also in the West state intervention was comprehensive. The state was involved in the economy through, for example, procurement of products (including military matériel), nationalised industries, regulation, providing services, research and education, guardianship of property, finance and currency control, and taxation.[5] In order to continue in business, MNEs were required to adapt to domestic policies in this period.

This book comments on how macroeconomic and political environments shape the form and content of MNEs by focussing on the question of organisational change and innovation. The central idea of the book is based on the underlying premise that the coming of the two World Wars, the devastating and long-term consequences of such total wars, and the ideological challenge of the Cold War acted as a pivot points in shaping the nature and character of the contemporary firm—or, more particularly, multinational firms. Given the tendency of European companies to adapt to local markets and to take on a more decentralised structure than their American counterparts it is surprising that the impact of the world wars on the European corporate structure has not received more attention.[6]

The framework of analysis that we advance here takes a broad approach in both temporal and geographical terms: it embraces the period from the late 19th to the late 20th century and it is global in scope. Only by tracing the various turns in global history—from the age of European empires and the high tide of imperialism, through to post-colonial nationalism and ideological conflict in the Cold War—is it possible to mark continuity and discontinuity in the course of the historical development of MNEs. This is important because much of the existing literature on the subject of political risk and MNEs has typically been focussed on the Third Reich or fascism and, to a lesser extent, on the First World War.[7] However, the issue, although evident also before 1914, was of significance during much of the interwar years, and after 1945. Any analysis should be concerned not just with Germany and occupied Europe but also with smaller neutral states, the Western Hemisphere (US, Canada and Latin America) and many parts of Africa and Asia.[8]

From a transnational and international perspective, the purpose of the current study is to enquire into the extent these organisational changes had elements of duration and continuity and how far strategic responses can be explained by sector or product specificity, by different national or supranational circumstances and institutional structures as well as by the geographical spread of interests of respective firms. The focus of this book is on the question of how MNEs organised themselves in relation to political risk, and especially the extreme political risk presented by war. This includes, for example, consideration of the following: the design of cloaking measures as a general practice among European MNEs; the impact of taxation on organisational structures and global strategies (not merely as an external factor, but as an integral element that helps to explain the competitiveness, domiciliary location and nationality of MNEs); and the impact of corporate law on organisational structures and global strategies (the implications beyond the point of view of conventional, corporate governance).

The Interpretative Model

The contention put forward here is that the significance of both the direct consequences of the total wars of the 20th century, and the real and imagined threats during the Cold War, have been largely overlooked as the key factor in explaining the shape of MNEs. During wartime, human capital, tangible and intangible assets, capital and financial assets are all likely to be damaged or depleted; the normal manufacture, flow and sale of many goods is diverted to the meet the needs of fighting the war, and services, networks and information flows are all disrupted.

The relationship between firms and nation states changed fundamentally during wartime. The coming of total war dictated the creation of war economies.[9] Government intervention in controlling the economy resulted in the removal of a high degree of the room for manoeuvre that firms experienced during peacetime. State intervention took various forms: the levying of new taxes or greatly raised levels of taxation, the expropriation or freezing of enemy-owned assets, the imposition of exchange-controls, export sanctions and blockades.

Not only did war have a direct and immediate effect on the environment in which firms attempted to carry out business, 20th-century conflicts had profound and long-lasting direct, and indirect, consequences for MNEs. Changes in the world order included a reconfiguration of territories and market conditions, the creation of new political and economic systems, and a restructuring of industries and the nature of competitiveness.

The modern MNE faced two world wars, nationalism, and the division of global markets in the first half of the 20th century; companies were forced to address these challenges organisationally and strategically. With enterprises in the defeated states in Europe hesitant about foreign direct investment after the sequestration of their assets abroad during First World War, international cartels were favoured as a means to direct investment in the interwar period.[10] A variety of unique, ownership control-structures (originally devised for tax purposes and the effective distribution of dividends to shareholders), became a strategic defence mechanism against confiscation of assets in Germany and the occupied countries, as well as in the Allied countries, during the Second World War, with long-lasting organisational consequences. Companies shifted part of their global business from the European continent to the Western Hemisphere as a result of their organisational adaptations and introduced innovative and complex legal systems to mitigate the risk of state control. From the interwar years onwards, MNEs were challenged by punitive levels of double taxation, threats of nationalisation from the political left and economic nationalism from the extreme right, and expropriation in former colonies. In other respects, pre-war distinctions between government and business were elided: international consortia pursued transnational interests, with political actors promoting the interests of business, whilst those representing business sought to reflect national or supra-national interests. Cold War security concerns also shaped the corporate form, ownership and governance structure of MNEs.

The simplified interpretative model presented in Figure 0.1 suggests that, through history, the organisational structure of MNEs—their ownership, control and inter-firm networks—has been determined as much by

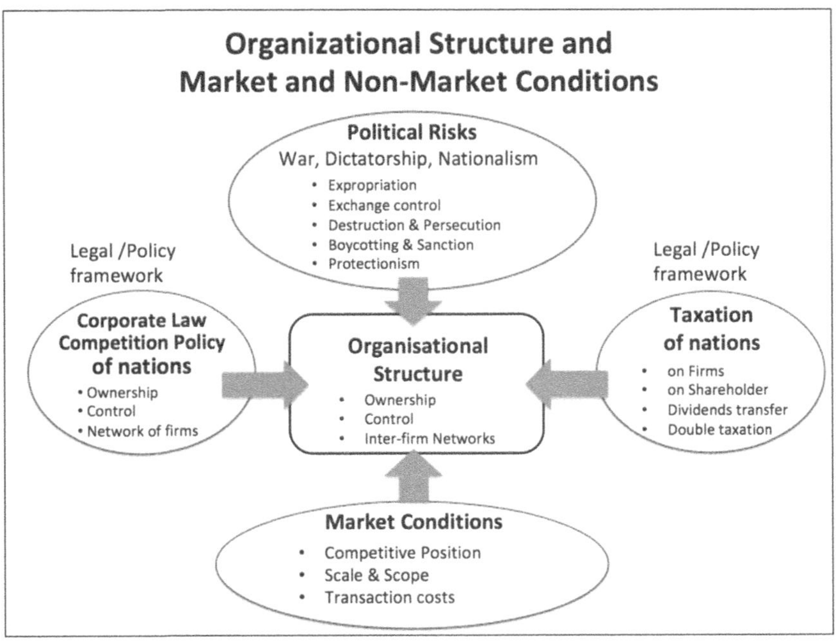

Figure 0.1

non-market forces as by questions of scale and scope, transaction costs, or managerial needs to allocate resources in response to market competition.[11] An MNE is, of course, an economic actor, but one that operates as a transnational business under political conditions and within several different national, legal frameworks. As such, it conducts business in a states-system comprising a multiplicity of sovereign entities and discrete jurisdictions. As a result, a dynamic of non-market forces is generated which creates opportunities and threats for MNEs and challenges for any one sovereign state. Tensions and conflicts are evident in various channels of interaction, especially in legal and policy arenas, namely the regulatory environment, accounting practice, corporate law, anti-trust law and, above all, taxation law. MNEs are economic actors, but they operate by definition within several different polities and national, legal frameworks and have to adapt to local political and legal conditions. These non-market forces created opportunities, challenges and threats, and formed political risks, all of which MNEs needed to address. The regulatory environment in different polities forced MNEs to respond strategically, which can explain organisational and legal innovations, and geographical shifts in international business in the long run.

Design of Organisational Structures

Capability to cope with the variety of political risks, namely expropriation, asset freezing, exchange control, economic blockade, boycotting and other, discriminatory actions, including persecution of individuals (managers, employees, shareholder and other stakeholders) became a crucial element in the survival and competitiveness of firms. Coping with these risks required MNEs to take conscious and calculated countermeasures in designing how businesses were structured and organised. Two interrelated considerations had to be taken into account: the geographical allocation of the business—its shareholders, assets and markets—and an organisational structure which, as far as possible, best served the geographical allocation.

These two dimensions of strategy and structure were discussed by Alfred Chandler.[12] However, the issue is broader than this because the nature and composition of a firm's shareholders and also the location of where it is registered should also be analysed. Three types of structural change are observable in the historical development of MNEs: first, a change of geographical distribution of business operations such as a withdrawal from or avoidance of a market, or diversification; second, reorganisation of the corporate structure in real terms resulting in evident change; third, reorganisation in nominal terms only, not intended to bring about fundamental change in the direction of the business. Whilst the first and second types have been discussed in the existing literature in terms of economic rationality and strategic management, the third development has received scant attention in business history literature, even though nominal change may itself have had an impact on the other types of change, and the changes interact with each other.

The concept of change in company structures that is no more than nominal may be viewed as a particular phenomenon that emerged as a political risk avoidance-strategy in the context of war and dictatorship. In the case of where the intention was to disguise ownership, the changes undertaken are described as 'cloaking' activities—a practice recognised as such by contemporaries. The first group of studies on cloaking—narrowly defined—focussed on German firms and those in neutral countries operating under conditions of war and dictatorship.[13] Actions to disguise either nationality (in terms of management, shareholders, employees and customers), or location (in terms of headquarters, registration, assets and markets), or both nationality and location were analysed. These studies took a critical view of such actions; the companies concerned were viewed through a lens of collaboration with the Nazi regime and were condemned on grounds of their ethical behaviour. A second group, of more recent studies, has revised this picture by emphasising that collaboration and accommodation in the Third Reich was often economically rational behaviour on the part of firms experiencing tension in their political relations with the Nazi regime.[14] In this context, cloaking is seen as a rational, management strategy to cope with not only host-country risk, but also home-country risk. Studies of Jewish-owned firms, firms in neutral countries, those domiciled in enemy states or occupied nations have supported this revised interpretation.[15]

Collectively, the relevant historiography has helped to clarify a number of issues. First, there was a diversity of forms and functions of cloaking; secondly, a variety of companies facing similar challenges adopted similar structures; thirdly, in many cases, the cloaking structures devised had no clear intention to disguise actions. Taking a narrow definition, cloaking structures and reorganisation of business to cope with the everyday challenges of normal trading activity have much in common. This suggests that the study of changes in organisational structures of business during wartime should be more firmly rooted in an understanding of the general requirements of strategic management.

Another implication of this approach is that the study of organisational design involving questions of nationality, the location of business and cloaking, should be placed in a wider context. This might include inter-company networks and business groups, international cartels, joint ventures or alliance strategies. The first wave of holding companies in Europe were set up from the 1880s to finance public utility business such as the development of electrification.[16] They were founded in Belgium and Switzerland especially because these countries were considered neutral in the aftermath of the First World War and continuing tension between Germany and France. It is possible to argue that the nominal reorganisation of structure to cope with political risk had very little impact on competitiveness. However, by way of contrast to such arguments, historians have shown how some MNEs established parallel holding-company structures with two headquarters, to address the Second World War division of global markets into two camps—the Allied and Axis powers—causing thereby a crisis of control. Similarly, a wide range of firms—from Germany, other Axis powers, and from neutral and Allied countries—all exemplify the long-lasting impact of structural reorganisation (for example, a policy of decentralisation) on competitiveness in global markets that stretched into the second half of the century.[17] This is yet more reason to examine in greater detail the organisational design of MNEs.

Taxation and MNEs

The impact of taxation is frequently mentioned in the research on cloaking.[18] More than a few cloaking schemes, which were mobilised to cope with political risks, were originally introduced to avoid or reduce taxation. The decisive watershed in the relationship between taxation and MNEs was the coming of the First World War. Until then, tariffs (custom duties) were the only taxation-related element which had a significant impact on MNEs. Due to the skyrocketing costs of the war, all belligerent nations were forced to change their tax policies and the overall tax burden in relation to the GDP sharply increased everywhere, with the exception of neutral states like the Netherlands and Switzerland. The latter two countries therefore became favourable destinations as domiciliary bases in order to minimise tax liabilities tax during the interwar period.[19] Suddenly, capability to manage tax became an essential element of the competitiveness of large, international companies.

In addition to the level of tax rates, international 'double taxation' became a serious problem after 1918.[20] Many firms transformed their foreign affiliates and branches into subsidiaries, with their own corporate status, to cope with the war and nationalism in the interwar period. It brought about the problem of double taxation: the profits of a subsidiary firm were taxed in the host nation and then, in the home country, the parent company was taxed on the dividends transferred by the subsidiary. As a result, it was not uncommon for firms to change the ownership structure of their group and review the legal status of their business. Both before and after the First World War, a few countries, for example the Netherlands, Switzerland and Liechtenstein adopted favourable tax laws to host the holding companies of MNEs, and emerged as important bases for constructing schemes to minimise taxation and to address the issue of political risk in general.

The introduction of tight exchange-controls, and the rise of international political tension during the 1930s, made the design of the financial structure of a group even more important.[21] A large number of MNEs changed the geographical allocation of their resources and reorganised the ownership structure of their business, in response to the increasing burden of taxation and constraints on profit transfer.[22] A variety of intermediaries, such as bankers, lawyers, accountants and even government officials were involved in this trend, giving shape to a new kind of global infrastructure for international business. Most of these constructions and institutional settings remained even after the Second World War and had a long-lasting impact on international business.

The relationship between taxation and MNEs has been discussed in both business and academic circles. In particular, the subject of international taxation has been studied by international business scholars and legal scholars.[23] However, in the field of business history, taxation has been treated as a marginal issue. The first steps to change this situation were taken by Mira Wilkins.[24] She argued that international taxation had some impact on the shift of British international business from a free-standing company structure to that of an MNE with a multidivisional structure. Since then, little research has been undertaken from this perspective, although recently some studies have helped to advance understanding of the question.[25] Just like political risk, tax has been regarded merely as an exogenous factor; rarely has it been discussed in the framework of the strategy and structure of firms. However, as mentioned above, the capability required, and the actual measures taken, to address problems posed by taxation was closely linked to the strategies devised to cope with political risks. This suggests that systematic and integrated research on the subject is needed.

Corporate Law and Other Legal Frameworks

As taxes on companies are levied within the legal frameworks of individual sovereign states, the premise underlying the actions undertaken by firms to cope with the political risks associated with taxation was that it was possible to distinguish between those jurisdictions which offered favourable conditions and those that did not. Both corporate law and anti-trust law had a close relationship with political risk and taxation and had an impact on corporate organisation and its governance. A focal point of research is the holding company. Holding-company structure played a pivotal role in the efforts to deal with political risks (cloaking and organisational set-ups with or without intention to disguise), international taxation, and exchange control.[26] In Europe, the holding-company form was used for international mergers and acquisitions, to adjust diverse interests among shareholders, who were represented by different nationalities and in different markets.

In the United States, the federal system created competition between states over the drawing up of corporate legislation and resulted in a diversity of flexible, legal frameworks that facilitated the emergence of big business.[27] In addition, the legal framework for competition policy had a significant impact on the international position of MNEs involving American interests. Beginning in the late 1930s, US legislators—motivated by the twin goals of implementing ant-trust law policy and, later, uncovering enemy assets—conducted extremely intensive investigations into the organisational structure of European MNEs.[28]

In Europe, some countries introduced flexible corporate law to attract foreign holding companies, by departing from the traditions of civil law. In a few countries, intensive debates on corporate governance appeared, reflecting the rise of nationalism and a fear of the growth of foreign influence.[29] From the 1920s through to the 1940s, as discussed in relation to cloaking, neutral countries such as Switzerland, the Netherlands and Portugal were used as convenient locations to set up holding companies to own and control foreign assets. The international infrastructure for these kinds of schemes had an even wider geographical reach. From the 1930s, and especially from the end of that decade, Latin America and South Africa became common places to host holding companies that had emigrated from Europe. In the course of that development, Panama, for example, adopted a flexible corporate law.[30]

In the academic tradition of business history, holding companies have often been positioned as 'loose' types of control of business. They have also been associated with the issue of family ownership. Studies on corporate governance and mergers and acquisitions have also discussed the function of holding companies from various perspectives. However, there is considerable potential for research on the legal form of companies from a perspective that combines political risk, taxation and competition policy. The aim of such research should be to study the interaction between strategic legislation enacted by competing sovereign states, on the one hand, and decisions taken by MNEs, on the other hand. More research, however, is needed into the rationale and historical role of holding companies, and how they were used as an entity to manage a firm's capital resources.

Geopolitical and Economic Geography Perspectives

Taking MNEs as the unit of analysis, and studying them through the lens of the 20th century, opens up the possibility of a more nuanced understanding in the evolving relationship between big firms and the development of the modern state and international order. In taking this approach, a range of disciplines may benefit from the insights business history is able to offer. In the fields of economics and management studies, for example, the nation state and national economies are frequently taken as standardised units of analysis with homogeneous features. In reality, of course, the historical record reveals that the world has been characterised by a much greater degree of heterogeneity: there is considerable diversity in the size of states and in the resources they are able to command; political governance may be exercised in a federal system where authority is devolved or, in a centralised state, control may be retained by national institutions. Similar diversity is observable in the role states play on the world stage. The 20th-century role of smaller states like the Netherlands, Switzerland and Hong Kong is remarkable in this respect. Why were these states often successful host and home countries of large MNEs?

The superstructure of the world's geopolitical and economic geography is asymmetrical, with financial and trading centres of varying importance and peripheral regions of less significance. At various times, economic blocs have emerged with countries bound together on the basis of sharing common tariffs and duties. Contrary to the Chandlerian view, national economies are not independent of each other but interact to varying degrees in this international arena; the exchange rate of a national currency, for example, may be fixed or tied in some way or free-floating; the power a state is able to project externally may be reflected in the relative position it occupies in the hierarchy of international organisations or membership of supra-national bodies. Thus, although a considerable number of comparative studies have been produced, relatively little work on relational studies has been undertaken. The purpose here, therefore, is to fill this epistemological gap by paying attention to the heterogeneous nature of the modern nation state and national economy, to large scale or regional geopolitical structures and to the issue of hierarchy in the world economy. Such factors need to be analysed not only by means of a comparative perspective, but also with a view to focussing on the relationship between diverse units of analysis.

Structure of the Book

This study is divided into three parts, each with its own particular emphasis. In several respects, the multinationals studied in Part I were directly impacted by specific events and developments that occurred during wartime. However, the focus in the first section is more generally on how the experience of war helped to determine the understanding of what geopolitical risks were, and the challenges that such risks posed to the way in which the companies organised themselves over the long-term.

In the opening chapter, Takafumi Kurosawa and Ben Wubs examine four multinationals which, in the course of the 20th century, grew to be major and important companies: Roche, Unilever, Nestlé and Philips. Covering various sectors of industry and producing a range of consumer goods, these companies remain 'household names'. Yet, domiciled, or partly domiciled, in two of Europe's smaller states, Switzerland and the Netherlands, these companies were exposed to extreme political risk and left with an acute sense of vulnerability, prompting their management boards to take a series of radical and, it was hoped, protective measures.

In the event of war, manufacturing companies could, at least, seek to relocate production facilities out of harm's way. A utility company, supplying gas to customers such as municipal authorities, had no choice but to adapt to the circumstances it found itself facing at any particular time; the alternative was the almost certain demise of the company. This was the case with the British-based multinational, Imperial Continental Gas Association. Ryo Izawa charts how this enterprise adapted to the extreme demands placed on it during the two world wars and the political turbulence that followed in the wake of the conflicts.

Mark Spoerer's study of C & A, the clothing retailer, focusses on how the coming of the Cold War impacted on corporate governance, and particularly the company's succession strategy. Yet, in the case of this multinational too, the decision-making of the controlling family, the Brenninkmeijers, can be understood only by taking into account what might be called 'family, corporate memory'. In this sense, the experiences of war acted over the long-term to influence, in a conscious and perhaps even unconscious way, strategy and organisational change.

Takeo Kikkawa considers how two foreign-owned oil companies, Rising Sun Petroleum and Standard Vacuum Oil, attempted to cope, during the 1930s, with regulations imposed under Japan's Petroleum Industry Law. The chapter assesses corporate, organisational structures in relation to investment, production and supply in the context of, first, Japan's drive to reduce dependency on imports before the Pacific War and, secondly, under US occupation following the war.

Multinational enterprises, by definition, undertake foreign direct investments. Part II of the book analyses what happens to those investments when the company's home country, or the country that hosts the investments, becomes a belligerent in war. In some cases, both home and host country go to war against each other. Luciano Segreto considers the example of Siemens—domiciled in Germany—and what befell the company's investments in Italy from the mid-19th century to the 1960s. In the course of this hundred-year period, relations between the two countries underwent seismic changes: enemies in the First World War, the two countries fought alongside each other in the Second World War.

Neil Forbes considers the case of the Spanish investments of Rio Tinto, a British-based, multinational mining company. Not dissimilar to the operations of a utility company, mining takes place in fixed locations that are geologically determined. Although Rio Tinto was able to protect its assets during the Spanish Civil War and Spain remained neutral in the Second World War, the danger of expropriation was never greater than under Franco's post-war dictatorship. The company felt it had little choice other than to divest itself of most of its Spanish assets and embark on a major reorganisation of its investments around the world.

Ray Stokes and Ralf Banken study the international industrial gases industry, focussing, in particular, on US-based Air Products. They show how the issue of political risk in the context of the Second World War and its aftermath was a key factor in shaping the dynamics of the industry. Their analysis confirms, in general, the hypothesis that war serves as a conduit not only for significant technological development but also transformational, organisational change,

The final part of the book considers the nature of political risk in the era of the ideological division that emerged after the Second World War and developed into the Cold War. Judit Klement examines the case of Siemens' subsidiary in Hungary after the Second World War II. In German ownership, the company became the property of the Soviet Union in 1946. However, the company enjoyed an afterlife: this chapter illustrates how an enterprise is not simply a legal entity but also embodies knowledge of production and management. It was not the firm but the (mostly former) Siemens employees who aimed to restart production and were ultimately successful in their efforts.

At the height of the Cold War, a combination of multinational oil companies envisioned the construction of an integrated pipeline system. Marten Boon's chapter examines why the Trans-European Pipeline was never constructed, even though it was technically and economically feasible. The explanation focusses on the efforts of the pipeline consortium to devise a legal and organisational structure that would protect the pipeline from political risks deriving from the geopolitics of oil during a period of heightened international tension.

Marcelo Bucheli's chapter analyses the evolution of the strategies of several multinational corporations in Chile throughout the period of the Cold War. The period encompassed development policies dominated by protectionism, rule of a right-wing open market-friendly military dictatorship, democratisation and a market-friendly regime. As well as adapting to such changes in the political and economic environment, the MNEs also responded to wider global shifts in existing paradigms on economic development. Altogether, the studies set out here demonstrate both the similarities and the differences in the organisational and strategic responses of MNEs to political risks and wars.

Notes

1 Francis Fukuyama, 'The End of History?' *The National Interest* 16 (1989): 3–18; Francis Fukuyama, *The End of History and the Last Man* (New York: Free Press, 1992).

2 Richard N. Langlois, 'The Vanishing Hand: The Changing Dynamics of Industrial Capitalism', *Industrial and Corporate Change* 12, no. 2 (1 April 2003): 351–385.

3 Mark Casson and Teresa da Silva Lopes, 'Foreign Direct Investment in High-Risk Environments: An Historical Perspective', *Business History* 55, no. 3 (2013): 375–404.

4 J. Adam Tooze, *Statistics and the German State, 1900–1945: The Making of Modern Economic Knowledge* (Cambridge: Cambridge University Press, 2001), 4–17.
5 Philip Scranton and Patrick Fridenson, *Reimagining Business History* (Baltimore: The John Hopkins University Press, 2013), 16–21.
6 Geoffrey Jones, *Multinationals and Global Capitalism From the Nineteenth to the Twenty-First Century* (New York: Oxford University Press, 2005), 174; Christopher Kobrak, 'Politics, Corporate Governance, and the Dynamics of German Managerial Innovation: Schering AG Between the Wars', *Enterprise & Society* 3 (2002): 429–461.
7 Neil Forbes, *Doing Business With the Nazis: Britain's Economic and Financial Relations With Germany, 1931–1939* (London and Portland: Frank Cass, 2000); Harold James and Jakob Tanner, *Enterprise in the Period of Fascism in Europe* (Aldershot: Ashgate, 2002); Christopher Kobrak and Per H. Hansen, eds., *European Business, Dictatorship, and Political Risk 1920–1945* (New York: Berghahn Books, 2004); Neil Forbes, 'Managing Risk in the Third Reich: British Business With Germany in the 1930s', in Kobrak and Hansen, *European Business*, 194–205; Francis R. Nicosia and Jonathan Huener, *Business and Industry in Nazi Germany* (New York: Berghahn Books, 2004); Joachim Lund, *Working for the New Order: European Business Under German Domination, 1939–1945* (Copenhagen: Copenhagen Business School Press, 2006).
8 Ivo J. Blanken, *The History of Philips Electronics N.V. Vol. IV. Under German Rule*, transl. C. Pettiward (Zaltbommel: European Library, 1999); Jana Wüstenhagen, 'German Pharmaceutical Companies in South America: The Case of Schering AG in Argentina', in Kobrak and Hansen, *European Business*, 81–102; Ben Wubs, *International Business and National War Interests: Unilever Between Reich and Empire, 1939–45* (Abingdon and New York: Routledge, 2008); Lukas Straumann and Daniel Wildmann, *Schweizer Chemieunternehmen im 'Dritten Reich'* (Zürich: Chronos, 2001); Roman Rossfeld and Tobias Straumann, eds., *Der Vergessene Wirtscahftskrieg. Schweizer Unternehmen in ersten Weltkrieg* (Zürich: Chronos, 2008); Pierre-Yves Donzé and Takafumi Kurosawa, 'Nestlé Coping With Japanese Nationalism: Political Risk and the Strategy of a Foreign Multinational Enterprise in Japan, 1913–45', *Business History* 55-8 (2013): 1318–1338.
9 Roger Chickering, 'World War I and the Theory of Total War. Reflections on the British and German Cases, 1914–1915', in *Great War, Total War*, eds. Roger Chickering and Stig Förster (Cambridge: Cambridge University Press, 2000), 35–53; Jeremy Black, *The Age of Total War, 1860–1945* (Santa Barbara: Praeger Publishers, 2006); Richard Overy, *Why the Allies Won* (London: Jonathan Cape, 1995); Chris Bellamy, *Absolute War: Soviet Russia in the Second World War* (New York: Penguin Random House, 2007); Hein Klemann and Sergei Kudryashov, *Occupied Economies: An Economic History of Nazi-occupied Europe, 1939–1945* (London and New York: Berg Publishers, 2012).
10 Harm Schröter, 'Risk and Control in Multinational Enterprise: German Businesses in Scandinavia, 1918–1939', *The Business History Review* 62, no. 3 (Autumn 1988): 420–443; Robert Fitzgerald, *The Rise of the Global Company: Multinationals and the Making of the Modern World* (Cambridge: Cambridge University Press, 2015), 156–178.
11 Although we do not want to under-estimate the important role that Alfred Chandler has played for the development of Business History as a discipline

wars and states do not play a big role in his analysis of 'managerial revolution' and the organisational ('structure') and strategic changes of big business in the 20th century. See, for example: Barry Supple, 'Essays in Bibliography and Criticism. Scale and Scope: Alfred Chandler and the Dynamics of Industrial Capitalism', *Economic History Review* (August 1991): 500–514.

12 Alfred D. Chandler, *Strategy and Structure: Chapters in the History of the Industrial Enterprise* (Cambridge, MA: The M.I.T. Press, 1962); Alfred D. Chandler, *The Visible Hand: The Managerial Revolution in American Business* (Cambridge, MA: The Belknap Press of Harvard University Press, 1977); Alfred D. Chandler, *Scale and Scope: The Dynamics of Industrial Capitalism* (Cambridge, MA: The Belknap Press of Harvard University Press, 1990).

13 Gerard Aalders and Cees Wiebes, *The Art of Cloaking Ownership: The Secret Collaboration and Protection of the German War Industry By the Neutrals: The Case of Sweden* (Amsterdam: Amsterdam University Press, 1996); Christiane Uhlig, Petrea Barthelmess, Mario König, Peter Pfaffenroth, and Bettina Zeugin, *Tarnung, Transfer, Transit Die Schweiz als Drehscheibe verdeckter deutscher Operationen (1939–1952)* (Zürich: Chronos, 2001); Mario König, *Interhandel Die schweizerische Holding der IG Farben und Ihre Metamorphosen—eine Affare um Eigentum und Interessen (1910–1999)* (Zürich: Chronos, 2001).

14 Mira Wilkins, *The History of Foreign Investment in the United States, 1914–1945* (Cambridge, MA: Harvard University Press, 2004); Mira Wilkins, 'Multinationals and Dictatorship: Europe in the 1930s and Early 1940s', in Kobrak and Hansen, *European Business*, 22–40; Christopher Kobrak and Jana Wüstenhagen, 'International Investment and Nazi Politics: The Cloaking of German Assets Abroad, 1936–1945', *Business History* 48, no. 3 (2006): 399–427.

15 Geoffrey Jones and Christina Lubinski, 'Managing Political Risk in Global Business: Beiersdorf, 1914–1990', *Enterprise & Society* 13, no. 1 (2012): 85–119; Martin Lüpold, 'Globalisierung als Krisenreaktionsstrategie. Dezentralisierung und Renationalisierung bei Nestlé 1920–1950', in *Globalisierung-Chancen und Risiken. Die Schweiz in der Weltwirtschaft 18.–20. Jahrhundert/ La globalisation-chances et risques. La Suisse dans l'economie mondiale 18e–20e siècles*, eds. Hans-Jörg Gilomen, Margrit Müller, and Béatrice Veyrassat, 211–234 (Zürich: Chronos, 2003).

16 Serge Paquier, 'Swiss Holding Companies From the Mid-nineteenth Century to the Early 1930s: The Forerunners and Subsequent Waves of Creations', *Financial History Review* 8, no. 2 (2001): 163–182; J. William Hausman, Peter Hertner, and Mira Wilkins, *Global Electrification: Multinational Enterprise and International Finance in the History of Light and Power, 1878–2007* (Cambridge: Cambridge University Press, 2008).

17 Wubs, *International Business*, 184–186.

18 König, *Interhandel*; Uhlig et al., *Tarnung, Transfer*; Kobrak and Wüstenhagen, 'International Investment', 411.

19 Jeroen Euwe, 'Financing Germany: Amsterdam's Role as an International Financial Centre, 1914–1931', in *Convergence and Divergence of National Financial Systems: Evidence From the Gold Standards, 1871–1971*, eds. Patrice Baubeau and Anders Ögren (London: Pickering & Chatto, 2010), 219–240; Gabriel Zucman, *The Hidden Wealth of Nations: The Scourge of Tax Havens* (Chicago and London: The University of Chicago Press, 2015), 8–12.

20 Sol Picciotto, *International Business Taxation: A Study in the Internationalization of Business Regulation* (London: Weidenfeld & Nicolson, 1992); Sol Picciotto, 'Offshore: The State as Legal Fiction', in *Offshore Finance Centres and Tax Havens*, eds. M. P. Hampton and J. P. Abbott (London: Palgrave Macmillan, 1999), 43–79.

21 Christopher Kobrak, 'Politics, Corporate Governance, and the Dynamics of German Managerial Innovation: Schering AG Between the Wars', *Enterprise & Society* 3 (2002): 429–461; Christopher Kobrak, Per H. Hansen, and Christopher Kopper, 'Business, Political Risk, and Historians in the Twentieth Century', in Kobrak and Hansen, *European Business*, 3–21.

22 Ryo Izawa, 'The Formation of Companies for Tax Avoidance: The Relationship Between UK Multinationals and International Double Taxation in the Interwar Period', *Business and Economic History Online*, 2015, www.thebhc.org/sites/default/files/Izawa_BEHO_Final%20Draft.pdf

23 Lorraine Eden, 'Taxes, Transfer Pricing, and The Multinational Enterprise', in *The Oxford Handbook of International Business*, ed. Alan M. Rugman (Oxford: Oxford University Press, 2009), 591–619; Klaus Vogel, *Klaus Vogel on Double Taxation Conventions: A Commentary to the OECD-, UN- and US Model Conventions for the Avoidance of Double Taxation of Income and Capital With Particular Reference to German Treaty Practice*, trans. John Mari (Deventer: Kluwer Law and Taxation Publishers, 1991).

24 Mira Wilkins, 'The Free-Standing Company, 1870–1914: An Important Type of British Foreign Direct Investment', *The Economic History Review* 41, no. 2 (May 1988): 259–282.

25 Simon Mollan and Kevin D. Tennent, 'International Taxation and Corporate Strategy: Evidence From British Overseas Business, Circa 1900–1965', *Business History* 57, no. 7 (2015): 1054–1081.

26 Kobrak and Wüstenhagen, 'International Investment', 411. Uhlig et al., 'Tarnung, Transfer, Transit',

27 Naomi R. Lamoreaux, 'Partnerships, Corporations, and the Limits on Contractual Freedom in U.S. History: An Essay in Economics, Law and Culture', in *Constructing Corporate America: History, Politics, Culture*, eds. Kenneth Lipartito and David Sicilia, 29–65 (Oxford: Oxford University Press, 2004).

28 Wyatt Wells, *Antitrust & the Formation of the Postwar World* (New York: Columbia University Press, 2002), 40; Neil Fligstein, *The Transformation of Corporate Control* (Cambridge, MA: Harvard University Press, 1990), 168.

29 Martin Lüpold, *Der Ausbau der "Festung Schweiz": Aktienrecht und Corporate Governance in der Schweiz, 1881–1961* (PhD. Diss. University of Zürich, 2010).

30 Niklaus von Deschwanden, *Das Aktienrecht von Panama* (Frankfurt am Main and Berlin: A. Metzner, 1961); Elmar Jerjen, 'Panama: Reasons for the Popularity of Private Interest Foundations', *Trusts & Trustees* 15, no. 5 (July 2009): 397–402.

Bibliography

Aalders, Gerard, and Cees Wiebes. *The Art of Cloaking Ownership: The Secret Collaboration and Protection of the German War Industry By the Neutrals.* The Case of Sweden. Amsterdam: Amsterdam University Press, 1996.

Bellamy, Chris. *Absolute War: Soviet Russia in the Second World War*. New York: Penguin Random House, 2007.

Black, Jeremy. *The Age of Total War, 1860–1945*. Santa Barbara: Praeger Publishers, 2006.

Blanken, Ivo J. *The History of Philips Electronics N.V. Vol. IV. Under German Rule*. Translated by C. Pettiward. Zaltbommel: European Library, 1999.

Casson, Mark and Teresa da Silva Lopes. 'Foreign Direct Investment in High-risk Environments: An Historical Perspective'. *Business History* 55, no. 3 (2013): 375–404.

Chandler, Alfred D. *Strategy and Structure: Chapters in the History of the Industrial Enterprise*. Cambridge, MA: The M.I.T. Press, 1962.

Chandler, Alfred D. *The Visible Hand: The Managerial Revolution in American Business*. Cambridge, MA: The Belknap Press of Harvard University Press, 1977.

Chandler, Alfred D. *Scale and Scope: The Dynamics of Industrial Capitalism*. Cambridge, MA: The Belknap Press of Harvard University Press, 1990.

Chickering, Roger. 'World War I and the Theory of Total War. Reflections on the British and German Cases, 1914–1915'. In *Great War, Total War*, edited by Roger Chickering and Stig Förster, 35–53. Cambridge: Cambridge University Press, 2000.

Deschwanden, Niklaus von. *Das Aktienrecht von Panama*. Frankfurt am Main and Berlin: A. Metzner, 1961.

Donzé, Pierre-Yves and Takafumi Kurosawa. 'Nestlé Coping With Japanese Nationalism: Political Risk and the Strategy of a Foreign Multinational Enterprise in Japan, 1913–45'. *Business History* 55–8 (2013): 1318–1338.

Eden, Lorraine. 'Taxes, Transfer Pricing, and The Multinational Enterprise'. In *The Oxford Handbook of International Business*, edited by Alan M. Rugman, 591–619. Oxford: Oxford University Press, 2009.

Fitzgerald, Robert. *The Rise of the Global Company: Multinationals and the Making of the Modern World*. Cambridge: Cambridge University Press, 2015.

Fligstein, Neil. *The Transformation of Corporate Control*. Cambridge, MA: Harvard University Press, 1990.

Forbes, Neil. *Doing Business With the Nazis: Britain's Economic and Financial Relations With Germany, 1931–1939*. London and Portland: Frank Cass, 2000.

Forbes, Neil. 'Managing Risk in the Third Reich: British Business With Germany in the 1930s'. In *European Business, Dictatorship, and Political Risk, 1920–1945*, edited by Christopher Kobrak and Per H. Hansen, 194–205. New York: Berghahn Books, 2004.

Fukuyama, Francis. 'The End of History?' *The National Interest* 16 (1989): 3–18.

Fukuyama, Francis. *The End of History and the Last Man*. New York: Free Press, 1992.

Hausman, J. William, Peter Hertner and Mira Wilkins. *Global Electrification: Multinational Enterprise and International Finance in the History of Light and Power, 1878–2007*. Cambridge: Cambridge University Press, 2008.

Izawa, Ryo. 'The Formation of Companies for Tax Avoidance: The Relationship Between UK Multinationals and International Double Taxation in the Interwar Period'. *Business and Economic History Online*, 2015. www.thebhc.org/sites/default/files/Izawa_BEHO_Final%20Draft.pdf

James, Harold and Jakob Tanner. *Enterprise in the Period of Fascism in Europe*. Aldershot: Ashgate, 2002.

Jerjen, Elmar. 'Panama: Reasons for the Popularity of Private Interest Foundations'. *Trusts & Trustees* 15, no. 5 (July 2009): 397–402.

Jones, Geoffrey. *The Evolution of International Business: An Introduction*. London: International Thomson Business Press, 1995.

Jones, Geoffrey. *Multinationals and Global Capitalism From the Nineteenth to the Twenty-First Century*. New York: Oxford University Press, 2005.

Jones, Geoffrey. 'The End of Nationality? Global Firms and "Borderless Worlds"'. *Zeitschrift für Unternehmensgeschichte /Journal of Business History* 51, Jahrg. H. 2. (2006): 149–165.

Jones, Geoffrey and Christina Lubinski. 'Managing Political Risk in Global Business: Beiersdorf, 1914–1990'. *Enterprise & Society* 13, no. 1 (2012): 85–119.

Klemann, Hein A.M. and Sergei Kudryashov. *Occupied Economies: An Economic History of Nazi-occupied Europe, 1939–1945*. London and New York: Berg Publishers, 2012.

Kobrak, Christopher. *National Cultures and International Competition: The Experience of Schering AG, 1851–1950*. Cambridge: Cambridge University Press, 2002.

Kobrak, Christopher. 'Politics, Corporate Governance, and the Dynamics of German Managerial Innovation: Schering AG Between the Wars'. *Enterprise & Society* 3 (2002): 429–461.

Kobrak, Christopher and Per H. Hansen, eds. *European Business, Dictatorship, and Political Risk 1920–1945*. New York: Berghahn Books, 2004.

Kobrak, Christopher, Per H. Hansen, and Christopher Kopper. 'Business, Political Risk, and Historians in the Twentieth Century'. In *European Business, Dictatorship and Political Risk 1920–1945*, edited by Christopher Kobrak and Per H. Hansen, 3–21. New York: Berghahn, 2004.

Kobrak, Christopher and Jana Wüstenhagen. 'International Investment and Nazi Politics: The Cloaking of German Assets Abroad, 1936–1945'. *Business History* 48, no. 3 (2006): 399–427.

König, Mario. *Interhandel Die schweizerische Holding der IG Farben und Ihre Metamorphosen—eine Affare um Eigentum und Interessen (1910–1999)*. Zürich: Chronos, 2001.

Lamoreaux, Naomi R. 'Partnerships, Corporations, and the Limits on Contractual Freedom in U.S History: An Essay in Economics, Law and Culture'. In *Constructing Corporate America: History, Politics, Culture*, edited by Kenneth Lipartito and David Sicilia, 29–65. Oxford: Oxford University Press, 2004.

Langlois, Richard N. 'The Vanishing Hand: The Changing Dynamics of Industrial Capitalism'. *Industrial and Corporate Change* 12, no. 2 (1 April 2003): 351–385.

Lund, Joachim. *Working for the New Order: European Business Under German Domination, 1939–1945*. Copenhagen: Copenhagen Business School Press, 2006.

Lüpold, Martin. 'Globalisierung als Krisenreaktionsstrategie. Dezentralisierung und Renationalisierung bei Nestlé 1920–1950'. In *Globalisierung-Chancen und Risiken. Die Schweiz in der Weltwirtschaft 18.–20. Jahrhundert/ La globalisation-chances et risques. La Suisse dans l'economie mondiale 18e–20e siècles*, edited by Hans-Jörg Gilomen, Margrit Müller, and Béatrice Veyrassat, 211–234. Zürich: Chronos, 2003.

Lüpold, Martin. *Der Ausbau der "Festung Schweiz": Aktienrecht und Corporate Governance in der Schweiz, 1881–1961*. PhD. Diss. University of Zürich, 2010.

Mollan, Simon and Kevin D. Tennent. 'International Taxation and Corporate Strategy: Evidence From British Overseas Business, Circa 1900–1965'. *Business History* 57, no. 7 (2015): 1054–1081.

Nicosia, Francis R. and Jonathan Huener. *Business and Industry in Nazi Germany*. New York: Berghahn Books, 2004.

Overy, Richard. *Why the Allies Won*. London: Jonathan Cape, 1995.

Paquier, Serge. 'Swiss Holding Companies From the Mid-nineteenth Century to the Early 1930s: The Forerunners and Subsequent Waves of Creations'. *Financial History Review* 8 no. 2 (2001): 163–182.

Picciotto, Sol. *International Business Taxation: A Study in the Internationalization of Business Regulation*. London: Weidenfeld & Nicolson, 1992.

Picciotto, Sol. 'Offshore: The State as Legal Fiction'. In *Offshore Finance Centres and Tax Havens*, edited by M. P. Hampton and J. P. Abbott, 43–79. London: Palgrave Macmillan, 1999.

Rossfeld, Roman and Tobias Straumann, eds. *Der Vergessene Wirtscahftskrieg. Schweizer Unternehmen in ersten Weltkrieg*. Zürich: Chronos, 2008.

Schröter, Harm. 'Risk and Control in Multinational Enterprise: German Businesses in Scandinavia, 1918–1939'. *The Business History Review* 62, no. 3 (Autumn 1988): 420–443.

Scranton, Philip and Patrick Fridenson. *Reimagining Business History*. Baltimore: Johns Hopkins University Press, 2013.

Smith Ring, Peter, Stefanie Ann Lenway, and Michele Govekar. 'Management of Political Imperative in International Business'. *Strategic Management Journal* 11, no. 2 (1990): 141–151.

Straumann, Lukas and Daniel Wildmann. *Schweizer Chemieunternehmen im 'Dritten Reich'*. Zürich: Chronos, 2001.

Tooze, J. Adam. *Statistics and the German State, 1900–1945: The Making of Modern Economic Knowledge*. Cambridge: Cambridge University Press, 2001.

Uhlig, Christiane, Petrea Barthelmess, Mario König, Peter Pfaffenroth, and Bettina Zeugin. *Tarnung, Transfer, Transit Die Schweiz als Drehscheibe verdeckter deutscher Operationen (1939–1952)*. Zürich: Chronos, 2001.

Wells, Wyatt. *Antitrust & the Formation of the Postwar World*. New York: Columbia University Press, 2002.

Wilkins, Mira. 'The Free-Standing Company, 1870–1914: An Important Type of British Foreign Direct Investment'. *The Economic History Review* 41, no. 2 (May 1988): 259–282.

Wilkins, Mira. *The History of Foreign Investment in the United States, 1914–1945*. Cambridge, MA: Harvard University Press, 2004.

Wilkins, Mira. 'Multinationals and Dictatorship: Europe in the 1930s and Early 1940s'. In *European Business, Dictatorship and Political Risk 1920–1945*, edited by Christopher Kobrak and Per H. Hansen, 22–40. New York: Berghahn, 2004.

Wubs, Ben. *International Business and National War Interests: Unilever Between Reich and Empire, 1939–45*. Abingdon and New York: Routledge, 2008.

Wüstenhagen, Jana. 'German Pharmaceutical Companies in South America: The Case of Schering AG in Argentina'. In *European Business, Dictatorship and Political Risk 1920–1945*, edited by Christopher Kobrak and Per H. Hansen, 81–102. New York: Berghahn, 2004.

Zucman, Gabriel. *The Hidden Wealth of Nations: The Scourge of Tax Havens*. Chicago and London: The University of Chicago Press, 2015.

Part I

Geopolitical Risks and Organisational Challenges

1 Swiss and (Anglo)-Dutch Multinationals and Organisational Change in the Era of Total War

Takafumi Kurosawa and Ben Wubs

Introduction

It has been suggested that the two world wars were a part of the cause of the decentralised corporate structure of European multinationals and that companies in the neutral states (the Netherlands, Sweden and Switzerland) enhanced their international competitive advantage.[1] However, research into multinational companies, based in neutral states, that might have capitalised on the war to gain a competitive edge is still scarce. Considering the tendency of European companies to demonstrate adaptation to the local market and to manifest a more decentralised structure than their American counterparts, an in-depth analysis of the impact of the two world wars on European corporate structure, together with the exogenous condition of the division into small national markets, has yet to be made.

This chapter aims to explore organisational change as a result of political and security risks of four major European multinationals—Roche (pharmaceuticals), Nestlé (food), Unilever (non-mineral oil, fats, food and soap), and Philips (incandescent lamps, electronics)—originating partly or wholly from two relatively small neutral countries at the time, namely Switzerland and the Netherlands, Both countries had highly developed, open economies with a high density of multinational enterprises. The chapter is based on four company archives, government archives, research results of the Independent Commission of Experts (ICE),[2] as well as corporate histories of the four companies. It addresses the following questions: how did both wars and nationalistic economic policy affect the organisational structures of these four multinationals, and to what extent did these organisational changes have elements of duration and continuity?

Despite their worldwide presence, the Swiss companies have not been studied much, even in Switzerland, compared to companies in other neutral states. It was as late as the mid-1990s that the study of the period from the 1930s to 1945 intensified in response to the international debate; the result was the establishment of ICE, and yet still relatively few research works are based on a business historical perspective.[3] The studies that do exist are hardly known outside Switzerland, and the amount of research on international comparisons is far from sufficient.[4] With regard to the Netherlands, Ben Wubs explored the case of Unilever, but the scope is mostly limited to analysing the UK, and German-dominated continental Europe.[5] Ivo Blanken published a study of Philips during the German occupation, but this research focusses particularly on the occupied Netherlands.[6] Although the four companies studied here showed similar organisational responses, a closer look shows that political circumstances between Dutch, Swiss and Anglo-Dutch companies differed greatly. The moment when managements decided to reorganise the companies in response to political risk also differed. Sometimes several exogenous pressures played a role at the same time. Generally, increased levels of taxation are key to understanding organisational change during the interwar period. Economic nationalism, and the threat of war and military occupation forced companies to take even more extreme measures. The four case studies focus particularly on the following significant themes: localisation (adaption to national circumstances), decentralisation, taxation, the formation of holding companies, twin corporate structures and geographical relocation of the businesses.

F. Hoffman La Roche in the Border City: From Foundation to the First World War

F. Hoffmann-La Roche & Co. was established in 1896 in Basel, a city at the junction of Swiss, German and French borders, a geopolitical fact which gave the company an international character from the beginning. German Patent Law called for the domestic exercise of a patent within three years of approval; this prompted Roche, since its founding, to locate its main plant in the nearby village Grenzach on the German side of the border. The company relocated successively most of its R&D function, sales organisation and patent management operation there by 1910.[7] It also started exporting its product and establishing its export agencies in each country and, from the early 20th century, it also increased the number of local subsidiaries and pursued localisation of packaging and legal compliance. It started, before its competitors, highly personal sales activities in each market by using medical representatives. With its subsidiaries and agencies in 35 countries, it had become Europe's second largest pharmaceutical enterprise next to IG Farben by 1929.[8]

For a company with such multinational characteristics, the First World War dealt it an unexpected major blow. The Swiss-German border was closed, the traffic between its biggest manufacturing base, Grenzach, and the headquarters was made difficult, and the supply of intermediate materials from Germany to Switzerland was disrupted. Since the company had its largest plant in Germany and a French name (after its founder), it was exposed to boycotts and the risk of blacklisting. Its French subsidiary tried to break through this deadlock by advertising its support of France. However, in July 1915, Emil C. Barrell, the then manager of the Grenzach plant in Germany and a future president of Roche, was detained and placed under house arrest in Berlin for the rest of the war, thereby undermining the company.[9]

Under these circumstances, Roche expanded its main factory at its Basel headquarters in Switzerland, renamed its subsidiaries, and kept a low profile in advertising. The German plant was restructured and given an independent corporate status—Chemische Werke Grenzach AG (Cewega)—in early 1916, under which Suddeutsch Diskont Gesellschaft became its shareholder, with an agreement that the shares would be bought back after the conclusion of a peace.[10] The existing plant management led by the Swiss was maintained, but most of the members on the auditing committee and the board of directors were replaced with Germans, and the employees were reshuffled between the Basel headquarters and the German production base, according to their nationalities. It was an attempt to pursue localisation and dilute its Swiss character.[11]

The company faced bankruptcy in 1919 because of difficulties during the First World War and the collapse of its foreign-currency asset value in the immediate post-war period. It was reorganised as F. Hoffmann-La Roche & Co. AG.[12] In the following year, after the demise of Fritz Hoffmann, the company founder, Barell returned from Germany to assume the presidency. Likewise, in 1921, the US subsidiary experienced financial difficulties, but Barell managed to steer through these by a drastic reduction in headcount, consolidated his authority by dispelling veteran and family board members and instated corporate governance under professional management.[13]

The company's penetration into the US market had begun with the establishment of a sales agency in 1895 and moved into higher gear with the founding of a subsidiary in 1905.[14] Following the crisis directly after the First World War, its US subsidiary made a staggering recovery in revenue under President Elmer H. Bobst, an American, surpassing the performance of the German subsidiary in 1926, and that of the Basel headquarters in 1929. After 1921, it kicked off a fully fledged local production unit, and relocated the production base from New York to Nutley, New Jersey, in 1929.[15]

Conversion to a Twin Corporation, Great Depression and Readiness for Another General War

The pre-war international economic order did not return after the end of the First World War and multinational companies were forced to adapt themselves to the new situation, which could be characterised by a heightened tone of retribution, mutual distrust and economic nationalism. National tax authorities started targeting the profits attributable to the in-country operations of foreign-domiciled companies, and increasingly prioritised their homegrown enterprises through economic policies such as the protection of intellectual property rights. In addition, wartime disruption of transport and communication, seizure and boycott of foreign firms were still fresh memories. These factors had noticeable impact on corporate governance and corporate organisational structures.[16]

One of the countermeasures taken by multinationals in such an environment was to reorganise their headquarters as a holding company. At Roche, the headquarters in Basel had directly owned the shares of its foreign subsidiaries but, after 1927, the shares were gradually transferred to a holding company called Sapac, which was established in Lichtenstein.[17] At that time, a Sapac share was deemed identical to a Roche share, and the Roche shareholders were assigned a Sapac share for every Roche share they owned. The two companies' shares were deemed inseparable. Roche shareholders received the dividend from both companies, but the Sapac shares were set aside and managed by trust businesses, so that the possibility of direct disposal of shares by Roche shareholders was excluded. The Roche group businesses were now reorganised as identical twins, taking a unique form, with each independent of the other, with no capital ties but sharing the same shareholder composition by their articles of incorporation. This double corporate form was intended to avoid the risk of seizure of foreign subsidiaries, tax claims on the parent company, blacklisting due to filiation, while maintaining integrity as a single corporate entity and ensuring equitable distribution of the group's profit to their shareholders.[18]

In March 1938, when Nazi Germany annexed Austria, Roche relocated Sapac to the Republic of Panama, away from Liechtenstein which now bordered the Third Reich. At the end of the same year, President Barell came back from the US and asserted that their business focus should be on the 'West', namely the Anglo-American world and Latin America. He made a decision to scale back the expansion plan of the research institute in Basel and to reallocate the resources to the UK and the US.[19]

The favourable setting of Panama can be seen in light of the fact that Nestlé had also chosen to set up its holding company there. Located at a geopolitically convenient setting between two oceans and two continents, it was not only far away from the warring states of Europe but, for a Latin American country, it also enjoyed a favourable political environment and an excellent economic infrastructure. It was virtually an American colony, with US sovereignty over the Canal Zone, and almost owing its independence to the interests of American capital.[20] During the Second World War, its political situation became temporarily destabilised, starting with the declaration of war against the Axis, and the advent of a short-lived, anti-American government. Nevertheless, Panama stayed within the American sphere of influence, both militarily and economically. Its company law and taxation system were extremely favourable to foreign holding companies, thus offering an ideal safe haven for companies originating in Switzerland, which, unlike the UK, France, Belgium and the Netherlands, lacked overseas colonies.[21]

Flight of President Barell to the US and the De Facto Double Headquarters System

On 15th September 1939, a fortnight after the outbreak of the Second World War, the Roche board, assuming a German invasion of Switzerland and the need to plan for contingencies, adopted a resolution to relocate its headquarters.[22] At the same time, letters of resignation by all board members were entrusted to legal counsel, and a document for invalidating board members' signatures was prepared, in readiness against aggression by the occupation forces. Barell insisted on relocating the headquarters to the US, but the other members objected to his proposal. Thus a relocation only to Lausanne was decided on for the time being, after which business operations were still carried out in Basel.[23] During the eight months of the Phony War, the board remained alert, but the situation drastically changed with the outbreak of war on the Western Front. On the eve of the collapse of the French army on 21st May 1940, Barell travelled to Genoa, and further to New York, accompanied by his family.[24] After Barell had left the country, business operations on the European continent were executed by a daily conference of the executive members that remained in Basel. Important decisions were made in the weekly board meetings at the consent of Brugger (a board member of Basler Handelsbank), as Barell's proxy. Barell found himself a base in the US subsidiary in Nutley, then his own office in New York, and kept in close communication with Basel via post, telegram and telephone, and stayed on top of the whole group. Most of the subsidiaries and agencies in the Allies' sphere of influence came under the supervision of Nutley, and a number of managers and researchers were transferred to the US from the autumn of 1940 to the following year. This way, Roche gradually transformed into a double headquarters system in order to cope with the division of markets into a western sphere and a Nazi-dominated sphere.

Most of the pharmaceuticals products had been produced in the US since the early 1920s, but the R&D function was also beefed up during the war to give the US subsidiary the position of the largest research base of the group. Roche grew to be the biggest vitamin provider to the Allies during the war, and started production of penicillin in 1943 at the request by the US Administration. The staffing level at the US subsidiary went up from 669 in 1940 to 2,000 in 1943, surpassing that of the Basel headquarters that grew from 800 to 1,200 during the same period.[25] In 1935, revenues of the Swiss market, the US subsidiary and the German subsidiary each represented a little under 20 percent of total group revenue. But, between 1935 and 1943, the revenue from the US subsidiary grew 17 times to the point where it represented half of the group's entire revenue.[26]

The double headquarters organisation developed without a formal restructuring having taken place and under conditions of rapid expansion in the nature of business; as a result, the corporate governance of Roche was destabilised. Bobst, general director of the US subsidiary, who had been manoeuvring for independence during the interwar period, attempted to list the subsidiary on the New York Stock Exchange. The board members of the Basel headquarters opposed this move, feeling apprehensive of a possible breakup of the group. The Financial Director, Fuchs, ran the risk of travelling to the US twice during the war to block this movement, and claimed that Bobst's authority should be restricted to production and sales within the US. This dispute was finally settled in Fuchs' favour with the resignation of Bobst.[27]

In Europe, on the other hand, the Berlin subsidiary enjoyed increasing sales thanks to exports to Germany and German-occupied areas and to the military demand, when two officers started to act arbitrarily on their own authority. In 1941, they attempted to take control of the subsidiaries in the areas under German control. However, the general manager of the Grenzach plant stood by the Swiss headquarters. The removal of the two German directors also helped Roche to survive this crisis.[28]

Reintegration With the Swiss Headquarters After the War

Roche built its double headquarters system during the war, on the existing twin corporate organisation, but it made an about-face in the post-war period and worked toward strengthening the centripetal force of the Swiss headquarters and reintegrating the organisation. At the beginning of 1946, Barrell returned to Basel. In June, a board meeting was convened with the attendance of the presidents of all the foreign subsidiaries in addition to the board members of the headquarters, where decisions on the re-centralisation of the group, and the streamlining of duplicated functions and the organisation was made. As a consequence, the R&D function was integrated at Basel, and at Welwyn Garden City in the UK and Nutley in the US, with increased mutual ties between them. On the other hand, a policy was set for each subsidiary to work independently for market-specific items, such as clinical trials. During the war, the Latin American subsidiaries under control of the US subsidiary, and the sales channels outside Europe, had been consolidated under Sapac. Immediately after the war, another hub was founded in Montevideo, the capital of Uruguay, to avoid intensification of taxation by the US government on overseas holding companies, which had their main income source from the business in the US. The group's account settlement organisation was set up in Montevideo, where an executive commercial manager at the Roche headquarters was stationed to oversee the operation. This measure made the structure of the group even more complicated, but Sapac remained in Panama until it was relocated to Canada in 1962.[29] In this way, the post-war period saw the reorganisation of Roche's global organisation and integration, but against the backdrop of the Cold War, the twin structure of Roche and Sapac was retained until 1989, when it renamed itself Roche Holding AG.[30]

For Roche, whose non-European market sales to its overall turnover had been merely at a 20 percent level before the war, the Second World War served as an important impetus for it to transform itself from a multinational firm based in Europe to a global multinational in the true sense of the word. The company managed to tide itself over (from the risk of a divided world market) through its twin corporate structure introduced in the pre-war period, and by the de facto double headquarters system it had established after the outbreak of war. Although its inclination toward the US market had put it on the verge of being broken up, it managed to sustain itself. While extending the R&D and sales organisation in the US, it managed to retain its identity as a multinational corporation by reintegrating the headquarters function at Basel in conservative Switzerland, albeit in a city bordering three countries, and at the same time by preserving the corporate culture that is sometimes described as family-based. This prompted the company to grow as a multinational that reflected the European market environment with its variety of sovereign states, by capitalising on its strength in marketing to cater closely for the uniqueness of each national market, whereas many American multinationals thrived on the potential for product innovation and competition offered by the size of the US domestic market.

Nestlé and Anglo-Swiss Condensed Milk Company, Ltd.

Nestlé was already a global multinational food company on the eve of the Second World War, having 22 subsidiaries in different countries, producing at 105 production bases in Europe, the Americas, Australia and Japan.[31] The history of Nestlé dates back to 1866, when two companies were founded. In this year, Charles Page, an American consul in Zurich, set up Anglo-Swiss Condensed Milk Co., a joint-stock company in Cham near Zurich, together with his brother, to start producing condensed milk. In the same year, in Vevey, on Lake Leman, Henri Nestlé, from Frankfurt am Main, started selling infant formula products under the name of Farine Lactée Henri Nestlé. After nine years, in 1875, Henri's business was sold to a group of local entrepreneurs, but the company continued to bear his name. These two dairy producers, in the eastern and western Switzerland, penetrated into each other's product areas through fierce competition before merging in 1905 as Nestlé and Anglo-Swiss Condensed Milk Co. (hereinafter called Nestlé).[32]

For 17 years between 1905 and 1922, Nestlé remained a single corporation with a multiple headquarters organisation.[33] At the headquarters in

Cham in the German-speaking area, the directors from the former Anglo-Swiss took charge of accounting, legal affairs, insurance and tax affairs, technology and manufacturing, logistics and sales in the German-speaking area. In the French-speaking area at Vevey, the executives from the former Nestlé were responsible for the sales in non-German-speaking areas in continental Europe, and the manufacturing at four plants in France and Switzerland. London, home to the sales base of both companies, had become a third headquarters that oversaw the UK and overseas businesses other than in North America. Nestlé's business management organisation was a minimal consolidation of the two companies' businesses organised by product and by strengths and weaknesses of each market, and thus was far from a unified management. The officers still comprised family members or relatives of the founders from the end of 19th century.[34]

Expansion During the First War, Post-War Management Crisis, and Unification of the Headquarters Organisation

The decisive element in enhancing Nestlé's multinational characteristics was the outbreak of the First World War in 1914.[35] Thanks to war-driven military orders and the industrialisation of foodstuff associated with the war, the demand for portable and long-lasting condensed milk and powder milk surged.[36] On the other hand, war also brought about a serious, raw materials procurement problem. Nestlé positioned the US as the key supplier of these products, which was the world's biggest condensed milk market, far away from the battlefields. After 1915, Nestlé outsourced its condensed milk and powder milk production to Boden and other American producers, and in 1917 it started to acquire factories in the US (owning 43 already in 1920), and it either started or expanded local manufacturing in Australia and Brazil. Nestlé's global production capacity doubled during the war, with American production reaching half of Nestlé's total production.[37]

However, when the war ended, Nestlé was left with excess stocks and suffered a management crisis, and had to sell most of its newly acquired American production plants. In May 1922, it hired Louis Dupple, a banker, to promote streamlining of the business and slashing liabilities. In that process, the headquarters' function, which had been scattered to four location, two headquarters in Switzerland, one in London (managing UK and its territories) and one in Paris (in charge of sales in continental Europe since 1919), was integrated in London. Two years later in 1924, the headquarters organisation in London was relocated to its place of origin, Vevey. In the following year, the executive board was replaced by professional managers, though the founding-family members and the owners from the 19th century were still on the board of directors.[38] The restructuring after 1922 had been a move to put a halt to the decentralisation process since the war and to seek to build an integrated management at the headquarters. However, free trade did not revive after the war; instead, trade barriers were raised by countries. This, in turn, prompted the company to localise production and sales further.[39] The move toward restructuring the business into a single subsidiary per country started and went into full swing in 1930.[40]

Two Holding Companies and Security Measures With the Coming of the Second World War

The restructuring in the 1930s stripped the headquarters of most of the markets under its direct management, such as the Swiss market. As a consequence, the headquarters was reorganised as a holding company called Nestlé and Anglo-Swiss Holding Company Limited (hereinafter called 'Nestlé Holding') in November 1936, and the former directly managed businesses, including the Swiss one, were transferred to the newly formed subsidiary in Vevey, called Nestlé and Anglo-Swiss Condensed Milk Company Limited.[41]

Simultaneously, a second holding company, Unilac Inc. (hereinafter 'Unilac'), was founded in Panama to manage business expansion inside Europe as well as security risks. The ownership of subsidiaries and affiliates in the Western Hemisphere was transferred to Unilac; the company's shares consisted of priority shares with voting right and ordinary shares. The former were solely owned by Nestlé Holding and the latter were distributed free of charge to Nestlé Holding shareholders. A Nestlé Holding share and a Unilac share had an identical serial number, and separate sale of each of them was prohibited. By this means, the two companies became twins, with an identical set of shareholders, just like Roche and Sapac.[42]

President Dupple passed away in July 1937, and Eduard Muller succeeded to his post. It was agreed that Muller and vice president Gustav Huguenin would be transferred to the US and that the rest of the board would remain in the Swiss headquarters, should contingencies occur.[43] This came into effect on the eve of the war, in August 1939, when Muller actually travelled across the Atlantic. Most of the overseas assets outside continental Europe now came under the ownership of Unilac,[44] by which time it no longer existed as a mere holding company. It set up its management system within the US subsidiary of Nestlé at Stamford, Connecticut, (a suburb of New York). Muller took charge of the whole group from this second—or, rather, first in terms of revenue and size of the areas under its discretion—world headquarters.[45] After this move, the subsidiaries in continental Europe were the only ones that remained under the umbrella of Nestlé Holding.

The most important purpose in founding Unilac, at the end of 1936, was said to be the reinforcement of the US business. However, the tense European situation must also have been a consideration. Yet Nestlé's measure was motivated by a need to protect the ownership of its shareholders, rather than a fear that the company might be endangered; preparedness against a direct seizure of assets by the Axis Power was not its main intention. This was because there was no way of preventing the confiscation of Nestlé's assets within the sphere of German influence, should Germany invade Switzerland, and because it was impossible for Germany to exercise virtual control over Nestlé's assets under the influence of the Allies, even if it did manage to confiscate its shares.[46] Rather, there was a risk that, under German occupation, Nestlé's subsidiaries and assets might be confiscated as enemy assets.

From this perspective, however, as long as the preferred shares (voting shares) of Unilac were in the hands of Nestlé Holding, this scheme without the complete separation of the two holding companies was not adequate. Therefore, Nestlé Holding set up a company called Uprona, in Uruguay, in December 1939, and transferred most of Unilac's preferred shares to it. The remainder was privately owned by the two top managers, who relocated themselves to the US, and by the president of the US subsidiary. These were measures to achieve a higher level of formal separation between the two holding companies, and to relocate both ownership and control from the European continent to Americas. As for the ownership of Uprona, another complicated scheme with trust indenture was introduced and its formal separation from Nestlé Holding was achieved.

Two Spheres of Influence and Two Headquarters

The Second World War saw a major expansion of the business of Nestlé under Unilac. The Latin American production bases were scaled up, and they expanded their sales by delivering to the military, including products like Nescafé.[47] It also maintained a favourable relation with the US government and escaped being put on the blacklist. The dividend was not transferred during the war due to quota restrictions imposed by the foreign exchange clearing agreement and was accumulated within Unilac as a secret reserve. As a result of difficulties in transportation and communication, its foreign subsidiaries increased their tendency toward local sourcing and sales.

Meanwhile in Europe, under the hegemony of Germany, Karl Avec (a Swiss national) vice president, served as chairman of the board of directors of Nestlé Holding, and Maurice Paternot (a French national) controlled the European operation as the acting chief executive officer of the board of directors. After 1940, the personnel traffic between the two headquarters in Europe and Stamford almost ceased, but communication via post and telegraph was relatively dense, and this sharing of a single global strategy was also supplemented by means of the Swiss diplomatic courier.[48]

In such circumstances the two Berlin subsidiaries, Deutsche Aktiengesellschaft für Nestlé Erzeugnisse [DAN] (dairy products) and Sarroti AG (chocolate manufacturer) expanded their area of management under

President Hans Riggenbach from Switzerland, simultaneously with the expansion of the German-controlled area. As leading firms on the German market, the two managed to expand sales under the Nazi administration. They faced no foreign competition and, responding fully to the procurement needs of the military, they were able to avoid reductions in staff numbers, factory closures, or complete compliance with Nazi ideology. Unlike Maggi (food company), Brown Boveri & Cie (BBC, the third largest electronics manufacturer in Germany) and some other Swiss companies, Nestlé could maintain control over its German subsidiary. This was done easily because three-quarters of the Nestlé group's revenue came from business under Unilac, and the revenue of its German subsidiary was not so conspicuous in Europe either.[49]

Reintegration After the Second World War and Security-Based Corporate and Organisational Structures

The post-war challenge for Nestlé, which was forced to decentralise under the pressure of war, was the reintegration of its two headquarters. Surprisingly, it was not until March 1947 that Muller finally returned to Switzerland, and only after the board meeting demanded this, hinting at his possible dismissal. He was apprehensive about the outbreak of a third world war against the USSR and, in May 1948, even proposed a complete dissolution of the two holding companies for security reasons. He was of the opinion that the operation should be integrated in the US—even the idea of a headquarters' detachment was to be discouraged—because of the large market and growth potential.[50]

However, his proposal was far from acceptable to the remaining directors in Switzerland. The executives who opposed relocation to the US based their argument on points such as how the history of Nestlé was deeply rooted in Switzerland, the US would be seemingly unable to escape from an outright participation in a next war, Switzerland's advantages as a neutral state, that 80 percent of the shareholders were Swiss, the existence of a favourable tax system in Switzerland, and lastly, the 'homecoming' in peacetime that had been promised in the board of directors meeting in 1940, when it voted to split the headquarters.

The strategy that Nestlé finally chose was to locate its headquarters in Switzerland, while enhancing its security measures.[51] Due partially to the transfer and repatriation of members from the US, the headcount swelled from 155 during the war to 490 in June 1947, though it was still a tiny headquarters for such a sizeable group.[52] A part of the US umbrella organisation of Unilac was kept for the top management to supervise in turn every half year, but after Muller died in the US in 1948, the move toward consolidating authority in Switzerland continued.[53]

Nonetheless, integration was a gradual process. The double structure was maintained for a long time both for the corporate form and ownership structure. In April 1947, Nestlé Holding merged with Uprona, where Unilac founder's shares had been transferred, reassuming control over Unilac, and bought out Alimentana, a Swiss company owning the Maggi brand, and renamed itself Nestlé Alimentana. The company also brought its subsidiaries in the Sterling bloc under its corporate umbrella in 1950, and toward 1953 it formed a dummy company in Canada and the Bahamas, which underpinned its security measures. In 1959, it issued registered shares for the exclusive sale to the Swiss, in an attempt to intensify its Swiss identity. It was in 1964 that the Swiss headquarters finally bought back the US subsidiary shares from Unilac, and it was as late as 1985 that the US subsidiary was dissolved with the clear prospect of the Cold War ending.[54]

The Anglo-Dutch Unilever: Two Companies Within a Single Management Organisation

Considered a British and Dutch company, Unilever was an offspring of a pan-European merger movement also involving companies in Czechoslovakia and France. In 1930, Lever Brothers and Margarine Unie/Union—a merger of Van den Bergh, Jurgens, Schicht, Hartog and Calvé-Delft two years before—set up two holding companies, Unilever Limited in London and Unilever NV in Rotterdam. They signed a so-called Equalisation Agreement aimed at an equal treatment of shareholders in Britain (Limited) and the Netherlands (NV), and to avoid double taxation.[55] After the merger, Unilever became one of the largest companies (measured by total capital) in Europe. Compared to Nestlé the Anglo-Dutch Unilever was a gigantic empire—it operated more than 500 businesses in more than 40 countries—achieving a dominant position in the non-mineral oil and fats, food and soap businesses in numerous markets all over the world.[56]

Unilever's legal dual form must not be confused with its organisational structure. The object of the merger agreement had been unity, as the company's name expressed. However, the formation of a centralised and unified company out of a conglomerate of former family businesses, managed directly from one centre (London) appeared much more complicated than the signing of an Equalisation Agreement. In fact, the formation of Unilever as a unified company would take another ten years, was violently disrupted by the Second World War and was continued after the war. Nevertheless, the Boards of Directors of Limited and NV were identical. From 1931 the Board meetings were regularly held in a new and impressive headquarters at Unilever House, in Blackfriars, London. Although professional managers played an important role in the 1930s, members of the old families were still well represented on the Board of Directors and had a good-sized share in the business until after the Second World War.[57] The Directors Conference, as Unilever's Board meetings were called, acted as an informal exchange of information and opinions once a week. It also had a more formal function: the allocation of capital expenditure.[58]

Final authority, however, was delegated to an executive body: the Special Committee. Initially it was a body of eight persons, but by 1938 it had been reduced to six, of whom the most important were the chairman of Limited, Francis D'Arcy Cooper, and the chairman of NV, from 1937, Paul Rijkens. Both D'Arcy Cooper and Rijkens were typical examples of professional managers; both were in charge as a result of their management qualities and not by accident of birth. The Special Committee was primarily responsible for Unilever's general business policy; it focussed on overall monitoring, planning and resource allocation. The members did not conduct the daily business of any specific unit, but were kept informed of, and advised and decided on, the more important matters that were submitted to them by other directors.[59] The Special Committee had meetings with various executive committees. The business in Britain was exceptionally managed by a Group Executive, organised by product: soap, margarine, oil mills, and foods. The Continental Committee supervised the continental business in Europe. The Overseas Committee looked after Unilever's business in the British Empire and North America, and the United Africa Company (UAC), the largest trading company in the world, had its own Board. The Unilever Group, however, was not organised according to product divisions. Only the British business was—by way of exception—grouped by products, which originated in 1926 in Lever Brothers, and could be called a multidivisional organisation. The Unilever Group outside Britain, however, was organised along the lines of national companies rather than functional divisions. In the 1930s, Unilever was a huge conglomerate of hundreds of operating companies, organised in a complex legal structure. It was a conglomerate because it rapidly diversified into several unrelated business areas as a result of the merger and a large number of acquisitions during that period.[60]

Preparing for War: Establishment of a Trust Scheme

In 1937, the subsidiaries under the two corporations in UK and the Netherlands were reshuffled, so that their profits were evenly shared to close the enlarging profit gap between them. This consolidated the highly profitable North American business, and overseas business outside the sphere of the British Empire under Mavibel, a holding company established by the Dutch NV, and the foreign business was placed under the direction of the NV Continental Committee and the Overseas Committee.[61]

The reorganisation was also done in the light of mounting tensions in Europe. NV was expected to keep its independence as a financial entity on the basis of the profits from its US subsidiaries even in case of an extreme contingency, as long as the Netherlands and the US remained neutral. However, with the prospect of a possible occupation of the Netherlands, additional security measures were implemented. Philips and Royal Dutch Shell planned to utilise the new Dutch law of April 1940 to relocate the place of registration to Curaçao, in the Dutch Antilles.[62] Unilever's solution, however, was to set up two holding companies in South Africa, in 1939, to which all overseas assets outside the British Empire would be transferred in case of emergency. These holdings were linked to London via trust contracts (named the 'White Hall Trust'—indicative of the close relations between the company and government).[63] This scheme was devised so that Unilever Limited in London was enabled to manage the group's foreign subsidiaries, which served most of its purpose during the war. Namely, the British administration tolerated the fact that Limited directly controlled NV's indirectly owned overseas subsidiary, which otherwise would have been legally subject to confiscation and management as 'enemy assets' under the German occupation.[64] As a result, a system came into being where two holding companies in the two blocs were to exercise control over their respective area of management.

Outbreak of the War: Conversion to the Two Headquarters System

Unilever's twin structure changed from a legal entity to a substantive two headquarters system due to the outbreak of the Second World War on September 1, 1939. NV in Rotterdam came to have its own board of directors separately from Limited in London, with their board members consisting solely of Dutch and British nationals respectively. At that time, Franz and Heinrich Schicht, from one of the Czechoslovakian founding families, who had received German nationality after the occupation of Sudetenland and had been on the identical boards of directors of the two companies, were sent to Berlin to be directors of the German headquarters and holding company, Margarine Verkaufsunion (MVU) in Berlin. Georg Schicht, the largest individual shareholder, who had been naturalised in the UK, remained as an executive officer of Limited. During the war, Limited maintained close communication with the British government and the Dutch government in exile in London, and supported the Allies' war effort. The Continental Committee, in control of the subsidiaries in continental Europe, was relocated from London to Rotterdam, after which it refrained from direct communication with the London headquarters.[65]

The situation changed again in May 1940 after the German invasion and occupation of the neutral Netherlands. The Jewish directors of NV fled the country, two of whom became executives of Limited. The board of directors of NV was revamped, after which Germans accounted for half of the members, including Karl Blessing, a former board member of the Reichsbank and board member of MVU in Berlin.[66]

Despite the Germanisation of NV, the most important positions in the board remained in Dutch hands. Pieter Hendriks, for example, held the chair of the Dutch board during the whole war period. Besides, all new German directors had had previous ties with NV before the outbreak of war.[67] Therefore, the organisational disconnection was only partial. This was why Limited in London and NV in Rotterdam managed to share a common strategy, despite their formal division and lack of communication. The German authorities in the occupied Netherlands restricted the action of the latter, but independence as a corporation was maintained to a certain extent. This was also a result of the doubling of the management headquarters on the European continent in Rotterdam and Berlin. While the German subsidiary increasingly made unauthorised decisions for itself, extending its control over subsidiaries in Central and Eastern Europe, the Dutch directors in Rotterdam were left with a certain room for manoeuvre. This was because the German directors had stationed themselves in Berlin, thereby positioning the German subsidiary as the core of the group. Western Europe and Scandinavia except Sweden, however, remained under the control of Rotterdam even after 1942.[68]

Hermann Göring's appointment of Hans Ernst Posse as a special Reichs Commissioner for the Unilever Group, in June 1941, involved the preparations to subsume Unilever NV's capital under that of a German syndicate. The appointment turned out differently from what had been planned in the 1940–1941 period by various German agencies, and the developments did not prove to be unfavourable to Unilever. The Reichs Commissioner protected the company against attacks by greedy competitors like Reemtsma and Reichwerke Hermann Göring, in their endeavours to acquire pieces of the Unilever conglomerate in occupied Europe. The formal relocation of the company's headquarters to Berlin, which was sought by various German government agencies and supported by some German Unilever managers, like Franz Schicht, also ended in complete failure as a result of the Reichs Commissioner's policies. Actually, Unilever benefited from the political infighting in the Third Reich and its contradictory economic strategies.

Liberation and Reunification of London and Rotterdam

In December 1945, Unilever went through a legal reunification. After the liberation of the Netherlands in 1945, Unilever Limited had made an application to the Bank of England for its approval for Limited to enter into a new Equalisation Agreement with NV.[69] The old agreement had been frustrated by the war.[70] During the war, Limited had paid 5 percent dividends on its ordinary shares; however, to fulfil the terms of the Equalisation Agreement it had set aside enough to take care of NV's shareholders dividends in the event that NV could not pay out. As a result, the company was able to make a financial settlement with its shareholders after the war.

After the liberalisation of the Netherlands, the German directors at NV and its subsidiaries were forced from office. All members of the Schicht family, except Georg, were dismissed from Unilever NV's board and their shares were confiscated by the Dutch government. Georg Schicht, a British citizen who had remained in London during the war, left the company in 1946 disaffected by the nationalisation policy in Eastern Europe and Unilever's settlement of the issue. The company lost many assets without compensation, but the Anglo-Dutch company no longer wanted to be associated with the reputation of the Schicht family in Eastern Europe. This development during and after the Second World War intensified the company's identity as an Anglo-Dutch company. Actually, in post-war publications, the Schicht pillar in the history of the company is hardly mentioned. Based on the inspection tours to subsidiaries outside the European continent during the war, the centralised Continental Committee and Overseas Committee were abolished after the war.[71] Support functions for the foreign subsidiaries were expanded by establishing a so-called contact director system. The governance of subsidiaries was confined to approval of annual business, expenditure plans, and appointment of the management; thus the decentralised system was maintained and even became one of Unilever's main business principles after the war.[72]

The comparative sales turnover figures showed a big shift in the distribution of sales worldwide, which was an important result of the war. Before the war, the European business had been most important to the company; with Africa coming second. By 1946, however, the sales figures of the German and the East European business had become null and void for the company; British sales figures had increased slightly, also in relative terms. The largest growth, however, came from the US and Africa. In the 1937–1946 period, sales in the US almost tripled, thereby doubling the share represented by that country in Unilever's total worldwide sales. Sales in the US had risen as a result of the booming American economy, beginning at the end of the 1930s and continuing throughout the whole war. The shift of Unilever's sales worldwide had also been a result of a deliberate strategy pursued at the end of the 1930s, when the board had taken steps to replace earning capacity, which might be lost on the continent, by developing new earning capacity on other continents.[73]

N. V. Philips' Gloeilampen Fabrieken

Philips & Company was established by the electrical engineer Gerard Philips in Eindhoven, in the south of the Netherlands, in 1891. Although the light bulb company was well organised technically, it incurred great losses until Gerard's younger brother Anton, trained as a financial specialist, joined the company in 1895. The combination of Gerard's technical skills combined with his brother's sales talent proved to be a success. The company began to sell incandescent lamps all over the Netherlands, and soon also across the border in Germany, in Westphalia and the Rhineland. By 1900, Philips & Company was able to pay back its original loans.[74]

As the European incandescent lamp market was fiercely defended by the big manufactures in Germany through cartels and patents, Philips sought new opportunities in North and South Europe, North and South America, Southeast Asia, Australia and South Africa. It aimed to build contact with sales agents, which in later years were taken over as sales companies.[75]

The constant growth of Philips & Co forced the company to look for a new management structure and stronger capital base. In particular, the older brother, Gerard Philips, who had no children, endeavoured to establish a limited company. In 1911, Henry van den Bergh, in London, one of the directors of the Dutch margarine manufacturer's family, advised Anton Philips to incorporate Philips in Britain, as Van den Bergh had done. According to him, it was still easier to find new capital in London than in Amsterdam. Nevertheless, in 1911 the London capital market was somewhat depressed, and in the Netherlands the introduction of preference shares a year before had been a great success. The interest of Dutch industrial companies in the Amsterdam stock exchange increased steadily. In 1912, the company was incorporated in the Netherlands and named N. V. Philips Gloeilampenfabrieken.[76]

Before the First World War, Philips was excluded from an agreement between the major German electrical firms like Siemens & Halse and AEG, organised in the *Patentgemeinschaft* (patent pool), and General Electric (GE). The purpose of this global entente was an exchange of patents and to carve out spheres of influence. In 1913, Philips was forced by the German bloc to sign a contract which limited the company's sales in Europe below its productive capacity. As a result, Philips expanded its exports to the United States which directly affected GE's sales in its home market. In 1916, GE therefore started negotiations with Philips about including the Dutch company in its network of licence holders if it stopped the export of incandescent lamps to the US. The 'Principal Agreement', as it was called, was signed in 1919 and brought Philips into the global inner circle of incandescent lamp manufacturers.[77] In addition, GE agreed to take a stake of 20 percent in Philips.[78] The agreement with General Electric was one of the main factors in Philip's post-war, foreign expansion within the incandescent lamp industry'.[79]

Another factor was the end of the dominant role of the *Patentgemeinschaft* as a result of the First World War. In the Allied countries, the agreements with the patent pool had become invalid. Factories belonging to Siemens in Britain and France, and to AEG in Italy, had been sequestrated as enemy property. Similar measures had been taken against German patents. In the major belligerent countries there had been scarcely any innovation in incandescent lamp manufacture. Moreover, German companies had lost a great deal of their export markets.[80]

Philips, on the other hand, had shown a formidable growth, as the German competition had fallen away during the war. Wartime conditions had forced the Dutch incandescent lamp manufacturer onto a road of vertical integration. Before the war, it had been dependent on foreign technology, raw materials and semi-manufactured goods. In 1914, on the eve of war, Philips had set up its own Physics Laboratory (NatLab), which developed in a short period of time into an important knowledge centre for the company.[81] In the course of the war, Philips had also set up its own factories for noble gases and glass bulbs. In addition, the war had proven that working through local agents made the export organisation vulnerable. Philips, therefore, created its own sales organisation abroad.[82] All these new developments, in combination with the company's strong financial position at the end of the war, put the Dutch incandescent lamp manufacturer in an extremely favourable position.[83] Moreover, Philips made handsome profits during and directly after the war, and paid out huge dividends to its shareholders.[84]

In 1920, Anton and Gerard Philips decided to change the company structure in the Netherlands and set up a holding company—N. V. Gemeenschappelijk Bezit van Aandelen Philips' Gloeilampenfabrieken—which prevented foreign shareholders from taking over the company. The holding company owned all Philips shares, with the exception of GE's stake, and was allowed to market new share issues. The six priority shares of the holding company were in the hands of Dutchmen, either directors or members of the Philips' supervisory board. The priority shareholders were entitled to make binding nominations for the appointment of the board of the operating company, Philips' Gloeilampenfabrieken.[85] The establishment of the holding company also marked the transformation from family company Philips to the Philips group, consisting of several domestic and foreign operating companies. In addition to the internationalisation of the Philips group, it sought legal protection against hostile and foreign take-overs.

Meanwhile, Philips' German competitors, AEG, the Deutsche Auergesellschaft and Siemens & Halske, had formed a single German incandescent lamp manufacturer—Osram GmbH. However, strong international competition and, in particular, Philips' expansionist policy in foreign markets, enforced the newly established German company towards an international incandescent lamp cartel. This fitted perfectly with the aims of GE to protect its American home market. Both the Americans and the Germans realised that such an agreement would not work without the expansion-oriented Philips. The latter chose stability instead of cutthroat competition. A little later, French and British manufactures joined the agreement. As a result, at the end of 1924 all major companies in the world ratified the 'General Patent and Business Development Agreement' in Paris, which later became known as the 'Phoebus' cartel.[86] It appeared to be one of the most successful interwar cartels, lasting until the outbreak of the Second World War.

Peace on the incandescent lamp market proved favourable to Philips as it offered new opportunities. Because of its excellent financial position it was able to diversify into new products and markets. In the early 1920s, Philips began to invest abroad, including France, Britain and Germany. However, the Phoebus cartel agreement did not allow Philips to produce incandescent lamps for the German market. Therefore, the company diversified in other directions and began to challenge the largest German electrotechnical firms, Siemens & Halske and AEG, with new products on their own home market.

The beginning of radio broadcasting in a number of European countries in 1923–1924, including the Netherlands, gave a powerful impulse to the development of a radio industry. Philips reacted rapidly to the rise in demand for radio valves, using its know-how from incandescent lamp manufacturing. Concentrating on mass production of radio valves of good quality soon put the company in a strong competitive position. In 1925, RCA tried to stop the expansion of Philips in its American home market and offered the Dutch company a licencing contract for various European countries if it undertook to stop expanding in the United States. After it had acquired C.H.F. Müller in Hamburg in 1927, a manufacturer of X-ray machines, Philips also obtained a factory of radio valves under the name Valvo, which had been set up in by Müller in 1924. Philips market share for radio valves in Germany increased to more than 30 percent.[87] Shortly after the take-over, Philips decided that research in X-ray technology should be continued in Eindhoven, but that the manufacturing would be done in Hamburg.[88] As a result of Philips' expansion abroad, particularly in Europe, and the several acquisitions it had made, the company had become a diversified electronics company during in the interwar period.

Economic Nationalism and National Trusts

Economic nationalism of the 1930s forced multinationals like Philips to rethink their organisational structure. In 1937, Philips' board in Eindhoven discussed the reorganisation of its international activities; power and functions had to be transferred to the various national organisations (localisation), which had to be given the greatest possible autonomy.[89] The reorganisation of Philips' international structure took place between 1937 and 1940 in several countries, including Germany. In November 1939, the Allgemeine Deutsche Philips Verwaltung Gesellschaft mbH (Alldephi) was set up to control all German and Austrian subsidiaries.[90] The German reorganisation, however, was not only the result of plans of the Philips board in Eindhoven, but it was also the consequence of pressure from the Nazi government, which endeavoured to bring about a Germanisation of the Dutch firm. As a major electronics firm in Germany, Philips was too important for Nazi war plans to be left in Dutch hands.

When tensions in Europe were mounting at the end of 1938 and beginning of 1939, Philips made legal provisions in Britain in case of war. The company realised that its factories in Britain would be possible targets for confiscation on the basis of the Trading with the Enemy Act if war were to break out between Britain and Germany. The solution found by Philips' legal advisers was to transfer its assets in the Commonwealth into the hands of a British trust. On May 1, 1939, Philips' management appointed the Midland Bank Executor & Trustee Company Ltd. as trustee. The purpose was to provide a legal structure under which Philips could operate its business in the commonwealth in the event of a German invasion. As long as Philips' management was able to control the business from Eindhoven ('Philips period'), the managing trustees had to act in accordance with instructions from the company's headquarters in the Netherlands. However, if the headquarters found itself in a position where it was unable to carry on management from Eindhoven as a result of the 'Specified Event' (i.e. the invasion of the Netherlands), the 'Shareholders period' would begin. From then on, the British trust would manage the assets exclusively in the interest of Philips' shareholders.[91]

A similar legal provision was set up in the US a few months later on August 25, 1939, to protect and manage Philips' assets in the US, Central and South America, with the exception of assets in Argentina which were transferred to the British trust. The Hartfort National Bank and Trustee Company was to be put in charge of Philips' assets in the Western Hemisphere in the event of a German invasion of the Netherlands. Similarly, to protect the valuable assets in the Netherlands, the company set up the N. V. Philips' Exploitatie Maatschappij, on May 1, 1939; if the Germans invaded, the plan was to hire out all the machinery and buildings owned by N. V. Philips' Gloeilampen to this new company. This would, according to Philips' legal advisers, prevent the enemy from confiscating the assets and simultaneously allow production in Eindhoven to continue.[92]

Transfer of Registered Office to Curaçao and Philips' Management to New York

In addition to the aforementioned provision, the company endeavoured to bring about the transfer of the registered offices of N. V. Philip's Gloeilampenfabrieken and the holding company, N. V. Gemeenschappleijk Bezit van Aandelen Philips' Gloeilampenfabrieken, which owned all the shares of the former, to Curaçao in the Dutch Antilles. However, a legal basis was lacking in the Netherlands for this transfer. The registered office of the company had already been transferred in February 1939 to the Hague—deemed a safer place than Eindhoven, which was located much closer to the German border. The Hague was situated inside the Fortress Holland, which was initially assumed a safe haven in case of a German invasion. However, the board decided a little later that this relocation would not be sufficient. As a result, it urged the Dutch government, together with BPM (Royal Dutch Shell) to prepare new legislation. Thereupon, the

Minister of Justice set up a mixed committee, consisting of government officials as well as Philips and BPM staff, to draft an emergency bill which would enable Dutch multinationals to transfer their registered offices to safer places in the Dutch Kingdom, namely, the overseas territories. A few weeks before the German invasion of the Netherlands, the law was signed.[93]

On the evening before the invasion of the Netherlands, deputy chairman Frans Otten received reliable information that a German attack was on its way. Thereupon the board decided to start with the evacuation of Philips' management, some selected staff, and some machinery to Fortress Holland. However, the greater part of the convoy never reached the western part of the country, except the group which included Anton Philips, Otten, Loupart, Van Walsum and some other senior staff members. The next day, Philips' senior management, together with the members of the Dutch government, sailed to the UK on board a British warship. Frits Philips, Anton's son, being a reserve officer in the Dutch army, was not allowed to leave the country. He went back to Eindhoven and took charge of the company's management in the Netherlands.

Immediately after the German invasion all legal provisions came into force: the company shifted its domicile to Willemstad in Curaçao, the agreement concerning the Exploitatie Maatschappij took effect, and both the British and American Trusts decided that the 'Shareholders period' had started. Shortly, Philips' board realised that from London it would be extremely difficult to manage Philips companies in neutral and unoccupied territories, and to stay in contact with Eindhoven. Formally, it was not even allowed to manage its companies in Britain according to the trust agreement. Consequently, Anton Philips, Otten and Loupart decided to move headquarters to New York. As a neutral state, the US offered ample opportunities to control the existing businesses around the world, and the possibility to expand Philips' business in North and South America.[94] In addition, the Advisory Committee of the American trust, which consisted of three American citizens, decided to set up a Board of Advice which included, exclusively, those Philips senior managers who had fled from the Netherlands.[95]

German Administrators in Eindhoven

As the company had great significance for the German war industry, Philips was put under German administration. Shortly after the occupation Dr. O Bormann and Dr. O. J. Merkel were appointed by the Ministry of Aviation as administrators (*Verwalter*) of Philips' German holding company Alldephi. Two months later, they were also appointed administrators of NV Philips' Gloeilampenfabrieken in Eindhoven. The new Dutch directorate in Eindhoven, chaired by Frits Philips, did not protest against the appointment of the two administrators, because both Germans had been on the supervisory Board of Alldephi before the occupation and could be seen as friendly business contacts. In particular, the appointment of Bormann, who had been a director of the incandescent lamp manufacturer Pintsch, a company that had had close business relations to Philips before the war, could not be seen as a real threat to the Dutch directors.[96]

In the first three years of the war, these German administrators helped Philips to defend itself against attempts of German competitors, like Telefunken and Bosch, which aimed to take over parts of the Philips organisation, or attempts by the Nazi state to Germanise Philips through mergers with other German companies. As agents for the Air Ministry, both administrators represented a faction in the polycratic Nazi regime that wanted Philips to manufacture components for military radio communication and to be split up and divided among German rivals. The price Philips, like all other Dutch multinationals, had to pay to survive the serious threats from competitors and various German government agencies, was manufacturing for and trading with the enemy. During the war, Philips' production of radio valves for military use grew dramatically. By 1942 the share of these radio valves had already increased threefold and it grew even further after 1943. Philips' sales of valves for the civilian market remained about the same during the war. Telefunken's share of military valves manufacturing only doubled, while its civilian production decreased. As a consequence, during the war Telefunken's parent company, AEG, complained to various German state agencies that its subsidiary company was being put at a disadvantage vis-à-vis Philips.[97]

Expansion in the Western Hemisphere and North American Philips Company

During the war, Philips expanded its activities tremendously in the Western Hemisphere. Latin America, in particular Argentina, Brazil and Chile, became of great importance for Philips' industrial activities. FAPESA (Fábrica Argentina de Productos Eléctricos) was Philips' biggest manufacturing company in Latin America, and was controlled first by the British trust, but in 1942 taken over by the American trust through a capital extension. Philips' extensive activities in Latin America led to distrust by the American secret service (OSS). The company was working on important war contracts in Britain and the US, but simultaneously it had contact with its businesses in neutral countries in Latin America and Europe (Switzerland, Portugal, Spain and Sweden), and indirectly, via these neutral states, contact even with occupied countries. Furthermore, it was not clear to OSS what had happened to the company's relations with the Phoebus cartel and whether it was still in existence during the war. In 1943, OSS published an extensive report which recommended 'investigation of and action against the concern'.[98] Eventually, the report had no negative consequences for Philips in the US. On the contrary, in organisational terms, the company continued on a path of aggrandisement.

As early as December 1940, director Loupart had presented his 'Work Plan' in which he had argued that Philips had to develop a substitute for Eindhoven in the US. Too many subsidiaries in the world relied too heavily on the technical input from headquarters in Eindhoven. The war situation had shown how dangerous this strategy could be. Therefore, the group had to develop a 'second power source' of know-how and semi-manufactured goods. However, as a result of agreements with GE and RCA, the company could not develop industrial activities in its core businesses (lamps, radio valves, radio sets), but it had to develop its US business in a different and new direction and preferably in joint ventures with American companies. In January 1942, the Philips board set up a new holding company for its US activities—the North American Philips Company (NAPC). Up until the autumn of 1944, NAPC's activities expanded tremendously, however, due to a fall in US war orders the company began to incur losses. Nevertheless, in 1946, Philips' board of management, which had returned to Eindhoven, stated that the group needed 'a permanent and active' presence in the US. In addition, the board decided that the continuation of the American trust would be an essential prerequisite for Philips' American identity and success in the country. The developing Cold War and outbreak of the Korean War convinced foe and friend alike that this was the right policy. But the separation of the US business and the group's strategy would lead to serious problem many decades later.[99]

Conclusion

Roche, Nestlé, Unilever and Philips survived the mounting nationalism and division of markets during the world wars by localising their corporate organisation, by introducing twin corporate structures, and by doubling or dispersing headquarter functions. As a result, these European firms all came to have a relatively decentralised form of organisation. In addition, security considerations kept on prescribing their organisational form, ownership and governance structure after the conclusion of the world wars.

Dutch and Swiss multinationals showed similar responses to political risk, the threats of war and finally war. The dual structure was a general phenomenon of these large corporations, originally meant as tax constructions in the 1920s and 1930s, it became a defence mechanism against sequestration in Germany and the occupied countries as well as Trading with the Enemy Acts in Allied countries. The new organisational structures of these corporations were strategic responses to the threating political conditions in the era of total war, which had long-lasting consequences. All four companies shifted part of their global business from the European continent to the Western Hemisphere as a result of their organisational adaptations. The differences between firm strategies and responses can be explained by sector product specificity, different national circumstances as well as geographical spread of their respective interests. Clearly, it was not a matter of one size fits all. However, the analysis here focusses more on the similarities than the differences, because the strategic response can be interpreted as a general phenomenon, which to a large extent explains the decentralisation of Swiss and Dutch big business for the greater part of the 20th century. It was only after the end of the Cold War that these legal and organisational defensive constructions became superfluous.

Golden share and multi-layered share ownership, strongly rooted in European countries, are generally considered to reflect perspectives on the market, company, or corporate governance; but the security background should also be taken into account. It is an interesting fact in the history of the world wars that both camps generally never took a hard line towards business activities within their sphere of influence despite their wariness against them. This suggest that the two camps accepted the separation of the twin holding companies and division of headquarters function as substantial to a certain degree, and, to that extent it can be interpreted as a success of companies' proactive efforts to cope with political risks. Interestingly, the formation of holding companies as a legal entity played a big role in this period. They were used as financial and legal constructs, but often they were also used as legal form to manage operational businesses. More research is needed into the historical role and multidimensional usage of these legal vehicles.

Roche and Nestlé, both based in Switzerland, pursued decentralisation and localisation (adaption to national circumstances) of their management organisation to address the nationalistic reactions in many countries during and after the First World War. They reorganised their headquarters into special dual-structured corporations in the interwar period to avert double taxation and prepared themselves against possible political and war risks. Unilever, based in the United Kingdom and the Netherlands, and Philips, headquartered in the Netherlands, also pursued complicated legal provisions and decentralised and localised their foreign operations in the interwar period. Just before the German occupation of the Netherlands and the threat of invasion of Switzerland by the Axis, the four companies all doubled their corporate organisational and headquarters functions, and continued their business in markets dominated by the Allies as well as the Axis. The ratio of business conducted in non-European markets, including the US market, increased due to the war, which paved the way for post-war global operations. During the Cold War, security concerns seemed to continue to determine their corporate form, ownership and governance structure.

The four case studies have revealed that the behaviour of the corporations based in neutral Switzerland had certain commonalities with multinational companies based in the Netherlands. The organisational and strategic countermeasures taken by Unilever and Philips against political and security risks were not so different from those taken by companies based in Switzerland. Neutral Switzerland, which appeared to be in an extremely precarious position confronted by the hegemony of Germany, was considered an unlikely shelter. Therefore, the US was selected as the safe haven for the world headquarters because of its security and the unparalleled market opportunities it provided. The Dutch Philips board also sought shelter in the US, while Unilever relied completely on the British state, nonetheless simultaneously redirecting its market strategy more to the US market. In this regard, the four case studies illustrate not only the impact of the world wars on corporate structure, but also the historic meaning of the world wars from a business perspective, namely the relative decline of Europe's position, and rise of the US as a hegemon.

Notes

1 Geoffrey Jones, *Multinationals and Global Capitalism From the Nineteenth to the Twenty-First Century* (Oxford: Oxford University Press, 2005), 81–83, 243–244.

2 In mid 1990s, the debate on the gold transactions between the Swiss National Bank and National Socialist Germany and the 'dormant assets' in Swiss banks had unexpectedly escalated to strong criticism from the outside, mainly US, on Switzerland. In this context, the Swiss Parliament and the Federal Council (executive branch of the government) decided to investigate these accusations and established *Independent Commission of Experts Switzerland—Second World War (ICE)* (www.uek.ch/en/index.htm). The outcome of this big research project was published as several interim reports and a series of publication of 25 volumes of monographs, which exceed more than 10,000 pages in total. The final report is published in four languages. See Independent Commission of Experts Switzerland—Second World War, ed., *Switzerland, National Socialism and the Second World War: Final Report* (Zurich: Pendo Verlag, 2002). Kurosawa published a Japanese translation of this final report, by adding follow-up research by several Japanese historians. See Takafumi Kurosawa, ed., *Churitsukoku Suisu to Nachizumu: Dainiji Sekaitaisen to Rekishi Ninshiki (Neutral Switzerland and National Socialism: The Second World War and Perception of History)* (Kyoto: Kyoto University Press, 2010).

3 An example of this kind of rare but intensive research is Hans Ulirch Wipf, *Georg Fischer AG 1930–1945: Ein Schweizer Industrieunternehmen im Spannungsfeld Europas* (Zürich: Chronos Verlag, 2001).

4 Historians' attention to corporate behaviour during the period of National Socialism and the Second World War intensified from the mid-1990s, and also focussed on other countries. The following research is worth mentioning. Harold James and Jakob Tanner, ed., *Enterprise in the Period of Fascism in Europe* (London: Ashgate, 2002); Joachim Lund, ed., *Working for the New Order: European Business Under German Domination 1939–1945* (Copenhagen: University Press of Southern Denmark, 2006); Christopher Kobrak and Per H. Hansen, eds., *European Business, Dictatorship, and Political Risk 1920–1945* (New York: Berghahn Books, 2004).

5 Ben Wubs, *International Business and National War Interests: Unilever Between Reich and Empire, 1939–1945* (London: Routledge, 2008).

6 Ivo J. Blanken, *The History of Philips Electronics N.V. Under German Rule*, Vol. 4 (Zaltbomme: European Library, 1999).

7 In 1914, among 700 employee of Roche, only 145 were working in Basel and most of its workforce for production was in Germany. Hand Conrad Peyer, *Roche- Geschichte eines Unternehmens 1896–1996* (Basel: Editiones Roche, 1996), 35.

8 Peyer, *Roche*, 116.

9 Peyer, *Roche*, 68; Lukas Straumann and Daniel Wildmann, *Schweizer Chemieunternehmen im «Dritten Reich' (Veröffenlichungen der UEK Bd.7 / Publications de la CIE Vol.7)* (Zürich: Chronos, 2001), 186.

10 Roche Historical Archive, Box Nr. AF.9_103182, Anzeige 'Cewega'. This document is a copy of Cewega's advertisement published in Münchener Medizinische Wochenschrift. It maintains that Cewega was a pure German company and its profit was in Germany. Additionally, it emphasises that the company is a competitor for Roche in the third country.

11 Though the case of Roche is the most prominent one, almost all Swiss multinational enterprises experienced the same kind of difficulties and they responded with similar measures. In regard to the impact of the First World War on Swiss firms, see Roman Rossfeld and Tobias Straumann, ed., *Der Vergessene Wirtschaftskrieg: Schweizer Unternehemen in Ersten Weltkrieg* (Zürich: Chronos, 2008). After the end of the war, in 1920, Roche bought back the shares of Cewega. Roche founded a local subsidiary company in Berlin (F. Hoffmann-La Roche & Co. AG) to control sales activities in Germany. Cewega was merged with this German subsidiary. Peyer, *Roche*, 70; Straumann and Wildmann, *Schweizer Chemieunternehmen*, 186.

12 Martin Lüpold, *Der Ausbau der 'Festung Schweiz', Aktienrecht und Corporate Governance in der Schweiz, 1881–1961* (PhD diss., Zurich University, 2008), 140.

13 Roche Historical Archive, *Organigramme 1922*, 'Schéma de l'organisation de la Centrale' dated 6 Jan 1922; Peyer, *Roche*, 69–70, 84–90, 125.

14 Mira Wilkins's intense and encompassing work on inward foreign investments in the US positioned the four companies studied here in a wider context. As she pointed out, the story of foreign investment in the United States is a subset of world economic history. Mira Wilkins, *The History of Foreign Investment in the United States 1914–1945* (Cambridge, MA: Harvard University Press, 2004).

15 In July 1929, at the peak of the bubble in the stock market boom in the US, Bobst visited Roche's headquarter in Basel along with investment bankers from New York. They proposed a shocking acquisition deal. One was an acquisition of the whole of Roche group for $25 million and the other was for the American subsidiary for $5 million. Both were immediately rejected. However, Bobst never gave up his ambition even afterwards, namely independence from the parent company in Switzerland. Peyer, *Roche*, 62, 73, 109, 115, 151.

16 Martin Lüpold's publication cited above traced the historical development of corporate governance in Switzerland. In this intensive work, he clarified the impacts of '*Überfremdung*' (excessive influence of foreigners and foreign capital) arguments on the transition of governance system and corporate form towards a more 'closed' system. The introduction of voting shares and *Vinkulierung* (restriction of transferability) during the interwar period was a direct result of this trend. Lüpold, *Der Ausbau der 'Festung Schweiz'*.

17 Peyer, *Roche*, 118; Roche Historical Archive, ed., *Aus meinem Berufsleben* (An autobiography written by a director of Roche). The Principality of

Liechtenstein formed a custom and currency union with Switzerland from 1924. The country legislated for very flexible corporate law ('Personen- und Gesellscahftrecht') in 1926, with a clear intention to attract the relocation of foreign enterprises into the country. Christoph Maria Merki, *Wirtschaftswunder Liechtenstein: Die rasche Modernisierung einer Kleinen Volkswirtschaft im 20. Jahrhundert* (Vaduz: Verlag des Historischen Verein für das Fürstentum Liechtenstein), 136–141.

18 See also: Roche Historical Archive, *Aus meinem Berufsleben.*

19 Peyer, *Roche*, 152, 177–178.

20 David Howarth, *The Goldeni Isthmus* (London: Reader's Union, 1967).

21 Panama had many advantages, not limited to widely used US dollars and English. Its joint-stock company law was enacted in 1927, just a year after the legislation of the above-mentioned corporate law in Liechtenstein. The law in Panama is also extremely flexible. The law is modelled after US corporate laws, breaking away from the system of continental law, which had been a tradition since the independence of the country. The tax system of the country is also very favourable for inward relocation of holding companies. The object of taxation was limited only to corporate profits gained by businesses based on Panama's inland resources. Therefore, the tax system exempted holding companies in Panama from taxation on income from dividends transferred by overseas subsidiaries. Additionally, when a foreign company moved into Panama and registered there, liquidation of the company in the original home country was not postulated; therefore, the company was able to maintain its contractual relationship. Niklaus von Deschwanden, *Das Aktienrecht von Panama* (Berlin and Frankfurt a.M.: A. Metzner, 1961), 1–6; Elmar Jerien, 'Panama: Reasons for the Popularity of Private Interest Foundations', *Trusts & Trustees*, 15, no. 5 (2009), 397–402.

22 An automatic change of place of register to the location of the government in exile was made possible by its amendment in the following month. Wipf, *Georg Fischer AG*, 144.

23 Straumann and Wildmann, *Schweizer Chemieunternehmen*, 179–180.

24 This abrupt departure of Barell can be explained not only by his memory of arrest and detention by the German authorities during WWI, but also by the fact that his wife was a Russian-German Jew. Two other executive officers of Basel out of six travelled to the US during the war. Peyer, *Roche*, 152–158.

25 Peyer, *Roche*, 159.

26 Straumann and Wildmann, *Schweizer Chemieunternehmen*, 181.

27 For the detail of this crisis of governance and Director Fuch's travel, see: Takafumi Kurosawa, 'Breaking Through the Double Blockade: Inter-Atlantic Wartime Communications at Roche', *Jahrbuch für Wirtschaftsgeschichte*, 56, no. 1 (2015), 227–256. Bobst later went to Warner-Lambert and nurtured it as a global pharmaceutical producer. Peyer, *Roche*, 162.

28 Peyer, *Roche*, 163.

29 Peyer, *Roche*, 171–172.

30 Peyer, *Roche*, 119.

31 Martin Lüpold, 'Globalisierung als Krisenreaktionsstrategie. Dezentralisierung und Renationalisierung bei Nestlé 1920–1950', in *Globalisierung-Chancen und Risiken. Die Schweiz in der Weltwirtschaft 18.–20. Jahrhundert/ La globalisation-chances et risques. La Suisse dans l'economie mondiale 18e–20e siècles*, ed. Hans-Jörg Gilomen, Margrit Müller, and Béatrice Veyrassat (Zürich: Chronos, 2003), 215; Jean Heer, *World Events 1866–1966: The First Hundreds Years of Nestlé* (Lausanne: Imprimeries Réunies, 1966), 168.

32 Heer, *World Events*, 87–89; Jean Heer, *Nestlé. Cent vingt-cinq ans de 1866 à 1991*(Vevey: Nestlé, 1991), 30–33, 50–80.

33 Jean Heer, *Weltgeschehen. 1866–1966. Ein Jahrhundert Nestlé* (Vevey: Nestlé, 1966), 111; Heer, *Nestlé. Cent vingt-cinq ans de 1866 à 1991*, 99; Jean Heer, *Nestlé 125 Years 1866–1991* (Vevey: Nestlé, 1991), 108.
34 Lüpold, *Globalisierung*, 215; Heer, *Weltgeschehen*, 159, 179–192; Heer, *World Events*, 140, 158–170; Heer, *Nestlé 125 Years*, 128, 164–166; Heer, *Nestlé. Cent vingt-cinq ans*, 131, 166–168.
35 Local production by foreign direct investment started during the 1870s. Anglo-Swiss Condensed Milk, which exported 70 percent of its products, was very keen on local production. Nestlé was more reluctant to relocate production during the 19th century, but it also increased rapidly the dependency on onsite production since 1898. Heer, *Nestlé 125 Years*, 59–80.
36 Thomas Fenner, 'Nestlé & Anglo-Swiss: Vom Schweizer Milchimperium zum Multinationalen Nahrungsmittelkonzern', in *Der Vergessene Wirtschaftskrieg. Schweizer Unternehmen in ersten Weltkrieg*, ed. Roman Rossfeld and Tobias Straumann (Zürich: Chronos, 2008), 317–343, 317–343, 323. After the company won an order for the British military, sales in the market of the Central Powers became extremely difficult. Two factories in Germany, which used to have English names as their trade names, were integrated into a newly established local subsidiary company with a German name. Its main product brand 'Milkmaid' was changed to 'Milchmädchen'.
37 Fenner, 'Nestlé & Anglo-Swiss', 326–337.
38 Heer, *Nestlé 125 Years*, 128, 164–166.
39 The Japanese market was an interesting example of this general trend. See: Pierre-Yves Donzé and Takafumi Kurosawa, 'Nestlé Coping With Japanese Nationalism: Political Risk and the Strategy of a Foreign Multinational Enterprise in Japan, 1913–45', *Business History*, 55, no. 8 (2013), 1318–1338.
40 Lüpold, *Globalisierung*, 211–234.
41 Heer, *Weltgeschehen*, 188; Heer, *World Events*, 166; Heer, *Nestlé 125 Years*, 173; Heer, *Nestlé. Cent vingt-cinq ans*, 175–176.
42 However, according to the ownership of the founder's shares, Unilac was a subsidiary of Nestlé Holding, which is a slight difference from the Roche's scheme. In the 1930s, Nestlé and Roche were partners in development and sales of vitamin tablets using concentrated milk as solvent. It should be considered that the corporate form of Roche was studied by Nestlé.
43 Heer, *Nestlé 125 Years*, 194. Heer, *Nestlé. Cent vingt-cinq ans*, 196.
44 As a result of transfer of ownership of the subsidiaries, Unilac bore liabilities to Nestlé Holding, which was repaid in instalments to Nestlé Holding within 1949. Christian Ruch, Myriam Rais-Liechti and Roland Peter, *Geschäfte und Zwangsarbeit. Schweizer Industrieunternehmen im «Dritten Reich' (Veröffenlichungen der UEK Bd. 6 / Publications de la CIE Vol.6)* (Zürich: Chronos, 2001), 183–188; Heer, *Weltgeschehen*, 188–189; Heer, *World Events*, 166–167.
45 Heer, *Weltgeschehen*, 189–192, 200; Heer, *World Events*, 167–170, 178; Heer, *Nestlé 125 Years*, 194–195; Heer, *Nestlé.Cent vingt-cinq ans*, 196–197.
46 Should Germany have occupied Switzerland and seized the headquarters of Nestlé, the ownership of Nestlé assets in other neutral states (such as the US before joining the war) could have been subject to transfer to the German government. As countermeasures to this possible contingency, the Swiss government ensured the companies would automatically relocate their place of register to the location of the Swiss government in exile by enacting a federal government decree in October 1939, which Nestlé took measure to accommodate. Lüpold, 'Globalisierung', 234.
47 Nescafe was successfully introduced into the Swiss market in 1938 and into the US market the following year and made a great success. Its US production

reached a million cartons in 1942. Heer, *Weltgeschehen*, 203–205; Heer, *World Events*, 180–182.

48 Ruch, *Geschäfte und Zwangsarbeit*, 274.

49 Because BBC sales depended much on military demand, and its German subsidiary was relatively big, i.e., close to its Swiss headquarters, it did not manage to drive a wedge in the abusive expansion strategy of its German subsidiary. Ruch, *Geschäfte und Zwangsarbeit*, 79–123, 166, 179–181, 183–188.

50 Lüpold, 'Globalisierung', 119–222.

51 Adopted was a complex scheme using a deposit agreement of the shares with voting rights, which was far more complex than the one used during the war. When transferring the subsidiaries from the Sterling area to its Swiss headquarters, it set up a dummy company in a third country, in order to prevent the British and American governments from confiscating its overseas assets, supposing a Russian occupation of Switzerland. Lüpold, 'Globalisierung', 225–226.

52 Heer, *Weltgeschehen*, 239; Heer, *World Events*, 212–213.

53 Lüpold, 'Globalisierung', 224.

54 Lüpold, 'Globalisierung', 227.

55 This scheme had also been also employed upon establishment of Margarine Unie / Union through merger in 1927, and in the corporate organisation of Van den Bergh, the other company in this merger. Wubs, *International Business*, 16.

56 Wubs, *International Business*.

57 Doreen Arnoldus, who researched into Van den Berg's firm, among others, states that Chandler simply ignores the family character of the Margarine Unie/union and Unilever in the early post-merger period. According to her, he failed to acknowledge how the Margarine Unie/Union was formed by former family firms, whose family members still exerted control in the firm. Doreen Arnoldus, *Family, Family Firm and Strategy: Six Dutch Family Firms in the Food Industry 1880–1970* (Amsterdam: Amsterdam University Press, 2002), 378.

58 Alfred D. Chandler, *Scale and Scope: The Dynamics of Industrial Capitalism* (Cambridge, MA: Harvard University Press, 1990), 384.

59 UAR, HIS 201, 1556, *Memorandum: Administration and Capitalisation of the Unilever Concern*, 24–8–1938.

60 Richard P. Rumelt, *Strategy, Structure, and Economic Performance* (Cambridge, MA: Harvard Business School Press, 1974), 23.

61 Rumelt, *Strategy*, 63–64.

62 Stephen Howarth and Joost Jonker, *A History of Royal Dutch Shell, Vol.2, Powering the Hydrocarbon Revolution, 1939–1973* (Oxford: Oxford University Press, 2007), 29–31.

63 In February 1939, Unilever set up a holding company in South Africa, under which it attached another holding company. During the German occupation of the Netherlands, the overseas assets of Unilever owned by Mavibel (excluding the ones in the British Empire and the Dutch East Indies) were transferred to this twice-removed subsidiary. At the same time, Unilever also established a trust body named White Hall Trust in London, to which it deposited the ownership of its said overseas assets. Half of the preferred registered shares with the voting right for board members of NV were transferred to the abovementioned South Africa holding company, while the other half was deposited in White Hall Trust as Limit's collaterals against liability to NV. Wubs, *International Business*, 62–65.

64 Wubs, *International Business*, 83.

65 Wubs, *International Business*, 77–78.

66 Wubs, *International Business*, 78–79.

67 After December 1941, the board of directors of Unilever NV comprised three Dutch expert managers and three Germans. Wubs, *International Business*, 84, 110.
68 Wubs, *International Business*, 79, 111–112, 120, 162–165.
69 Unilever Archive London (UAL), MDC, 6 December 1945.
70 Unilever Archive London (UAL), MDC, 11 October 1945.
71 Wubs, *International Business*, 181.
72 Wubs, *International Business*, 158–165. For Royal Dutch Shell, the war is believed to have worked as a trigger to dissolve the imbalance between the Netherlands and the UK, to streamline the management organisation, and to change over to a strategy focussed on the Western Hemisphere. Howarth and Jonker, *A History of Royal Dutch Shell, Vol. 2*, 1–103.
73 Wubs, *International Business*.
74 Part of the information for the Philips case is based on information in the Office of Strategic Services (OSS) which was collected during the war. We are grateful to the Dutch radio programme Argos (VPRO) and its journalist Gerard Leenders who handed over to us this recently declassified material. National Archives and Records Administration (NARA), RG226, Records of the Office of Strategic Services, A1–210, file number WM14534, declassified NND974345, 'The Philips Concern'.
75 A. Heerding, *The History of Philips Electronics N.V. A Company of Many Parts*, Vol. 2 (Cambridge: Cambridge University Press, 1988), 340–341.
76 Heerding, *A Company of Many Parts*, 291–298.
77 Ivo J. Blanken, *The History of Philips Electronics N.V. Under German Rule*, Vol. 4, 7–8; Heerding, *A Company of Many Parts*, 168.
78 Ivo J. Blanken, *The History of Philips Electronics N.V. The Development of N.V. Philips' Gloeilampenfabrieken Into a Major Electrical Group*, Vol. 3 (Zaltbommel: European Library, 1999), 58.
79 Heerding, *A Company of Many Parts*, 335.
80 Ivo J. Blanken, *Philips'Gloeilampenfabrieken Into a Major Electrical Group*, 12.
81 Kees Boersma, 'Tensions Within an Industrial Research Laboratory: The Philips Laboratory's X-Ray Department Between the Wars', *Enterprise & Society*, 4, no. 1 (2003), 73.
82 Ivo J. Blanken, *Under German Rule*, 7–8; Heerding, *A Company of Many Parts*, 8–9.
83 Quoted in: Ivo J. Blanken, *The Development of N.V. Philips' Gloeilampenfabrieken*, 21.
84 Heerding, *A Company of Many Parts*, 337.
85 Heerding, *A Company of Many Parts*, 338.
86 Its members had set up a company with this name in Geneva to manage the daily affairs of the cartel, i.e. Phöbus S.A. Compagnie industrielle pour le développement de léclairage. Günther Luxbacher, *Massenproduktion im globalen Kartell. G, Radioröhren und die Rationalisierung der Elektroindustrie bis 1945* (Diepholz: GNT-Verlag GmbH, 2003), 364–365.
87 Luxbacher, *Massenproduktion im globalen Kartell*, 442–443.
88 Boersma, 'Philips Laboratory's X-Ray Department', 82–83.
89 Ivo J. Blanken, *Under German Rule*, 91.
90 Philips Company Archives (PCA), 882, Alldephi 1939-, *10 November 1939, Notariele akte van Alldephi Verwaltung Gesellschaft ondertekent door O.M.E. Loupart.*
91 Ivo J. Blanken, *Under German Rule*, 114–116; National Archives and Records Administration (NARA), RG226, 'The Philips Concern', 27–41.
92 Ivo J. Blanken, *Under German Rule*, 118–119; NARA, RG226, 'The Philips Concern', 27–41.

93 Ivo J. Blanken, *Under German Rule*, 118–121; NARA, RG226, 'The Philips Concern', 33.
94 Ivo J. Blanken, *Under German Rule*, 126, 144; NARA, RG226, 'The Philips Concern', 33.
95 NARA, RG226, 'The Philips Concern', 34–35.
96 Ivo J. Blanken, *Under German Rule*, 137–144.
97 Luxbacher, *Massenproduktion im globalen Kartell*, 446–447.
98 The report was published in August 1943 and consisted of more than 400 pages. NARA, RG226, 'The Philips Concern'.
99 Ivo J. Blanken, *Under German Rule*, 300–314.

Bibliography

Arnoldus, Doreen. *Family, Family Firm and Strategy: Six Dutch Family Firms in the Food Industry 1880–1970*. Amsterdam: Amsterdam University Press, 2002.

Blanken, Ivo J. *The Development of N.V. Philips' Gloeilampenfabrieken Into a Major Electrical Group*, Vol. 3. Zaltbommel: European Library, 1999.

Blanken, Ivo J. *The History of Philips Electronics N.V. Under German Rule*, Vol. 4. Zaltbommel: European Library, 1999.

Boersma, Kees. 'Tensions Within an Industrial Research Laboratory: The Philips Laboratory's X-Ray Department Between the Wars', *Enterprise & Society*, 4, no. 1 (2003), 65–98.

Chandler, Alfred D. *Scale and Scope: The Dynamics of Industrial Capitalism*. Cambridge, MA: Harvard University Press, 1990.

Donzé, Pierre-Yves and Takafumi Kurosawa. 'Nestlé Coping With Japanese Nationalism: Political Risk and the Strategy of a Foreign Multinational Enterprise in Japan, 1913–45', *Business History*, 55, no. 8 (2013): 1318–1338.

Fenner, Thomas. 'Nestlé & Anglo-Swiss: Vom Schweizer Milchimperium zum Multinationalen Nahrungsmittelkonzern', in *Der Vergessene Wirtschaftskrieg. Schweizer Unternehmen in ersten Weltkrieg*, edited by Roman Rossfeld and Tobias Straumann, 317–343. Zürich: Chronos, 2008.

Heer, Jean. *Nestlé 125 Years 1866–1991*. Vevey: Nestlé, 1991.

Heer, Jean. *Nestlé. Cent vingt-cinq ans de 1866 à 1991*. Vevey: Nestlé, 1991.

Heer, Jean. *Weltgeschehen. 1866–1966. Ein Jahrhundert Nestlé*. Vevey: Nestlé, 1966.

Heer, Jean. *World Events 1866–1966: The First Hundreds Years of Nestlé*. Lausanne: Imprimeries Réunies, 1966.

Heerding, A. *The History of N.V. Phillips' Gloeilampenfabrieken, vol.2, A Company of Many Parts*. Cambridge: Cambridge University Press, 1988.

Howarth, David. *The Golden Isthmus*. London: Reader's Union, 1967.

Howarth, Stephen and Joost Jonker. *A History of Royal Dutch Shell, Vol.2, Powering the Hydrocarbon Revolution, 1939–1973*. Oxford: Oxford University Press, 2007.

Independent Commission of Experts Switzerland—Second World War, ed. *Switzerland, National Socialism and the Second World War: Final Report*. Zurich: Pendo Verlag, 2002.

James, Harold and Jakob Tanner, eds. *Enterprise in the Period of Fascism in Europe*. London: Ashgate, 2002.

Jerien, Elmar. 'Panama: Reasons for the Popularity of Private Interest Foundations', *Trusts & Trustees*, 15, no. 5 (2009): 397–402.

Jones, Geoffrey. *Multinationals and Global Capitalism From the Nineteenth to the Twenty-First Century*. Oxford: Oxford University Press, 2005.

Kobrak, Christopher and Per H. Hansen, eds. *European Business, Dictatorship, and Political Risk 1920–1945*. New York: Berghahn Books, 2004.

Kurosawa, Takafumi. 'Breaking Through the Double Blockade: Inter-Atlantic Wartime Communications at Roche', *Jahrbuch für Wirtschaftsgeschichte*, 56, no. 1 (2015), 227–256.

Kurosawa, Takafumi. *Churitsukoku Suisu to Nachizumu: Dainiji Sekaitaisen to Rekishi Ninshiki (Neutral Switzerland and National Socialism: The Second World War and Perception of History)*. Kyoto: Kyoto University Press, 2010.

Lund, Joachim, ed. *Working for the New Order: European Business under German Domination 1939–1945*. Copenhagen: University Press of Southern Denmark, 2006.

Lüpold, Martin. *Der Ausbau der "Festung Schweiz", Aktienrecht und Corporate Governance in der Schweiz, 1881–1961*. PhD diss., Zurich University, 2008.

Lüpold, Martin. 'Globalisierung als Krisenreaktionsstrategie. Dezentralisierung und Renationalisierung bei Nestlé 1920–1950', in *Globalisierung-Chancen und Risiken. Die Schweiz in der Weltwirtschaft 18.–20. Jahrhundert/ La globalisation-chances et risques. La Suisse dans l'economie mondiale 18e–20e siècles*, edited by Hans-Jörg Gilomen, Margrit Müller, and Béatrice Veyrassat, 211–234. Zürich: Chronos, 2003.

Luxbacher, Günther. *Massenproduktion im globalen Kartell. G, Radioröhren und die Rationalisierung der Elektroindustrie bis 1945*. Diepholz: GNT-Verlag GmbH, 2003.

Merki, Christoph Maria. *Wirtschaftswunder Liechtenstein: Die rasche Modernisierung einer Kleinen Volkswirtschaft im 20. Jahrhundert*. Vaduz: Verlag des Historischen Verein für das Fürstentum Liechtenstein, 2007.

Peyer, Hans Conrad. *Roche- Geschichte eines Unternehmens 1896–1996*. Basel: Editiones Roche, 1996.

Rossfeld, Roman and Tobias Straumann, eds. *Der Vergessene Wirtschaftskrieg: Schweizer Unternehemen in Ersten Weltkrieg*. Zürich: Chronos, 2008.

Ruch, Christian, Myriam Rais-Liechti, and Roland Peter. *Geschäfte und Zwangsarbeit. Schweizer Industrieunternehmen im 'Dritten Reich' (Veröffenlichungen der UEK Bd. 6 / Publications de la CIE Vol.6)*. Zürich: Chronos, 2001.

Rumelt, Richard P. *Strategy, Structure, and Economic Performance*. Cambridge, MA: Harvard Business School Press, 1974.

Straumann, Lukas and Daniel Wildmann. *Schweizer Chemieunternehmen im 'Dritten Reich' (Veröffenlichungen der UEK Bd. 7 / Publications de la CIE Vol.7.)*. Zürich: Chronos, 2001.

Von Deschwanden, Niklaus. *Das Aktienrecht von Panama*. Berlin and Frankfurt a.M.: A. Metzner, 1961.

Wilkins, Mira. *The History of Foreign Investment in the United States 1914–1945*. Cambridge, MA: Harvard University Press, 2004.

Wipf, Hans Ulrich. *Georg Fischer AG 1930–1945: Ein Schweizer Industrieunternehmen im Spannungsfeld Europas*. Zürich: Chronos Verlag, 2001.

Wubs, Ben. *International Business and National War Interests: Unilever Between Reich and Empire, 1939–1945*. London: Routledge, 2008.

2 Municipalisation, War, Tax and Nationalisation

Imperial Continental Gas Association in an Era of Turmoil, 1824–1987

Ryo Izawa

Introduction

Utility companies are incessantly confronted with non-market forces. Privately owned multinational enterprises, in particular, have been affected by political uncertainties, as described in a recent history of global electrification.[1] The assets located in host countries were sometimes given up without any compensation in the waves of municipalisation or nationalisation. Combinations of domestic laws in different countries also caused issues for these companies across multiple jurisdictions. In contrast, most of the enterprises did not give up their businesses even after their overseas business was taken without compensation. This implies that these companies managed to use their remaining resources to survive.

The Imperial Continental Gas Association (ICGA) was established in London as a gas provider in 1824. The business purpose written on the first prospectus was to provide an 'admirable' English gas system to the principal towns of continental Europe. Then, the Imperial Continental Gas Association Acts legislated by Parliament restricted its business area to foreign countries. In the late 19th century, the company provided gas service to about 10 major European cities in the Netherlands, Austria, Germany, France and Belgium. However, their bright success was overshadowed by two changes: technologically, the advent of the electric light reduced the demand for gas for illumination and, politically, municipal authorities in continental Europe began to question the privileged contracts granted to foreign-owned utility companies. ICGA, as a result, advanced into the electricity business and divested some business areas; however, it endeavoured to minimise the effects of political uncertainties. Such corporate reactions towards changes in the external environment were repeated throughout the company's history. Eventually, ICGA survived as one of the largest energy providers in Belgium and as a liquefied petroleum gas (LPG) supply in the UK until 1987, when the company demerged into two companies, Contibel Holdings and Calor Group.

This study presents a brief history of the ICGA, mainly from the viewpoint of its relationship with political uncertainties such as municipalisation, war, tax and nationalisation. In analysing how the company dealt with the political environment for 164 years, this study is based on an ICGA company history published in 1974,[2] two typescripts[3] and relevant archival sources.[4]

Political Uncertainties and Corporate Capabilities

Recent studies on political risk management, particularly in the field of international business, show a growing interest in firm-specific facets to the political environment.[5] Political risk is regarded as not exclusively an exogenous variable but one that is partially, if not completely, endogenous.[6] However, insights such as these which rely on quantitative data analysis should be complemented by qualitative research and case studies which, in turn, can explore causal mechanisms and overlooked factors.[7] In particular, historical approaches contribute to 'help us better understand the processes at work in capabilities origins and development over time'.[8] In analysing ICGA's history, it is possible to follow how it faced political uncertainties and nurtured its political capabilities; corporate strategy was shaped through experience and a process of trial and error.

Issues related to free-standing companies and international taxation are of importance to this study. In so far as we define a free-standing company as a firm 'set up in one country for the purpose of doing business outside that company', ICGA was surely a free-standing company, albeit with over-centralism.[9] In addition, Mollan and Tennet (2015) maintained that in response to international double taxation in the early 1930s, the company became a holding company and made the transition from a free-standing company to a multidivisional, multinational structure. However, their findings about ICGA were supported only by an article in the *Financial Times*. Moreover, what effects these organisational changes brought about has not been clarified. As the authors mentioned, a firm-level investigation of international corporate tax planning and its impacts on corporate behaviours would be of great value.[10] For this reason, one section in this study focusses on how the free-standing company with over-centralism changed its corporate structure and management in the face of international double taxation.

Heyday and Decline as a Gas Company (Late 19th Century–1913)

After it was formed in 1824, ICGA steadily expanded its operations into continental Europe.[11] The first operation was started in Ghent, where ICGA agents reported to head office that a crowd, too many to be counted, celebrated the bright gas light and praised the company on commencing the supply of gas. By 1828, ICGA was supplying 6,000 lights through four undertakings: Ghent, Berlin, Hanover and Rotterdam. The company successfully concluded new contracts with about 10 city authorities from the 1830s to 1840s, extending its business area to Austria and France. There was little resistance from city authorities to the idea of awarding contracts for lighting to a British company.[12]

However, these favourable conditions were not perpetuated mainly because local authorities wanted to pressure the company to reduce the gas price or just end the contracts. The company lost contracts with seven major cities between the 1850s and 1880s. In the case of the Rotterdam contract, the company had to concede to substantial price reductions at the time of renewal in 1859 as the contract was put up for public tender. Moreover, the city authority had extensive powers of requiring additional lighting and reserved the right to cancel the contract after five years on payment of compensation. Eventually, the city council decided to form a municipal undertaking in 1883. Although ICGA was permitted to continue its business until the municipal undertakings were in operation, it had to withdraw from the business in May 1887. The city did not purchase any assets of ICGA or pay compensation.[13]

Meanwhile, ICGA was able to exploit the existing contracts and conclude new contracts with smaller towns, at least until the early 1890s. It also acquired gas undertakings from other companies or even municipalities (e.g. Nancy, Flushing). By 1875, over one million 'lights' on the continent were supplied by ICGA.[14] Furthermore, in 1897, the company achieved the supply of 2,669,624 lights in 12 major European cities and 29 small towns. It received 41.4 percent of its trading profits from Austria–Hungary, 29.4 percent from Germany, 13.7 percent from the Netherlands, 9.0 percent from France, 6.1 percent from Belgium.[15]

In hindsight, the year 1897 signalled the climax of ICGA as a gas provider. The waves of electrification and municipalisation acted to demolish the company's gas business. To compensate for the technological transition of street lighting, the company started to provide gas services for other uses such as gas ovens. The effort was partially rewarded as we can see from the historical trend of the gas industry. In parallel with the enlargement of its original business, ICGA entered into the electricity business. While it is unknown whether this change was caused by entrepreneurial motivation, the company gradually and steadily moved in this new direction.

Besides the adaption to the technological climate, ICGA undoubtedly struggled to cope with the political environment. Prompted by the intention to form municipally owned utility companies, the authorities of Amsterdam and Vienna terminated contracts in 1898 and 1899, respectively. Although, in 1883, the company succeeded in renewing the Amsterdam contract for a period of a further 35 years, the city authorities gave notice to terminate it by August 1897. ICGA received £1,385,000 for the sale of its establishment in Amsterdam.[16] In Vienna, a new mayor, Karl Leuger, determined the fate of ICGA's Vienna business. He criticised ICGA for not providing a reasonable price and quality, questioning the fact that a British company monopolised gas services. Right after his inauguration, he decided to take over the gas plants when the contract expired in 1899. The lengthy negotiation of sale price, which included mediation by the Prime Minister of Austria, was ultimately in vain. The mayor decided to construct a brand new gas establishment.[17] Naturally, ICGA did not get any compensation from the Viennese authorities, as in the case of Rotterdam.

The loss of undertakings in Amsterdam and Vienna quickly caused a deterioration in ICGA's financial condition as its overall trading profits slumped from £781,000 in 1897 to £483,000 in 1900. The breakdown shows that profits from Austria–Hungary decreased from £323,000 in 1897 to £52,000 in 1900 and the profits from the Netherlands decreased from £107,000 to £17,000.[18] The yearly dividend rate also reduced from 12 percent in 1895 to 10 percent in 1897 and further to 8 percent in 1909,[19] though ICGA was still one of the leading utility companies in the UK.[20]

Furthermore, ICGA endeavoured to adopt a more political strategy and shifted its investment policy. This meant that the company started to review its reliance on directly controlled branches. In 1900, the company purchased 75 percent of the shares in a Hungarian company. After 1908, the Frankfurt business was operated by a German company in which ICGA had a major interest. More importantly, in 1907, it established a French subsidiary, Compagnie Continentale du Gaz, which grouped all the small French works which had been acquired by ICGA over many years. The wholly owned company was registered under French law with a fixed capital of 10 million francs.[21] It appears that over-centralisation, as summarised by a company historian as characteristic of the ICGA until 1900, started to wane from the turn of the 20th century.[22] Nonetheless, the Directors of ICGA and Compagnie Continentale du Gaz were common to both firms.[23] The effective control of the French company had been grasped by the parent company. However, the change of the company's management policy was interrupted or, rather, accelerated by the outbreak of World War I.

World War I and Compulsory Liquidation (1914–1924)

The beginning of the 165th half-yearly Ordinary General Meeting held on 3 November 1914 must have surprised ICGA shareholders. The Chairman, Charles J. Jessel, stated that the company could not report 'any half-yearly accounts, nor a scheme for the division of profits'.

The First World War severed ICGA's channels of communication with its stations on the continent.[24] Consequently, 91 percent of its revenue (65 percent from Germany, 20 percent from Belgium and 6 percent from

France) was immediately cut and the vast majority of the revenue sources fell into belligerent hands.[25] In the absence of a balance sheet, the chairman ended up being unable to declare a dividend. Meanwhile, the company tried to appease shareholders who were concerned about the news that the German government might take over the English gas works. The chairman explained that there were no such facts reported in German newspapers as far as company staff were able to see.

As the war dragged on, information on the situation on the continent gradually reached the head office. The Chairman in the 166th meeting reported that the company had a grasp of the picture of French undertakings. As of May 1915, despite the fact that the cities (e.g. Lille, Nancy) suffered German bombardment, the factories and gas lines in France were left nearly intact. The company also announced that information on the Berlin station and German circumstances was channelled through the Netherlands, which had proclaimed neutrality. The company secretary of ICGA was despatched to Amsterdam, in November 1914, to communicate with the Agent and Chief Engineer at Berlin, 'with the full knowledge and consent of the Foreign Office' and the German counterpart. It was revealed that business in Germany was being carried on as usual and with great civility, even though under state control. The report of the Chief Engineer, Herr Ernst Körting, the third generation to serve the ICGA, satisfied the company. The Chairman noted that: 'Not one single personal complaint came to my ears either by letter, word of mouth, or through the newspapers against any officer of the Association—German or English'.[26] He anticipated a future 'no less satisfactory and no less creditable'.[27]

Arguably, until 1916, ICGA was content with its method of withdrawing from business. In 1915, the company successfully sold the whole of its interest in the Frankfurt business to the local authority. The deal was profitable. The total sum paid to ICGA was £941,320, whereas the value of the shares on the books of the company stood at around £465,650.[28] In addition, the Flushing station, the sole remaining undertaking under the control of the head office, was a small but brilliant earner of profits. The company was able to employ neutral steamers, mainly Dutch, to export coal from the UK to Flushing.[29]

However, the situation changed on 31 July 1916 when the German government established the compulsory registration of enemy property and inaugurated the liquidation of British enemy property.[30] A year later, ICGA was ordered to liquidate its undertakings in Hanover and Berlin.[31] The former business was knocked down for 6 million marks (£300,000) by the sole bidder, the town of Hanover. The company not only lost the contract, which extended to 1950, but also received less than its total past investment of 10 million marks. The latter work was sold for 85.2 million marks to the 'County Council', which set up a company operating its gas service and appointed Körting as the manager. In 1918, the Belgian undertakings, about which little information was provided to shareholders during the first half of the war, were also liquidated. However, in the case of Belgium, King Albert I signed a decree making all such enemy orders since 4 August 1914 null and void.[32]

Eventually, by 1925, ICGA received £7,376,807 from the Enemy Debts Clearing Office as compensation for the confiscated properties.[33] This was the result of the company repeatedly lodging claims for reparations with the British Foreign Office during and after the war. Nevertheless, the compensation did not match the original claims in 1916 of £15,713,949 or the amended claims in 1920 of £13,134,214 (Germany: £10,869,473; Belgium: £1,773,599; Austria: £491,141).[34] At last, in 1921, the company resumed dividend payments at 10 percent per annum. Besides regular dividends, ICGA could declare special dividends paid from the German money.[35]

After the First World War, ICGA's remaining business area was mainly limited to France and Belgium. As for the French business, the company finally realised by 1918 that its works could not be run as before. Gas lines in the towns of Armentières and Estairs were completely destroyed. The up-to-date electrical equipment in Lille was also stripped by the Germans. Moreover, the bombardment between both camps greatly damaged the Nancy undertaking.[36] In 1920, the company consolidated all its interests in France into a subsidiary, Compagnie Continentale du Gaz.[37] In contrast, the Belgian stations returned to ICGA were deployed as directly owned branches as before. However, another factor produced by domestic and international politics encouraged the company to alter the management structure of its Belgian business.

International Taxation and Holding Company (1925–1939)

The effort of ICGA to keep up with the times continued into the late 1920s and 1930s. Technologically, the business portfolio was increasingly inclined towards electricity. A newspaper reported, 'the present title of the Imperial Continental Gas Association is something of a misnomer, for nowadays this old but virile undertaking is deeply engaged also in the supply of electrical energy'.[38] Faced with a rising tide of municipalisation, the company went for small undertakings in Essegg (1926), Flushing (1934), Prague (1935) and Graslitz (1938).[39]

However, the major concern of ICGA at that time must have been its Belgian business and the emergence of international double taxation problem. At the annual meeting in 1931, the company called itself 'one of the most unfortunate victims of double taxation'. For example, Belgian taxation authorities deducted 22 percent from the gross amounts of its dividends, and British authorities deducted 22.5 percent from the remainder. The reason ICGA suffered from this severe tax burden was because there was only partial international double taxation relief in the UK. Despite the fact that corporate income tax rates in many countries had skyrocketed and remained high since 1914 (UK: 5.8 percent in 1913, 30 percent in 1918, 22.5 percent in 1931; US: 1 percent in 1913, 12.5 percent in 1918, 12 percent in 1931), the British government provided a foreign tax deduction relief only inside the Empire.[40] The UK's tax regime was inferior to some other national tax relief systems that provided, for example, foreign tax credits or extraterritorial income exclusion.[41]

In fact, by the time of ICGA's annual meeting in 1931, where the chairman first publicly raised complaints about international taxation, the company had already taken two measures to alleviate double taxation. First, in 1927 the company launched a private British financial company called the Utility Loan Company (ULC).[42] ULC's purpose was to be the channel through which the company financed its associated companies for the very good reason that ICGA sought to 'avoid a large part of the foreign taxation which would otherwise be borne'.[43] The tax planning was to take advantage of differences in the taxation of dividends and interest. Belgian law defined companies without offices or permanent establishments in Belgium as foreign companies and taxed interest paid to foreign companies at the reduced rate of 5 percent. Therefore, ICGA established ULC to lend money to its Belgian subsidiaries.[44] In 1927, when ULC revenue was not reflected, interest revenue from Belgium was only £518. However, this amount increased to £13,824 in 1928. The percentage of Belgian total revenue was approximately 25 percent at its peak in 1933, when interest revenue was £101,941.[45]

ICGA's second action, in 1930, was to convert branch offices in Belgium into Belgian subsidiaries. International double taxation arose when overseas subsidiaries remitted dividends; however, no tax was applied when subsidiaries retained their profits. In contrast, after 1914, the British authorities taxed the profits of overseas branches, whether remitted or not. Therefore, by converting its branches into subsidiaries, ICGA could retain profits in Belgium. The company decided 'not to press the subsidiary companies for dividends in excess of the sum required to yield a reasonable rate of dividend'. Under the policy it encouraged subsidiary and associated companies to build up internal reserve.[46]

More importantly, ICGA's 1930 reorganisation propelled the decentralisation of management. The intention was publicly announced by the Chairman in the 1929 Annual Meeting, where he stated that 'direct branch establishments of an English Company had become an anachronism'. He subsequently said 'local capital and local interest ought to be given the opportunity to associate themselves with their undertakings' and ICGA 'was assuming more the character of a holding company'. He also reminded shareholders that in the past the company had owned some foreign companies in Hungary, France and Germany.[47] Furthermore, ICGA created a new Belgian position of 'Liaison Officer for ICGA and its Associated Companies' and appointed a Belgian, Maurice Périer, in December 1930.[48] The 'effective management' rule, which the British tax authority adopted, must have influenced the decision: British multinationals could not escape their potential income tax liability based on their profits unless all their activities, management and control occurred abroad.[49]

Eventually, decentralism and personnel reshuffle along with corporate reorganisation brought great success to ICGA in the 1930s. When the company renegotiated its contract with communes in Antwerp in 1931, Périer and his young and capable staff in a new, small office found that the taxes on profits and dividends would be extremely low if the gas or electricity distribution subsidiaries of ICGA formed profit-sharing joint associations with the communes. The later-termed 'intercommunale' system was implemented immediately and was concluded between a Belgian subsidiary, Antwerpsche Gsmaatschappij, and the communes of Antwerp in 1932. In the case of the subsidiary, the dividend tax was 22 percent in 1930, 5 percent in the contract year 1932 and nil in 1935.[50] The system, which also protected the interests of both ICGA and local authorities, ended up being applied to all former concessions by 1936. The company, released from the pressure of a heavy tax burden and contract termination, formed a holding company in Belgium called Compagnie Belge et Continentale de Gaz et d'Electricité (Contibel) in 1933.[51] It goes without saying that Perier was appointed the Managing Director of Contibel.[52]

Additionally, the review in the 1930s was not limited to corporate reorganisation. The company was able to extend its operations to the United Kingdom because the request to amend the Imperial Continental Gas Association Act was passed in 1936.[53] In the same year, the company acquired a 28 percent share in Edmundsons Electricity Corporation, which was repatriated from a US multinational utility company, Utilities Power and Light Corporation, and had substantial interests in electricity production and distribution, mainly in the Midlands, East Anglia, the West Country and South Wales. In 1938, the company raised 59.3 percent of its gross revenue in Belgium, 24.2 percent in France and 16.5 percent in the UK.[54] It appeared that ICGA started to step into a new era as a European holding company.

War, Nationalisation and New Ventures (1940–ca. 1987)

ICGA's new start in the 1930s was stopped yet again by other political calamities in the 1940s. In May 1940, German troops invaded and occupied Belgium, forcing the defeat of France the following month. Direct communication with Belgium ceased abruptly on the day of the German attack, and, for news, the head office had to rely on reports from the personnel of subsidiary companies who had fled to the UK.[55] Head office received a letter dated 5 July 1941 from the Foreign Office informing that the Belgian companies were 'not under sequestration and continued their activity'. The letter further stated, 'only the management of the ICGA's participation in the Companies is entrusted to the care of a German Administrator' who 'is regarded as a member of the Board of Directors'. The Administrator also 'checked any documents handed to the members of the Board'.[56] With regards to the French situation, it appears more difficult to access the information. The Chairman, at the 1942 meeting, mentioned only that the situation seemed to be the same in France. Of course, dividends were 'out of question' in the circumstances.[57]

On the other hand, the impact of the German occupation administration during the Second World War on ICGA was limited. Unlike during the First World War, practically all the company's interests in Belgium and France were in the form of investments in local companies. Therefore, those companies were left comparatively unmolested by the Germans.[58] On the contrary, sales of gas and electricity in Belgium recovered to their pre-war levels in 1942 and increased until the beginning of 1944. Sales of gas in France also increased by 69 percent during the war.

Rather, new threats arose after peace. The French and British governments legislated for the nationalisation of gas and electricity between 1946 and 1949. All the company could do was to receive £6.5 million in compensation for all the shares in both Compagnie Continentale du Gaz and Edmundsons Electricity, though the company negotiated with the French government over the amount of compensation. The fear of nationalisation in Belgium made ICGA launch a new company in 1947, the Société Italo-Belge Pour le Commerce et l'Industrie (Belcomin), to which were transferred all 'non-nationalisable assets'.[59]

Finally, the compensation received for nationalisation reshaped the ICGA's activities. The company diversified into new markets and business areas in the 1950s. The company invested in water heaters, paints, catering equipment and even sewing machines. Furthermore, it acquired Canadian utility companies Gatineau Power (£1.5 million) and Calgary Power (£0.5 million). By 1960, 71 percent of its income came from Belgium while 12 percent and 17 percent came from North America and the UK, respectively. However, the 1960s saw the company retreat from most businesses it had invested in the 1950s. The retained profits were poured into more promising businesses: oil and gas business in the North Sea and LPG sales in the UK. Holding around 10 percent shareholder of Petrofina—an oil and gas company as well as one of the largest corporations in Belgium—ICGA enjoyed unprecedented economic success along with the exploitation of oil and gas in the North Sea. In addition, the company took over all the shares of the Calor Gas Group in 1969, which was also one of the largest LPG suppliers in the UK.[60] Happily, the company was selected as an original member of the FTSE 100 Index in 1984. Then, ICGA brought down the curtain in 1987 by splitting itself into a Belgian energy company (Contibel Holdings) and a British LPG supplier (Calor Group). These companies are now owned by SHV and Tractebel, respectively.[61]

Conclusion

This study followed the brief history of a British multinational enterprise whose original business was as a gas provider for continental Europe. As we saw, the company, Imperial Continental Gas Association, passed through successive waves of technical and political changes throughout its life.

In particular, political issues or non-market forces such as municipalisation, wars, international taxation and nationalisation, had a critical impact on its corporate decisions. Various local, national and international political events seen in the Netherlands (Rotterdam, 1887; Amsterdam, 1898), Austria (Vienna, 1899), Germany (Berlin and Hanover, 1916), France (1946) and the UK (1948–1949) directly forced the company to divest its works. The fear of municipalisation, nationalisation and international double taxation prompted the company to reorganise its corporate structure whereby ICGA gradually shifted from an over-centralised company to a pure holding company with decentralism taking place during the first half of the 20th century. Arguably, the political capabilities of ICGA nurtured by these experiences contributed to the survival of its Belgian business. The fructified, intercommunal system prevented not only (wholly) nationalisation but also the imposition of serious tax burdens. Thanks to its reliable stronghold in Belgium, ICGA could succeed in investing in oil and gas business in the 1960s and 1970s. Nevertheless, it should be pointed out that ICGA's business scope mostly remained focussed on 'gas utility' and Europe. This limitation or discretion on investment mitigated political uncertainties and supported decisions regarding technological selection. In other words, the political capabilities of a firm should be placed in the context of industrial characteristics, geographical peculiarities, corporate strategy and business policy.

Naturally, this study has limitations. First, the cognitive perspective of managers was not analysed: the entrepreneurial activities of top or middle management are known to be key in trying to gain a better understanding of the firm's ability to sense and seize opportunities as well as to reconfigure when change occurs.[62] Secondly, this study has scarcely mentioned competitors' behaviour or mimetic process.[63] Thirdly, the corporate political activity of ICGA in attempting to change political institutions or situations themselves has not been analysed.[64] Notwithstanding these qualifications, and on the basis of the evidence available, the 164 years of ICGA's history show a robust spirit not easily defeated by political uncertainties.

Notes

1 Hausman, Herterner and Wilkins, 2008.
2 Anon, 1974. According to the Forward by an anonymous writer of the ICGA official history, the small book was based on the works referenced in footnote 3.
3 Hill, 1950; Bourne-Paterson, 1970. The former typescript is held at the British Library. The latter one is located in the London Guildhall Archives.

4 Historical materials of the ICGA are held at the London Metropolitan Archives (LMA).
5 See Holburn and Zelner, 2010; Blake and Moschieri, 2017.
6 Jiménez, Luis-Rico and Benito-Osorio, 2014.
7 George and Bennett, 2005, 21.
8 Jones and Wadhwani, 2016, 23.
9 Wilkins, 1998, 3. Wilkins (1988) mentioned that 'fundamental to free-standing company was its inherently weak managerial structure at origin, causing it to depend on outside providers of services'. The finding appears to make Jones (1986), who relied on the embryonic ideas of Wilkins and the official ICGA's history book, write that before 1914 ICGA was 'a vigorous "free-standing" venture' but had 'many features of a modern multinational'. At least in 1900, all decisions and ICGA's day-to-day administration were carried out by its London office under the guidance of the Board of Directors. See Wilkins, 1988, 279; Wilkins 1998, 45; Jones, 1986.
10 Mollan and Tennet, 2015, 1063, 1069.
11 The Association was promoted in 1824 by William Congreve, who was the inventor of Congreve rockets. The Imperial Continental Gas Association Act was firstly legislated in 1833. Subsequently, the Act was supplemented and amended by the Acts, 1836, 1843, 1845, 1847, 1851, 1853, 1870, 1878, 1879, 1884, 1893, 1916, 1929 and 1936. See CLC/B/122/MS23323: Acts of Parliament, LMA, 1916, 1.
12 Anon, 1974, 1–8.
13 Hill, 1950, 119, 173–174.
14 ICGA concluded compensation contracts with municipal authorities. City authorities must have provided the gas service to private customers. However, there were no data about usage of lights. Having said that, the number of consumers in 1881 was 99,913. See Hill, 1950, appendix Xb.
15 Anon, 1974, 12, 14–15; Hill, 1950, 205.
16 Anon, 1974, 15; Hill, 1950, 172–173, 195–196.
17 Geehr, 1990, 55. Furthermore, Leuger pushed municipalisation of electricity work and public transport systems. As a social reformer, the battle with ICGA was a battle that could not be lost.
18 Hill, 1950, 219.
19 *The Financial Times*, 25 August 1910, 31.
20 The share capital value on the London Stock Exchange was £7,524,000 in 1900. While it should be noted that ICGA was a utility company, the value easily meets the definition of big business as suggested by Youssff Casis: a yardstick of 10,000 employees and/or a share capital of £2 million before 1914. See Cassis, 2008.
21 Anon, 1974, 25–26.
22 Hill, 1950, 229.
23 Anon, 1974, 22.
24 Report of the proceedings at the 165th half-yearly Ordinary General Meeting of proprietors held 3 November 1914, in CLC/B/122/MS23344/003: Circulars to shareholders. Include annual reports and accounts for the years 1900–1914, 2.
25 Anon, 1974, 23–24.
26 Report of the 166th meeting, 11 May 1915, CLC/B/122/MS23344/003, 4.
27 Report of the 167th meeting, 11 Nov. 1915, in CLC/B/122/MS23344/004: Circulars to shareholders. Include annual reports and accounts for the years 1915–1927, 8.
28 Anon, 1974, 17.
29 Report of the 168th meeting, 24 May 1916, CLC/B/122/MS23344/004, 4.
30 Caglioti, 2014, 6.
31 Report of the 169th meeting, 1 May 1917, CLC/B/122/MS23344/004, 7–8.

32 Report of the 170th meeting, 7 May 1918, CLC/B/122/MS23344/004, 4–8.
33 Anon, 1974, 25–26.
34 Report of the 172nd meeting, 5 May 1920, CLC/B/122/MS23344/004, 10. The claims on Belgium were modified by the return of the works and immovable properties in Brussels and Antwerp. The company claimed for materials, stocks and cash confiscated by the Germans. ICGA also claimed for 'the cash assets invested by the Austrian Government, and for a loan to the Central Gas Company of Budapest' (172nd, 10).
35 *The Financial Times*, 15 April 1924.
36 Report of the 171st meeting, 6 May 1919, CLC/B/122/MS23344/004, 12.
37 172nd, 7.
38 *The Financial Times*, 7 May 1931.
39 Anon, 1974, 30.
40 Peden, 2000, 44, 94, 149, 207, 212, 268, 287; Taylor, 2013, 287–288; Avery-Jones, 2013; Only within the British Empire, Article 27 of the Finance Act 1920 provided foreign tax credit and limited it to a maximum half credit (Avery-Jones, 2013, 1).
41 For example, let the income of a corporation of Nation A earned in Nation B be 100 and let A's tax rate be 20% and B's tax rate be 10%. Under the foreign tax credit, income after tax = 100 – (100 × 0.1) – {100 × (0.2 – 0.1)} = 80. Under foreign tax deduction, income after tax = 100 – (100 × 0.1) – {(100 – 100 × 0.1) × 0.2} = 72.
42 'Company No: 226976; Utility Loan Company Limited Vols 1 and F. Incorporated in 1927. Dissolved in 1960', BT 31/38033/226976, The National Archives (UK).
43 Proceedings at the 183rd Ordinary General Meeting of the Proprietors of the Association, 20 May 1931, in CLC/B/122/MS23344/005: Circulars to shareholders. Include annual reports and accounts for the years 1931–1937, 11.
44 Bourne-Paterson, 155. The financial company could sometimes charge higher rates than were politically possible for ICGA.
45 Bourne-Paterson, 1970, Appendix 3a.1. The Belgian revenues were £326,203 (total revenue of ICGA: £499,126) in 1927, £410,791 (£755,631) in 1931 and £387,645 (£748,940) in 1933.
46 Proceedings at the 184th Meeting, 25 May 1932, CLC/B/122/MS23344/006, 11. The amount placed in Belgium was Frs. 67,759,225 (approximately £500,000) during 1936–1940 (Bourne-Paterson, 232).
47 Proceedings at the 181st Meeting, 29 May 1929, in CLC/B/122/MS23344/005: Circulars to shareholders. Include annual reports and accounts for the years 1931–1937, 8–9.
48 Bourne-Paterson, 192.
49 Picciotto, 1992, 7–9.
50 Bourne-Paterson, 190, 210.
51 Anon, 1974, 32–33.
52 Bourne-Paterson, 231.
53 Anon, 1974, 34.
54 Bourne-Paterson, Appendix 4a.1.
55 Proceedings at the 192nd meeting, 7 June 1940, CLC/B/122/MS23344/006, 1.
56 Minutes of the Board of Direction held on Friday, the 25th July, 1941, in CLC/B/122/MS23327/061: Board of directors' minute book, April 1938–December 1952, 993.
57 Proceedings at the 194th meeting, 12 June 1942, CLC/B/122/MS23344/006, 1–2.
58 Proceedings at the 197th meeting, 15 June 1945, CLC/B/122/MS23344/006, 2. The ICGA's shareholding itself was regarded as enemy property. Then, the dividends were handed over to the German Custodian of Enemy Property

during the war. After liberation, the company estimated that the dividends, rents, etc. paid to the German Custodian was B. Frs. 48,600,254 (£ 274,578). The dividends, interests, etc., less expenses not paid to the Germans, were calculated to be B. Frs. 60,399,608 (197th, 2).

59 Anon, 1974, 37–38.
60 Anon, 1974, 39–45.
61 *The Economist*, 14 March 1987, 84; Moore, J., 'Who's still standing in the FTSE 100 today?', *The Independent*, 3 January 2014, www.independent.co.uk/news/business/analysis-and-features/who-s-still-standing-in-the-ftse-100-today-9038180.html, accessed 1 May 2017.
62 Teece, 2007; Leih and Teece, 2013.
63 DiMaggio and Powell, 1983.
64 Rajwani and Lawton, 2013.

Bibliography

Anon, *The Imperial Continental Gas Association, 1824–1974*, 1974.

Avery-Jones, J. F., 'Sir Josiah Stamp and Double Income Tax', in J. Tiley (ed), *Studies in the History of Tax Law*, Volume 6, Oxford: Hart Publishing, 2013.

Blake, D. J. and Moschieri, C., 'Policy Risk, Strategic Decisions and Contagion Effects: Firm-specific Considerations', *Strategic Management Journal*, 38(3), 2017, 732–750.

Bourne-Paterson, R. A., *The Imperial Continental Gas Association in the Twentieth Century* [Unpublished typescript], London Guildhall Archives, 1970.

Caglioti, D. L., 'Property Rights and Economic Nationalism', in U. Daniel et al. (eds), *1914–1918-online, International Encyclopedia of the First World War*, 2014, https://encyclopedia.1914-1918-online.net/article/property_rights_and_economic_nationalism, accessed 1 May 2017.

Cassis, Y., 'Big Business', in G. Jones and J. Zeitlin (eds), *The Oxford Handbook of Business History*, Oxford: Oxford University Press, 2008.

Dimaggio, P. J. and Powell, W. W., 'The Iron Cage Revisited: Institutional Isomorphism and Collective Rationality in Organizational Fields', *American Sociological Review*, 48(2), 1983, 147–160.

Geehr, R. S., *Karl Lueger: Mayor of Fin de Siecle Vienna*, Detroit: Wayne State University Press, 1990, 55.

George, A. L. and Bennett, A., *Case Studies and Theory Development in the Social Sciences*, Cambridge, MA: MIT Press, 2005, 21.

Hausman, W. J., Herterner, P. and Wilkins, M., *Global Electrification: Multinational Enterprise and International Finance in the History of Light and Power, 1878–2007*, Cambridge: Cambridge University Press, 2008.

Hill, N. K., *The History of the Imperial Continental Gas Association, 1824–1900*, [Unpublished Ph.D. thesis], University of London, 1950.

Holburn, G. L. F. and Zelner, B. A., 'Political Capabilities, Policy Risk, and International Investment Strategy: Evidence From the Global Electric Power Generation Industry', *Strategic Management Journal*, 31(12), 2010, 1290–1315.

Jiménez, A., Luis-Rico, I. and Benito-Osorio, D., 'The Influence of Political Risk on the Scope of Internationalization of Regulated Companies: Insights From a Spanish Sample', *Journal of World Business*, 49(3), 2014, 301–311.

Jones, G., *British Multinationals: Origins, Management and Performance*, Aldershot: Gower, 1986.

Jones, G. and Wadhwani, R. D., 'Historical Change and the Competitive Advantage of Firms: Explicating the "Dynamics" in the Dynamic Capabilities Framework', *Harvard Business School Working Paper*, No. 17–052, December 2016, 1–32.

Leih, S. and Teece, D. J., 'The Functions of Middle and Top Management in the Dynamic Capabilities Framework', *Kindai Management Review*, 1, 2013, 1–25.

Mollan, A. M. and Tennet, K. D., 'International Taxation and Corporate Strategy: Evidence From British Overseas Business, Circa 1900–1965', *Business History*, 57(7), 2015, 1054–1081.

Peden, G. C., *The Treasury and British Public Policy 1906–1959*, New York: Oxford University Press, 2000.

Picciotto, S., *International Business Taxation*, London: Weidenfeld and Nicolson, 1992.

Rajwani, T. and Lawton, T., 'Corporate Political Activity: A Literature Review and Research Agenda', *International Journal of Management Reviews*, 15(1), 2013, 86–105.

Taylor, J., 'Corporation Income Tax Brackets and Rates, 1909–2002', *IRS, Statistics of Income Bulletin*, 2013, 284–290.

Teece, D. J., 'Explicating Dynamic Capabilities: The Nature and Microfoundations of (Sustainable) Enterprise Performance', *Strategic Management Journal*, 28(13), 2007, 1319–1350.

Wilkins, M., 'The Free-standing Company, 1870–1914: An Important Type of British Foreign Direct Investment', *Economic History Review*, 41(2), 1988, 259–282.

Wilkins, M., 'The Free-standing Company Revisited', in M. Willkins and H. Schröter (eds), *The Free Standing Company in the World Economy, 1830–1996*, Oxford: Oxford University Press, 1998, 3.

3 Go West

C&A's Motives and Strategies for Expansion From Europe Into the Western Hemisphere, 1945–1962

Mark Spoerer

Introduction[1]

C&A is today still one of the world's largest clothing retail chains. The firm was founded in 1841 in the Netherlands by two German nationals, the brothers Clemens and August Brenninkmeyer. Since its beginnings, C&A has been exclusively operated and owned by direct descendants of the Brenninkmeijers (as the family name is written in Dutch), now in the sixth generation. In the course of its company history, C&A stood several times at crossroads where it had to decide whether it should expand into a foreign country. The firm took a leap into Germany in 1911, into the United Kingdom in 1922 and into the United States in 1946. After the foundation of the European Economic Community, C&A soon expanded into other countries, both in the EEC and elsewhere.

In this chapter, it will be argued that, first, there is a systemic link between the corporate governance of C&A, and in particular the succession strategy of the Brenninkmeijer family, and the necessity to expand into other countries; secondly, the choice of the Western Hemisphere after 1945 was clearly a consequence of the emerging Cold War.

The following section describes the fate of the company until the end of World War II, with a focus on the decisions to expand the branch network from the Netherlands to Germany and the UK. The third section analyses the strategic problems faced by the Brenninkmeijer family and C&A after 1945. The following two sections are devoted to C&A's costly retail trade adventure in the United States and the family's much more successful move to safe havens in Canada and Curaçao (Dutch Antilles).

Family Dynamics: C&A's Expansion Abroad Until 1945

In the first half century of its existence, C&A Brenninkmeijer remained a small business based in Sneek (Frisia). Clemens and August were pedlars who sold fabrics to customers in the countryside. They opened their first stores in Sneek (1860) and in nearby Leeuwarden (1881). A big step forward was the move of the second Brenninkmeijer generation to

Amsterdam, the commercial capital of the Netherlands, in 1893. Within 11 years, sales more than tripled.[2]

But the most important move was a radical change in the targeted customer group which started in 1906. The traditional mark-up in the clothing retail business was 100 percent, which implied that clothes should be sold at twice their purchase price. In nearly all stores and even most warehouses, selling clothes or fabrics incurred high transaction costs. Prices were not fixed but a result of bargaining between the salesperson and the customer. The latter could expect that the purchased goods would be tailored, if necessary, delivered and be paid for by credit. As a consequence, lower-class customers usually bought clothing at the second-hand market.[3]

In contrast, the Brenninkmeijers[4] switched to a marketing strategy that a few pioneers like the warehouse chain Vroom & Dreesmann had already introduced. They reduced the frills, refused to give any credit and reduced the mark-up to a mere 25 to 33 percent. The loss of profit per piece was more than compensated for by volume, which was fuelled by aggressive marketing. C&A became famous for its 'meiden mantels', coats that even maids could afford. Both sales and profits soared and, by 1910, C&A was running ten stores—in the aforementioned three cities, in Groningen and in Rotterdam. C&A offered primarily ladies' wear, but from 1897 increasingly menswear as well.[5]

The fast growth of C&A from the early 1890s resulted in important changes in the firm's corporate governance. In 1910, six Brenninkmeijers of the second and third generations ran the company, and nine members of the third generation were already trainees or 'aspirants'. Whenever one of the partners retired or died or an aspirant was co-opted to become partner, the partnership contract had to be renewed. In order to avoid costly transactions, C&A changed its legal form and became a joint-stock company, like many other Dutch companies at the time.[6] The shares were distributed exclusively among the partners. When they retired or died, they or their heirs had to sell the shares to existing or newly entering partners. This guaranteed that both ownership and control were in the hands of a small and exclusive group of Brenninkmeijer entrepreneurs. The company charter guaranteed that no outsider could acquire C&A shares or had a chance of being co-opted into the inner circle which ran the company.

These partners—who were all either brother, cousin, nephew or uncle to each other—also established a set of informal binding rules amongst themselves. There was no primogeniture; in contrast, every Brenninkmeijer son who descended in an unbroken, direct line from Clemens or August was given the chance to become a member of the partnership which ran C&A. If, during his years as a trainee and an aspirant, he demonstrated the potential to become an able entrepreneur, a young Brenninkmeijer would be co-opted into the inner circle in his late 20s (or, if not, he had to leave the firm, which occurred only in a very few cases before the 1960s). Starting after World War I, all partners had to retire at the age of 55 and to sell their shares as described above. These rules helped to overcome the succession problem which is typical of the family firm—the Buddenbrook effect.[7] Rather than hiring the most able executives on the labour market, the members of the inner circle stood in an 'intense, noble performance-orientated competition'[8] among themselves. The top positions were filled by those judged as the most able by their brothers, cousins, nephews and uncles. In the terms of the principal-agent model, the Brenninkmeijers traded the risk of choosing sub-optimal entrepreneurs from a very restricted and exclusive pool of family members for fewer information asymmetries and fewer control problems which executives or partners from outside the family would have caused. The Brenninkmeijer family, which always stressed 'unitas', an extremely tight sense of togetherness, certainly serves as an excellent example for the 'stewardship' theory.[9]

The main problem by the end of the first decade of the 20th century was that the pool of Brenninkmeijers was becoming ever larger. In the following few years, a dozen Brenninkmeijer sons would have needed positions that enabled them to enjoy the standard of living they were used to. These positions were either being director of one of the large stores in Amsterdam or Rotterdam or acting as a coat buyer for a number of stores. The Netherlands had become too small for the prolific Brenninkmeijer family.

Thus, it was the growing pool of actual and prospective partners that pushed the Brenninkmeijers to look at foreign options for expansion. Whether they ever discussed an alternative to Germany (Belgium, for example) is not clear, as company records are silent on the matter. Yet Germany was an obvious choice. At the time, every Brenninkmeijer was born or raised in Mettingen, a village in northwestern Germany where the family had its roots since at least the early 17th century. Hence, German was their mother tongue. Moreover, as the Netherlands did not dispose of a competitive clothing industry,[10] the Brenninkmeijers were used to placing large orders in Berlin. At the time, Berlin was Germany's centre for ladies' wear, with many, often Jewish, firms that ran hundreds of sweatshops throughout the city.[11] Not only did the Brenninkmeijers know the producers and the local clothing retail market, they also had a business concept which was fairly new to the city. In 1911, C&A opened its first shop in Berlin, which soon became very successful. In the years up to 1914, C&A expanded much faster in Germany than in the Netherlands. In late 1914, C&A ran 11 shops in five Dutch cities and five shops in four large German cities.

World War I and its aftermath confronted the Brenninkmeijers for the first time with what is termed political risk. Germany had lost the war and had to bear a yet unknown reparation burden. Moreover, the country was torn by political upheaval provoked by communist and revanchist movements; on several occasions it was on the brink of civil war and was certainly not the place to invest safely. Moreover, the rapid devaluation of the German currency made business prospects look very uncertain. C&A's German subsidiary did not expand its branch network but tried to acquire the buildings in which it ran its stores. Moreover, it followed its Dutch sister company and integrated vertically into the production of ready-made clothing. While C&A Holland had acquired a small factory in Amsterdam, C&A Germany set up a subsidiary in 1921 which had clothing produced by a number of sweatshops in Berlin run by independent middlemen.[12]

As prospects in Germany were uncertain, the Brenninkmeijers discussed expansion to the United Kingdom. On the one hand, the country had won the war and was still Europe's leading economy. On the other, it was not clear whether the commercial conditions and the business culture were similar to those of the Netherlands and Germany. The older generation was reluctant, as their pensions depended on the welfare of the C&A concern. The younger generation was willing to take the risk. Following the advice of a small team which assessed the business conditions as favourable, the owners decided to set up C&A Modes in London. As the building in which the first store was established was rented, the commercial risks were manageable. As in Germany, where conditions improved from 1924, the new British subsidiary expanded quickly. By April 1940, C&A was operating 56 branches which were nearly evenly distributed between the three sister companies in the Netherlands, Germany and the United Kingdom. In the course of World War II and the immediate post-war years, 23 of them were lost either by destruction or nationalisation (eastern Germany and Wroclaw in Poland).[13]

Family, Firm and Geopolitics in the 1940s

Immediately after the surrender of the Netherlands on May 15, 1940, the Brenninkmeijers who were based in London offered part of their British C&A headquarters to the exiled Dutch government. As a consequence, they had many opportunities to discuss the political situation with Dutch ministers, officials and other high-level functionaries—sometimes in air raid shelters. As the war dragged on, fears increased that the Soviet Union or communist parties would seize power in Western and central Europe.[14]

After the end of the war, the Brenninkmeijers living in the Netherlands and Britain were finally able to hold joint meetings again, typically around important Catholic holidays, when the whole family got together. The most important point was the long-term future of C&A and the personal assets of the family. The Brenninkmeijers living in Germany were prevented from attending by Allied travel restrictions and because, in spring 1947, the British occupation forces in Germany regarded them as collaborators with the Nazi regime.[15]

The difficult relationship with the Nazi regime was the only experience of political risk that the Brenninkmeijers had had so far. On the one hand, the economic upswing in post-1933 Germany was welcomed, and opportunities to acquire real estate cheaply in the course of the 'aryanisation' were eagerly seized by C&A Germany. On the other hand, Nazi economic policy hindered warehouses and large retail chains like C&A from fully participating in the boom. Moreover, since 1931, it had become difficult to transfer profits abroad. Many other foreign companies faced similar problems such as the Dutch Unilever group or IBM.[16]

In their efforts to open a store in Leipzig against the will of local authorities, the Brenninkmeijers came into contact with Hermann Göring in 1938 who, as Plenipotentiary for the Four Year Plan, was in charge of the economy at the time. The Brenninkmeijers started to corrupt Göring who, in turn, helped them overcome the local resistance in Leipzig and later also on other occasions. It was very probably Göring who, after the occupation of the Netherlands, advised auditors of the *Feindvermögensverwaltung* (enemy property control) to handle 'the affairs of the Brenninkmeyer firm in an accommodating manner'.[17]

Despite their partial collaboration with the regime, the Brenninkmeijers considered Germany to be different from the Netherlands and the United Kingdom, and to be a less safe country. While their main assets in these two countries were under control of a joint holding company, Nederlandsche Bedrijfs-Unie NV (Nebu, see Figure 3.1 below), the German assets were held directly by the Brenninkmeijers running the business there and a Dutch-based holding, Beleggings Corporatie Mettam NV. The Dutch and British firms were joint-stock companies, while the legal form of C&A Germany often changed following German corporation and tax laws. In order to avoid the comparatively high corporate taxation in Germany, and in particular to circumvent the restrictions of profit transfers out of Germany, the Brenninkmeijers established holdings in Liechtenstein and Switzerland. The owners of these holdings, which lent capital to C&A Germany, were family members not residing in Germany. As a consequence, the interest payments of C&A Germany to these holdings were tax-deductible and formally not hidden distribution of profits in the strict sense of the tax laws.

Figure 3.1 illustrates the separation of the Brenninkmeijers' assets in Britain and the Netherlands—countries where capitalism was not under threat in the interwar period. The German assets were held separately, so that losses there would not affect the structure of the West European C&A group.[18] Had C&A Germany been expropriated by the Nazis (or, after the war, by the allies), the Brenninkmeijer entrepreneurs would have had distributed the losses amongst themselves. In other words, the political risk was shared among all individual Brenninkmeijers, regardless of whether a family member worked and resided in Germany or not.

The figure also illustrates how the Brenninkmeijers handled their private wealth (gray boxes). Given that all three businesses yielded decent profits

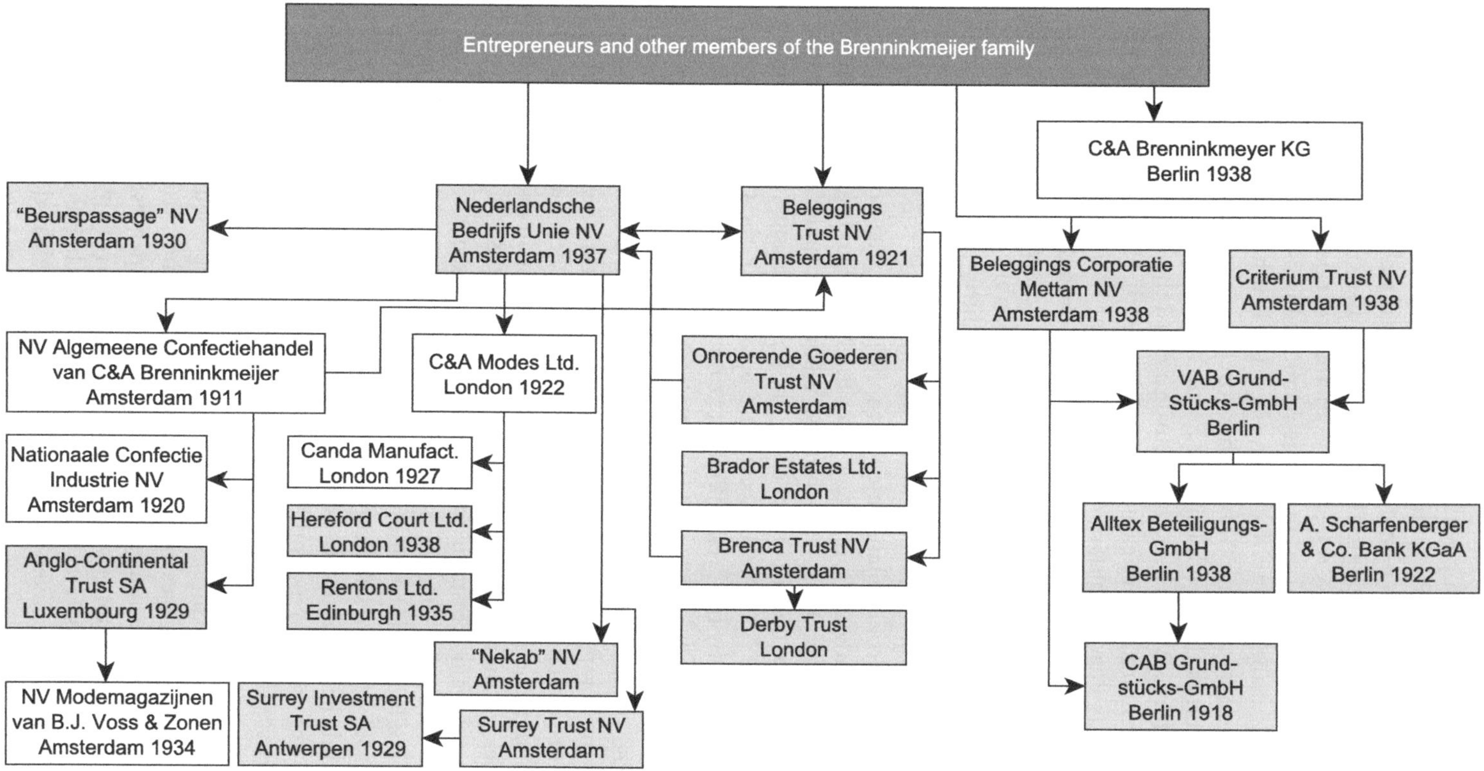

Figure 3.1 The C&A group in mid-1939

Source: Tax audit report C&A Brenninkmeyer KG, March 21, 1940, sheet 4, 23, Bundesamt für zentrale Dienste und offene Vermögensfragen, shelf 8/6, No. 19.

Notes: 'Other members' of the family are those without controlling rights. Insignificant companies not pictured. Retail and production companies white; property, holding, asset management and financial companies gray.

(close to ten percent on sales before taxes)[19] and the family's wealth was growing, this was an important issue which also concerned the running business of the three C&A retail companies NV Algemene Confectiehandel NV, C&A Modes Ltd. and C&A Brenninkmeyer (Germany). When Brenninkmeijer entrepreneurs left the inner circle, either because of premature death or the self-imposed retirement age of 55, they or their heirs had to trade the shares with voting rights for assets without any control over the running of the business. For these reasons the Brenninkmeijers also created a network of asset management companies which administered their personal wealth and that of their families. During this period, there was no clear separation between the Anglo-Dutch operating concern and the asset management concern. Both the Beleggings Trust NV (Beltru) and the Brenca Trust NV held shares (without voting rights, of course) in the Nebu, the core holding of the Dutch and British businesses.[20] Typically enough, there were no asset management companies of the Brenninkmeijers in Germany. If profits from Germany were to be distributed, they flowed as tax-deductible interest payments to the holdings in Switzerland and Liechtenstein and from there to the Brenninkmeijers not resident in Germany who held the shares of these holdings. There are no accessible archival holdings which reveal how these flows were distributed among all individual Brenninkmeijers.

In 1945, the Third Reich was defeated, but it seemed as if the reconstruction of Europe would take a long time. Additionally, with the supremacy of the Soviet Union, a new spectre had appeared on the horizon. One Eastern European state after another fell into the Soviets' sphere of influence. Moreover, communists and socialists had been strengthened in Western Europe—the Labour Party had, after all, won the British general election of 1945. The Brenninkmeijers' business model, which had proved so successful in the past, was based on a capitalist order that seemed to be coming under threat everywhere in Europe. The Cold War, which had already become a reality by 1947, appeared to confirm these anxieties. Amidst the first Berlin blockade from June 1948 to May 1949, the Brenninkmeijers even considered making copies of all their important business documents and storing them in a second British head office and transferring the management of their assets to South Africa.[21] In the years that followed, provisional plans were drawn up concerning how the family could flee to South Africa via Ireland. Two companies were founded whose main tasks consisted of quickly mobilising liquid assets in case of a crisis.[22] But the main focus of the Brenninkmeijers was on the Western Hemisphere.

C&A Inc., New York

In 1945, North America was a beacon that seemed to guarantee free markets.[23] Members of the Brenninkmeijer family had returned from business trips to the United States in 1923, 1932 and 1935 with new ideas concerning issues like organisation, logistics and advertising. Now, as 1945 faded into 1946, the idea arose of establishing a foothold in the US similar to C&A's successful start in Britain. In America, all wartime price restrictions and most production restrictions had already been lifted or released by late 1946.[24] The market was gigantic and would offer business opportunities for generations of Brenninkmeijers to come.

In March 1946, a three-man commission of the third generation, all of whom had extensive experience with C&A Modes, flew to New York. There, and also in Chicago and St. Louis, they visited a variety of department stores, chain retailers and garment producers. To their amazement, they found out that even in the wealthy United States many products were scarce, and that procuring goods was, before even quality and price, one of the biggest concerns of clothing retailers. The scarcity was the result of the price controls still in place from the wartime economy. Producers focussed on those articles of clothing for which the difference between the highest allowable price and costs was most advantageous. Back in Europe, the three Brenninkmeijers advised against relocating the entire family to the US, citing hurdles like the need for visas, the problem of the 'dollar gap' in Western Europe and the fact that many of the Brenninkmeijers had been born in Mettingen—that is, in Germany. But they did think it would be worth setting up a business in America.

In mid-June 1946, after overcoming numerous difficulties with acquiring the currency required from the Dutch central bank, the Brenninkmeijers founded C&A Brenninkmeyer Inc. in New York. The Brenninkmeijers were prepared to invest 3.5 million dollars in the project—2 million for the first branch and 1.5 million as reserves and for a second branch, which was deemed crucial because it would allow the company to negotiate bulk discounts from suppliers and for advertising. The search for a suitable location, however, proved difficult. By the end of 1946, the backers in the family were becoming impatient. They wanted to open a less than ideal shop sooner rather than an ideal shop in more than a year's time. In April 1947, C&A was finally able to rent a building on Brooklyn's Fulton Street, together with the building next door and a further property on the corner of Fifth Avenue and 38th Street in Manhattan.[25]

By late May 1947, the Brenninkmeijers were convinced that the focus of their business would inevitably drift toward Anglo-Saxon countries. They were sure that they would be able to establish a chain of branches as quickly in the United States as they had in Germany as of 1911 and Britain as of 1922.[26]

Even though the location question had been solved in spring 1947, numerous other problems retarded the opening of the first American C&A store. One of them was recruiting young leaders for the middle management. In America, C&A encountered a culture that placed less emphasis on loyalty than on quick changes of jobs. The Brenninkmeijers hit upon the idea of directly asking the sons of the female side of the second generation, who had been blocked by the self-imposed rules described above from joining the firm's inner circle, if they would be interested in careers in the United States.[27] In light of the poverty and lack of opportunities in Germany directly after the war and the uncertain future of Europe as a whole, including the Netherlands, the idea was far from absurd. But the inner circle never followed through on this idea, which implied that future partners would not have the last name Brenninkmeijer.

On 15 April 1948, C&A finally opened its first American branch in Brooklyn.[28] It was followed by a second branch in an ambitiously conceived new building on Fifth Avenue in early 1950. The company believed it was on its way. But the firm's success in Europe, where all three sister companies boomed, could not be transferred directly to its two New York branches. Wages were two to three times higher than in Europe, but prices were not, and there was a lot more competition. The business results were disastrous.[29] By the autumn of 1950, catastrophic financial results had already left the disappointed company leadership admitting that it was tougher to compete in the United States than in Europe. They argued that personalities ready to do battle and aggressive advertising campaigns would be needed to gain a foothold in New York. As a consequence, publicity campaigns were expanded, and particular bargains from all C&A departments were to be featured in display windows to entice shoppers into branches.[30] Between 1951 and 1956, C&A Brenninkmeyer Inc. extensively re-organised—but to no avail. In June 1954, the newly built branch of Fifth Avenue was sold at a loss of $700,000.[31]

The Brenninkmeijers continually debated the future of the money-losing US subsidiary throughout the 1950s. In mid-1955, they drew some self-critical conclusions. They had underestimated the difficulties in America, primarily the higher wages and the problems with establishing long-term relations with suppliers. In addition, business in Europe had developed better than expected shortly after the end of the war, 'noticeably cooling' the 'enthusiasm for America'.[32]

Yet despite continuing losses, the Brenninkmeijers opted to stick to the project because they definitely wanted a foothold in the Western Hemisphere. A number of new factors started to play a role. Liberalised international trade relations removed hindrances that had been significant in the late 1940s. Moreover, C&A was concerned that 'big capital'—to which the Brenninkmeijers despite their wealth did not feel themselves to belong—was increasingly penetrating the retail sector. This was a dangerous tendency with respect to the family's business in Europe which had to remain absolutely independent from external capital (and control). Therefore it was important to keep C&A in the United States and monitor possible developments first-hand. Finally, the Cold War was in full swing. In case war or revolution broke out, the plan was now to move the company head office to Curaçao in the Dutch Antilles (as Philips—the Dutch, electrotechnical company—had done in 1940), where C&A had already set up holding companies for tax purposes (see following section). For logistical reasons, it was thus important to have family members present in the United States. Nonetheless, those who already worked in New York had problems adjusting to American society and lived eight years after their arrival in a 'complete isolation' that took its toll on their psyche and constitution. But C&A Brenninkmeijer Inc., with its branch on Fulton Street, remained the company's 'bridgehead' in America.[33]

In 1956, turnover at the Fulton Street branch had risen to $2 million (while the combined turnover of the three European C&A companies was $215.4 million in the same year).[34] The following September, C&A again opened a second American branch, this time in the Jamaica section of Queens. One main reason for the choice of this location was that the local Brooklyn sections of New York newspapers also included Jamaica, allowing C&A's relatively high advertising costs to be split between the two branches. After the Brooklyn branch was expanded in the late 1950s, both outlets offered ladies' wear and menswear. As of 1958, the Brooklyn branch even sold electrical household appliances while the European branches stuck strictly to ready-made clothing. The attempt to establish a third outlet in a new shopping centre on Long Island failed.[35]

Ten years after the first American branch was opened, C&A was still running at a loss there. For years, C&A Modes and C&A Brenninkmeyer GmbH (Germany) had been transferring half of their net profits to their Dutch group headquarters, which in turn supported C&A Brenninkmeyer Inc. in New York.[36] The Brenninkmeijers' willingness to burn more money in America rose and fell inversely to the political climate in Europe.[37] Still, even when European political tension was relaxed, they remained convinced that America would be an important arena for the upcoming fourth generation of Brenninkmeijers and that the lessons learned stateside would prove crucial in the 'Euromarkt' (European market), a concept first used in the meeting minutes in July 1958.[38] But management positions in New York were far from popular among the young Brenninkmeijers: whilst it was part of their job that they were transferred from one (European) branch to another at only several days' notice, the chronically deficit-ridden American business was so unpopular that young entrepreneurs made an agreement with their uncles not to be sent to the US against their will.[39]

In late 1958, during the second Berlin crisis, an internal commission recommended acquiring an existing American retail chain rather than pursuing a business strategy that had theretofore failed. In the autumn of 1959, C&A Brenninkmeyer Inc. took out advertisements in major newspapers, proclaiming that an 'established business' was interested in taking over a chain of clothing retailers. But the offers that materialised were not attractive enough.[40] In January 1962, following three years of searching and negotiating with various companies, C&A took over Ohrbach's, a chain of stores that members of the Brenninkmeijer family had intensely examined while on a business trip all the way back in 1932. With its slogan 'turnover in millions and profit in pennies', Ohrbach's was the US chain that most closely resembled C&A. With Ohrbach's four stores in the New York and Los Angeles areas, its turnover of $53 million and its net return on sales of 1.7 percent, C&A thought it had finally gained its coveted foothold in America.[41] By mid-1964, C&A had closed both of its own New York branches.[42]

Canada and Curaçao: Atlantic Tax Havens

While the Brenninkmeijers had regarded Germany as the main source of political risk in the interwar period, Europe as a whole came under threat after 1945. The group structure that had evolved in the 1930s (see Figure 3.1 above) was vulnerable both in the case of a conventional or a nuclear war. Until the late 1950s, the Americas, at least, seemed safe from a nuclear attack by the Soviet Union. Thus the reasons for the Brenninkmeijers' leap across the Atlantic were not confined to their core business at the time, the clothing retail trade, but included also the safeguarding of both the assets of the operating group as well as those of the asset management group.

The reorganisation of the whole Brenninkmeijer group was a long runner in the meetings of the inner circle. Two issues were at stake. First, the assets of the family and the C&A group needed to be protected against the dangers arising from the Cold War. Second, the Brenninkmeijers considered it as unsatisfactory that a portion of the capital intended for asset accumulation and for supplying payments in cases of inheritance was being used via loans to finance the on-going business.[43] The constant restructuring of the group in the 1950s led to a stricter separation of the operating business and the family's asset management companies. Toward the end of the period for which archival material is accessible, this process had been largely, but not entirely, completed.

Figure 3.2 is a dramatically simplified presentation of the relationships among the companies in the group; in particular, asset management companies that did nothing else are not pictured. The core of the group in the second half of the 1950s was Unicena (*Uni*tas and *C en A*). It took over the role that had been fulfilled by Nebu up to that point, which had transferred its shares in the operating companies to Unicena.[44] At the end of the 1950s, the shares of the Dutch, British and American retail trade companies that had voting rights were all united in Unicena. Moreover, it owned Mateor, which was supposed to lay the groundwork for starting up business in Belgium, as well as all the voting shares in Locanda NV in Curaçao.[45] The debt instruments (amounting to 35 million guilders) of Antibella, which was likewise located in Curaçao, flowed into Locanda. This connection between Antibella and Locanda, both founded in 1958, was the last crossover point between the operating C&A business and the family's asset management companies pictured in gray in Figure 3.2.

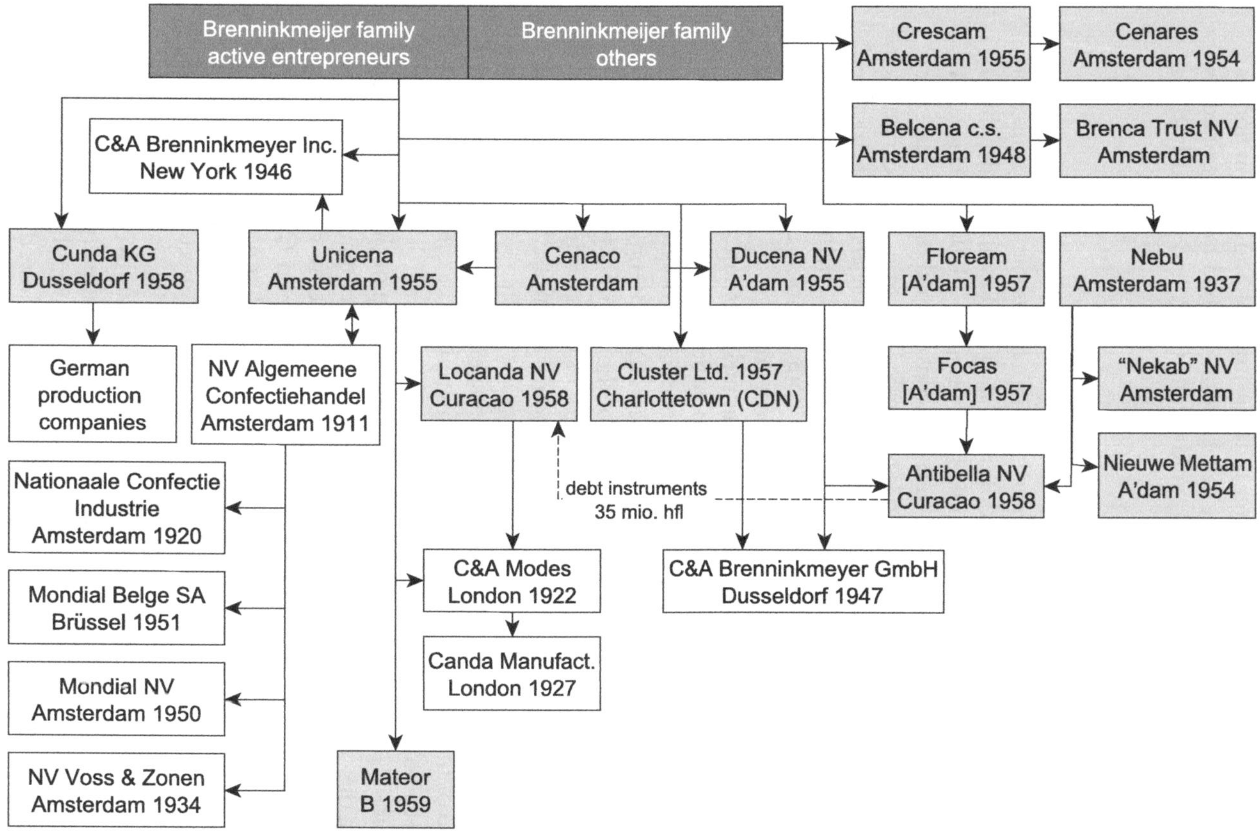

Figure 3.2 The C&A group at the end of 1959

Source: 'Overzichten juridische structuur' 1959.10 and 1959.12, both DCM, Sig. 122784.

Notes: Insignificant companies not pictured. Retail, wholesale and production companies white; property, holding and asset management companies gray. The only cross-holdings were between Confectiehandel and Unicena.

The German business, C&A Brenninkmeyer GmbH, was controlled through Ducena NV (*Du*itsland and *C en A*).[46] The profit distributions, however, not only flowed into Ducena but also into Cluster Ltd. in Charlottetown. This little town is located on Prince Edward Island, which is part of Canada. Charlottetown was about one hour's flight from Gander (Canada) and a half hour's flight from Bangor (Maine, USA), two airports important for the connection to Europe at the time. This arrangement ensured that a portion of the proceeds of the three European companies flowed into tax oases that were located in the Western Hemisphere. If the Soviet Union had invaded Western Europe, large parts of the C&A financial assets would have been out of its reach—the name Antibella was probably not chosen without forethought. When the group was restructured, the experts at Unicena were very particular about making sure that the shareholders of the asset management companies would continue to have no controlling rights over the companies that ran the operating business.[47]

In addition to the Atlantic safety net, the Brenninkmeijers created a war account of 1.25 million Swiss francs at a Swiss banking company in Zurich in the summer of 1961. It was intended to provide the necessary cash to enable family members and high-ranking employees of the C&A group to flee to the West.[48]

Thus both main objectives of the reorganisation were at least partially achieved by the beginning of the 1960s. A large part of the profits earned by the three European sister companies flowed directly to Canada or Curaçao. The controlling rights of these companies were in the hands of the active Brenninkmeijer entrepreneurs who could decide whether the money was reinvested in Europe or not. Moreover, these overseas companies formed a safety net in case of a war in Europe. Although there is no direct archival evidence for this, one can assume that the group lawyers in Amsterdam had plans which would have allowed them to transfer the property rights of the most important European companies to the Western Hemisphere within a few days.

Conclusion

John Dunning has listed, in his 'eclectical paradigm', the most important motives for firms to become multinationals: firms want to gain access to resources or markets, they want to improve their efficiency, they seek to secure strategic assets, they have to provide support to foreign customers or they want to evade political risk.[49] None of these apply in the case of the Brenninkmeijers, the exception being political risk, which, although it was not a motive as such, played a role in the question of where to expand (or not).

Rather, as argued in the second section, becoming a multinational enterprise was an inherent consequence of the peculiar corporate governance structure of C&A. The Brenninkmeijers solved the succession problem of the family firm by giving a chance to every son in direct and unbroken descent of the company founders Clemens and August. As the profoundly Catholic family was very prolific, each of the first four generations had at least double the number of sons than the one preceding it (2, 8, 24 and 51).[50] This had the advantage that the Brenninkmeijer entrepreneurs of the inner circle had the opportunity to select the most able among their generation and the one following, and that they did not have to look for partners outside the family, with all the typical principal-agent problems involved. The other side of the coin was that this strategy—combined with the generative behaviour of the family—made it necessary to expand continuously. As shown above, this self-induced pressure was the main reason to expand into Germany in 1911 and into the United Kingdom in 1922. Being a family firm was not at all an impediment to the internationalisation of the business, as not only Alfred D. Chandler has maintained.[51]

For the Brenninkmeijer generations active in the interwar years, political risks were mainly confined to post-WWI Germany. While the Netherlands and Britain remained profoundly pro-capitalist, Germany was shaky. Throughout its short existence, the political order of the Weimar Republic was always threatened by right and left-wing groups. Reparations, a legacy of the Empire which had risked war in 1914 and had collapsed in 1918, imposed heavy psychological and fiscal burdens on the young republic. When the Brenninkmeijers built up a network of asset management companies from the mid-1920s to administrate the growing wealth of the family, Germany was excluded. The political risks in Germany increased when the Nazi Party came to power in 1933. Although their economic policy turned out to be less anti-capitalist than their propaganda, business conditions became a very delicate matter. C&A Germany profited from the economic upswing and the opportunities to acquire real estate in the course of 'aryanisation'. Yet, as Catholics, foreigners and capitalists, the Brenninkmeijers residing in Germany felt themselves to be threatened by the Nazi Party and thus gained the protection of Hermann Göring, who appreciated personal wealth more than national socialist purism.

After World War II, Germany soon became as pro-capitalist as the other two countries in which C&A operated fast-expanding branch networks. But now the political risks affected Europe as a whole. Hence leaping to the United States in 1946 was a consequence both of C&A's corporate governance and the increase in geopolitical risks. In the second half of the 1940s, the Brenninkmeijer family envisaged its future to be in the United States, the standard-bearer of enterprise capitalism. Although they soon had to realise that they had underestimated the difficulties of the US clothing retail market, they continued to fuel their American adventure from the profits of the three European sister companies.

Two further motives for the turn to the Western Hemisphere were the safeguarding of the family's assets and tax avoidance. While the United States was not attractive in these respects, Canada and Curaçao were. Hence the Brenninkmeijers founded overseas holding companies which served two purposes, saving taxes and forming a safety net in the case of political upheaval or war in Europe. In contrast to the interwar period, when the Brenninkmeijers outsmarted the German tax authorities, after the Second World War, tax savings models were discussed in advance with the Dutch tax authorities.[52]

Due to the reduction of tensions between the United States and the Soviet Union, the Atlantic safety net was never used. While the objective to reduce taxes was certainly fulfilled, the hopes to make money in the United States materialised only for a short period. Ohrbach's stores acquired in 1962 were located in neighbourhoods that declined in the course of the 1960s and 1970s. In the subsequent decades, the Brenninkmeijers built up an extensive fashion empire in the United States and Canada by acquiring five further clothing chains. In 2004, C&A withdrew from the North American clothing market in order to focus on its core business in Continental Europe.

Notes

1 This chapter has originated from a larger study on the company history of C&A for which the Brenninkmeijer family generously permitted unlimited access to archival holdings up to 1961. For the years thereafter, the chapter draws on newspaper articles and a book by a journalist, Weiguny, *Die geheimnisvollen Herren.*

2 See Spoerer, *C&A*, 414–415.

3 See, e.g., Segers, Loyen, Dejongh, and Buyst, *Op weg naar een consumptiemaatschappij.*

4 The notion 'the Brenninkmeijers' pertains to those members of the family who were active entrepreneurs (partners) in the inner circle which led the C&A group.

5 See Spoerer, *C&A*, 42–58; Hondelink, 'Vroom en Dreesmann', 163.

6 See Arnoldus, *Family*, 374.

7 See Rose, 'Beyond Buddenbrooks'.

8 Rudolf Brenninkmeijer (1892–1955) in his annual report for the German subsidiary 1943, sheet 1, Draiflessen Collection, Mettingen (DCM), Sig. 109760 (my translation, M. S.).

9 See Davis, Schoorman, and Donaldson, 'Towards a Stewardship Theory of Management'; Colli, 'Family Firms', 588.—On the Brenninkmeijers' 'unitas' principle see Spoerer, *C&A*, 339–341, 371.

10 See Wolff-Gerzon, *Au bonheur des dames*; de Leeuw, *Kleding in Nederland.*

11 See Westphal, *Berliner Konfektion*; Schnaus, *Kleidung zieht jeden an.*

12 See Spoerer, *C&A*, 68, 107–113.

13 See Spoerer, *C&A*, 90–96, 230.

14 See Bernard Brenninkmeijer's diary, sheets 3–4, 6, 8–9, 24–25, DCM, Sig. 128096; see also Interview Martin Brenninkmeijer (2008), lines 2163–2181, DCM, Sig. 128634; Minutes of Meeting, June 6, 1955, sheet 4, DCM, Sig. 122770.

15 See for details Spoerer, *C&A*, 270–273.

16 See Black, *IBM*, 122–123, Wubs, *International Business*, 47–49, 176, and in general: Forbes, *Doing Business with the Nazis*, 138–141.
17 Letter Kramer to Deutsche Revisions und Treuhand AG, April 20, 1942, Bundesarchiv, R 177/1246 (my translation, M. S.).
18 Unilever, which also held most of its assets in the UK, the Netherlands and Germany, found a similar solution, see Wubs, *International Business*, 180–181.
19 See Spoerer, *C&A*, 418–419.
20 See 'Übersicht über interne Rechtsverhältnisse und Kapitalaufbau des C. & A. Brenninkmeijer Konzerns, zu Bericht über die Nederlandsche Bedrijfs Unie N.V., Amsterdam', Bundesarchiv Berlin, R 177/1246, sh. 7.
21 See Minutes of Meeting, October 14, 1948, sheet 1, DCM, Sig. 122767.
22 See Minutes of Meetings, February 19–22, 1952, sheet 11, and July 8–10, 1952, sheets 11–12, both DCM, Sig. 122768. Valuable documents were also taken to Ireland; see Minutes Board Meeting C&A Modes, December 10, 1951, February 28, 1952, and August 27, 1952, all DCM, Sig. 113310.
23 See Interview Martin Brenninkmeijer (2008), lines 2163–2181, DCM, Sig. 128634; see also Bernard Brenninkmeijer's diary, sheets 3–4, 6, 8–9, 24–25, DCM, Sig. 128096.
24 See Rockoff, *Drastic Measures*, 108, 150–154; idem, 'The United States', 109–110.
25 See Minutes of Meetings, January 30 to February 1, 1947, sheet 4, September 22–24, 1947, sheet 1, and September 9–10, 1948, sheet 1, all DCM, Sig. 122767 and 122768.
26 See Minutes of Meetings, May 28–30, 1947, sheet 2, June 4, 1955, sheet 4, and October 6–7, 1959, sheet 3, DCM, Sig. 122770, 122774, respectively.
27 See Minutes of Meeting, May 28–30, 1947, sheet 3, and December 18–19, 1947, sheet 4, both DCM, Sig. 122766.
28 See 'Opens First Brooklyn Store', *New York Times*, April 16, 1948.
29 Detailed figures are not available. All three European C&A subsidiaries produced extensive internal business data since at least 1926, but the company archives in Mettingen (DCM) do not dispose of similar holdings for the US subsidiary. In February 1963, the central administrative office for the Netherlands, which at the time also disposed of archival holdings of the other subsidiaries, was destroyed in a fire.
30 See Minutes of Meeting, October 12–13, 1950, sheets 1–2, DCM, Sig. 122768.
31 The newly constructed building cost $2.8 million. It brought in 2.1 million when it was sold. See Minutes of Meetings, February 17–19, 1953, sheet 4, and July 6–8, 1954, sheet 11, both DCM, Sig. 122769 and 122770.
32 Quotes from Minutes of Meeting, June 4, 1955, sheet 5, DCM, Sig. 122770.
33 See Minutes of Meeting, June 4, 1955, sheet 4, DCM, Sig. 122770. On Philips, see Blanken, *History of Philips*, 120–128; Klemann, *Nederland 1938–1948*, 44.
34 See Spoerer, *C&A*, 418, 428.
35 See Minutes of Meetings, July 4–5, 1957, sheets 6–7, October 1–2, 1957, sheet 3, and March 18–19, 1958, sheet 5, all DCM, Sig. 122772 and 122753.
36 See Minutes of Meeting, December 10–11, 1957, sheet 11, DCM, Sig. 122772.
37 See Minutes of Meeting, December 9–10, 1958, sheet 6, DCM, Sig. 122773.
38 See Minutes of Meetings, July 8–10, 1958, and sheet 8, October 6–7, 1959, sheet 5, both DCM, Sig. 122772 and 122773.
39 See Minutes of Meeting, October 6–7, 1959, sheets 4–5, DCM, Sig. 122773.
40 See Minutes of Meeting, October 6–7, 1959, sheet 2 ('een bestaand concern'), DCM, Sig. 122773.
41 See Minutes of Meeting, July 11–12, 1961, sheets 7–8, DCM, Sig. 122774; Blaisse and Dekkers manuscript, sheet 220, DCM, Sig. 128926.
42 The Fulton Street (Brooklyn) branch closed in early summer 1964, see *New York Times*, May 30, 1964. On the development of C&A business in America

during the 1960s, see Blaisse and Dekkers manuscript, sheets 211–214, 217–220, DCM, Sig. 128926.
43 See Minutes of Meetings, January 30 to February 1, 1947, and July 12, 1951, both DCM, Sig. 122766 and 122768.
44 See Minutes of Meeting September 25–26, 1956, sheet 2, DCM, Sig. 122771.
45 On the taxation there, see Sutterer, *Die internationalen Basisgesellschaften*, 74–75.
46 See Minutes of Meeting, September 20–21, 1955, sheet 3, DCM, Sig. 122770.
47 'het stemrecht in de vennootschappen van het werkconcern uitsluitend wordt uitgeoefend door de winstdeelgerechtigde leden' of the group of owners, Minutes of Meeting, July 8–10, 1958, sheet 5, DCM, Sig. 122773.
48 See Minutes of Meeting, July 11–12, 1961, sheets 5–6, DCM, Sig. 122775.
49 See Dunning, *Multinational Enterprises*, 82–83; see also Geoffrey Jones, *Multinationals*, 7–10.
50 See Spoerer, *C&A*, 320.
51 See Chandler, jr., *Scale and Scope*, 235–237, 595; see on the issue also Lubinski, Fear, and Fernández Pérez, 'Family Multinationals', 3, 11; Colli, 'Family Firms', 583, 587.
52 See, e.g., Minutes of Meetings, February 16–18, 1954, sheet 6, and April 5–6, 1961, sheet 1, both DCM, Sig. 122769 and 122774.

Bibliography

Arnoldus, Doreen. *Family, Family Firm, and Strategy: Six Dutch Family Firms in the Food Industry 1880–1970*. Amsterdam: Aksant, 2002.

Black, Edwin. *IBM and the Holocaust: The Strategic Alliance Between Nazi Germany and America's Most Powerful Corporation*. London: Little, Brown, 2001.

Blanken, Ivo J. *The History of Philips Electronics N.V., Vol. IV: Under German Rule*. Zaltbommel: European Library, 1999.

Chandler jr., Alfred D. *Scale and Scope: The Dynamics of Industrial Capitalism*. Cambridge, MA: Harvard University Press, 1990.

Colli, Andrea. 'Family Firms Between Risks and Opportunities: A Literature Review'. *Socio-Economic Review* 11 (2013): 577–599.

Davis, James H., F. David Schoorman, and Lex Donaldson. 'Towards a Stewardship Theory of Management'. *Academy of Management Review* 22 (1997): 20–47.

de Leeuw, Kitty P. *Kleding in Nederland, 1813–1920. Van een traditioneel bepaald kleedpatroon naar een begin van modern kleedgedraag*. Hilversum: Uitgeverij Verloren, 1992.

Dunning, John H. *Multinational Enterprises and the Global Economy*. Wokingham: Addison-Wesley, 1992.

Forbes, Neil. *Doing Business With the Nazis: Britain's Economic and Financial Relations With Germany, 1931–1939*. London: Cass, 2000.

Hondelink, H. Philippe. 'Vroom en Dreesmann, de oprichters en hun onderneming 1887–1912'. *Jaarboek voor de geschiedenis van bedrijf en techniek* 9 (1992): 159–184.

Jones, Geoffrey. *Multinationals and Global Capitalism: From the Nineteenth to the Twenty-first Century*. Oxford: Oxford University Press, 2005.

Klemann, Hein A.M. *Nederland 1938–1948. Economie en samenleving in jaren van oorlog en bezetting*. Amsterdam: Boom, 2002.

Lubinski, Christina, Jeffrey Fear, and Paloma Fernández Pérez. 'Family Multinationals. Entrepreneurship, Governance, and Pathways to Internationalization'. In *Family Multinationals: Entrepreneurship, Governance, and Pathways to Internationalization*, edited by *idem*, 1–18. Abingdon: Routledge, 2013.

Rockoff, Hugh T. *Drastic Measures: A History of Wage and Price Controls in the United States*. Cambridge: Cambridge University Press, 1984.

Rockoff, Hugh T. 'The United States: From Ploughshares to Swords'. In *The Economics of World War II: Six Great Powers in International Comparison*, edited by Mark Harrison, 81–121. Cambridge: Cambridge University Press, 1998.

Rose, Mary B. 'Beyond Buddenbrooks: The Family Firm and the Management of Succession in Nineteenth-century Britain'. In *Entrepreneurship, Networks, and Modern Business*, edited by Jonathan Brown and Mary B. Rose, 127–143. Manchester: Manchester University Press, 1993.

Schnaus, Julia. *'Kleidung zieht jeden an': die deutsche Bekleidungsindustrie 1918–1973*. Berlin: De Gruyter, 2017.

Segers, Yves, Reginals Loyen, Guy Dejongh, and Erik Buyst (eds.). *Op weg naar een consumptiemaatschappij. Over het verbruik van voeding, kleding en luxusgoederen in België en Nederland (19–20e eeuw)*. Amsterdam: Aksant, 2002.

Spoerer, Mark. *C&A: A Family Firm in Germany, the Netherlands and the United Kingdom, 1911–1961*. Munich: C.H. Beck, 2016.

Sutterer, Hermann. *Die internationalen Basisgesellschaften und ihre steuerrechtliche Behandlung. Dargestellt am Steuerrecht der Schweiz, des Fürstentums Liechtenstein, des Großherzogtums Luxemburg, des Königreichs der Niederlande und der Bundesrepublik Deutschland*. Ph.D. thesis Mannheim, 1969.

Weiguny, Bettina. *Die geheimnisvollen Herren von C&A. Der Aufstieg der Brenninkmeyers*. Frankfurt on Main: Eichborn, 2005.

Westphal, Uwe. *Berliner Konfektion und Mode. Die Zerstörung einer Tradition 1836–1939*, 2nd edn. Berlin: Ed. Hentrich, 1992.

Wolff-Gerzon, Alice. *'Au bonheur des dames'. Uit het Nederlandse kledingbedrijf van de laatste honderd jaar*. Amsterdam: Spiegel, 1949.

Wubs, Ben. *International Business and National War Interests. Unilever Between Reich and Empire, 1939–45*. London: Routledge, 2008.

4 Foreign Oil Majors in Japan and the Second World War

Takeo Kikkawa

Introduction

As far as large MNEs with worldwide networks are concerned, especially in cases where the host country is either small or less developed, the company may have the power to influence the host country, in economic, political or strategic terms. This may hold more true if the home country of the MNE is a powerful state or, in the case of the MNE, controls strategic material. Studies on Latin America and Iran have revealed how MNEs can have such an impact on sovereign states, and demonstrate the importance of examining the mutual interaction between MNEs and states.[1]

As emphasised in the introduction to this volume, the rivalry among sovereign states plays a pivotal role: it may affect the business environment of MNEs, and in extreme cases, it may escalate into a war. This has to be considered also in the context of the measures taken by MNEs to address political risks. The political and economic relationship between the host and the home nations, or various diplomatic relationships between them (from alliance to hostility) influence the bargaining power against the host country and the freedom of action of MNEs within it. If an MNE has sufficient leverage on its home government, and its home government has in a strong diplomatic, economic, or military position against the host country, it may successfully utilise its home government to create a favourable situation for itself in the host country.

In the early 20th century, Japan opened its door to inward foreign direct investment (FDI) through legislative change. Multinationals from major Western countries, such as Standard Oil, Western Electric, General Electric, Westinghouse, Siemens, American Tobacco, Singer Sewing Machine, J & P Coats and Nestlé set up branches, joint ventures, or subsidiaries in Japan.[2] At the same time, local competitors emerged by taking advantage of the First World War and upgraded their business during the 1920s and 1930s. In the 1930s, by following worldwide trends, the Japanese government adopted a series of industrial policy measures to foster 'national' industries.[3] In the course of military expansion and the escalating confrontation with the US, the situation described above materialised in the oil business to a significant extent.

Oil became the most important strategic material in the 20th century. In Japan, oil drilling and refining began in the late 19th century through technology transfer from the west. However, due to the scarcity of competitive oilfields and limited organisational capability of local firms, American and Anglo-Dutch MNEs established a dominant position. The result was that Japan, which was seeking not only the establishment of national industries but also energy security, was highly dependent on the import of crude oil and oil products. Eighty-two percent of domestically refined crude oil in 1934 was imported.[4] Moreover, it was controlled by MNEs from potential enemies: 70 percent of Japan's crude oil imports at the time were sourced from America.[5] If a crude oil embargo on Japan had been realised, it would have dealt a significant blow to domestic refiners who were greatly dependent on crude oil imports.

In such a context, policy measures to enhance control of oil were introduced in Japan, including licencing of oil business, compulsory stockpiling, price control and policy instruments to facilitate oil refining in Japan. MNEs responded to it by taking multiple measures, including a private oil embargo on Japan and requests to their home governments to introduce a state-level oil embargo. The latter request was declined by home-country governments for diplomatic reasons. But the oil embargo imposed by the US government in August 1941 triggered the Japanese attack on Pearl Harbor and, in order to contain Japanese military aggression in the region, elucidates both the strategic importance of oil and the context of the struggle between foreign MNEs and the Japanese government. While foreign oil MNEs were pressurised by nationalistic economic policy, they also had the power and capability to counteract it.

In this respect, how can we analyse this struggle over oil from the perspective of organisational structures? There are two dimensions: first, the mode of entry into the host country and forms of ownership and control of the business there; secondly, the geographical allocation of actual operations and the design of the value chain, including the degree of vertical integration. In terms of the first dimension, it is known that MNEs used a variety of forms of partnership with local actors in the host country, such as joint ventures or various alliances, to reduce political risks, or to exploit economic advantage. The share of ownership and degree of control were also at stake. Both in the 1930s and the second half of the 1940s, choice about these factors turned into important issues of strategic decision-making for the foreign oil businesses in Japan.

The second dimension, the allocation of actual operations is also an important issue both for the strategy of oil companies and for policy goals of the host country. In the case of foreign oil companies in Japan, there was a choice: either to import and sell refined petroleum product, using refinery plant located in their home country or in a third country near an oil field ('production-area refinery model'), or to import crude oil and refine it in Japan ('consumption-area refinery model'). Because refining in the host country required huge, fixed capital investments, this decision was closely related to the above-mentioned choice between solo-investment or joint ventures. On the other hand, from the viewpoint of the host government in a country with limited crude oil production, it is a choice between petroleum product import and crude oil import. Although both mean import dependency, the import of crude oil means larger reserves of oil, more industrial activity, greater value added in the country, and control of a wider part of the value chain including, theoretically, a greater chance to integrate parts of the value chain upstream (e.g. oil field in the third country). Both in the 1930s and 1940s, Japanese governments looked to the 'consumption-area refinery model', despite Japan's totally changed position in the world order.

This chapter analyses two of the largest foreign oil companies in Japan. Rising Sun Petroleum Company (hereafter 'Rising Sun'), which belonged to the Anglo-Dutch Royal Shell Group, and Standard Vacuum Oil Company (hereafter 'Stanvac'). Rising Sun was founded in 1900 as an independent spin-off from the British trading firm, M. Samuel & Co.'s petroleum division, which had made inroads in Japan. It subsequently came under the umbrella of Asiatic Petroleum Company, part of the Royal Shell Group.

As for Stanvac, it was established in 1933 as a fifty-fifty joint subsidiary of New Jersey Standard (Standard Oil Company of New Jersey) and Socony-Vacuum, which in turn had been founded in 1931 through the merger of Vacuum Oil Company and Socony (Standard Oil Company of New York), which had opened a succession of branches in Japan in 1882–1883. A glance at market shares in Japan's gasoline market in the early 1930s shows Rising Sun in first place, at around 30 percent, with Stanvac in third, at around 20 percent. In terms of the value of their assets on the eve of the Pacific War in 1941, among all the foreign-backed corporations with a foreign capital ratio of 50 percent or more at that time in Japan, Rising Sun was ranked highest, followed by Stanvac in second place.[6]

In this context, this chapter analyses negotiations between the Japanese government and these two firms. Firm strategy materialised as actual investments and other decisions and behaviour, and thus eventually as organisational structure. The process of negotiation reveals not only the perception and expectation of relevant actors but also the conditions they faced.

The first section of this chapter provides a historical overview of the Japanese oil industry, focussing on the period leading up to the Second World War. The following section analyses the efforts by Rising Sun and Stanvac to cope during the period that the Petroleum Industry Law was enforced. In the final section, attention is turned to the period after war, examining the process by which foreign oil companies, including the two named, took the lead in creating the Japanese oil industry's post-war structural framework.

1. *Early History and the 'Consumption-Area Refinery Model'*[7]

Foreign oil companies penetrated deep into the Japanese oil market immediately after the industrial inauguration in the late 19th century. They drove the newly born domestic oil companies into a disadvantageous position. Socony, which took charge of exports anew for the Asian region in the US Standard Oil Group, shifted from the conventional commission sales model to the direct sales model to compete against Russian kerosene, which was rising in the Asian market, and opened a branch office in Japan in 1893. M. Samuel & Co. was in charge of Russian kerosene imports in the Japanese market, but the oil division of the trading company became an independent enterprise in 1890, and Rising Sun Oil was established as a company incorporated in Japan. Shortly after its foundation, Rising Sun came under the umbrella of Asiatic Petroleum, which had been established in 1903, as part of the British and Dutch-origin Royal Dutch Shell Group. In response to this situation, Nippon Oil Corporation (hereafter 'Nippon Oil'), which was founded in 1888 as a domestic oil company, and Hoden Oil Company (hereafter 'Hoden Oil'), which was founded in 1893 as a domestic oil company, promoted a vertical integration strategy that started from the upstream sections (oil exploration) to developing the downstream sections (oil refining) and advanced into the oil sales business as well. However, they failed to establish a competitive advantage over foreign oil companies due to technical backwardness and latecomer disadvantage. The Four Companies Agreement, a kerosene cartel agreement that was signed in 1910, determined that the shares of the domestic market sales should be 43 percent for Socony, 22 percent for Rising Sun Oil, 21 percent for Hoden Oil Company and 14 percent for Nippon Oil Corporation.

Domestic oil companies employed the consumption-area refinery model to compete against foreign oil companies in the mid-1920s. As early as the 1920s, Nippon Oil and Ogura Oil set up refinery facilities in Japan, while foreign oil companies exported petroleum products to Japan by using their refineries close to the oilfields in US or Dutch East Indies (today's Indonesia). This strategy of domestic firms worked partially, but did not go as far as to change the large shares held by foreign MNEs. A gasoline cartel agreement on the Japanese market signed, in 1932, determined that the sales shares should be 32 percent for Rising Sun, 21 percent for Socony-Vacuum Oil, whereas Nippon Oil Corporation had 24 percent, Ogura Oil Company had 13 percent, Mitsubishi Oil Co. had 7 percent and other companies had 3 percent.

The establishment of Stanvac in 1933 improved the importance of the Japanese market in two ways. Before this reorganisation, the oil companies had made America, where they were headquartered, and to a lesser extent Europe, their prime business territory; the Japanese market did not have that much weight. In contrast, Stanvac conducted its business activities in overseas regions east of Suez and did not make America, where it was headquartered, or Europe, part of its business territory. So, for Stanvac, it can be said that the Japanese market had considerable weight. Even in 1941, when the US government imposed the oil embargo on Japan and sales dropped sharply, the share of sales in Japan (including Korea, Taiwan and Manchuria) in Stanvac's total sales was almost 6 percent.[8] According to data collected by Irvine H. Anderson, Stanvac's sales in 1937 and 1939 also shows that Japan was the largest market in East Asia and Southeast Asia, elbowing out China.[9]

For Stanvac, therefore, the Asia-Pacific region was its prime business territory; in contrast to Socony and Socony-Vacuum, who struggled to secure sales channels for kerosene, the company instead had a hard time securing sales channels for gasoline. It is only natural that Stanvac would put strategic emphasis on the Japanese market, where there was exceptionally great demand for gasoline, unlike most of the Asian region.

In addition, after the establishment of Stanvac, the supply base of petroleum products for the Japanese market changed from refineries in America to the ones in the Dutch East Indies. This means that both Rising Sun and Stanvac, who had refineries in Asia,[10] did not find good reasons to have second ones in Japan. Under this situation, the consumption-area refinery model was not a choice for these companies and they had good reason to resist the Japanese government's policy of pursuing this model.

2. *The Petroleum Industry Law of 1934 and Foreign MNEs*[11]

The 1930s were a turning point in Japan of economic thought and policy, and in ideology in Japan. In the process of modernisation and Westernisation since the 1870s, especially after massive privatisation of state-owned enterprises in the 1880s, economic liberalism was the norm in the country, and there was little direct intervention in industrial activities. However, in the course of depression after the 1929 economic crisis and the worldwide trend towards protectionism and economic nationalism, the economic ideology and policy framework in Japan also started to change towards state-interventionism. The Petroleum Industry Law in 1934 was the first and most prominent example of this trend.

The Petroleum Industry Law (hereafter PIL) was announced on 28 March 1934 and came into effect on 1 July of that year. The law contained a number of important stipulations: (1) petroleum refining and importing businesses were subject to the government's licencing system and the government allocated the volume of product sales for each business; (2)

petroleum refiners and importers had a requirement to retain a fixed amount of petroleum reserves; and (3) the government, when required, had the right to adjust the supply and demand, and change the price of oil.

By mid-1934, two issues, in particular, regarding the PIL had become clear: (1) the assigned amounts of petroleum product sales volumes were advantageous for domestic refiners but disadvantageous for petroleum product importers, and (2) oil reserve requirements imposed an immense burden on oil companies. The Japanese government required petroleum reserves of three months' worth to be held until 1 April 1935 and six months' worth until 1 October 1935, based on the volume of petroleum imports over the preceding 12 months (in the case of Rising Sun and Stanvac, two months' worth of petroleum reserves exceeded normal business requirements).

By facing this disagreeable situation, Rising Sun and Stanvac were reluctant to comply with the law requirements. They did not submit the business planning forms for 1935, which made up part of the material used each year to decide the approval of business as determined in the PIL. They submitted only sales plans and not the importation or storage plans that directly dealt with fulfilling petroleum storage requirements.[12] The two foreign oil companies not only ignored the 30 September 1934 deadline, but also the re-established deadline of 15 November.[13]

In order to resolve the confrontation, a meeting between the two MNEs and ministry officials was held on 20 November 1934, and it brought about a compromise. From the ministries, Yoshino, as Vice-Minister of Commerce and Industry, and Kurusu, as the Commerce Bureau Chief of the Ministry of Foreign Affairs, attended the meeting. Their counterparts were T. G. Ely of Rising Sun and J. C. Goold of Stanvac's Japan Branch. At this meeting, Yoshino proposed a compromise whereby the 1935 business plans would be fully submitted with a postscript attached to the effect of 'contents revisable depending on a future change in conditions'.[14] The two foreign oil companies accepted Yoshino's proposal and on 30 November submitted their business plans for 1935. One month later, the assigned amounts of petroleum product, sales volumes for 1935 were announced, but in contrast to the allocations for the second half of 1934, 30 percent of new, increased demand in gasoline was allocated to the petroleum product importers Rising Sun and Stanvac.

In January 1935, with tensions between the Japanese government and foreign oil companies somewhat reduced, F. Godber, an executive from Rising Sun's parent company Royal Dutch Shell, George S. Walden, Chairman at Stanvac's head office in New York, and Philo W. Parker, President of Stanvac, visited Japan and began earnest negotiations with Yoshino and Kurusu. The negotiations took place from 9 January to 13 April 1935, and included 17 meetings in total.[15] The negotiations faced difficulties but a tentative agreement called the 'Five-Point Memorandum' was reached. The central points in this memorandum were: (1) in regard to assigned amounts of petroleum product sales volumes, one-third of new, increased demand in gasoline would thereafter be distributed to petroleum product importers; and (2) petroleum storage requirements would be for three months' worth of petroleum and adjustments made by the Japanese government would end by 1 October 1935 (until adjustment was complete, the two foreign oil companies would not be burdened with fulfilling oil storage requirements).[16] In this way, a tentative compromise was reached between both sides.

However, after April 1935, the implementation of the Five-Point Memorandum turned out to be difficult. Yoshino and Kurusu were unsuccessful in convincing other actors in the government. Despite the promised reduction of petroleum storage requirements from six months' worth of petroleum to three months, the Japanese government eventually decided to maintain it for six months, while taking the following three measures: (1) the final deadline for achieving petroleum storage requirements would be extended by nine months to 1 July 1936, (2) in order to lessen the burden on foreign oil companies, the price of gasoline would be increased, and (3) for the same reason, a subsidy would be provided in relation to the fulfilment of petroleum reserve requirements.[17]

However, Rising Sun and Stanvac expressed strong opposition in part by arguing that the second and third measures did not offer sufficient compensation.[18] What added fuel to the fire of the two foreign oil companies' opposition was the Petroleum Tariff Amendment Proposal that surfaced in November 1935, which was much more disadvantageous for importers (the tariff amendment was implemented on 1 June 1936).

From the autumn of 1935, though bitter exchanges continued between the two foreign oil companies, who called for a return to the Five-Point Memorandum', and the Japanese government, who refused, eventually on 23 December 1935 Kojima Arakazu, the Mining Bureau Chief of the Ministry of Commerce and Industry, denied the validity of the Five-Point Memorandum.[19] In this way, the confrontation between both sides increased once again.

In 1936, the contrast became clear between the domestic oil companies[20] who had basically achieved the six months' petroleum storage requirements, and the foreign oil companies (Rising Sun and Stanvac) who refused to fulfil it. The assigned amounts of petroleum product sales volume for 1936 took place on a quarterly basis, and the two foreign oil companies, who failed each time to meet the petroleum storage requirements and were thus noncompliant, faced the threat of losing part of their existing amounts to domestic oil companies who had complied with the petroleum storage requirements.

Despite their policy of non-compliance, both Rising Sun and Stanvac were basically able to maintain their existing assigned amounts. This was because the two foreign oil companies pursued a compromise plan that established a petroleum holding company within Japan, with joint investment provided by Mitsui & Co., to fulfil the two companies' petroleum reserve requirements. This compromise plan was first rumoured within Stanvac from around November 1935 and appears to have been seriously considered when Kurusu had endorsed the idea of business cooperation with Japanese capital, at a meeting in December 1935 between American embassy staff and representatives of the two foreign oil companies.

In this way, Japanese government and foreign oil companies continued their confrontation while also aiming to once again reach a compromise. However, the principal supporters of the Japanese government's efforts at compromise, Kurusu and Yoshino, both left the negotiating stage one after the other. Kurusu was transferred to the post of Japanese Ambassador to Belgium in April 1936, withdrawing from negotiations on the PIL. Kurusu's role was taken over by Yoshino, although on 7 October 1936, Yoshino also left his post as Vice-Minister of Commerce and Industry and ceased to be a party to the negotiations.[21] Just before this, in a meeting held on 19 September with representatives of Rising Sun, Stanvac and Mitsui & Co., Yoshino made verbal guarantees about the future in order to satisfy the two foreign oil companies.[22]

After Yoshino left his position, two foreign oil companies temporarily strengthened their opposition towards the Japanese government. This was for four reasons: (1) on 21 November 1936 the Ministry's Mining Bureau declined to confirm in writing the guarantees given by Yoshino to the two foreign oil companies in September; (2) revisions made in December 1936 to the assigned amounts of kerosene sales volumes for the second half of 1936 led to a decrease in assigned amounts for importers (foreign oil companies); (3) in December 1936, a new Petroleum Tariff Amendment Proposal further strengthened the advantages of the imported, crude oil refining process over the petroleum product import method, and (4) the 1937 petroleum product sales quota for Korea saw a significant reduction in Rising Sun's and Stanvac's volume amounts.[23]

However, in the long-term, this period saw the confrontation between the Japanese government and foreign oil companies over the PIL head towards resolution. This was because the following points could be confirmed: (1) from November 1936 the Mining Bureau no longer demanded, as before, that Rising Sun and Stanvac achieve their petroleum storage requirements (for this reason, negotiations between the two foreign oil companies and Mitsui & Co. to establish a new petroleum holding company stopped progressing from around November 1936, and eventually fizzled out); (2) in regards to the 1937 sales quota announced in late December 1936, the two foreign oil companies secured their existing volume; (3) on 15 January 1937, the Japanese Ministry of Foreign Affairs, in place of the Ministry of Commerce and Industry, confirmed in writing the future guarantees made to the two foreign oil companies by Yoshino, and (4) at that time, the Ministry of Foreign Affairs also made clear that the difference in the treatment of domestic and foreign oil companies in relation to the assigned amounts of kerosene sales volumes for 1936 was an exceptional measure accompanying an increase in domestic crude oil production. Even the final issue of disagreement regarding assigned amounts for petroleum product sales volumes in Korea was resolved when the Ministry of Foreign Affairs gave an answer on 29 May 1937 that was satisfactory to the two foreign oil companies.

As sketched above, as the result of non-compliance with the storage requirement of PIL, Rising Sun and Stanvac experienced a slow but steady decrease in their market share. On the other hand, the Japanese government was unable in the end to force the companies to comply with the six-month petroleum storage requirements.[24] At the same time, while the two companies were noncompliant, they were still able to maintain existing sales volumes and continue their operations in Japan, and their share was still very high, even in the late 1930s. The Japanese government was also able gradually to realise its highly important, political priority of importing and refining crude oil. Therefore, after a meeting on 29 May 1937 between representatives from the Ministry of Foreign Affairs and the two companies, hardly any negotiations took place between the Japanese government and foreign oil companies over the PIL.

What kind of interpretation can be placed on the negotiation process described above? First, the bargaining power of two parties was defined both by economic capability and world politics. The Japanese government had a fundamental dilemma. The self-sufficiency of oil and petroleum products was their ultimate goal, together with energy security in the event of war. The consumption-area refinery model and the requirement of oil storage were instruments for achieving this goal. However, without having sales of oil by foreign MNEs, in other words being dependent on them, these goals were unachievable. For example, Rising Sun and Stanvac were important suppliers of heavy oil to the Japanese Navy. In 1933, for instance, Rising Sun's share of heavy oil sales on the Japanese market was 31 percent, and Stanvac's share of heavy oil sales was 12 percent. On the other hand, for foreign MNEs, both compliance with the storage requirement regulation and the additional investment for the refining plan were difficult choices to make. Especially under the high-level of uncertainty in the future political situation, the choice of a low-risk and low-return strategy seemed reasonable to them to remain in the Japanese market, even if it was accompanied with a gradually decreasing market share. This, one may suppose, was another reason for the quickly abandoning the plan to undertake a joint venture for a refinery plant with Mitui.

The impact of world politics is also evident. After withdrawal of Japan from the League of Nations and the revocation of the Washington and London treaties, apprehension over the instability of foreign relations ('the Crisis of 1935–6') had spread widely at the time within the Japanese government. As noted above, the negotiation between the Japanese government and foreign MNEs ended up with a very ambiguous compromise. This was intentional and means that the Japanese government did not want to destabilise the existing balance, in which Japan could continue with oil imports and build up their oil storage and refining capacity, even if the pace was slow, especially because of the growing tension in international politics. From November 1936 to the US oil embargo in the summer of 1941, notwithstanding the escalating diplomatic tension between Japan and Allies, the Mining Bureau and Fuel Bureau (from 1937 onward) of the Ministry of Industry and Commerce did not intervene in the business of foreign MNEs, despite their non-compliance with PIL regulations.[25]

Secondly, the emergence of the ambiguous compromise was a result of rivalry among foreign oil companies. Rising Sun and Stanvac supported in some cases the crude oil embargo against Japan while also trying to protect their vested interests in importing petroleum product into Japan. On the other hand, Californian oil companies, such as Socal (Standard Oil Company of California), Associated Oil Company, Union Oil sought to continue to expand oil exports to Japan up until the very end. For example, when Stanvac, Asiatic Petroleum (the parent company of Rising Sun) and Texaco tried to boycott crude oil bids for the Manchurian Petroleum Company in 1934, and thus tried to put pressure on the Manchurian government to make regulations more favourable for them, the boycott soon lost its effectiveness as Socal and Union began supplying crude oil to Manchurian Petroleum in place of Stanvac.

This rivalry among private companies also had some effect on the possibility of an official oil embargo by their home-country governments. From August to December 1934, the parent companies of Stanvac and Rising Sun opposed the application of the PIL in Japan and urged the American and British governments to impose a crude oil embargo against Japan. However, this request was rejected by a reluctant American government, giving consideration to the interests of the Californian oil companies.

3. *The Post-War Era: Re-Entry of MNEs and Tie-Ups With Japanese Firms*

With the outbreak of the Pacific War in 1941, Rising Sun and Stanvac were forced to abandon the Japanese Market entirely. After Japan's defeat in 1945, Japan was placed under occupation by GHQ/SCAP (General Headquarters/Supreme Commander for the Allied Powers, hereafter GHQ). Rising Sun Petroleum and Standard Vacuum Oil returned to Japan as members of the Petroleum Advisory Group (hereafter, PAG) established by Staff Group 4 at GHQ (hereafter G-4). In October 1948, Rising Sun Petroleum changed its name to Shell Sekiyu (hereafter, Shell).

It is noteworthy that PAG's membership consisted of representative from foreign oil companies, including Caltex, Stanvac, Shell, Tidewater and Union. Caltex was founded in 1936 as a fifty-fifty joint venture by California Standard and Texaco. These foreign oil companies played a central role in constructing a post-war structural framework for the Japanese oil industry, characterised by foreign capital participation and use of the consumption-area refinery model.

In light of this, the question is what kind of changes occurred in the political risks that caused these companies to abandon the market completely and reject the requests by the government of the country where they had made inroads (the Japanese government), to fortify the system for greater self-sufficiency in oil? What kind of effects did these changes have on the organisational form (mergers or tie-ups) when foreign capital once more made inroads?

In the early day of the occupation, 'the harshest among the occupation's measures were directed at the Japanese oil industry',[26] This was clearly manifest in an order issued by GHQ on 21st January 1946, banning crude oil importation (SCAPIN640)[27] and another issued later that year on 27 September, banning the operation of refineries along the Pacific Coast (SCAPIN1236).[28] In examining GHQ's oil policies, the most important point here is to elucidate when and how these 'harsh policies' were transformed. Without having this transformation, the oil business by foreign multinationals in Japan would have been in a totally different form of market entry and organisational structure.

Among various policy papers on the occupation, the final Pauley Report (by Edwin W. Pauley, an oil financier from California) on the issue of war reparations, written in April 1946 and released the following November, has the greatest importance, because it embodies the turning point in the draconian occupation policy. It designated the refinery facilities with a crude oil, processing capacity in excess of 40,000 barrels a day, and storage facilities with a capacity of more than 10 million barrels, as assets that could be used in reparations.[29] The final Pauley Report differed from previous reports, including Pauley's interim report (released in December 1945) and the Far Eastern Commission's interim plan for reparations (adopted in September 1946), that did not mention removal of refineries for reparations. In being the first to recommend this, the Pauley Report sent shock waves through the Japanese oil industry. A more important point, though, is that the final Pauley report indicated criteria for allowing facilities to remain, recognising the import of crude oil on a substantially large scale and the operation of refineries on the Pacific coast.

GHQ's approval, in December 1946, of letting Pacific coast refinery facilities stay, is significant as the beginning of a transformation in the severe oil policies imposed by GHQ that aimed to remove Japan's Pacific coast refineries. Furthermore, GHQ's stance of allowing, as a general rule, crude oil imports and operations at refineries to start up again never changed after that.

If the beginning of the transformation of GHQ's oil policies is postulated as December 1946, one problem immediately arises. That is the question of why the second Strike Report, published in March 1948, set out to have all of Japan's oil refineries shut down.

Following Pauley's committee, the 'reparations mission' led by Clifford S. Strike, who had come to Japan at the request of the US Department of the Army, published two reports, the first in February 1947 and the second in March 1948. These reports determined that, overall, both the refining and storage capacities in Japan came up short of the limits set by standards in Pauley's final report for facilities to be spared, and exempted the refineries from removal for reparations. From that time on, never again were Japanese refineries listed as targets for reparations.

There were more aspects to the Strike Report, however, that caused the Japanese oil refining industry to lose hope than there were aspects that gave them hope. The reason is that the second Strike Report stressed the outdatedness and inefficiency of Japan's refineries and recommended that the refinery facilities be scrapped entirely, with the country switching over solely to importation of refined oil products, regardless of the question of reparations.[30]

However, this proposal to scrap all refinery facilities did not mean a second turn of the oil-related occupation policy, and the basic stance of the final Pauley Report, especially the clause which allowed the operation of refineries in Japan, was maintained throughout this period. In so far as one looks at the GHQ/SCAP documents, it would never appear that the Strike Mission was acting in concert with GHQ or affiliates of the oil majors regarding Japanese oil policies. Data contained in GHQ/SCAP documents show that on 26 March 1948, just after the second Strike Report was released, there was no retreat from their previously established principle of letting Japan's refineries stay.[31] Furthermore, on 6 June that year, GHQ fielded queries from the US Department of the Army as to whether (1) they would agree to the second Strike Report's recommendation to scrap the refineries, (2) they would propose adding the refinery facilities to the reparations list, and (3) they thought it would be advantageous, from the viewpoint of conserving foreign currency, to have oil products refined in Japan during the occupation. In response, GHQ said 'no' to the first two questions, but 'yes' to the third.[32] After that, GHQ's posture of ignoring the second Strike Report's recommendation to close the refineries never changed.[33]

As is clear from these developments, the Strike Mission called for the scrapping of all of Japan's refineries, not on the basis of views of sections within GHQ connected with oil policies (G-4 and ESS), but rather as an outsider, so to speak. The real reason why the Strike Reports were published after GHQ's oil policies began changing might be found by considering organisational deficiencies within the US government and its agencies.

If we posit that GHQ's oil policies started to shift in favour of allowing crude oil importation and the operation of Pacific coast refineries in December 1946, one problem still remains. That is the question of what the significance was of the Noel Report, written in March 1949. This report asserted the necessity of crude oil imports and the operation of Pacific coast refineries.

To answer that question, we must first turn our attention to the conditions within GHQ, where G-4 and ESS had differences of opinion regarding specific developments in oil policies. GHQ organised a 'Petroleum Study Committee' in September 1948, and set to work determining the capacities of the facilities were being allowed to remain in Japan.[34] This committee comprised five representatives from ESS, four from G-4 (including two from the Petroleum Advisory Group), one from the Natural Resources Section and one from the Reparations Section;[35] but the actual goal of organising the committee was to reconcile the differing opinions of ESS and G-4.

After intensive coordination, ESS and G-4 reached an agreement on 7 October on points such as (1) allowing a storage capacity equivalent to one-third of annual domestic demand to remain in Japan, (2) not adopting a policy of removing or scrapping Japanese refiners' equipment for military-related reasons, (3) enabling crude oil imports to resume and the operations of Pacific coast refineries to start up again, rescinding the former orders banning crude oil importation (SCAPIN640).[36]

Differences of opinion still remained, however, between ESS and G-4 as to whether there should be limits on the level of operations to be allowed at Pacific coast refineries. To resolve the differences in ESS's and G-4's views, Henry M. Noel, an oil refining technician at Standard Oil of New Jersey, was brought to Japan.[37] From December 1948 to March 1949, Noel undertook a vigorous survey of refineries throughout Japan.[38] He wrote up the 'Noel Report', as it was called, in March 1949. The report completely refuted the SCAPIN640 order banning crude oil importation and the recommendations of the second Strike Report to scrap the refineries.[39] Meanwhile, ESS at GHQ wrote a draft memorandum to the Japanese government giving approval for the resumption of crude oil imports and operation of Pacific coast refineries.[40] This draft memorandum set no upper limit on Japan's refining capacity. It amounted to the realisation of ESS's principles.[41] In January 1949, ESS handed the draft memorandum to G-4, and G-4 approved it.[42]

When restarting operations at the Pacific coast refineries, GHQ chose which refineries would get the nod for restoration. Exerting an important influence in this was Noel, who had returned to Japan in June 1949. For example, on 22 August that year, Nakahara, who served as the president of Toa Nenryo Kogyo (one of the predecessors of the currently existing JXTG Holdings) from January 1944 to February 1962, wrote in his diary, 'As Mr. Noel will return to America after a week, and as the refineries are to be determined by then, it seems all of the companies are campaigning intensely'. In his final report, written in October 1949, Noel spelled out his criteria for selecting Pacific coast refineries to be approved for the resumption of operations.[43]

The foreign oil company members of PAG, which was established in GHQ's G-4 division, had originally appraised the Japanese oil market at the beginning of the occupation as suitable for receiving refined products rather than crude oil, based on the production-area refinery model that had been adhered to since before the war. That was indicated distinctly by the unanimous support expressed by the PAG-member representatives of four companies, Caltex, Stanvac, Shell and Tidewater, for GHQ's ban on crude oil imports in January 1946 (SCAPIN640).[44]

However, the position taken by foreign oil companies, including the major ones, with regard to the Japanese market changed swiftly as Middle Eastern crude oil production burgeoned and the consumption-area refinery model spread increasingly throughout Western Europe. The diary of Nobuhei Nakahara, is extremely useful in understanding the timing of such change: November 1946 or earlier was proposed, approximately the same period when the change in GHQ's oil policies began to occur (December 1946). Further, in April 1947, British Embassy staff in America reported to the British government that foreign oil companies appeared prepared for an advance into the Japanese refining business.[45]

The change in the Oil Majors' strategy for Japan took the specific form of partnerships with Japanese refiners, based on adoption of the consumption-area refinery model. Table 4.1 lists the series of foreign capital partnerships promoted by Japanese refineries from 1949 to 1952.

Partnerships between the oil majors and Japanese refiners had advantages for both sides. For example, in Japan, the tie-up between Toa Nenryo Kogyo, which had refineries but lacked the ability to supply crude oil and had no sales network for its products, and Stanvac, which had the ability to supply crude oil and had a sales network for products but lacked refinery facilities, was natural because it was reciprocal. Likewise, the principle of reciprocity functioned in the partnership between Nippon Oil Corporation, which had plenty of strength in refining and product sales but deficiency in crude oil provision, and Caltex, which had plenty of strength in crude oil provision but lacked refinery facilities and a product sales network.

Focussing on the tie-up between Stanvac and Toa Nenryo Kogyo, it was highly significant to Stanvac for expanding its crude oil sales. Stanvac's in-house journal can be found at the US Library of Congress in Washington D.C.; the lead article on the first page of the journal in 1949, when the establishment of the tie-up with Toa Nenryo Kogyo was being proclaimed boldly, emphasised the 15 percent increase in Stanvac's crude oil throughput resulting from the operation of Toa Nenryo Kogyo's refinery facilities in Shimizu and Wakayama. In fact, Stanvac's crude oil throughput was

Table 4.1 Major foreign capital tie-up contracts with Japanese refineries from end of World War II until 1952

Partner companies	*Date concluded*	*Contract details*	*Foreign capital contractor*
Toa Nenryo Kogyo Stanvac	1949. Feb. 11 1951. Jul. 1	Capital tie-up contract [51%] Technical tie-up contract	Stanvac Stanvac
Nippon Oil Corp. Caltex	Mar. 25 Apr. 21 May 16	Oil product consignment sales contract Crude oil consignment refining contract Contract to found jointly funded [50%] subsidiary (Nippon Petroleum Refining Co.)	Caltex Japan Caltex Japan Caltex Products
Mitsubishi Oil Tidewater	1949. Mar. 31	Capital tie-up contract [50%]	Tidewater
Showa Oil Shell	Jun. 20 1951. Jun. 28 1952. Dec. 3	Crude oil consignment refining contract Capital tie-up contract [26%] Capital tie-up contract [50%]	Shell Japan Shell Japan Shell Japan
Koa Oil Caltex	Jul. 13 1950. Jul. 20	Crude oil consignment refining contract Capital tie-up contract [50%]	Caltex Japan Caltex Japan
Maruzen Petroleum Union Oil	1949. Oct. 21	Crude oil supply and oil product consignment sales contract	Union Oil
Maruzen Petroleum Shell	1951. Jun.—	Crude oil consignment refining contract	Shell Japan

Source: prepared by author based on data from a variety of sources.

Notes:

1. [Bracketed figures] indicate foreign capital stake in capital tie-up contracts.
2. '—' indicates date unknown.
3. Only major content is included under 'Contract details'.
4. 'Caltex Japan' indicates Caltex Oil (Japan) Limited. 'Caltex Products' indicates Caltex Oil Products Company. 'Shell Japan' indicates Shell Company of Japan, Limited.

up by 11 percent year-on-year in 1950, due to the start of operations at Toa Nenryo Kogyo's two refineries, despite production slowdowns at refineries outside of Japan.

Even though Stanvac and Shell (Rising Sun Petroleum before the war) had ultimately been forced to abandon the Japanese market prior to the Pacific War, they made new inroads into the Japanese market after the war by establishing joint ventures and made sizeable investments in facilities. They had determined that, by forming joint ventures, it would be more difficult to abandon their investments than before the war, but it could be said that the changed international order after the war, and spread of the consumption-area refinery model worldwide, including Japan, brought, if anything, reduced political risks for multinational enterprises. Under the consumption-area refinery model, concluding crude oil consignment refining contracts was natural, so to speak, but this reduction in political risks was occurring in the context of further inroads by foreign oil companies, who were concluding capital tie-up contracts and sometimes even technical tie-up contracts.

Conclusion

What confronted Rising Sun Petroleum and Standard Vacuum Oil directly in the period leading up to the Second World War was the Petroleum Industry Law, enacted by the Japanese government in 1934 as a legislative means for exerting wartime control. It instituted rationing of sales and an obligation to stockpile petroleum. Both companies continued their business activities in the Japanese market while vigorously resisting the law's enforcement. With the outbreak of the Pacific War in 1941, however, both companies were forced to abandon the Japanese market for the time being. After the war ended, Rising Sun and Stanvac returned to the Japanese market as advisers to GHQ, playing a central role in the construction of a post-war system for the Japanese oil industry

Between the pre-war and post-war situations a certain kind of inevitable connection exists. The tenacious measures to deal with risks by Rising Sun Petroleum Company and Standard Vacuum Oil Company in the pre-war period showed a deeper understanding of the Japanese oil market by both of these companies. The knowledge they had accumulated became one factor that enabled foreign oil companies, including these two, to change their strategy promptly in the post-war Japanese market. Affected by the changes in the situation before and after the Second World War, in the form of more vigorous application of the consumption-area refinery model in Western Europe and large oil field discoveries in the Middle East, the foreign oil companies were able to construct in an extremely short time a post-war system for the Japanese oil industry represented by foreign capital participation and application of the consumption-area refinery model.

When observing the relationship between multinational enterprises and political risks, there are two possible approaches: one from the point of view of the enterprise and one from the point of view of the risks. In the course of research to date, the approach from the point of view of the enterprise has produced a great deal of knowledge. In contrast, this chapter has tried an approach from the point of view of the risks, namely the perception and action of the host country, and tried to elucidate the mutual interaction among multiple political and economic entities. It will be up to the reader to decide whether or not this new approach has been effective.

Notes

1 See, for example, Marcelo Bucheli, 'Multinational Corporations, Business Groups, and Economic Nationalism: Standard Oil (New Jersey), Royal Dutch Shell, and Energy Politics in Chile 1913–2005', *Enterprise & Society*, 11, no. 2 (2010): 350–399; Regina Lee Blaszczyk, 'Synthetics for the Shah: DuPont and the Challenges to Multinationals in 1970s Iran', *Enterprise & Society*, 9, no. 4 (2008): 670–723.

2 Takeshi Yuzawa and Masaru Udagawa, *Foreign Business in Japan Before World War II: Proceedings of the Fuji Conference* (Tokyo: University of Tokyo Press, 1990).

3 See, for example, Pierre-Yves Donzé and Takafumi Kurosawa, 'Nestlé Coping With Japanese Nationalism: Political Risk and the Strategy of a Foreign Multinational Enterprise in Japan, 1913–45', *Business History*, 55, no. 8 (2013): 1318–1338.

4 'The Fuel Bureau's Survey on production amount of oil products in the main islands of Japan by type of source oil produced in Japan and overseas' included in the 'Petroleum Industry Law Related Documents' (1937).

5 The Records of the Bureau of Far Eastern Affairs, State Department dated August 3, 1934 (Records of the US Department of State, file number 894.6363/88, abbreviated below as 894.6363/88).

6 Masaru Udagawa, 'Senzen Nihon no Kigyo Keiei to Gaishikei Kigyo (Corporate Management and Foreign-backed Corporations in Pre-war Japan), Parts 1 and 2', *KEIZAI SHIRIN: The Hosei University Economic Review*, 24, no. 1 and 2, Hosei University, 1987.

7 The descriptions in the following section are a summary of Kikkawa Takeo, *Nihon Sekiyu Sangyo No Kyosoryoku Kouchiku* (Nagoya: Nagoya University Press, 2012).

8 TFR-500 Original Reports, Series A II, Folder: Standard Vacuum Oil Co. (RG265, B556). Washington National Records Center.

9 Irvine H. Anderson, Jr., *The Standard-Vacuum Oil Company and United States East Asian Policy, 1933–1941* (Princeton: Princeton University Press, 1975), 220, Table B-1.

10 Memorandum, S. P. Coleman to E. J. Sadler, August 6, 1940 (Henry J. Morgenthau, Jr.'s Diary, Volume 292, pp. 268–270, owned by the Franklin D. Roosevelt Library, Hyde Park, New York, USA).

11 As material, this section relies mostly on the General Records of the Department of State, Record Group Number 59 of the National Archives in Washington, DC. For annotating US State Department documents in this section, the record group number (59) has been abbreviated to the file number only.

12 Letter by Tsuneo Fukuda, Chief of the Mining Bureau, Ministry of Commerce and Industry, to J.C. Gould (General Manager of Stanvac's Japanese branch), dated October 13, 1934 (894.6363/107); letter dated November 5, 1934, from the Mining Bureau to Stanvac (894.6363/141); memorandum written by Stanvac's Japanese branch dated November 21, 1934, on talks the previous day with the Mining Bureau (894.6363/152); letter by Joseph C. Grew, American Ambassador to Japan, to the US Secretary of State, dated November 30, 1934 (894.6363/153).

13 Memorandum written by Stanvac's Japanese branch dated November 21, 1934, on talks the previous day with the Mining Bureau (cited above); letter by Grew to the US Secretary of State, dated November 30, 1934 (also cited above).

14 Memorandum written by Ely on November 21, 1934, regarding the four-party talks the previous day (894.6363/153).

15 Held in Britain's National Archives, class F.O 262; British Embassy/Consulate document, file number 269, dated 1935; *Oil Japan*, Part 4, *Minutes of Meetings between Companies and Officials.*
16 *Oil Japan,* Part 4, *Minutes of Meetings between Companies and Officials*; letter by Grew dated April 19, 1935, to the US Secretary of State (894.6363/199).
17 Letter dated October 4, 1935, from Edwin L. Neville (US Charge d'affaires ad interim in Japan) to the US Secretary of State (894.6363/213); memorandum on the talks of November 6, 1935 (894.6363/226).
18 Neville's letter to the US Secretary of State, dated October 4, 1935 (cited above), and memorandum on the talks of November 6, 1935 (also cited above).
19 Memorandum on Kojima's reply on December 23, 1935 (894.6363/242).
20 Mitsubishi Oil, which was established as a fifty-fifty joint venture by Mitsubishi and America's Associated Oil Company, was treated within Japan at the time as a domestic oil company. Therefore, this paper considers Mitsubishi Oil to be a domestic oil company.
21 Letter by E. R. Dickover (US Charge d'affairs in Japan) to the US Secretary of State, dated October 14, 1936 (894.6363/294).
22 Memorandum on talks with Kurusu on 27 December, 1935 (894.6363/245).
23 This reduction in assigned amounts was due to predictions of an increase in petroleum production in Korea and the beginning of the manufacturing of synthetic oil. Therefore, it was not just RS and SV, but domestic producers who also saw a decrease in their allotments.
24 Both Mira Wilkins and Irvine H. Anderson, Jr. emphasise that the two foreign oil companies were able to continue their operations within Japan up until the outbreak of the Pacific War, despite not having met the petroleum storage requirements of PIL. Mira Wilkins, 'The Role of U.S. Business', in *Pearl Harbor as History: Japanese-American Relations, 1931–1941*, eds. Dorothy Borg and Shumpei Okamoto (New York: Columbia University Press, 1973), 352–375; Anderson, *The Standard-Vacuum Oil Company.* Although such a view holds true, this chapter equally stress that Japanese government achieved at least partially their policy goal, and the share of foreign MNEs had to be gradually declined.
25 For instance, the temporary American charge d'affaires, Edwin L. Neville, made a prediction in September 1935 that if the Japanese government recognised that 'the Crisis of 1935–6' was not going to be realised, it most likely would have softened its stance towards foreign oil companies in relation to the application of the PIL. On this point, see Neville's letter to the Secretary of State, dated 20 September 1935 (894.6363/211).
26 Ministry of International Trade and Industry, ed., *Shoko Seisakushi, Vol. 23, Kogyo (Part II)* (Tokyo: Syoko Seisakushi Kanko Kai, 1980), 242.
27 In its analysis, this section uses resources such as GHQ/SCAP documents stored at the US National Archives, especially Record group number (abbreviated as RG below) 331 among GHQ/SCAP records. To facilitate resource searches, the box number and folder number (below abbreviated as B and F) are included with each reference. Memorandum, Allen to Imperial Japanese Government, January 21, 1946, RG331, B7310, F12.,
28 Memorandum, John B. Cooley to Imperial Japanese Government, September 27, 1946, RG331, B7310, F12.
29 Notes re: Pauley Report, undated, RG331, B7310, F15.
30 Toa Nenryo Kogyo KK, ed., *Tonen Jugonenshi* (Tokyo: Toa Nenryo Kogyo KK, 1956), 640–641.
31 Memorandum, H. M. Fish to Cruse, March 26, 1948, RG331, B7310, F15.
32 W. A. Thurman, Teleconference between FEC and DA, June 2, 1948, RG331, B7310, F15.

33 R. C. Ludlum, 'Some Considerations Affecting the Proposed Rebirth of Japan's Petroleum Refining Industry', August 2, 1948, RG331, B7310, F15.
34 H. B. Overton, Conference Report, September 4, 1948, RG331, B7310, F12.
35 Overton, Memorandum, undated, RG331, B7339, F18.
36 Overton, Minutes of Petroleum Study Committee Meeting, October 7, 1948, RG331, B7339, F18.
37 Overton, Memo for Record, December16, 1948, RG331, B7254, F10.
38 Noel, Memo for Record, January 3, 1949, RG331, B7254, F10, Letter, Noel to Roy R. May, February 10, 1949, RG331, B7254, F10, Noel, Memorandum for File, February23, 1949, RG331, B7254, F10, and Noe1, *Survey of Petroleum Refineries of Japan*, RG331, B7254, F10.
39 ESS, GHQ, SCAP, *The Petroleum Refineries of Japan*, March 25, 1949, RG331, B7203, F6.
40 Draft of Memorandum for Japanese Government, undated, RG331, B7309, F18.
41 W. F. Marquat, Memorandum for Chief of Staff, January 11, 1949, RG331, B7339, F18.
42 Checknote No.7, G-4 to ESS, June 3, 1949, RG331, B7339, F18.
43 Noel, *Final Report, Petroleum Refinery Operations*, October 24, 1949, RG331, B6339, F3.
44 Webster Anderson, Memorandum, May 25, 1946, RG331, B7310, F15.
45 Letter, C. E. H. Druitt to C. Elias, April 21, 1947, held by the British National Archives POWE33, Petroleum: Correspondence and Papers, Ref. No. 1414.

Bibliography

Anderson, Irvine H. Jr., *The Standard-Vacuum Oil Company and United States East Asian Policy, 1933–1941*. Princeton: Princeton University Press, 1975.

Blaszczyk, Renina Lee, 'Synthetics for the Shah: DuPont and the Challenges to Multinationals in 1970s Iran', *Enterprise & Society*, 9, no. 4 (2008): 670–723.

Bucheli, Marcelo, 'Multinational Corporations, Business Groups, and Economic Nationalism: Standard Oil (New Jersey), Royal Dutch-Shell, and Energy Politics in Chile 1913–2005', *Enterprise & Society*, 11, no. 2 (2010): 350–399.

Donzé, Pierre-Yves and Takafumi Kurosawa, 'Nestlé Coping With Japanese Nationalism: Political Risk and the Strategy of a Foreign Multinational Enterprise in Japan, 1913–45', *Business History*, 55, no. 8 (2013): 1318–1338.

Kikkawa, Takeo, *Nihon Sekiyu Sangyo no Kyosoryoku Kouchiku*. Nagoya: Nagoya University Press, 2012.

Ministry of International Trade and Industry, ed., *Shoko Seisakushi, Vol. 23, Kogyo Part II*. Tokyo: Syoko Seisakushi Kanko Kai, 1980.

Toa Nenryo Kogyo KK, ed., *Tonen Jugonenshi*. Tokyo: Toa Nenryo Kogyo KK, 1956.

Udagawa, Masaru, 'Senzen Nihon no Kigyo Keiei to Gaishikei Kigyo, Part 1(Corporate Management and Foreign-backed Corporations in Pre-war Japan, Part 1)', *The Hosei Journal of Business*, 24, no. 1 (1987): 15–31.

Udagawa, Masaru, 'Senzen Nihon no Kigyo Keiei to Gaishikei Kigyo, Part 2 (Corporate Management and Foreign-backed Corporations in Pre-war Japan, Part 2)', *The Hosei Journal of Business*, 24, no. 2 (1987): 29–40.

Wilkins, Mira, 'The Role of U.S. Business', in *Pearl Harbor as History: Japanese-American Relations, 1931–1941*, edited by Dorothy Borg and Shumpei Okamoto. New York: Columbia University Press, 1973, 352–375.

Yuzawa, Takeshi and Masaru Udagawa, *Foreign Business in Japan Before World War II: Proceedings of the Fuji Conference*. Tokyo: University of Tokyo Press, 1990.

Part II

Total War and Long-Lasting Impact

5 Mutual Attraction

Siemens Activities in Italy 1855–1968

Luciano Segreto

Introduction

'It is better to be enemies than allies'. This could be the paradoxical slogan for Siemens investments in Italy and particularly the impact on them of the First and the Second World War. This chapter will outline the evolution of the strategies of the German electromechanical firm between the end of the 19th century and the early 1960s, when the consequences of the new strategies established as the result of the Second World War became evident. It will consider how the company reacted to political risk, and especially the extreme political risk presented by war.[1] However, in the case of the post-war period, the chapter will show that some of the decisions taken by the firm were the direct result of the attitude of the host country—Italy—which tried to use the dramatic consequences of the war to redefine the national interests in some of the sectors where Siemens was involved. From this point of view, the highest political risk did not strictly correspond to the years 1939–1945. It rather reached its peak in the immediately following years, when Siemens suffered the most dramatic attempts to reduce its influence and its role in the Italian market.

We will subdivide the period of about half a century of Siemens initiatives in Italy into the following four sub-periods. Each of them corresponds to a different strategy and structure of the firm both in Germany and in Italy—one of the countries where the company made its most significant foreign direct investments until 1945:

1) 1853–1918: commercial penetration into the Italian electromechanical sector and indirect investments into the electrical sector; the weak consequences of the Great War for Siemens' direct investments and the loss of all financial investments;
2) 1920s–1943: reinforcement and diversification of the direct investment into the telecommunication sector; the opening of industrial factories and the acquisition of small and medium-sized Italian advanced technology companies;

3) 1943–1959: confiscation and 'nationalisation' of Siemens investments in Italy without losing contact with the headquarters in Germany;
4) 1960–: re-establishment of German direct control over the Italian company.

The chapter will follow these segments representing the different moments of a long-term strategy that had to be modified in connection with the outcome of two world wars and their short- and long-term consequences. Finally, we will be also providing some conclusions that should permit comparisons with others included in this volume.

Investing in a Developing Country (1853–1914)

The Italian electrification process took place between the 1890s and the years before the First World War. In those years, the electrical sector showed a very high dynamism due to a series of factors. The acceleration of Italian industrialisation from the mid-1890s, after a false start in the early 1870s, offered many opportunities for social and economic development that included all the sectors of the Second Industrial Revolution.[2] The need for new forms of power for a country practically without coal (almost more than 90 percent was imported from Great Britain) was a more specific incentive for the important effort made to electrify manufacturing production. The strong tradition of an electrotechnical engineering culture in both the Polytechnics of Milan and Turin offered the opportunity to prepare highly qualified human capital for the different branches of the production and distribution of electricity.[3] Finally a sort of symbolic struggle among small and big towns to have electric light in the public areas helped to create the pre-conditions for a strong demand for energy.[4]

In this framework, a very weak point of the country was the electromechanical production: generators, turbines, alternators and most of the small parts of big electric machines were largely imported from Germany, Switzerland, France, the United States and Great Britain.[5] This situation is readily explained by the technological superiority of all these countries compared with the general economic backwardness of Italy, which was still part of the developing periphery of Europe. Nevertheless, there were also some more precise reasons—mainly the strong control over the most important patents and a sort of cartel among the world giants of this sector (General Electric, Westinghouse, AEG, Siemens, Brown Boveri)—that contributed to explaining the difficulties in setting up a national industry. The situation in the electromechanical sector was just more evident than in others because of the strategic importance of the energy sector.[6]

The strong political and diplomatic relations existing between Germany and Italy from the early 1880s, and the positive perspectives that Italy offered in the early 1890s, pushed all the Reich's economic and financial establishment to consider this country as a privileged (and to some extent captive) market for many German industrial and manufactured goods. In fact, Germany slowly became Italy's most important commercial partner between the 1880s and the 1890s, a position that has actually never changed, with the exception of a very short period after the Second World War. In the early 1890s, the German share of total Italian imports was already higher than 10 percent, but ten years later it reached more than 16 percent.[7] In the electromechanical sector, Italian dependence on Germany was even more impressive, so that after the first export of machines for the first Italian electrical firms in the early 1880s, this sector was largely controlled by that country: in 1913, almost 60 percent of Italian imports came from Germany.[8]

The Siemens Company was established in Berlin in 1847 by a former Prussian officer, Werner Siemens, and a mechanical engineer, Johan Georg Halske, under the official name of Siemens & Halske. Its first activity was participation in the telegraph business. Werner Siemens patented a new system, called 'Siemens rapid'. The model invented by Siemens was a telegraph using a needle to point to the right letter, instead of the Morse code. It was based on synchronism with automatic transmission and a five-unit code. The company developed an international strategy strictly connected with the sector in which it was involved. The first important contract concerned the construction of the telegraphic line between Paris and Brussels. The first country where the company directed its initiative was Russia. Czar Nicolas I asked the company to instal the telegraph network in the whole country (the length of the lines was 5,000 km). This explains why, in 1853, the firm opened an administrative branch in St Petersburg, under the supervision of Carl Siemens, the brother of the company's founder. At the beginning, the Russian branch just assembled the different individual pieces produced in Berlin. In the following years, other important achievements confirmed the success of Siemens & Halske products: in 1858, Werner Siemens supervised the layout of the submarine cable between India and the Gulf of Aden; in 1867, the company built the line between Berlin and Tehran and one year later started the works to build a 10,000-km network between London and Calcutta. It is quite self-evident that Great Britain became in that period one of the most important markets for the firm. From 1853, a British branch of the company started its activities under the same business model adopted in Russia: Carl Wilhelm Siemens, another one of Werner Siemens' brothers, worked in England as the commercial representative of the firm. Products were manufactured in Germany and sent to Great Britain. It was not until 1863 that Siemens & Halske established a first factory in Woolwich, near London, for the production of telegraph cables to link the United Kingdom with North America. This strategy was later followed in Russia, where the company moved to industrial activities between 1880 and 1882.[9]

In Italy, the first telegraphic network was established in 1847 by the government of the Grand Duque of Tuscany. The telegraph system developed quite quickly in the following years, covering different parts of the peninsula, not yet politically unified, however. It is in this framework that Siemens & Halske established in 1855 the first links with Italy, actually even before the national unification process of 1861. The contacts—to establish a telegraphic line between Sardinia and Algeria—were with the Kingdom of Sardinia, the political entity that started the unification process under the lead of Prime Minister Cavour.[10]

The boom of modern infrastructure (railways and telegraph) after the unification process brought about new opportunities for increasing commercial relations with Italy. There were reasons to establish a representative office of the company in Italy too. Since the most relevant contracts were with the public administration (the ministry of Post and Communications, the ministry of War and the Navy), the logical choice was to establish an office in Rome, in 1878. In that same year, the Italian army passed an order to Siemens for telegraphic materials. Two years later, in 1880, Siemens & Halske signed a contract for the general representative of all their products with the company G. Taddei from Turin.[11] However, only one year later Taddei renounced this charge. The service was taken over by a manager with experience in the metal industry, Luigi Langer, and a Dutch engineer, Carlo Maleschott, who was for some years the general consul of his country in Rome. As Langer later resigned, Maleschott remained the only representative agent of Siemens between 1883 and 1891, but he continued to work for the German firm until 1897.[12]

However, this structure did not permit Italy to have an important role until the end of the century. There are many reasons for this situation, mainly associated with the generally quite conservative strategy of the company envisaged by the founder. Siemens remained for many years strictly linked with the first low-voltage products, being quite sceptical about the potential of the other segment of the electrical market. This also explains why AEG was able to take over quite rapidly a large part of the high-voltage market.

There were also some more specific reasons why the Italian market was of less importance in those years. According to Peter Hertner, the first historian to study Siemens activities in late 19th-century Italy, the death in 1880 of Robert Wedekind, a Roman private banker, who was a relative of Werner Siemens and informally supervised the company's business in Italy, reduced the importance of the links with Italy. It is possible that some important networks he had been able to establish no longer functioned without him.[13]

Italian economic development accelerated in the 1880s with the introduction of protectionist tariffs, as in many other European countries. However, new industrial sectors like the electrical one became protagonists for this new phase of economic growth, not just those sectors directly interested in the restrictive trade policy. From the early 1880s, many local electrical companies became active. The most important one was Edison

General Electric Company, established in Milan in 1883 by the European branch of the American Edison company. Soon many other towns, big and small, imitated Milan: electricity and lighting of city centres were the new frontiers of the modernisation process. Electrification of public transportation and of many manufacturers was the next step. The 1891 successful experiment in Laufen (Germany) of long-distance electricity transportation enlarged the market in many European countries, including Italy, where the orography was largely based on rivers running from the Alps and the Apennines toward the sea.[14]

Investments in the electrical industry needed many investors and intermediates. From the very beginning, they had an international character: international companies, banks and other financial intermediates were among the first actors in this process. They were particularly active in the 1880s. In the following decade, new kinds of investors started to play a decisive role in the development of the electrical industry at the global level. Manufacturers started to intervene directly in the sector, in a sense creating their own market. Initially, this strategy was limited to the national level. From the mid-1890s, almost all the biggest electromechanical producers (General Electric, Westinghouse, Allgemeine Elektricitäts-Gesellschaft, Siemens & Halske, Brown Boveri) founded financial companies to make fund-raising easier in different countries, where they wanted to extend their initiatives with the creation of an electric company. In the case of the German and the Swiss manufacturing companies, the new financial holding companies were usually organised in Switzerland, and sometimes in Belgium, that is, in neutral countries with many financial and fiscal advantages, and very solid professional traditions in the banking sector.[15]

Thus, AEG founded, in 1895 in Zurich, the Bank für Elektrische Unternehmungen, simply known as Elektrobank, with the financial support of a consortium of German banks, the Credit Suisse, and the Geneva branch of the Banque de Paris et des Pays Bas. The Swiss electromechanical firm Brown Boveri reached, in the same year, an agreement with some German and Swiss banks and the biggest German metal trader to set up a holding company called Motor. In 1896, Siemens set up a holding company in Basel called Schweizerische Gesellschaft für elektrische Industrie (Swiss company for electrical industry), later simply known as Indelec, with the intervention of a group of German and Swiss banks headed by Basler Handeslbank and Leu & Co. of Zurich. Schuckert was the only exception. Its financial holding, Continentale Gesesllschaft fur elektrische Unternehmungen, was founded in 1895 in Nuremberg.[16]

The strategy established by the German and the Swiss manufacturers consisted of a complex financial and commercial structure, based on very strict legal constraints. The electrical firms created and financed by the holding companies bought, on an exclusive contract basis, all electrical machinery (turbines, alternators, generators, transformers) from the electromechanical producer controlling the electro-financial holding of the manufacturer company. De facto, in this way, the electromechanical companies created a sort of international captive market, granting themselves a quite regular flow of production. This system was internationally known by the German term *Unternehmensgeschäft*.[17]

In Italy, the crisis of the late 1880s to early 1890s reduced for some years the interests of foreign investors. Many sectors were damaged, including the banking sector, and wholesale reform became necessary. The Bank of Italy was established in 1893, while the Italian government requested that the German authorities prompt the German banks to intervene in Italy to reorganise the main banks, and to create a better and more efficient image of the most important financial actors, in order to attract foreign investors again.[18]

The slow beginning of a recovery in Italy, together with the decision, taken in Berlin, to reorganise the international structure of the company, pushed Siemens to reconsider how to keep the contacts with clients and even more how to win new ones. In 1890, the company set up so-called technical offices. In 1903, there were already 30; eight of them were abroad and one was in Italy. In 1898, the Italian office was transformed into a stock company called Società Italiana Siemens per Impianti Elettrici. This change gave new momentum to the Italian business. From the early 1890s onwards, the first electric tramways in Genoa and Turin were running thanks to Siemens' technology. However, the most relevant change in the interest concerning the Italian business took place from 1895 after the company secured the concession for a hydroelectric plant near Ivrea (less than 60 km north of Turin). The objective was to produce electricity for the industrial town of Biella, one of the most important centres of the Italian wool industry. To run this business, Siemens set up, in early 1896, S.A. Alta Italia. The German company established, in Turin, Società Elettrica Alta Italia, subscribing 100 percent of its nominal capital of 1.9 million lira. In 1897, Siemens won another important contract for the electricity service in the town of Alessandria. For that purpose, they decided to set up a specific company, S.A. Elettricità Alessandrina, which provided electricity with a thermal plant.[19]

In the following years, the Alta Italia Company increased its capital to 15 million lira (only 5 million lira completely subscribed). Siemens asked its holding company, Indelec, to participate in supporting the financial efforts required by the new investments' programme of the Italian electrical firm. Nevertheless, the relationships between the mother and holding companies were quite tempestuous. The Italian component of the firm, represented by the banker Roberto Cattaneo, chairman of the Banco Sconto e Sete (one of the oldest and most important banks in Turin), played an important role in permitting the company to develop, but this had a cost, the relative autonomy of the holding company from the mother firm. For instance, the company gave a preference to material manufactured by Siemens & Halske only if it was sold at a more convenient price. De facto, the *Unternehmensgeschäft* was thus broken. Moreover, different evaluations on the effectiveness of some very expensive and risky investments made by Alta Italia Company produced some friction that finally calmed down only in 1901, when Siemens agreed to pass all its shares in that electrical company to Indelec. The most critical aspect was Siemens financial difficulties in the early 1900s, which pushed the German company to ask for the intervention of the second Italian bank, Credito Italiano, and of one of the biggest Swiss banks, Basler Handelsbank, to subscribe to the bonds issued by Alta Italia.[20]

The development of the Italian business implied that the Italian technical office should be transformed into a more formalised structure. Thus, in 1899, Siemens set up in Milan a company called Società Siemens per Impianti Elettrici (Siemens Company for electric plants). Its role was a commercial one, channelling all the orders to the mother company in Germany and offering a sort of pioneering after-sale service. In the same year, Siemens moved to another region for a new investment in the Italian electrical industry. The new company was the S.A. Elettrica Umbra (capital 1.2 million lira) for the production and distribution of electricity in Perugia, and the surrounding area. A few months later, but already in 1900, a new investment was made at a local level. The S.A. Elettricità Toscana was established in Pisa (capital 800 thousand lira). A little later, the three companies of Alessandria, Perugia and Pisa were sold by Siemens to Siemens Elektrische Betriebe, a holding company set up by Siemens & Halske and Indelec in Germany to reduce the risks of long-term investments.[21]

In general, Siemens economic and financial profile was reinforced in the coming years thanks to a new, very important financial partner, Deutsche Bank, but even more thanks to two mergers. The first one, in 1897, with Halske, was because of the transformation in a stock company—Telegraphen-Bauanstalt Siemens & Halske—which specialised in the telegraph industry. Even more important was the second merger that took place in 1903 with Schuckert, the third German competitor by size in the electromechanical sector. The very deep crisis of 1901–1902 in Germany, as well as in the US, provoked a strong wave of mergers and acquisitions, which involved the entire electromechanical sector. It produced also important consequences in Italy, and particularly in the northwestern part of the country, where Schuckert, with much bigger investments, had until then been a very dangerous competitor for Siemens. Many of Schuckert's direct investments, as well as those undertaken through Continentale Gesellschaft and an Italian sub-holding company, Società Nazionale per Industrie e Imprese Elettriche, no longer represented a challenge, as they were all now part of the same group. The merger with Schuckert implied also the reorganisation of the Italian commercial branch. In 1903, Società Italiana di Elettricità Siemens-Schuckert (SIESS) commenced operations.[22]

In the following years, Siemens became the most important supplier for the Italian telephone industry. To some extent, the company rediscovered its origins in low-voltage products. This sector had started on a very weak basis in the 1890s, but it was significantly reorganised in 1906–1908, when the government tried to establish new rules for the sector, permitting private companies to run the business only at the town level, while keeping under state control the long-distance calls. From the 1890s, Siemens & Halske controlled the most important company, Società Telefonica Alta Italia, based in Milan, where the telephone network was much more developed. In 1903, the company installed the most modern switching device in the Milanese central exchange. However, the management of the company was always in Italian hands. In 1907, the sector was nationalised. The German firm remained one of the most important suppliers of the national network with its technology, selling telephones, central switches and junction boxes. From 1910, SIESS distributed also the products of Gesellschaft für drahtlose Telegraphie m.b.H., System Telefunken, simply known as Telefunken, a joint venture company set up in 1903 by Siemens & Halske and AEG in the very advanced (for that time) field of wireless telecommunication.[23]

The decision taken by the Italian government to push the electrification of the railways system offered another opportunity to the German multinational. This process was a part of the economic modernisation of the country during the 15–20 years before the First World War. However, as in some other high tech sectors, Italy's development was relatively behind that of West European nations. Italian State Railway (nationalisation took place in 1905) had mainly Italian steam locomotives (the largest producer was Breda company in Milan, which was very competitive and also active in some Balkan countries), whilst before 1918–1920, electric locomotives were largely imported from Germany, and particularly those produced at the Siemens Werke in Berlin.

In the years before the First World War, when Italy was experiencing its 'first economic miracle', Siemens-Schuckert had consolidated its structure both in Germany and in Italy. In the peninsula, its financial holding Indelec was increasing its activities mainly in the same geographical areas (the north and the northwest of the country), while the commercial branch SIESS, which had still a very light structure, organised all the imports of goods from the firm's factories in Germany. However, this structure could have been much stronger if the company had accepted, in 1903, the proposal by a dynamic but not very big Italian electromechanical firm from Milan, Gadda & Co, to merge. This would have given Siemens a more solid presence, particularly in the manufacturing sector. The Swiss electromechanical company Brown Boveri & Cie accepted the proposal. A new, big actor thereby occupied part of the sector: Tecnomasio Brown Boveri, the name of the new firm after the agreement, became the biggest producer of the sector for many years ahead.[24]

Expropriation During the First World War

In May 1915, ten months after the beginning of the conflict, Italy entered the war against the Austro-Hungarian Empire, while the declaration of war against Germany came only in August 1916. The government seized temporarily all properties belonging to the enemy. Under these conditions, officially only SIESS and its eight branches located in eight Italian towns were among the companies involved in this procedure. Nevertheless, the impact was very little, because all the economic sectors not directly linked with the war effort suffered from much-reduced business activity. More relevant was the process of 'Italianisation'—a very early, but still partial process of 'domestication'[25]—experienced by the electrical sector, wherein 1913 all the foreign investors (Swiss, German, French and Belgian) controlled about 40 percent of the top 50 electrical companies and 29.77 percent of the total sector, whose total value was 515.2 million lira. More particularly, Indelec investments had been evaluated at 20.49 million lira (distributed in five companies), the second biggest amount after the Swiss holding Elektrobank (22.42 million). However, if this data are correlated with the shares directly controlled by Siemens (2 million, in two companies), those in the hands of Alta Italia (280 thousand lira) and those of Schuckert's holding Continentale, since 1902 controlled by Siemens, 18.2 million lira (distributed in six companies), it appears clearly that Siemens had the largest portion of all foreign direct investments in the Italian electrical sector, more than 41 million lira, equivalent to 7.96 percent of all investments in this sector, and to 26.77 percent of the foreign investments in the Italian electrical industry.[26]

Most of these investments could not be considered German from the legal point of view. They belonged to a Swiss company, Indelec, and therefore they were considered of neutral ownership. However, this condition did not protect them completely. Siemens had to face a complete transformation of the ownership structure of all the companies where the German company was directly and especially indirectly involved. The 'forced' Italianisation of the shares controlled by the German companies and their holdings provoked considerable losses, which are not easy to calculate, because the assets were on the balance sheet at their nominal value, while the sale was made under the political pressure. The dramatic conditions of the war permitted the potential buyers to impose their evaluations during the negotiations, usually taking place in Switzerland. Moreover, after the war, all the electrical holdings, including Indelec, suffered many losses due to the devaluation of all their foreign investments, not only the Italian ones. Their complete reorganisation passed through a recapitalisation that the original mother companies were not ready to support. Thus, only the intervention of the Swiss banking system permitted the rescue of these holdings. De facto, this process was equivalent to another loss of assets for the German firms. The 'Switzerlandisation' of Elekrobank and

Indelec was just the other face of the 'Italianisation' of their investments in the Peninsula.[27]

The same process occurred in Great Britain. All German companies were confiscated. In 1916, after the passing of the Trading with the enemy Act, the Public Trustee took over Siemens' works at Stafford. Only in 1929 did Siemens re-establish contacts with this very important market. However, the absence of German competitors in the domestic market was only partially exploited by the English electromechanical groups. A wide reorganisation of the sector in this country, which included also a closer relation with the American Westinghouse, did not succeed despite the efforts made by a group of firms and entrepreneurs headed by Dudley Docker, the flamboyant industrialist and financier who wanted Metropolitan Vickers to become the new British national champion in the electromechanical industry.[28]

In the end, Siemens was 'surprised' by the events. The change of strategy provoked by the war was unexpected, and it could neither be prepared for nor its impact avoided. To some extent the reorganisation of Siemens both in Germany and abroad, opened a new era for the company, while the general economic, financial and monetary conditions determined the borders of this transformation.[29]

A New Beginning in the Telecommunication and the New, Advanced Electrical Devices Sector

Re-establishing contact with the Italian clients was not so easy. The reinforcement of the Italian industrial structure in the years before the First World War and the impressive development in the 1915–1918 period, particularly in the military sector, changed the framework for all the foreign investors. In particular, in the decade following the end of the war, the Italian electromechanical industry gained in importance and technological capabilities. Italy no longer needed to import relevant machinery. The successful process of import substitution was one of the best consequences of the war for the Italian economic system.[30]

Moreover, the procedure to eliminate the seizure of the SIESS with the payment of a fee seemed to take too much time. For this reason, the Berlin headquarters decided to set up a new company, Siemens Società Anomima (Siemens S.A.), in 1921. The capital of the new firm was subscribed to only by Siemens & Halske and by Siemens-Schuckert. On the one hand, the new approach in corporate governance reflected the new business climate. The Chairman and General Manager of the company was an Italian, Giovanni Giamminola, as was one of the three technical directors (the other two were German). On the other hand, Giamminola was the only non-German in the board of directors of five members.[31] The main activities of the firm were concentrated in the classical sectors of low-voltage products, especially all the devices for the telephone network, which was in a phase of new development. This trend became more evident after 1923, when the first Mussolini government reprivatised the electrical sector and reorganised the service in an oligopolistic way, subdividing the country in three macro-areas (North, Centre, South and the Islands), controlled by three different big capital groups (Stipel, Telve and Timo, the two latter later controlled by Sip—Società Idroelettrica Piemonte, the new name for Società industriale elettrochimica di Pont Saint Martin that, at the end of the war, emerged as the new, big actor in the northwest Italy). Nevertheless, telephone companies remained largely dependent on foreign technology. In this expanding market, Siemens was facing the competition of two other, very big foreign producers, the Swedish Ericsson and the American Face Standard. All of them, in those years, were just exporting to Italy, through their sales companies, the products requested by the Italian telephone groups.[32]

Thus, when Siemens started the new phase of its Italian experience, the company suffered from the same problem that had arisen from its pre-1914 strategy: the absence of its own manufacturing plant. However, this time Siemens took a new direction: the acquisition of some Italian manufacturing companies. The explanation for this new strategy lies in the economic consequences of the war. Already practically absent from France before 1914 because of political tensions between the two countries following the Franco-Prussian War and the proclamation of the German Empire in the Hall of Mirrors at Versailles in 1871, the geographical profile of Siemens' European markets had changed considerably. The disappearance of the very promising Russian market, the expulsion from the British market, the weakness of the Spanish and the Portuguese markets, all increased the relative importance of the Italian market, notwithstanding the many difficulties that existed in the peninsula. However, the choices made in Italy, once again, were mostly the consequences of a new strategy at home.[33]

Siemens & Halske made another acquisition in Germany, by taking the complete control of Isaria Zahlerwerke, a firm that had some specific knowledge and market share in the production of electrical counters. Automatically, the branch that already existed in Italy, Isaria Contatori Elettrici, which had a small factory in Milan, also passed into the control of Siemens. In that plant, Siemens started the first industrial production in Italy under the name of Officine Siemens (Siemens Workshop). There, the company produced electrical counters and table telephones.[34] This initiative did not change, however, the strategic vision of the company: the main market remained Germany. The foreign branches were just bodies completely dependent on the mother company. This attitude arose not only out of choice but also from a constraint: the insufficient liquidity of the company, connected with the process of stabilising the German currency, did not permit huge financial resources to be used to start a completely different strategy.[35]

A similar situation—the establishment of a commercial branch, by adopting a wider strategy of diversification and the acquisition of a specialised firm—appeared some years later. In 1925, Siemens bought the electro-medical devices producer Reiniger Gebert & Schall. In the same year, the Società Italiana Apparecchi Medicali e Affini (SIAMA) was established in Rome. At the end of the 1920s, it became clear that the success of this company would be more secure if it could produce directly in Italy. Therefore, at the end of the same decade the firm merged with the Luigi Gorla Company, a firm specialised in X-ray devices and radioscopic instruments.[36]

Two collateral areas remained weak: the lamps production, and the telephone devices production. Siemens entered the lamp production just after the First World War. The biggest German electromechanical companies decided to share their knowledge and technologies in this field. In 1919, Siemens & Halske, AEG and Deutsche Gasglülicht, together with a Berlin banker, Leopold Koppel, formed a new firm, called OSRAM Werke GmbH Kommanditgesellschaft. One year later, this firm opened a commercial branch in Milan by setting up a new firm, Osram Società Anonima, which soon became one of the most competitive companies for the use of lamps in public areas, streets and monuments. Italy was one of the first countries where OSRAM established a foreign commercial branch.[37]

Siemens reinforced its presence in Italy in 1928. The firm acquired the control (62 percent of the shares) of a very promising company, Officine Lombarde Apparecchi di Precisione (Lombardy Workshops Precision Equipment), simply known as OLAP, a company mainly working for the Italian Navy. The results did not meet the company's expectations. However, the investment had an advantage. It helped to stop the initiative of the American multinational, ITT, which in the early 1930s was ready to invest in Italy in the telephone sector, opening a factory with 5,000 workers. Mussolini personally intervened to support the Siemens' interests, because, according to a Siemens & Halske's manager, 'Siemens gave a lot of favours to the Italian government'.[38]

The following step was the take-over of another firm, Alfieri & Colli Company, in the late 1920s, specialised in telephone devices and low- or high-voltage dispatching. This allowed Siemens to have a semi-monopolistic position across the telephone devices' sector in Italy. By 1941, the company controlled through its different 'branches' around 70 percent of the Italian market.[39] In the same year, Siemens, through Siemens Plania Werke AG, acquired one of the most important industrial companies in central-southern Italy, the Società dei Forni Elettrici e dell'Elettrocarbonium (SFEE). This company was a sort of monopolist in the production of amorphous coal and graphite, two components for the electrodes.[40]

Thus, in the 1930s, Siemens had a quite complex structure in Italy, one of the most important and very promising foreign markets. Its new specialisation in lamps, advanced technology medical devices, and telephone devices, including dispatching structures, showed the new capabilities of Siemens to act in electrical mass (light or mainly light) production, whilst the idea of basing heavy electromechanical manufacturing in a country which, from an industrial point of view was far more technologically advanced than before the First World War, was much less attractive.

Following the onset of the Great Depression in 1929, the general structure of the company was reorganised in Germany and, in the meantime, in the rest of the world, according to two big divisions: 'light & power' and 'electrical devices'. Included in electrical devices was the production of the Telefunken radio transmitters. In Italy, that firm had existed since 1910 as a commercial branch of the German mother company. When, from the early 1930s, the production structure of Siemens in Italy had become more complete, Siemens OLAP also manufactured the Telefunken radio-telegraphic devices. However, its commercial activities remained in the hands of Siemens S.A.[41]

From Military Ally to Economic Competitor

Italy entered the Second World War in June 1940 as an ally of Germany. At that moment (the data are for 1941), Siemens's employed about 5,600 staff. The structure of the group had a sort of main company, the official branch of Siemens & Halske, Siemens S.A., and a series of semi-independent companies. Some of them were just the commercial branches of a German mother company, and others had a very qualified manufacturing profile. The development of new products and technologies was mainly concentrated in Germany, but some of the Italian-controlled companies like OLAP or SFEE, thanks to their previous tradition and experience, had their own R&D departments.[42]

In 1942, this structure was dramatically modified. All the companies, except for Gorla & SIAMA, and Radion SA (established in Milan in 1941 to act as a substitute for Telefunken activities in the country, after the agreement signed in that year between Siemens and AEG in Germany, by which AEG was to become the only shareholder of Telefunken) merged into Siemens S.A. The new company had the lion's share among the employees of the group in Italy: 4,056 out of 5,600 were working in this enterprise.[43]

One year later, when in September 1943 Italy exited the war—without becoming a new ally of the anti-Nazi fascist alliance—and the fascist regime collapsed, Siemens activities were suddenly in danger. The assets that were in the regions progressively liberated by the Allies were confiscated by the Italian Finance Ministry, but the largest ones were in the north of the country, which remained under the control of the Third Reich until the German army surrendered in April 1945.[44] However, once Germany was finally defeated, an international committee for the liquidation of the goods of the defeated nations decided to transfer the management of all Siemens properties in Italy to the Italian Finance Ministry.

Now Siemens' presence in Italy was challenged much more than in the past, especially in the telephone sector. The pressure of the American government during the reconstruction period permitted two Italian companies controlled by US firms, Autelco Mediterranea (in the hands of Automatic Electric Corp. of Chicago) and Fabbrica Italiana Apparecchi Telefonici e Elettrici, simply known as FACE (a branch of ITT) to have an important role in the modernisation of the telecommunication sector in Italy. Another company, Fabbrica Apparecchi Telefonici e Materiale Elettrico, better known as FATME, controlled by the Swedish firm Ericsson, also contributed to the reduction of Siemens' market share in post-war Italy.[45]

Nevertheless, the most important telephone company, STET, a financial holding controlled by the state-holding IRI, embarked on a very different trajectory. Some circles in the Italian political and economic establishment, and particularly the one connected with the role of the State in the economy, wanted the country to reach a more independent position in this field. In 1947, long and tough negotiations took place between ITT and the Italian government about a comprehensive modernisation of the telecommunication sector. It appeared to be very advantageous to have one single counterpart, provided with the most advanced technological solutions, and quite obviously well positioned to channel some financial aid as part of the Marshall Plan. The Minister for Budget and Economic Planning (and, from 1948, President of the Republic), the well-known economist, Luigi Einaudi, strongly criticised the deal under discussion, because it would have given too much power to ITT in the Italian telecommunication sector, frustrating the attempt to improve national production. However, it appears quite clear that the real aim of the US firm was not to have a better position among the numerous firms working in this very important sector. Rather, ITT's strategy was to eliminate its biggest competitor—Siemens, still under forced state-management, which before the war had controlled 70 percent of the Italian telephone market—by asking the Finance Ministry to transfer its control over the Siemens group to the US firm. This could possibly have been the reason why, in spring 1947, the workers in Siemens' Italian plants went on strike several times. They wanted to see the old manager, Mr. Mantellassi (pro-German, but untainted by collaboration with the Nazis during the Wehrmacht's occupation), brought back, and the man who represented the provisional owner, the Italian State, Mr. Fulvio Furani, fired as he was not supported by the workers and their representatives in the company's workers' council. However, in 1948 the Finance Ministry of Treasury named a new manager, Aganippo Brocchi, who started the reconstruction of the company.[46]

In the end, STET, which was against the ITT strategy also because 60 percent of its telephone exchanges had adopted the Siemens model, refused to sign an agreement with ITT. By contrast, they started to talk about cooperation with Siemens S.A., still under state confiscation. In the meantime, the US, Great Britain, France and Italy signed an agreement pushing the Italian government to sell the companies and the foreign goods under sequestration. Despite these pressures, it was very difficult and even impossible for STET to acquire the control of just the telephone manufacturing activities of Siemens S.A. The only way was to buy all Siemens' activities in Italy. The agreement was finally reached in 1950. Thus Siemens S.A., despite keeping strategic links with the parent company, particularly from the technological point of view, became part of the STET group. Siemens' capital was split in order to give a better balance of power inside the IRI universe: 49 percent of the shares remained in STET, 49 percent were given to SIP (the biggest telephone company controlled by STET), and 2 percent to IRI, a decision that, according to Bruno Bottiglieri, can be explained logically only by a desire to avoid STETT becoming overly weighty. After this new distribution of the shares, Siemens S.A. was renamed Società Italiana Telecomunicazioni Siemens (later known simply as SIT-Siemens). This ownership structure lasted until 1963, when the nationalisation of the electrical industry pushed SIP (which had been involved in this sector) to sell back its SIT-Siemens shares to STET.[47]

In a few years, the new company STET-Siemens achieved the leading role in the Italian telephone market, followed by the Pirelli Group and Swedish Ericsson. Its strong position was even enhanced by the complex links and its financial shareholdings in some of the companies controlled by its two main competitors.[48] Nevertheless, the inclusion of the whole Siemens S.A. in STET also provoked some problems. Already in 1947, just at the beginning of the negotiations about the acquisition of Siemens by STET, IRI considered splitting the telephone and telecommunication production from that connected with the electromechanical automation. At that moment, the suggestion was to include those activities in the recently established Finmeccanica, the IRI holding for the mechanical sector. This solution was abandoned after the completion of the negotiations, but, immediately after, IRI started the process of separating the non-telephone branches of Siemens from those directly linked with the telephone sector, which was the strategic one for STET. This process took many years to be completed. Before the end of the decade, the non-telephone branches were finally merged in a new company, Siemens Elettra, formed in 1960. During the reorganisation process, in 1959, the company Gorla-SIAMA, which had been sold to a private group in 1950, was sold back to Siemens Elettra, and, later, in 1963, it merged with this company.

The other strategic change had already occurred three years before. In 1960, Siemens Elettra was sold by IRI to Siemens & Halske and to Siemens Schukertwerke. More than 2,000 staff were employed at that moment in the company. The company mainly produced mass consumer goods (TV, radio, cinema projectors) and a wide range of industrial electrical devices (counters, high- and low-voltage machinery, measuring instruments). The telephone production remained in Italian hands under the name of Società Italiana Telecomunicazioni Siemens, simply known as Sit-Siemens, official representative of Siemens in Italy for this sector. This company employed, in the early 1960s, more than 4,400 staff.[49] The process of European integration, which facilitated trade relations and was strongly supported by the German and Italian governments, made the deal easier and to some extent the logical conclusion of the post-war strategy of Siemens and STET that was always based on mutual respect.[50]

The 'coming home' strategy was completed with a total Germanisation of the corporate governance structure. An *Aufsichtsrat* (the board of Directors with representatives of Siemens & Halske and Siemens-Schuckert) and a *Vorstand* (the managerial structure) were set up, usually comprising a large majority of German citizens. The Siemens headquarters in Munich (where the company moved after the Second World War), kept the right to nominate all the members of the two bodies.[51]

For a large part of the 1960s and 1970s, the leading role was given to the sales department, a sort of heritage of the original structure of early Siemens' investments in the country, when the Italian branch had been mainly a commercial firm charged only to collect the orders and to offer a post-sales service. Despite the increasing importance of Milan in the central organisation of the company in Italy, during the 1950s and 1960s many commercial branches and representatives started their activity in different towns and regions of the peninsula.[52]

During the second part of the 1960s and through the 1970s, following the merger in Germany between the three Siemens companies (Siemens & Halske, Siemens-Schuckert, and Siemens-Reiniger), which occurred in 1966, all the foreign branches were reorganised. The new Siemens AG, as with many other big European companies in those years, adopted a multidivisional structure. The foreign branches were, of course, included in this process. This permitted them to become part of a global strategy of the German group, by increasing their role in R&D and manufacturing. In Italy, this process went ahead in parallel to a progressive 'Italianisation' of the management. Seventy years after entering the Italian market, Siemens was more German, but also more Italian, than it had ever been before.[53]

Conclusions

Siemens investments in Italy are paradigmatic of the company's strategies. Until the First World War, Italy was still a developing country, and highly technologically dependent. Siemens, as well as many other foreign firms in the electromechanical as well as in other advanced industrial sectors, took advantage of the situation. However, because of the size of the Italian market and some conservative attitudes still prevailing in Berlin, the peninsula was not placed among the top destinations for Siemens' foreign direct investments. Commercial penetration was preferred. This helps to explain the development of the *Unternehmensgeschäft* strategy, which permitted the company to secure important deliveries of big electromechanical devices through financial control of the customers.

Although the consequences of the First World War were relatively unimportant for the company's direct investment position, they were quite important for the financial investments through the German and the Swiss electric holding companies. However, from the point of view of the company, looking to define a post-war strategy, losing the war was more devastating than entering the war. The financial losses and the mark devaluation reduced the possibilities of a new wide-investment phase. The company adapted quite well to the new constraints. Italy became a sort of preferential market and the place where most of the new domestic strategies (particularly in the case of mergers and acquisitions) had a direct effect. The potential to expand the capacity of the Italian market, from the 1920s the most relevant in Europe after the domestic one, especially in the telecommunication sector, offered Siemens the possibility to become the most important actor in this rapidly developing area. The next step was to create manufacturing activities in Italy, not as direct investment but through the financial control of very promising Italian firms in electromechanical manufacturing activities as well in some strategic production.

The consolidation and the reorganisation of all investments in Italy occurred during the Second World War. As in the case of the Great War, the most relevant negative effects came with the end of the war. For about 15 years, Siemens could no longer control its Italian assets. This time, the strength of Italian national interests was directly represented by the state-owned companies and their controlling holding companies (IRI and STET). Thus, the example of Siemens tends to confirm that—in some cases—the dramatic effects of the beginning of the war were less important than those provoked by the end of the conflict. The political risk could be accepted and, to some extent, it was included in the variety of tactics a company had to pursue. Much less predictable—and difficult to evaluate—were the economic and financial long-term consequences. The probability of resisting and succeeding, at the very end of a process that can sometimes be very long, depends on how firms adapt to changing economic and political conditions and how effectively they respond to a sort of Darwin's invisible hand.[54]

Notes

1 Casson, Mark and da Silva Lopes, Teresa, 'Foreign Direct Investment in High-Risk Environments: An Historical Perspective', *Business History*, 2013, 55:3, 375–404; Ring, Peter Smith, Stefanie, Ann Lenway and Govekar, Michele Govekar, 'Management of the Political Imperative in International Business', *Strategic Management Journal*, 1990, 11:2, 141–151. Kobrak, Christopher, Per H. Hansen and Kopper, Christopher, 'Business, Political Risk, and Historians

in the Twentieth Century', in Christopher Kobrak and Per Hansen (eds.), *European Business, Dictatorship and Political Risk, 1920–1945*, New York: Berghahn, 2004: 3–21.

2 Mori, Giorgio, 'L'economia italiana dagli anni Ottanta alla prima Guerra mondiale', in Giorgio Mori (ed.), *Storia dell'industria elettrica in Italia, 1. Le origini. 1882–1914*, Rome-Bari: Laterza, 1992: 1–106.

3 Guagnini, Anna, 'The Formation of the Italian Electrical Engineers: The Teaching Laboratories of the Politecnici of Turn and Milan: 1887–1914', in F. Cardot (ed.), *1880–1980. Un siècle d'électricité dans le monde*, Paris: Presses Universitaires de France, 1987: 283–300; Lacaita, Carlo G., 'Politecnici, ingegneri e industria elettrica', in Giorgio Mori (ed.), *Storia dell'industria elettrica in Italia, 1. Le origini. 1882–1914*, op. cit.: 603–644.

4 Segreto, Luciano, 'Imprenditori e finanzieri', in Giorgio Mori (ed.), *Storia dell'industria elettrica in Italia, 1. Le origini. 1882–1914*, op. cit.: 259–271.

5 Hetrner, Peter and Doria, Marco, 'L'industria elettrotecnica', in Giorgio Mori (ed.), *Storia dell'industria elettrica in Italia, 1. Le origini. 1882–1914*, op. cit.: 571–580.

6 Giannetti, Renato, *La conquista della forza: risorse tecnologia ed economia nell'industria elettrica italiana (1883–1940)*, Milano: Franco Angeli, 1985; Vasta, Michelangelo, 'Innovazione e sviluppo economico: l'uso dei brevetti nell'analisi del settore elettrotecnico italiano nel periodo 1895–1914', in *Rivista di storia economica*, 1990, VII:1, 47–74; Vasta, Michelangelo, *Innovazione tecnologica e capitale umano in Italia (1880–1914). Le traiettorie tecnologiche della seconda rivoluzione industriale*, Bologna: Il Mulino, 1999; Barbiellini Amidei, Federico, Cantwell, John and Spadavecchia, Anna, 'Innovation and foreign technology', in Gianni Toniolo (ed.), *The Oxford Handbook of the Italian Economy Since Unification*, Oxford: OUP, 2013: 378–400.

7 Capanna, Adriano and Messori, Oreste, *Gli scambi commerciali dell'Italia con l'estero dalla costituzione del Regno ad oggi*, Roma: Unione Editori d'Italia, 1940: 34–35; Hertner, Peter, 'La Germania alla conquista del mercato italiano tra gli anni ottanta e la vigilia della prima guerra mondiale', in *I Convegno nazionale di storia del commercio in Italia, Mercati e consumi: organizzazione e qualificazione del commercio in Italia dal XII al XX secolo, Reggio Emilia 6–7 giugno1984 e Modena 8–9 giugno 1984*, Bologna: Analisi, 1984: 236–243.

8 Capanna, Adriano and Messori, Oreste, *Gli scambi commerciali dell'Italia con l'estero dalla costituzione del Regno ad oggi*, op. cit.: 34–35; Hertner, Peter, 'La Germania alla conquista del mercato italiano', op. cit.: 236–243.

9 Feldenkirchen, Wilfred, *Werner von Siemens: Inventor and International Enrepreneur*, Columbus: Ohio University Press, 1994: 45–83; Holzer, Georg S., *The German Electrical Industry in Russia: From Economic Entrepreneurship to Political Activism 1890–1918*, Lincoln: University of Nebraska, Unpublished Thesis; Kirchner, Walther, 'The Industrialization of Russia and the Siemens Firm 1853–1890', in *Jarbuch fur Geschichte Osteuropas*, 1974, 22, 321–357; Kirchner, Walther, *Siemens and AEG and the Electrification of Russia, 1890–1914*, Berlin: Seiner, 1982.

10 Giuntini, Andrea, *Sul filo della comunicazione. La telegrafia nell'Ottocento fra economia, politica e tecnologia*, Prato: Istituto di studi storici postali, 2004; Giuntini, Andrea (ed.), *Communication and Its Lines: Telegraphy in the 19th Century Among Economy, Politics and Technology*, Prato: Istituto di studi storici postali, 2004; Fari, Simone, *Una penisola in comunicazione. Il servizio telegrafico dall'Unità alla Grande Guerra*, Bari: Cacucci, 2008.

11 Siemens Archives, Berlin, 68/Ld 851, Wagner, Joseph, *Geschichte des Hauses Siemens im Ausland, Italien*, Teil A, Band 1.

12 Hertner, Peter, 'Il capitale tedesco nell'industria elettrica italiana', in Bruno Bezza (ed.), *Energia e sviluppo. L'industria elettrica italiana e la Società Edison*, Turin: Einaudi: 216.
13 Ibidem.
14 Segreto, Luciano, 'Elettricità ed economia in Europa', in Giorgio Mori (ed.), *Storia dell'industria elettrica in Italia, 1. Le origini. 1882–1914*, op. cit.: 697–750; Hausman, William J., Hertner, Peter and Wilkins, Mira, *Global Electrification: Multinational Enterprise and International Finance in the History of Light and Power, 1878–2007*, Cambridge: Cambridge University Press, 2008: 75–82.
15 Ibidem, 46–55.
16 Hertner, Peter, 'Les sociétés financières suisses et le développement de l'industrie électrique jusq'à la première guerre mondiale', in *1890–1980. Un siècle d'électricité dans le monde*, op. cit. 327–340; Segreto, Luciano, 'Capitali, tecnologie e imprenditori svizzeri nell'industria elettrica italiana: il caso della Motor (1895–1923)', in Bruno Bezza (ed.), *Energia e sviluppo*, op. cit., 180–182.
17 Hertner, Peter, *Il capitale tedesco in Italia dall'Unità alla prima guerra mondiale. Banche miste e sviluppo economico italiano*, Bologna: il Mulino, 1984: 45–55.
18 Ibidem, 61–70; Mori, Giorgio, 'L'economia italiana', op. cit., 40–56.
19 Hertner, Peter, 'Il capitale tedesco nell'industria elettrica italiana', op. cit.: 218–220 and 233–234; Caligaris, Giacomina, *L'industria elettrica in Piemonte dalle origini alla prima guerra mondiale*, Bologna: il Mulino, 1993: 31, 69–84.
20 Ibidem, 118–119; Segreto, Luciano, 'Imprenditori e finanzieri', op. cit.: 297–298.
21 Caligaris, Giacomina, *L'industria elettrica in Piemonte dalle origini alla prima guerra mondiale*, op. cit.: 101–133; Confalonieri, Antonio, *Banca e industria in Italia*, Bologna: il Mulino, 1994, vol. 2: 233–234.
22 Hertner, Peter, 'Il capitale tedesco nell'industria elettrica italiana', op. cit.: 228–2247.
23 Ibidem, 219–224; Bottiglieri, Bruno, *SIP. Impresa, tecnologia e Stato nelle telecomunicazioni italiane*, Milan: Franco Angeli, 1990: 32–37; Segreto, Luciano, *Giacinto Motta. Un ingegnere alla testa del capitalismo industriale italiano*, Rome-Bari: Laterza, 2003: 45–50; Balbi, Gabriele, *Le origini del telefono in Italia. Politica, economia, tecnologia, società*, Milano: Bruno Mondadori, 2011.
24 Licini, Stefania, 'E. Marelli e Tecnomasio Italiano dalle origini agli anni Trenta: un tentativo di comparazione', in Fondazione ASSI, *Annali di storia dell'impresa*, 5/6, Bologna: il Mulino, 1990: 299–315; Hertner, Peter and Doria, Marco, 'L'industria elettromeccanica', op. cit.: 582.
25 For this concept see Hausman, William J., Hertner, Peter and Wilkins, Mira, *Global Electrification*, op. cit.: 233.
26 Segreto, Luciano, 'Imprenditori e finanziari', op. cit.: 332–334.
27 Segreto, Luciano, 'Du "Made in Germany" au "Made in Switzerland". Les sociétés financières suisses pour l'industrie électrique dans l'entre-duex-guerres', in Monique Trédé (ed.), *1880–1980. Electricité et électrification dans le monde*, Paris: Presses Universitaires de France: 347–368; Segreto, Luciano, 'Gli assetti proprietari', in Giuseppe De Rosa (ed.), *Storia dell'industria elettrica in Italia, 3. Espansione e oligopolio. 1926–1945*, Rome-Bari: Laterza: 1993: 94–110.
28 Davenport Hines, Richard P.T., *Dodley Docker: The Life and Times of a Trade Warrior*, Cambridge: Cambridge University Press, 1984: 200; Hausman, William, Hertner, Peter and Wilkins, Mira, *Global Electrification*, op. cit.: 134–135.

29 'La Siemens compie 125 anni', in *Elettra*, n. 3:dicembre 1972, 8–9; Siegrist, Hannes, 'Strategie delle grandi imprese tedesche dopo la prima guerra mondiale', in Giorgio Mori and Peter Hertner (eds.), *La transizione dell'economia di guerra dall'economia di pace in Italia e in Germania dopo mondiale*, Bologna: il Mulino: 269–277; Giannetti, Renato, *La conquista della forza*, op. cit.: 94–96.
30 Pescarolo, Alessandra, *Riconversione industriale e composizione di classe. L'inchiesta sulle industrie metalmeccaniche del 1922*, Milan: Franco Angeli, 1979: 287; Hertner, Peter, 'Un investimento tedesco in Lombardia tra le due guerre mondiali: le Officine Lombarde Apparecchi di Precisione', in *Storia in Lombardia*, 1, 1986: 9–11.
31 Siemens Archives, 'Die Wiederaufnahme der geschaftigkeit und das Ende des Siemens-Schuckertwerke, 1919–1921', in *Geschichte des Hauses Siemens im Ausland, Italien*, Teil B, Band 9: 90–97.
32 Bottoglieri, Bruno, *SIP*, op. cit.: 74–120.
33 Chandler, Alfred D., *Scale and Scope: The Dynamics of Industrial Capitalism*, Cambridge, MA: Harvard University Press, 1990: 543–545.
34 Siemens Archives, Berlin, 'Personelle und organisatorische Veränderungen bei der Siemens S.A.', in *Geschichte des Hauses Siemens im Ausland*, op. cit., Teil B, Band 9: 139–145; 'Einrichtung einer nachrichtentechnischen Fertigung', ibidem, Band 5: 128–129.
35 Hertner, Peter, 'Un investimento tedesco in Lombardia', op. cit.: 9.
36 Siemens Archives, Berlin, 'Die weitere geschäftliche Entiwickulng, 1927–39', in *Geschichet des Hauses Siemens im Ausland*, op. cit., Teil B: 147–154; Durante, Raffaele, Alberoni, Francesco and De Maio Adriano, *Siemens 1899–1999. Cento anni in Italia*, Milan: Franco Maria Ricci, 1999: 110–112.
37 Giannetti, Renato, 'The Power Equipmente Cartels', in Takashi Hara and Aiko Kudo (eds.), *International Cartels in Business History*, Tokyo: University of Tokyo Press, 1992: 190–209; Hertner, Peter, 'How They Changed their Strategy. The German Electromechanical Industry and the Italian Market Before the Second World War', in Geoffrey Jones and Harm Schroeter (ed.), *The Rise of Multinational in Continental Europe*, London: Adershot, 1993: 155–172; Heerding, *The History of N. V. Philipps Gloeilampenfabrik, Volume 2, A Company of Many Parts*, Cambridge: Cambridge University Press, 1988: 112–125. In 1924 Osram joined the Phoebus cartel, set up in that year, together with General Electric Company, Tungsram, Compagnie di Lampe, and Philips.
38 Hertner, Peter, 'Un investimento tedesco', op. cit.: 24.
39 Hertner, Peter, 'Un investimento tedesco', op. cit.: 15–20; ibidem. 'How They Changed their Strategy', op. cit. 155–172.
40 Siemens Archives, Berlin, 'Personelle und organisatorische Veränderung bei der Siemens *Elettra* Milano', in *Geschichte des Hauses Siemens im Ausland*, op. cit., Teil B, Band 9: 139–145; Durante, Raffaele, Alberoni, Francesco and De Maio Adriano, *Siemens 1899–1999*, op. cit.: 112–115; Crepax, Nicola, *Storia dell'industria in Italia. Uomini, imprese, prodotti*, Bologna: il Mulino, 2002: 267–268.
41 Durante, Raffaele, Alberoni, Francesco and De Maio Adriano, *Siemens 1899–1999*, op. cit.: 113; Thiele, Heinrich, *Telefunken dopo 100 anni: l'eredità di un brand mondiale*, Berlin: Nicolai Editore, 1993; Friedewald, Manfred, 'Telefunken e la radio nave tedesca, 1903–1914', *Rivista aziendale*, 2001, n. 1, 27–57.
42 Durante, Raffaele, Alberoni, Francesco and De Maio Adriano, *Siemens 1899–1999*, op. cit.: 113–116; Siemens Archives, Berlin, 'Die italienische Siemens-Gesellschafi im 2. Weltkrieg', in *Geschichte des Hauses Siemens in Ausland*, op. cit., Teil B, Band 9: 155–165.

43 *Siemens. Cento anni in Italia*, op. cit.: 13–116; Siemens Archives, Berlin, 'Die italienische Siemens-Gesellschaf im 2. Weltkrieg', in *Geschichte des Hauses Siemens in Ausland*, op. cit., Teil B, Band 9: 155–165.
44 Kilinkhammer, Lutz, *L'occupazione tedesca in Italia 1943–45*, Turin: Boringhieri, 1993; Rieder, Maximiliane, 'I rapporti economici italo-tedeschi tra alleanza, occupazione e ricostruzione', in Vera Zamagni (ed.), *Come perdere la guerra e vincere la pace*, Bologna: il Mulino, 1997: 309–340.
45 *Siemens 100 anni Anni in Italia*, op. cit.: 114–115; Feldenkirchen, Wilfried, '160 Years of Siemens', in *Siemens-World Siemens*, October 2007: 3–4; 'Der Verlauf des Krieges in Italien und das Schicksal der Siemens SpA (1943–1945)', in *Geschichte des Hauses Siemens in Ausland*, op. cit.: 173–176.
46 Harper, John L., *America and the Italian Reconstruction 1945–1948*, Cambridge: Cambridge University Press, 1986: 70–71; 'Dimostrazione di operai in Via Fabio Filzi', *Corriere della Sera*, 9/10.05.1947; 'I lavoratori decisi a salvare la Siemens', *l'Unità*, 10.05.1947; 'Democristiani e nazisti all'assalto della Siemens', ibidem, 4.06.1947; 'Il sequestratario della Siemens confermato nella carica', *Corriere della Sera*, 28/29.06.1947.
47 Siemens Archives, Berlin, 'Die sequesterbehörde verkauft die Aktien der italienischen Siemens—Siemens SpA baut ehnchtentechnischen Fabrik Zusammenarbeit mit S&H-SSW und SRW 1950–1960', in *Geschichte des Haus Siemens*, op. cit.: 187–192; Bottiglieri, Bruno, *STET. Strategie e struttura delle telecomunicazioni*, Milan: Franco Angeli, 1987: 259–260.
48 Ibidem, 219–249.
49 Mariotti, Sergio, 'Le telecomunicazioni dal monopolio tecnologico ai mutamenti degli anni Ottante e Novanta, alle privatizzazioni', in Franco Russolillo (ed.), *Storia dell'Iri, 5, Un gruppo singolare. Settori, bilanci, presenza nell'economia italiana*, Rome-Bari:Leterza, 2015: 1550–1570.
50 Vordemann, Christian, *Deutschland-Italien, 1949–1961. Die diplomatischen Beziehungen*, Frankfurt am Main: Peter Lang, 1994; Guiotto, Maddalena and Lill, Johannes, *Italia-Germania, Deutschland-Italien, 1948–1958. Riavvicinamenti-Wiederannäherungen*, Firenze: Olschki, 1997; Masala, Carlo, *Italia und Germania. Die deutsch-italienischen Beziehungen, 1963–1969*, Köln: S-H Verlag, 1998; Rieder, Maximiliane, *Deutsch-italienische Wirtschaftsbeziehungen. Kontinuitäten und Brüche, 1936–1957*, Frankfurt am Main: Campus Verlag, 2003.
51 Siemens Italia Archives. Milan, Comitato di Direzione Siemens *Elettra* Milano No. 5/61, 1 febbraio 1961 e Comunicazione No. 21, 6 aprile 1961; 'Vorstand/Comitato di Direzione e Comunicazione Siemens Elettra Milano, No 16, 30 gennaio 1962, in Die Geschäfisleitung (Comitato di Direzione) und die Vertriebs- und Verwaltungsbereiche', in *Geschichte des Hauses Siemens im Ausland*, Teil B, Band 9, op. cit.: 266–269.
52 Siemens Archives, Berlin, 'Zweigniederlassungen, Technischen Büros und Verkaufsbüros', in *Geschichte des Hauses Siemens im Ausland*, op. cit.: 277–283; 'Che cosa Facciamo noi della Siemens Elettra', *Elettra, periodico aziendale della Siemens Elettra SpA*, n. I:dicembre 1968, 4–5.
53 Siemens Archives, Berlin, 'Personelle und organisatorische Veraenderungen bei der Siemens Elettra Milano', in *Geschichte des Hauses Siemens im Ausland*, op. cit.: 263–266; Organisationsplan Siemens Elettra Mailand—Stand 1/10/1969, ibidem: 269; 'La parola al nostro amministratore delegato Hans Verlohr e Siemens Elettra SpAS, la nuova organizzazione dal 1 ottobre 1968', *Elettra*, n. 4:dicembre 1969, 2–5.
54 Johnson Dominic D.P. Price, Michael E. and Van Vugt, Mark, 'Darwin's Invisible Hand: Market Competition, Evolution and the Firm', *Journal of Economic Behavior & Organization*, 90: June 2013, 128–140.

Bibliography

Balbi, Gabriele, 2011, *Le origini del telefono in Italia. Politica, economia, tecnologia, società*, Milan: Bruno Mondadori.

Barbiellini Amidei, Federico, Cantwell, John and Spadavecchia, Anna, 2003, 'Innovation and Foreign Technology', in *The Oxford Handbook of the Italian Economy Since Unification*, edited by Gianni Toniolo, 378–400, Oxford: Oxford University Press.

Bottiglieri, Bruno, 1987, *STET. Strategie e struttura delle telecomunicazioni*, Milan: Franco Angeli.

Bottiglieri, Bruno, 1990, *SIP. Impresa, tecnologia e Stato nelle telecomunicazioni italiane*, Milan: Franco Angeli.

Capanna, Adriano and Messori, Oreste, 1940, *Gli scambi commerciali dell'Italia con l'estero dalla costituzione del Regno ad oggi*, Rome: Unione Editori d'Italia.

Casson, Mark and da Silva Lopes, Teresa, 2013, 'Foreign Direct Investment in High-Risk Environments: An Historical Perspective', *Business History*, 55:3, 375–404.

Chandler, Alfred D., 1990, *Scale and Scope: The Dynamics of Industrial Capitalism*, Cambridge, MA: Harvard University Press.

Communication and Its Lines: Telegraphy in the 19th Century Among Economy, Politics and Technology, 2004, edited by Andrea Giuntini, Prato: Istituto di studi storici postali.

Confalonieri, Antonio, 1994, *Banca e industria in Italia*, Bologna: il Mulino, vol. 2.

Davenport-Hines, Richard P.T., 1984, *Dodley Docker: The Life and Times of a Trade Warrior*, Cambridge: Cambridge University Press.

'Democristiani e nazisti all'assalto della Siemens', *l'Unità*, 4.06.1947.

'Dimostrazione di operai in Via Fabio Filzi', *Corriere della Sera*, 9/10.05.1947.

Durante, Raffaele, Alberoni, Francesco and De Maio, Adriano, 1999, *Siemens 1899–1999. Cento anni in Italia*, Milan: Franco Maria Ricci.

Fari, Simone, 2008, *Una penisola in comunicazione. Il servizio telegrafico dall'Unità alla Grande Guerra*, Bari: Cacucci.

Feldenkirchen, Wilfred, 1994, *Werner von Siemens: Inventor and International Enrepreneur*, Columbus: Ohio University Press.

Feldenkirchen, Wilfried, 2007, '160 Years of Siemens', *Special Edition of Siemens-World Siemens*, October 2007.

Friedewald, Manfred, 2001, 'Telefunken e la radio nave tedesca, 1903–1914', *Rivista aziendale*, n. 1, 27–57.

Giannetti, Renato, 1985, *La conquista della forza: risorse tecnologia ed economia nell'industria elettrica italiana (1883–1940)*, Milano: Franco Angeli.

Giannetti, Renato, 1991, 'The Power Equipment Cartels. The International Agreement and the Italian Case in the Thirties', in *International Cartels in Business History*, edited by Takashi Hara and Haiko Kudo, 190–209, Tokyo: University of Tokyo Press.

Giuntini, Andrea, 2004, *Sul filo della comunicazione. La telegrafia nell'Ottocento fra economia, politica e tecnologia*, Prato: Istituto di studi storici postali.

Guagnini, Anna, 1987, 'The Formation of the Italian Electrical Engineers: The Teaching Laboratories of the Politecnici of Turn and Milan: 1887–1914', in *1880–1980. Un siècle d'électricité dans le monde*, edité par Fabienne Cardot, 283–300, Paris: Presses Universitaires de France.

Guiotto, Maddalena and Lill, Johannes, 1997, *Italia-Germania, Deutschland-Italien, 1948–1958. Riavvicinamenti-Wiederannäherungen*, Firenze: Olschki.

Harper, John L., 1986, *America and the Italian Reconstruction 1945–1948*, Cambridge: Cambridge University Press.

Hausman, William J., Hertner, Peter and Wilkins, Mira, 2008, *Global Electrification. Multinational Enterprise and International Finance in the History of Light and Power, 1878–2007*, Cambridge: Cambridge University Press.

Heerding, A., 1988, *The History of N. V. Philipps Gloeilampenfabrik, Volume 2, A Company of Many Parts*, Cambridge: Cambridge University Press.

Hertner, Peter, 1984, *Il capitale tedesco in Italia dall'Unità alla prima guerra mondiale. Banche miste e sviluppo economico italiano*, Bologna: il Mulino.

Hertner, Peter, 1984, 'La Germania alla conquista del mercato italiano tra gli anni ottanta e la vigilia della prima guerra mondiale', in *I Convegno nazionale di storia del commercio in Italia, Mercati e consumi: organizzazione e qualificazione del commercio in Italia dal XII al XX secolo, Reggio Emilia 6–7 giugno1984 e Modena 8–9 giugno 1984*, 236–243, Bologna: Analisi.

Hertner, Peter, 1986, 'Il capitale tedesco nell'industria elettrica italiana', in *Energia e sviluppo. L'industria elettrica italiana e la Società Edison*, edited by Bruno Bezza, 213–257, Turin: Einaudi.

Hertner, Peter, 1986, 'Un investimento tedesco in Lombardia tra le due guerre mondiali: le Officine Lombarde Apparecchi di Precisione', *Storia in Lombardia*, 1, 7–37.

Hertner, Peter, 1987, 'Les sociétés financières suisses et le développement de l'industrie électrique jusq'à la première guerre mondiale', in *1890–1980. Un siècle d'électricité dans le monde*, edité par Monique Trédé, 327–340, Paris: Presses Universitaires de France.

Hertner, Peter, 1993, 'How They Changed their Strategy. The German Electromechanical Industry and the Italian Market Before the Second World War', in *The Rise of Multinational in Continental Europe*, edited by Geoffrey Jones and Harm Schroeter, 155–172, London: Adershot.

Hetrner, Peter and Doria, Marco, 1992, 'L'industria elettrotecnica', in *Storia dell'industria elettrica in Italia, 1. Le origini. 1882–1914*, edited by Giorgio Mori, 571–602, Bari-Rome: Laterza.

Holzer, Georg S., *The German Electrical Industry in Russia: From Economic Entrepreneurship to Political Activism 1890–1918*, Lincoln: University of Nebraska, Unpublished Thesis.

'I lavoratori decisi a salvare la Siemens', *l'Unità*, 10.05.1947.

'Il sequestratario della Siemens confermato nella carica', *Corriere della Sera*, 28/29.06.1947.

Johnson, Dominic D.P., Price, Michael E. and Van Vugt, Mark, 2013, 'Darwin's Invisible Hand: Market Competition, Evolution and the Firm', *Journal of Economic Behavior & Organization*, 90:June, 128–140.

Kilinkhammer, Lutz, 1993, *L'occupazione tedesca in Italia 1943–45*, Turin: Boringhieri.

Kirchner, Walther, 1974, 'The Industrialization of Russia and the Siemens Firm 1853–1890', *Jarbuch fur Geschichte Osteuropas*, 22, 321–357.

Kirchner, Walther, 1982, *Siemens and AEG and the Electrification of Russia, 1890–1914*, Berlin: Seiner.

Kobrak, Christopher, Per, Hansen H. and Kopper, Christopher, 2004, 'Business, Political Risk, and Historians in the Twentieth Century', in *European Business,*

Dictatorship and Political Risk, 1920–1945, edited by Christopher Kobrak and Per Hansen, 3–21, New York: Berghahn.

Lacaita, Carlo G., 1992, 'Politecnici, ingegneri e industria elettrica', in *Storia dell'industria elettrica in Italia, 1. Le origini. 1882–1914*, edited by Giorgio Mori, 603–644, Rome-Bari: Laterza.

'La parola al nostro amministratore delegato Hans Verlohr e Siemens Elettra SpAS, la nuova organizzazione dal 1 ottobre 1968', *Elettra*, n. 4:dicembre 1969, 2–5.

'La Siemens compie 125 anni', *Elettra*, n. 3:dicembre 1972, 8–9.

Licini, Stefania, 1990, 'E. Marelli e Tecnomasio Italiano dalle origini agli anni Trenta: un tentativo di comparazione', in Fondazione ASSI, *Annali di storia dell'impresa*, 5/6, 299–331, Bologna: il Mulino.

Mariotti, Sergio, 2015, 'Le telecomunicazioni dal monopolio tecnologico ai mutamenti degli anni Ottante e Novanta, alle privatizzazioni', in *Storia dell'Iri, 5, Un gruppo singolare. Settori, bilanci, presenza nell'economia italiana*, edited by Franco Russolillo, 201–276, Rome-Bari: Laterza.

Masala, Carlo, 1998, *Italia und Germania. Die deutsch-italienischen Beziehungen, 1963–1969*, Köln: S-H Verlag.

Mori, Giorgio, 1992, 'L'economia italiana dagli anni Ottanta alla prima Guerra mondiale', in *Storia dell'industria elettrica in Italia, 1. Le origini. 1882–1914*, edited by Giorgio Mori, 1–106, Rome-Bari: Laterza.

Pescarolo, Alessandra, 1979, *Riconversione industriale e composizione di classe. L'inchiesta sulle industrie metalmeccaniche del 1922*, Milan: Franco Angeli.

Rieder, Maximiliane, 1997, 'I rapporti economici italo-tedeschi tra alleanza, occupazione e ricostruzione', in *Come perdere la guerra e vincere la pace*, edited by Vera Zamagni, 309–340, Bologna: il Mulino.

Rieder, Maximiliane, 2003, *Deutsch-italienische Wirtschaftsbeziehungen. Kontinuitäten und Brüche, 1936–1957*, Frankfurt am Main: Campus Verlag.

Ring, Peter Smith, Stefanie, Ann Lenway and Govekar, Michele Govekar, 1990, 'Management of the Political Imperative in International Business', *Strategic Management Journal*, 11:2, 141–151.

Segreto, Luciano, 1986, 'Capitali, tecnologie e imprenditori svizzeri nell'industria elettrica italiana: il caso della Motor (1895–1923)', in *Energia e sviluppo. L'industria elettrica italiana e la Società Edison*, edited by Bruno Bezza, 175–210, Turin: Einudi.

Segreto, Luciano, 1991, 'Du "Made in Germany" au "Made in Switzerland". Les sociétés financières suisses pour l'industrie électrique dans l'entre-duex-guerres', in *1880–1980. Electricité et électrification dans le monde*, edited by Monique Trédé, 347–368, Paris: Presses Universitaires de France.

Segreto, Luciano, 1992 'Imprenditori e finanzieri', in *Storia dell'industria elettrica in Italia, 1. Le origini. 1882–1914*, edited by Giorgio Mori, 249–338, Rome-Bari: Laterza.

Segreto, Luciano, 1993, 'Gli assetti proprietari', in *Storia dell'industria elettrica in Italia, 3*. Espansione e oligopolio. 1926–1945*, edited by Giuseppe De Rosa, 89–174, Rome-Bari: Laterza.

Segreto, Luciano, 2003, *Giacinto Motta. Un ingegnere alla testa del capitalismo industriale italiano*, Rome-Bari: Laterza.

Siegrist, Hannes, 1983, 'Strategie delle grandi imprese tedesche dopo la prima guerra mondiale', in *La transizione dell'economia di guerra dall'economia di pace in Italia e in Germania dopo mondiale*, edited by Giorgio Mori and Peter Hertner, 269–300, Bologna: il Mulino.

Thiele, Heinrich, 1993, *Telefunken dopo 100 anni: l'eredità di un brand mondiale*, Berlin: Nicolai Editore.

Vasta, Michelangelo, 1990, 'Innovazione e sviluppo economico: l'uso dei brevetti nell'analisi del settore elettrotecnico italiano nel periodo 1895–1914', *Rivista di storia economica*, VII:1, 47–74.

Vasta, Michelangelo, 1999, *Innovazione tecnologica e capitale umano in Italia (1880–1914). Le traiettorie tecnologiche della seconda rivoluzione industriale*, Bologna: Il Mulino.

Vordemann, Christian, 1994, *Deutschland-Italien, 1949–1961. Die diplomatischen Beziehungen*, Frankfurt am Main: Peter Lang.

6 Reinventing the Rio Tinto Company

Spain, Political Risk and Corporate Strategy Before and After the Second World War

Neil Forbes

Introduction

The intention in this chapter is to analyse the relationship between corporate strategy and political risk in the context of the Spanish mining operations of the British-domiciled Rio Tinto Company between the 1930s and the 1950s. In the first half of the 1930s, the company was forced to try to manage politically motivated strikes by its workforce. But, from 1936, the political risks faced by Rio Tinto then became extreme in nature: the rise of nationalism and Franco's victory in the Spanish Civil War, the impact of the Second World War and the development of economic nationalism under the post-war Francoist dictatorship, imposed a succession of existential threats to the company.

Rio Tinto was confronted with the dilemma of how it could both protect its investments in a potentially hostile environment to the satisfaction of its shareholders and simultaneously contribute to the defence of the values of capitalism and liberal democracy. In one respect, upholding liberal values afforded Rio Tinto some degree of protection from attacks by the Nationalist regime: the company undertook a number of measures in order to demonstrate that it was a responsible employer. These included fair wages and the maintenance of reasonable living standards for its Spanish miners and their dependants.

However, as the international political crisis developed in the course of the 1930s, and the possibility of war in Europe grew ever more likely, British multinational businesses, especially those with a global reach, were expected to play their part in preparing to defend the nation. As a major international mining company, Rio Tinto was an important producer and supplier of several minerals and metals, such as copper, sulphur and pyrites. Although the market for many key commodities was volatile in the interwar years, Britain's imports of copper doubled between 1930 and 1938; vehicle manufacturing, the electrical industries and finally rearmament all created a demand for the metal. Britain consumed, for example, approximately one-half of the output from Northern Rhodesia—a major copper producer—whilst about one-third of the output was bought by Germany.[1]

Although plans for conducting economic warfare in the event of conflict with Germany had been drawn up in Britain from the turn of the 20th century, the strategy was abandoned at the outbreak of war in 1914.[2] Nevertheless, the nature of industrial warfare in the modern age quickly demonstrated the futility of attempting to carry on with 'business as usual'; on the contrary, defeating the enemy depended on being able to mobilise all of society's resources. One of the many lessons of what became the world's first total war was that access to, and control over, global trade in strategic raw materials was for Britain, and also for potential enemy powers, a vital national interest—and one that had to be secured well before the outbreak of any major conflict.

After the Second World War, Sir Auckland Geddes was to recall that it was in his capacity as Chairman of Rio Tinto that, in1928, he was asked by Stanley Baldwin, the Prime Minister, to try to promote commercially the supply of copper and cobalt under British control, on a scale that would be adequate for the needs of defence. Although it could not be publicly acknowledged, there was a growing anxiety that isolationism in the United States might, in the event of war, create great difficulties in the supply of essential metals that were under American control.[3] In 1929, the Board of Trade began to make plans for the requirements in *matériel* in order to be able to fight a future war. Non-ferrous metals such as zinc, lead, tin and copper were deemed to be particularly important.[4] As armament industries geared up for war, the ability to ensure the security of supplies of a vital material such as copper and, in the event of hostilities, the denial of supplies to an enemy, assumed ever more military and strategic significance. As far as the United States was concerned, there was, in one respect at least, an ironical outcome to Baldwin's anxieties: even by 1939 that country's military planners had neglected to consider chemicals used in explosives and propellants as strategically important; plans to procure products such as sulphuric acid—vital for the rearmament effort—had to be devised.[5] The international cartel arrangements, and particularly deals between American and German firms, that had been set up during the interwar years, were aimed at avoiding competition in markets, thereby reducing the risk of producing surplus or excess output. Consequently, with the outbreak of war in Europe, various key industries in the United States were left without the plant capacity, and related up-to-date technological know-how, to produce essential war materials.[6]

Although Franco's government extended material and ideological support to Hitler at the outbreak of war in Europe, the Spanish state did not join the Axis powers in 1939–1940 and remained a non-belligerent throughout the Second World War. As a result, the impact of the war on Rio Tinto was much less damaging than had been feared. Nevertheless, in the immediate post-war years, the Spanish operations were becoming increasingly uneconomical and the company began to consider how it might dispose of most of its investments. In one sense, the company's problems were common to many mining operations around the world. In studying British Columbia, Jeremy Mouat observed that in the decades that followed the end of the 19th century, mining managers sought efficiency gains and cost reductions in ore recovery and production in order to offset the depletion of easily worked deposits.[7] In addition to the question of commercial viability, political issues compounded the problems facing Rio Tinto. Although the company was able to demonstrate a record of social responsibility and had established its political legitimacy, thereby successfully navigating the dangerous waters of reputational risk, the threat of expropriation under the post-war, Francoist dictatorship loomed ever larger.

In a spirited critique of Alfred Chandler's methodology, Leslie Hannah took issue with Chandler's unsubstantiated assertions that, by the beginning of the 20th century, Rio Tinto was so weak that it had permanently lost the opportunity to become a major player in the global copper oligopoly. Instead, Hannah points out, the company is a compelling example of the staying power of an entrenched oligopolist, demonstrating at various points throughout the 20th and 21st centuries that it is a global leader by market capitalisation or sales turnover.[8]

This chapter will analyse how Rio Tinto could conduct business in such challenging conditions and how the experience of coping with extreme political risk impacted upon corporate governance and organisational structures and policies, and decision-making over foreign direct investments. In her commanding history of foreign investments in the United States, Mira Wilkins points to how some multinational enterprises, including Rio Tinto, have invested in and then withdrawn from the US, only to reinvest at a later period.[9] In his study of the fall of Courtaulds—once a world-leading textile manufacturer—Geoffrey Owen comments that there is not one best way for a company to adjust to disruptive change in its external environment, nor is there a single set of characteristics that explain why some firms adjust successfully and others do not.[10] In this sense, survival might depend on a company's entrepreneurial capacity to bring about a sufficient level of innovation in the organisation; this might take the form of mitigating the negative effects of the external environment, producing existing goods and services more efficiently, developing new markets or products or some combination of such behavioural change. Royal Dutch Shell is an example of a company that grew spectacularly in its early history because it was so successful in finding and deploying the right mix of such factors. Similarly, the successful changes and adaptations made by Unilever during the Second World War not only allowed the company to cope with the challenges brought by the war but also to continue on a trajectory of growth after it.[11] The contention advanced here is that Rio Tinto survived and prospered in the years following the Second World War only because, in choosing decisively on a radical change of direction, the company effectively reinvented itself.

Rio Tinto and the Spanish Civil War

There is a certain assumption that British economic and financial interests supported the Nationalist cause in Spain: from the first months of the Civil War, the trading relationship with Nationalist Spain seemed to offer British interests a greater degree of security than the relationship with the Republic.[12] Britain was the largest foreign investor in Spain with assets amounting to some £40 million, or 40 percent of total inward foreign direct investments.[13] British-owned mining interests represented the most significant part of those investments, and the Rio Tinto Company was the largest of all the businesses operating in Spain. In the case of British banks, Tom Buchanan has suggested that the reaction to the Civil War was very largely one of extreme caution. He observes that there was certainly little sympathy for the Republic, and a willing complicity with the policy of the British government in the policy of Non-Intervention. However, Buchanan found no reliable evidence of any conspiracy against the Republic, nor any particular desire to invest in a victory by Franco.[14]

In his important study of Rio Tinto, Charles Harvey reached the conclusion that, while Franco endeavoured not to be drawn too closely into the German economic orbit, the placing of Anglo-Nationalist relations on a more secure basis was important in helping to resist this tendency. Not only was British policy in Spain directed towards the containment of the Civil War but, according to Harvey, the policy was also most successful in preserving Spanish freedom of action in the political and economic spheres. More than this, Harvey claims that,

> In the economic sphere, the sovereignty of British companies in the pyrites trade was preserved, supplies to Britain were not restricted during or after the civil war, and as early as May 1939 Rio Tinto was not penalized for refusing to supply Germany.[15]

This interpretation is, perhaps, a somewhat partial one. To characterise Rio Tinto as a sovereign entity is to suggest that the company not only retained ownership of its investments in Spain but that it also enjoyed a high degree of agency in its relations with the Francoist regime. But, as a recent study by Pierpaolo Barbieri underlines, as a result of early German pressure, the junta passed a decree allowing the generals to seize minerals, industrial production and foreign exchange; the measures targeted the production of raw materials from foreign-owned companies such as Rio Tinto.[16]

As Rowena Olegario and Christopher McKenna have argued, for firms operating within authoritarian, political structures, the licence to operate is granted by the regime and the firm needs to signal that it is at least not in active opposition to the regime's values and objectives.[17] Indeed, as this chapter attempts to argue, the company struggled to retain control over its operations in Spain and its trade with Germany. It required the company to perform an extremely difficult balancing act—compliance with the dictates of the Nationalist regime that was just sufficient to ensure an adequate level of company autonomy.

The increasingly unstable political conditions under the Second Spanish Republic brought industrial unrest to the Rio Tinto mines. Writing in 1933, J. W. Cooper, the British manager of Spanish operations, complained to a colleague in London that 'Things were not what they were in the "good old days" when matters ran smoothly in the Mines'. Relations between the different sections of the workforce were full of friction because, Cooper maintained, of the 'class war which is waged under the Socialist regime'.[18] By 1936, the position of Britain's direct investments in Spain was in fundamental ways analogous to the position of foreign direct investments in Germany in 1932: the foundations of a liberal, capitalist economy were being undermined by ideological challenges from both ends of the political spectrum. The threats included disruption caused by labour disputes and strike action organised and inspired by the political left, or a possible loss of control and autonomy if a nationalist, interventionist regime were to achieve political power; the clamour constantly heard on both the extreme left and right was that foreign economic interests should be nationalised.

Rio Tinto seemed to believe, however, that there was little in its record as an employer that exposed the company to a heightened level of political risk. The question of 'labour' was regularly discussed at Board meetings in London. Mining is an inherently dangerous occupation, and the Board noted the name of every Spanish worker who suffered a fatal accident. At the same time, the company congratulated itself on a remarkable improvement in its record during the preceding years, claiming that a high standard of safety had been reached in comparison to mining companies in the USA. The mines were also employing an estimated 600 men who, though deemed to be surplus to requirements, could not be made redundant under the Spanish government's regulations.[19]

In 1936, Rio Tinto understood that, at the very least, a long period of unrest in Spain lay ahead and expected that foreign firms operating in the country would be the first to suffer: a very large proportion of Spain's industrial production was in the hands of comparatively few foreign companies.[20] In view of this state of affairs, Rio Tinto had suspended the payment of dividends on its Ordinary Shares.[21] By May 1936, Rio Tinto had become so concerned about the deteriorating political conditions in Spain that it decided a new policy was needed to try to prevent the gradual destruction of the capital value of the company's property. This involved taking the lead in setting up an interest group—the Association of

Foreign Businesses in Spain—with the objective of trying to persuade the governments of the various countries represented in the Association to urge the Spanish government to do everything possible to preserve foreign economic interests.[22] In June and July, strikes and stoppages periodically halted production at Rio Tinto's mines. News then reached London of the outbreak on 18 July of a 'Revolution' that brought out on strike the company's entire Spanish workforce. The port of Huelva was handed over to what was described as the 'Insurgents', and the company's employees there returned to work. But the conditions were thought to be so dangerous that all British women and children at the mines and at Huelva were evacuated to Gibraltar on 24 July by the Royal Navy destroyer, HMS Boreas.[23] By 26 August, the Nationalist forces had occupied the mines region without facing any opposition and were proposing that the British staff should return. In London, the Rio Tinto Board authorised the Chairman, Sir Auckland Geddes, to send a telegram to General Queipo de Llano, one of the leading military conspirators and commander of the base at Seville, asking for the utmost clemency to be extended to the company's workers.[24]

From the outset of the Civil War, access to raw materials from Spain provided the Nationalists with an opportunity to secure weapons and war *materiél* from Nazi Germany. With Spain's gold and foreign currency under the control of the Republican government, the Nationalists looked to the trade in ores, pyrites, copper and sulphur as means of compensation for the support received from the Third Reich. At the same time, with the establishment of the Four Year Plan under Göring, as plenipotentiary, Germany had an ever-growing need to import strategic raw materials for its rearmament programmes, but severely limited reserves of foreign currency to pay for such imports.[25] There were even attempts by the Third Reich, in 1937 and 1938, to gain greater control of Spanish raw materials by investing directly in mining and production enterprises. But these attempts were resisted by the Nationalists: Franco's reluctance to be drawn too closely into the German economic orbit allowed existing foreign-owned companies such as Rio Tinto to continue to occupy a preeminent place in the minerals and metals export trade.[26]

To some extent, Franco's policy worked to the benefit of Britain's strategic interests: just as Germany sought to ensure greater security in the supply of raw materials, so it was calculated that the more the Third Reich depended on trade channelled via British multinationals, the more chance Britain had of depriving Germany of such materials in time of war. Engaging in international trade in strategic raw materials during peacetime helped to facilitate rearmament in Nazi Germany. But, in the minds of British policy-makers, imposing constraints or limitations on such trade would have been counter-productive: it would have encouraged Germany during peacetime to seek to establish alternative sources of supply which might then have been more difficult to disrupt during wartime. Yet not only was this policy stance contentious in itself, it created a dilemma for the strategists: even if it proved to be possible to predict with any degree of accuracy the point in the future when war was going to break out, an assessment would have to be made of how far in advance of hostilities any trade in vital raw materials should be stopped.[27]

Moreover, the idea of imposing limitations or, even worse, sanctions on the activities of British companies, thereby rendering those companies less commercially viable, was anathema to the Britain's National Government: it would hardly have helped to bring about the return of a strong economy—increasingly seen as Britain's fourth arm of defence. In addition, the Treasury held firmly to the view that it was vital to maintain a positive trade balance and secure the foreign exchange earnings for the purchase of raw materials upon which Britain depended.[28]

It seems to have been understood by the British government that there would, inevitably, be a price to pay for being allowed to retain the ownership of—if not full control over—British investments in Spain. For the mining companies, this meant that it would become impossible to avoid contributing to the Nationalist war effort. Initially, Rio Tinto attempted to keep above the fray. Rio Tinto's London-based directors made frequent and lengthy visits to Spain in order to inspect, at first hand, the company's mining operations, to determine the condition of its considerable investments, and to open and maintain a dialogue with the new Francoist authorities. Very detailed reports on what was found on the visits were then drawn up and circulated to the Rio Tinto Board. In terms of the impact of the Civil War on the lives and living standards of the local population, the reports bear witness to the terrible consequences of the conflict. By early 1937, an increasing level of destitution amongst the population was noted; a large number of widows and orphans, for example, had become entirely dependent on charity. The company made donations to the charitable efforts that had been initiated to relieve distress and contributed to a stamp tax, levied largely in order to support the provisions of soup kitchens and similar facilities. But further charitable donations were recommended as a matter of 'good policy'.[29]

The Board discussed whether such a financial contribution should be made, via the Huelva Mining Association, to the Nationalist Army. It was decided that 'the Company must closely observe the strictest canons of neutrality'. The proposal was rejected. Instead, the Board authorised the expenditure of one million Pesetas on charitable work and the relief of distress in Nationalist-held areas. This was a sizeable amount of money. Currency exchange rates for both the Republican and Nationalist peseta naturally fluctuated considerably in the course of the war: in September 1937, one pound sterling could purchase 80 Nationalist pesetas, and an average 55 pesetas by June 1938.[30] Some Pts 0.5 million was made available to the manager at the mines to give assistance 'especially to our own people, and with a view to helping as many unemployed and their families as possible to leave the district'. The Board also wanted the manager to apply for permits to import rice and clothing materials for sale in the company's stores. The company's representative in Spain, Captain Charles, was also authorised to draw on a further Pts 0.5 million for the charitable relief of distress in Burgos and Salamanca.[31]

In the course of 1937, the evidence related to living standards was carefully researched. Under-nourishment among the population was evident. The company was aware that its workforce was becoming considerably worse off as the men had to support unemployed or widowed relatives, and were required to contribute one day's earnings each month to a fund for supporting dependants of men on military service.[32] This was one reason why the company did not feel confident that it had a clear picture of the relationship between the workers' earnings and their needs. For although wages had risen by some 20 percent over the pre-war figures, so had the cost of living, and the company had benefitted from instituting six-day rather than five-day working. Nevertheless, the company noted, in April 1938, that men applied to work at the mines from far afield, as 'It is generally recognized that wages and conditions at Rio Tinto compare favourably with those in any other industry in any part of Spain'. Furthermore, with 'two good meals a day' provided to widows and orphans by the soup kitchens that had been established in all the villages in the province of Huelva, the problem of under-nourishment had receded. However, the costs of this relief were borne not just by the company but also by weekly contributions from the wages of the workers. Rio Tinto employed men on a basis of both piece work and day wages; the report concluded that the lower-paid workers had no margin at all over what was required for subsistence. A few months before the outbreak of the Civil War, there were 8,508 men on the company payroll. By April 1938, this had decreased to 6,618 men, with an additional 727 absent on military service (unspecified). An estimated 600 of the company's men had been killed in the fighting.[33]

This policy of charitable giving seems to have continued until the end of the Civil War in 1939: in March of that year, the Board authorised a 'substantial contribution' to the National Fund for Catalan Relief.[34] Nevertheless, as the tide of war turned in Franco's favour, Rio Tinto alone was to supply the Nationalists with goods and services to the value of £2,850,000 by the end of the conflict. Moreover, there was no doubt, according to Harvey, that 'Franco's policies regarding the production and distribution of pyrites and iron ore contributed much to his ultimate victory'.[35] It is difficult to assess precisely which goods and services were brought into the calculation in order to arrive at the total valuation cited by Harvey. But it is more important to consider the impact on the financial health of Rio Tinto of compliance with Franco's coercive policy. As the Nationalist armies began to establish control over the regions of Spain in which Rio Tinto's mines and facilities were located, the effect of the

Civil War on the company's fortunes immediately became clear: pyrites and ores produced by the company were requisitioned by the military authorities.

The pyrites and ores requisitioned by Nationalist Spain were exported to Italy and, in particular, to Germany—Rio Tinto's most important European market apart from the UK market. All of the company's ores destined for Europe (except the UK and Ireland and also Spain and Portugal), were sold under contracts in the name of the European Pyrites Corporation Ltd. (EPC), or its subsidiary, Schwefelkies GmbH. EPC had been incorporated in December 1926, with a shareholding that was divided equally between Rio Tinto and the Frankfurt-based Metallgesellschaft AG.[36]

Rio Tinto took immediate action to try to safeguard its interests. Geddes cabled J. N. Buchanan, the Finance Director, who at that point was in Estoril, Portugal. Geddes asked Buchanan to travel to Burgos in order to press the authorities to re-establish the smooth working of the trade with Germany. Renewed efforts were to be made to persuade the Nationalists to allow the company to conduct its own ore business with Germany. This involved securing buyers before shipment, and also Reichsmark credits equivalent to the full contract value which the company would then place at the disposal of the authorities in exchange for pesetas. Geddes argued that this would allow for a progressive increase in deliveries on the basis of more organised and regular shipments.[37] Rio Tinto was also concerned that by requisitioning the production of copper and, especially of pyrites, that was destined for Germany, the sales organisations of the company and its subsidiaries would be so disrupted that existing, large customers would be neglected with the result that they would resort to sourcing supplies from competing countries and important markets would be lost to Spain.[38]

In November 1936, Head Office in London was informed that no payment had been received from the authorities in Seville for production valued at pesetas 5m. The company's representatives in Spain pressed for payment, but without success. Trade between Nationalist Spain and Germany was channelled via a payments clearing agreement. For Rio Tinto, this posed a grave threat: as the company was compelled to accept payment entirely in pesetas on the basis of a valuations of ore shipments, sterling resources became paralysed. In turn, the company told Metallgesellschaft that it was forced to pay any commissions or remuneration owed to German agents in pesetas rather than sterling as,

> a position has developed of such abnormality that the power to make £ payments lies not with us but with those who regulate directly or indirectly commercial transactions in our mining area.[39]

Given the course of events in Spain, Rio Tinto felt that it had no choice other than to continue to impose this policy on its trading organisation—regarded as 'a large family'. The rise in world copper prices in the second half of the 1930s, driven by demand arising from the rearmament boom, brought no relief. Rio Tinto thought it was preposterous that the rise in copper values did nothing to help their sterling currency trading position as the more valuable the copper in the ore, the more sterling they were forced to deliver to the Franco government.[40]

In the course of 1937 and 1938, Rio Tinto enlisted the support of the British government in attempts to recover payment for its requisitioned products. In February 1937, the company decided to prepare a claim against the German government for the equivalent tonnage of fine copper contained in the precipitate that had been requisitioned up to that point. A similar claim was prepared against the Italian government. Geddes told the Rio Tinto Board that representations were being made through diplomatic channels to both the German and Italian governments, and to General Franco.[41] As McKenna and Olegario have argued, the reputational element may be of key importance when looking at the how markets and hierarchies function.[42] Holding various high, political offices during the First World War, and sitting in the British Cabinet in 1919–1920 as President of the Board of Trade, few businessmen in the interwar years disposed of more 'reputational capital' than Geddes. This afforded the company the best possible opportunity to engage in corporate political activity—strategies that seek to use personal connections, networks and formal lobbying to advance a firm's interests. In appointing Geddes, the company was clearly seeking to augment its organisational capabilities. In this respect, Rio Tinto was, of course, far from unique: major British-based companies frequently looked to appoint to their boards former high-ranking figures from the world of politics, the military or the civil service. However, as Andrew Perchard has observed, firms supplying strategic raw materials may well have been profoundly affected by their relationship with the state.[43] The history of Rio Tinto in the years before and after the Second World War certainly supports such an interpretation of business-government relations.

There is a tendency in some of the scholarship on the subject of corporate political activity to claim that the non-market environment has, in the contemporary era, become far more complex and multidimensional than it was in the past.[44] But the history of multinational enterprise in the interwar years would suggest that complexity is hardly a recent phenomenon. In the context of an international political environment that was rapidly deteriorating, Rio Tinto's political activity—however notable for its powers of persuasion with government—stood a vanishingly small chance of achieving any success. Rio Tinto would certainly never have to worry that, as a result of its corporate political activity, it would become locked into a non-market, path dependency which would, thereby, render the company less flexible and less focussed on alternative markets.[45]

For the démarche was completely ineffective. Indeed, by the time the British Foreign Office received a reply from the German government, in

May 1937, a further 500,000 tonnes of pyrites had been requisitioned, and the company asked the British government to present a fresh protest to Germany.[46] In early 1938, Rio Tinto wanted the Foreign Office to make similar protests to the Spanish authorities, and to draw attention to the 'flagrant discrimination' against the company as a result of the continuing requisitions of pyrites for Germany and Italy.[47]

There is no doubt that the impact of the Spanish Civil War on Rio Tinto was severe. In presenting the Annual Report and Accounts in April 1938, Geddes commented that the accounts told the story of the year with painful clarity. The total of sterling and goods of sterling value delivered by order of General Franco's government since the outbreak of the war, and for which the company had been required to accept pesetas or the promise of pesetas, was in excess of £1.75m. The inescapable, but nonetheless distressing, conclusion reached by the chairman was that 'If it were not for its investments outside Spain, the Company would have had great difficulty in standing this financial strain'.[48] Those investments were principally the company's large shareholdings in the South African-controlled Rhokana Corporation, with its copper mining firms operating in the altogether more benign political conditions of the British colony of Northern Rhodesia. Copper production had expanded considerably in Northern Rhodesia, with the result that, by the mid-1930s, the country had become one of the most important producers of the metal in the world. Nearly all the concentrates were smelted locally, and the output was of an exceptionally pure quality.[49]

At the same time, Geddes was ebullient in trying to downplay the political risk facing the company in Spain. He castigated those who had pictured the Board as violent Fascists, and reiterated that the company's stance was one of neutrality. Rather than having to contend with the threat of expropriation, Geddes maintained that the company's legal and moral position in Spain was strong, based on the legitimate acquisition of its assets, its exemplary record as an employer and Spain's need for its mining expertise. Finally, Geddes believed that a Franco victory would lead to a 'phalango-traditionalist' political system that would differ importantly from other totalitarian forms of government.[50] Given that Spain did not enter the Second World War alongside the other dictatorships, this assessment proved to be accurate. But, the idea that Franco's regime was in any way distinct from totalitarianism would have been risible to many who lived in Spain after 1939.

In the calendar year 1938, some 360,000 tonnes of ore mined by Rio Tinto was delivered to Germany and over 18,000 tonnes of ore was delivered to Italy. Payment was made in pesetas, which the company calculated would have provided a notional profit of £64,753. In May 1939, as Harvey stated, Rio Tinto refused to allow any further supplies to be delivered to Germany. However, in the first five months of that year, approximately 100,000 tonnes had already been supplied and Italy had received over 82,000 tonnes. The company records reported this trade as a net loss.[51]

It seems likely that the reason the company insisted in 1939 that supplies to Germany should cease had as much, if not more, to do with the problems over payment than it did with any issue over the coming of war. In May 1938, representatives of Rio Tinto and Metallgesellschaft met in London to negotiate an extension to the EPC agreement, which was due to expire at the end of the year. At that stage, Rio Tinto made it very clear that the company was most anxious that the agreement should continue; the response of Metallgesellschaft was equally enthusiastic.[52]

Rio Tinto and the Second World War

At the outbreak of Second World War in September 1939, Rio Tinto composed a secret memorandum for the Ministry of Economic Warfare—the government department that had operated covertly in peacetime but was now publicly acknowledged—on Germany's situation in respect of pyrites. The document offers an opportunity to assess what British strategic policy and Rio Tinto's corporate strategy had achieved in the course of the Spanish Civil War and the growing international crisis of the late 1930s. Germany was not only the greatest consumer in Europe of pyrites (consuming some 2 million tonnes per annum) but it was well equipped in the capacity for treating the residues from pyrites: there were copper extraction plants in several locations and also plants for the conversion of pyrites iron residues into iron ore suitable for blast furnaces. The level of stocks at the consumer works was believed, in the case of those belonging to IG Farben, to be equivalent to a supply over a period of 10 months.

Consequently, in respect of industrial processes that depended on utilising these raw materials, German war production hardly faced a position of severe shortages. In this context, any analysis that emphasises an 'early' stoppage of Rio Tinto's pyrites trade with Germany becomes highly questionable: it is rather more pertinent to consider whether the company should have continued to supply Germany with such vital raw materials until as late as May 1939. The issue for the Ministry was to consider where the enemy would turn for alternative supplies and what, if anything, could be done to disrupt the movement of such supplies. In the last year of peace, Germany had consumed almost one million tonnes of pyrites from Spain alone. With the loss of this trade, Germany was compelled to turn to Norway and Sweden; shipments from their mines had reached a peak in 1937 of one million tonnes, though this had been achieved by drawing heavily on stocks in order to take advantage of the artificial shortages created by the Spanish Civil War.[53] There was some hope, in 1939, that Britain could do something to forestall German attempts to gain control of Norwegian production; the possibility of preventing Swedish production from going to Germany was, however, considered to be so remote that the policy was regarded as a lost cause.

In the first months of the war, Rio Tinto nervously defended its record of dealings with the Third Reich. At the AGM in May 1940, the company announced that no copper had been exported during the year as it was all required in Spain; reports of shipments of some 35,000 tonnes of copper per month to Germany were, the Board declared, falsehoods presumably designed to suggest that the loss of decency on the part of the directors was such that they had been prepared to help the mortal enemy of the nation.[54]

There were also immediate concerns over what the coming of the Second World War would mean for the Spanish mining industry and, consequently, the company's considerable investments in that country. It was feared that the loss of the German market coupled with the assumed loss of the company's annual pyrites shipments, of up to 400,000 tonnes, to the USA, would create great difficulties for the mines in Spain. Nevertheless, both Britain's policy of Non-Intervention and Rio Tinto's corporate strategy in managing the crisis posed by the Spanish Civil War played a part in enabling Britain to survive the Nazi onslaught at the beginning of the Second World War. Once it became clear that Franco would not join forces with Hitler and that Spain would not be incorporated in, or that any of the company's production would be exported to, Nazi-dominated Europe, Rio Tinto maintained a substantial UK staffing in the country. The irony is that, by the end of the war, with Franco remaining in power as the sole surviving fascist dictator, the company began to doubt whether it had a future in Spain and began to prepare to withdraw from the country.

What is notable is that, even in the midst of the war, Rio Tinto's senior management began to form the view that the most profitable course of action in terms of the interests of the company's shareholders would be to dispose of the Spanish mines if a suitable offer could be secured. The development which triggered this train of thought was a projected new mining law in Spain which made provision for the expropriation of assets without mentioning compensation. The future looked bleak. In terms of costs, the mines were run down and new investment would be required at the same time as Spanish costs were rising and the copper content of the ore was declining. After the war, there would also be the problem of paying for scarce shipping capacity to transport pyrites across the Atlantic to supply the USA. As for prices, the company didn't believe that copper and sulphur would be produced competitively, and the German market for pyrites would take a long time to recover. Furthermore, even if any profits were made, Rio Tinto feared that a large proportion would be swallowed up by taxes both in the UK and in Spain.[55]

Rio Tinto and the Post-War Exit From Spain

By the end of the war, the company had entered into discussions with a Spanish banking group that was interested in purchasing the assets. Inventories were made available and tours arranged to inspect the mines. Rio

Tinto took particular note of what it probably regarded as an irresistible rise of nationalistic sentiment—that the ownership of the mines should be in Spanish hands. The public face of the company was that the Board had every sympathy with such an aspiration. This stance was conveyed to Captain Charles in Spain, along with the minimum terms and conditions that the company was prepared to accept for any sale, in order to protect shareholders' interests. In what appeared to be an extraordinary turn-around, the company declared that it was not interested in considering a proposition to sell shares in Rio Tinto as its interests outside Spain were so large that such an arrangement would hardly be possible. Such assertions of strength should, perhaps, be viewed as predictable tactics on the part of the company at the outset of negotiations. Nevertheless, in spite of the travails imposed by the Spanish Civil War and the Second World War, by 1945 Rio Tinto clearly felt sufficiently confident about its prospects for growth outside Spain to construct a complete exit strategy from the country.[56]

For Geddes, a point had been reached in the life of the company which called for a vital decision. He saw three possible courses: first, to continue in Spain and be taxed and hampered by the Spanish government; secondly, to sell for whatever sum in sterling they could get, clear out of the business and proceed laboriously to wind up the company; thirdly, to adapt to the possibilities available and go forward vigorously to new developments and renewed prosperity. Hardly surprisingly, Geddes dismissed the first two courses of action as a choice between, respectively, a slow and painful death and the sudden death of the company.[57]

The negotiations for the sale dragged on into the early-1950s. Rio Tinto was careful, however, to try to keep developments from becoming public knowledge: in March 1952 the company flatly denied reports that the Spanish government was proposing to re-purchase the mines.[58] But there was a palpable sense that a turning point for the global pyrites industry had been reached. An analysis by the *Economist* pointed out that the Spanish pyrites industry had been in decline since 1936 as a result partly of the extension of mining in other countries, of the cheapness of US sulphur and of the extraction of sulphur from other sources. The process of bringing plant and equipment up to modern standards had been held up by the Spanish government, particularly by delays in issuing import licences for machinery—much of it from Britain. In terms of labour, it was difficult both to attract new miners or to get back those lost in the 1930s. The result was that total exports of pyrites for all producers in Spain reached a total of 1.2–1.3 million tonnes in 1950, compared to an average 2.65 million tonnes in the late 1920s. For the Rio Tinto mines, 650,000 tonnes was produced in 1950, compared to 1.2 million tonnes in 1937.[59]

But, if Rio Tinto had come to a decision that its Spanish operations were no longer commercially viable, it was political factors that were to dictate the terms and conditions under which the company disposed of its assets. By the early 1950s, a political climate inimical to the interests of multinational mining enterprise had begun to develop in some parts of the world: nations endowed with natural resources were becoming more and more critical of foreign-owned companies in the extractive industries. As Espen Storli has commented, the nationalisation drive in Bolivia that swept up, in 1952, a large proportion of that country's tin mining industry heralded what was to come.[60] From the outset of 1954, Rio Tinto was keen to push on with negotiations as quickly as possible as the political conditions were deteriorating. In the words of Lord Bessborough, the Chairman who had succeeded Geddes in 1947, the company 'was fully conscious that the present anti-British attitude of the Spanish Government may result in an unpropitious atmosphere'. If anything, this understated the position: Franco had apparently referred to Rio Tinto as the 'economic Gibraltar'. The company turned, once again, to the British government for advice on how Anglo-Spanish relations might be improved. Like Geddes, Bessborough was well connected politically: as a former Member of Parliament and, in the 1930s, Governor General of Canada, the new Chairman was in a position to mobilise political support yet, at the same time, be aware that diplomatic action might yield few, if any, positive results. Following a conversation between Bessborough and Sir Anthony Eden, the Foreign Secretary, the company decided that it would be better to get out of Spain on the most favourable terms that it could secure rather than face a forced sale in a hostile environment.[61] There can be no doubt that this proposed course of action did not arise as a result of any lack of support by the British government: Anthony Eden had, himself, served as a director on the Rio Tinto Board when he had been in opposition from 1945.[62]

By July, the Board was forced to confirm rumours that Spanish interests had made an approach with a view to acquiring a majority shareholding in the mines; the chance that the company could liquefy its Spanish interests led to an instant 12 percent jump in prices of the ordinary shares.[63] Under the terms of the sale that was finally agreed later in 1954, a new company was set up. Rio Tinto effectively received £8 million in cash by selling two-thirds of its assets to a majority shareholding group headed by Banco de Santander; Rio Tinto retained the remaining one-third shareholding, and maintained technical services in Spain and commercial services in London. As the Board valued its assets in Spain to be £20 million and claimed that its properties were 'one of the major mining enterprises of the world', it would seem that the company was prepared to make a considerable sacrifice in order to withdraw very largely from the country.[64]

Conclusion

The argument advanced in this brief study is that as a result of the Second World War and its legacy in Spain—the continuation of Franco's dictatorship—Rio Tinto underwent a period of change that transformed the company. After the war, the company committed itself to fulfilling the aim set out by Geddes of withdrawing from Spain. The intractable circumstances in which the company found itself convinced the Board that Rio Tinto would be trapped in a downward spiral unless radical action was taken to bring in fundamental, organisational change. In 1948, Lord Bessborough announced the reorganisation of the Board of directors. This involved the retirement of long-serving directors; whether the emotional wrench of withdrawing from the historic heartlands and the critical change of direction proved to be too much for them or whether the company believed that it was an appropriate time to dispense with their services is unclear. But it is certainly the case that Rio Tinto was looking to bring in directors with a range of new and relevant business experience.[65]

By 1954, when Rio Tinto completed the sale and transfer of two-thirds of its Spanish assets, the company had developed interests in other countries that, it was hoped, would more than compensate for the loss of its Spanish mines. There was no capital distribution to Rio Tinto's long-suffering shareholders following the disposal of the Spanish mines. Instead, the intention was to retain the proceeds to finance exploration—prospecting for deposits, particularly of uranium. Offices had already been established in Darwin as a base for setting up an operation to explore for uranium in Australia. Whilst the investments in the Rhodesian copper companies had enabled the company to survive in the 1930s and 1940s, and this block of shareholding remained at the core of Rio Tinto's business, the way was now open for the company to attempt to expand and diversify, not just in Australia and in various parts of Africa but also in Canada. At the beginning of 1955, a consortium led by Rio Tinto, which included the London Rothschilds, made what was thought to be the largest single investment of British capital in any Canadian mining enterprise. This was the Algom mines group in Northern Ontario, and the expectation was that the new company would become one of the world's largest uranium producers.[66]

The story of Rio Tinto from the period of the Spanish Civil War to the mid-1950s points to one way to conceptualise the role of multinational enterprise. In the context of an international political economy experiencing the most extreme conditions, Rio Tinto provides an example of a company that was able to operate in a multi-governmental way, commanding a whole range of resources in attempting to ensure long-term survival. Not least among those resources was the company's considerable social and political capital, exemplified by the reputation and status of the leading executives and their readiness to exploit their close connections to the British government. However, given the context of the international crisis that led to the Second World War, and the ideological complexion of Spain in the post-war years, the British government could do little practically to support Rio Tinto. But, far from suffering a decline, the company's response to the challenges of the war and post-war years was to reinvent itself, and it has since grown to become a leading mining enterprise on a global scale.

Notes

1 Lawrence J. Butler, *Copper Empire: Mining and the Colonial State in Northern Rhodesia, c.1930–1964* (Basingstoke: Palgrave Macmillan, 2007), 21.
2 Nicholas A. Lambert, *Planning Armageddon: British Economic Warfare and the First World War* (Cambridge, MA: Harvard University Press, 2012), 499.
3 Sir Auckland Geddes, *The Forging of a Family: A Family Story Studied in Its Genetical, Cultural, and Spiritual Aspects, and a Testament of Personal Belief Founded Thereon* (London: Faber & Faber, 1952), 336–337.
4 Simon Ball, 'The German Octopus: The British Metal Corporation and the Next War 1914–1939', *Enterprise & Society*, 5, no. 3 (2004), 478.
5 Paul A.C. Koistinen, *Planning War, Pursuing Peace: The Political Economy of American Warfare, 1920–1939* (Lawrence: University Press of Kansas, 1998), 178.
6 Wyatt Wells, *Antitrust and the Formation of the Postwar World* (New York: Columbia University Press, 2002), 58.
7 Jeremy Mouat, *Roaring Days: Rossland's Mines and the History of British Columbia* (Vancouver: University of British Columbia Press, 1995), 151.
8 Leslie Hannah, 'Strategic Games, Scale, and Efficiency, or "Chandler Goes to Hollywood"', in *Business in Britain in the Twentieth Century*, eds. Richard Coopey and Peter Lyth (Oxford: Oxford University Press, 2009), 19–21.
9 Mira Wilkins, *The History of Foreign Investments in the United States, 1914–1945* (Cambridge, MA: Harvard University Press, 2004), 602.
10 Geoffrey Owen, *The Rise and Fall of Great Companies: Courtaulds and the Reshaping of the Man-Made Fibres Industry* (Oxford: Oxford University Press, 2010), 9.
11 Joost Jonker and Jan Luiten van Zanden, *From Challenger to Joint Industry Leader, 1890–1939: A History of Royal Dutch Shell* (Oxford: Oxford University Press, 2007), 495; Ben Wubs, *Unilever between Reich and Empire: International Business and National War Interests* (Abingdon: Routledge, 2008), 177–179.
12 Christian Leitz, *Economic Relations Between Nazi Germany and Franco's Spain: 1936–1945* (Oxford: Clarendon Press, 1996), 72.
13 Enrique Moradiellos, 'The Origins of British Non-Intervention in the Spanish Civil War: Anglo-Spanish Relations in Early 1936', *European History Quarterly*, 21 (1991), 343–344.
14 Tom Buchanan, 'The Republic Besieged? British Banks and the Spanish Civil War, 1936–39', in *Crisis and Renewal in Twentieth Century Banking: Exploring the History and Archives of Banking at Times of Political and Social Stress*, eds. Edwin Green, John Lampe and Franjo Stiblar (Aldershot: Ashgate, 2004), 100.
15 Charles E. Harvey, *The Rio Tinto Company: An Economic History of a Leading International Mining Concern 1873–1954* (Penzance: Alison Hodge, 1981), 284–285. See, also, Charles E. Harvey, 'Politics and Pyrites During the Spanish Civil War', *Economic History Review* 31, no. 1 (1978): 89–104.
16 Pierpaolo Barbieri, *Hitler's Shadow Empire: Nazi Economics and the Spanish Civil War* (Cambridge, MA: Harvard University Press, 2015), 142.
17 Rowena Olegario and Christopher McKenna, 'Introduction: Corporate Reputation in Historical Perspective', *Business History Review*, 87, no. 4 (Winter 2013): 649.
18 By courtesy of Rio Tinto and the London Metropolitan Archives (hereafter LMA), CAR 9, letter, 24 August 1933, Cooper to Beecher.
19 LMA 4543/01/02/01/016, Board minutes of 8 June and 13 July 1936.
20 LMA, SSR 2272 10/0/1/13, letter, 13 May 1936, Company Secretary to FR Phillips, Central Mining & Investment Corp. Ltd.

21 LMA 4543/01/07/01/001, Operating Committee Minutes, 23 April 1936.
22 LMA 4543/01/02/0 SSR/16, Board Meetings Minutes Book, 11 May 1936.
23 Ibid., 10 August 1936.
24 Ibid., 14 September 1936.
25 Adam Tooze, *The Wages of Destruction: The Making and the Breaking of the Nazi Economy* (London: Penguin Books, 2006), 223–230.
26 Glyn A. Stone, *Spain, Portugal and the Great Powers, 1931–1941* (Basingstoke: Palgrave Macmillan, 2005), p. 36.
27 Neil Forbes, 'The Foreign Office, Foreign Policy and Commerce: Anglo-German Relations in the 1930s', in *The Foreign Office, Commerce and British Foreign Policy in the Twentieth Century*, eds. John Fisher, Effie G. H. Pedaliu and Richard Smith (London: Palgrave Macmillan, 2016), 201.
28 Joe Maiolo, *Cry Havoc: The Arms Race and the Second World War, 1931–1941* (London: John Murray, 2010), 144.
29 LMA, RTC 118, Report of Visit, 22–31 January 1937, by W.G. Gray.
30 Julio Ponce Alberca, *Gibraltar and the Spanish Civil War, 1936–39: Local, National and International Perspectives* (London: Bloomsbury Publishing, 2015), 98.
31 LMA 4543/01/02/01/016 (formerly SSR/16), Board Meetings Minutes Book, 8 March 1937.
32 LMA, RTC 118, Report of Visit, 20 October to 6 November 1937, by W.G. Gray.
33 Ibid., Report of Visit, April 1938, by Preston & Gray.
34 Ibid., 19 March 1939.
35 Harvey, *Rio Tinto*, 286.
36 LMA, RTC 7 10-B-07, Memo, dated 8 January 1935.
37 LMA, RTC 118 100-A-34, telegram, 23 September 1936, Geddes (London) to Buchanan (Estoril).
38 Ibid., translation of letter, 29 September 1936, Jose Sanchez Mora (Rio Tinto) to the President, Official Chamber of Commerce, Industry and Navigation, Huelva.
39 LMA, RTC 95 80-A-13, letter, 22 December 1936, Beecher (Company Secretary) to Metallgesellschaft (Frankfurt).
40 Ibid., letter, 12 March 1937, Beecher (Company Secretary) to Metallgesellschaft (Frankfurt).
41 LMA 4543/01/02/0 SSR/16, Board Meetings Minutes Book, 8 February 1937.
42 Christopher McKenna and Rowena Olegario, 'Corporate Reputation and Regulation in Historical Perspective', in *The Oxford Handbook of Corporate Reputation*, eds. Michael L. Barnett and Timothy G. Pollock (Oxford: Oxford University Press, 2014), 268.
43 Andrew Perchard, *Aluminuimville: Government, Global Business and the Scottish Highlands* (Lancaster: Crucible Books, 2012), 80.
44 Thomas C. Lawton, Jonathan P. Doh and Tazeeb Rajwani, eds., *Aligning for Advantage: Competitive Strategies for the Political and Social Arenas* (Oxford: Oxford University Press, 2014), 9.
45 See, for example, the discussion in Jan Siedentopp and Albrecht Söllner, 'Path Dependence Through Corporate Political Activity', in *The Hidden Dynamics of Path Dependence: Institutions and Organizations*, eds. George Schreygögg and Jörg Sydow (Basingstoke: Palgrave Macmillan, 2010), 72–73.
46 LMA, 4543/01/07/01/001, Minutes of the Operating Committee, 27 May 1937.
47 LMA, 4543/01/02/0 SSR/16, Board Meetings Minutes Book, 14 February 1938.
48 LMA, RTC 78 30-C-41, Report & Accounts, 29 April 1938.
49 Butler, *Copper Empire*, p. 76; Imperial Institute, Mineral Resources Department, *The Mineral Position of the British Empire* (London: Imperial Institute, 1937), 113–114.
50 LMA, RTC 78 30-C-41, Report & Accounts, 29 April 1938.

51 LMA, CAR 170 Parts I & II, 'RTC Profit on Sales of Produce', 1938 and 1939.
52 LMA, RTC 95 80-A-13, note of discussion, 24 May 1938.
53 LMA, CAR 7, 'Secret and Confidential for Ministry of Economic Warfare—Situation of Germany September 1939 in respect of Pyrites'.
54 *Economist*, 11 May 1940, p. 879, Issue 5046.
55 LMA, RTC 134, 'Note for Chairman—Confidential', 18 November 1943.
56 Ibid., Company Secretary to Charles, 19 July 1945.
57 Ibid., Geddes memo to Directors, 'The Rio Tinto Company', 2 December 1945, Pitlochry.
58 *Financial Times*, 12 March 1952, p. 5.
59 *Economist*, 7 July 1951, p. 48.
60 Espen Storli, 'The Birth of the World's Largest Tin Merchant: Philipp Brothers, Bolivian Tin and American Stockpiles', in *Tin and Global Capitalism: A History of the Devil's Metal, 1850–2000*, eds. Mats Ingulstad, Andrew Perchard, and Espen Storli (Abingdon: Routledge, 2015), 202–203.
61 LMA, RTC 134., Bessborough, secret memo, 'Rio Tinto', 4 January 1954; Notes, 22 and 26 January 1954.
62 *Financial Time*, 13 June 1945.
63 Ibid., 1 July 1954, p. 1, Lex column.
64 LMA, RTC 134, Summary of Mines' Activities, 7 January 1954.
65 *Economist*, 29 May 1948, p. 907, Issue 5466.
66 Ibid., 12 February 1955, p. 560, Issue 5816.

Bibliography

Alberca, Julio Ponce. *Gibraltar and the Spanish Civil War, 1936–39: Local, National and International Perspectives*. London: Bloomsbury Publishing, 2015.

Anglo-German Relations in the 1930s'. In *The Foreign Office, Commerce and British Foreign Policy in the Twentieth Century*, edited by John Fisher, Effie G. H. Pedaliu and Richard Smith, 189–209. London: Palgrave Macmillan, 2016.

Ball, Simon. 'The German Octopus: The British Metal Corporation and the Next War 1914–1939'. *Enterprise & Society*, 5, no. 3 (2004): 451–489.

Barbieri, Pierpaolo. *Hitler's Shadow Empire: Nazi Economics and the Spanish Civil War*. Cambridge, MA: Harvard University Press, 2015.

Buchanan, Tom. 'The Republic Besieged? British Banks and the Spanish Civil War, 1936–39'. In *Crisis and Renewal in Twentieth Century Banking: Exploring the History and Archives of Banking at Times of Political and Social Stress*, edited by Edwin Green, John Lampe and Franjo Stiblar, 87–103. Aldershot: Ashgate, 2004.

Butler, Lawrence J. *Copper Empire: Mining and the Colonial State in Northern Rhodesia, c.1930–1964*. Basingstoke: Palgrave Macmillan, 2007.

Forbes, Neil. 'The Foreign Office, Foreign Policy and Commerce: Geddes, Sir Auckland. *The Forging of a Family: A Family Story Studied in Its Genetical, Cultural, and Spiritual Aspects, and a Testament of Personal Belief Founded Thereon*. London: Faber & Faber, 1952.

Hannah, Leslie. 'Strategic Games, Scale, and Efficiency, or "Chandler Goes to Hollywood"'. In *Business in Britain in the Twentieth Century*, edited by Richard Coopey and Peter Lyth, 15–47. Oxford: Oxford University Press, 2009.

Harvey, Charles E. 'Politics and Pyrites During the Spanish Civil War'. *Economic History Review* 31, no. 1 (1978): 89–104.

Harvey, Charles E. *The Rio Tinto Company: An Economic History of a Leading International Mining Concern 1873–1954*. Penzance: Alison Hodge, 1981.

Jonker, Joost and Jan Luiten van Zanden. *From Challenger to Joint Industry Leader, 1890–1939: A History of Royal Dutch Shell*. Oxford: Oxford University Press, 2007.

Koistinen, Paul A. C. *Planning War, Pursuing Peace: The Political Economy of American Warfare, 1920–1939*. Lawrence: University Press of Kansas, 1998.

Lambert, Nicholas A. *Planning Armageddon: British Economic Warfare and the First World War*. Cambridge, MA: Harvard University Press, 2012.

Lawton, Thomas C., Jonathan P. Doh and Tazeeb Rajwani, eds. *Aligning for Advantage: Competitive Strategies for the Political and Social Arenas*. Oxford: Oxford University Press, 2014.

Leitz, Christian. *Economic Relations Between Nazi Germany and Franco's Spain: 1936–1945*. Oxford: Clarendon Press, 1996.

Maiolo, Joe. *Cry Havoc: The Arms Race and the Second World War, 1931–1941*. London: John Murray, 2010.

McKenna, Christopher and Rowena Olegario. 'Corporate Reputation and Regulation in Historical Perspective'. In *The Oxford Handbook of Corporate Reputation*, edited by Michael L. Barnett and Timothy G. Pollock, 260–277. Oxford: Oxford University Press, 2014.

Moradiellos, Enrique. 'The Origins of British Non-Intervention in the Spanish Civil War: Anglo-Spanish Relations in Early 1936'. *European History Quarterly*, 21 (1991): 339–364.

Mouat, Jeremy. *Roaring Days: Rossland's Mines and the History of British Columbia*. Vancouver: University of British Columbia Press, 1995.

Olegario, Rowena and Christopher McKenna. 'Introduction: Corporate Reputation in Historical Perspective'. *Business History Review*, 87, no. 4 (Winter 2013): 643–654.

Owen, Geoffrey. *The Rise and Fall of Great Companies: Courtaulds and the Reshaping of the Man-Made Fibres Industry*. Oxford: Oxford University Press, 2010.

Perchard, Andrew. *Aluminuimville: Government, Global Business and the Scottish Highlands*. Lancaster: Crucible Books, 2012.

Siedentopp, Jan and Albrecht Söllner, 'Path Dependence Through Corporate Political Activity'. In *The Hidden Dynamics of Path Dependence: Institutions and Organizations*, edited by George Schreygögg and Jörg Sydow, 71–93. Basingstoke: Palgrave Macmillan, 2010.

Stone, Glyn A. *Spain, Portugal and the Great Powers, 1931–1941*. Basingstoke: Palgrave Macmillan, 2005.

Storli, Espen, 'The Birth of the World's Largest Tin Merchant: Philipp Brothers, Bolivian Tin and American stockpiles'. In *Tin and Global Capitalism: A History of the Devil's Metal, 1850–2000*, edited by Mats Ingulstad, Andrew Perchard, and Espen Storli, 202–220. Abingdon: Routledge, 2015.

Tooze, Adam. *The Wages of Destruction: The Making and the Breaking of the Nazi Economy*. London: Penguin Books, 2006.

Wells, Wyatt. *Antitrust and the Formation of the Postwar World*. New York: Columbia University Press, 2002.

Wilkins, Mira. *The History of Foreign Investments in the United States, 1914–1945*. Cambridge, MA: Harvard University Press, 2004.

Wubs, Ben. *Unilever between Reich and Empire: International Business and National War Interests*. Abingdon: Routledge, 2008.

7 War and Industry Dynamics

The Case of the Industrial Gases Industry After 1940

Ray Stokes and Ralf Banken

Introduction

'Industry' is a concept that is widely viewed as self-explanatory and unambiguous. But in fact the boundaries delineating an industry are as vaguely defined as they are protean, and the firms that comprise them often have interests and activities in more than one industry, interests and activities that can also change over time.[1] This blurriness does not mean that industries do not exist—they most certainly do: as loci of competition among firms;[2] in the heads of actors in firms operating within a self-defined industry; in the form of trade associations; and in statistics compiled by governments and other organisations. The key points are these, however: that they are constructed in different ways by different people and organisations; and that these constructions change over time. Agency and history matter.

But how are the boundaries that define an industry, however vaguely, established, and how does the definition of a particular industry shift over time? Many factors can play a role, including but not limited to markets, international trade conditions, management techniques and personnel, technological development and economic cycles. The constellation of shaping factors acting over a given time frame often results in slow, incremental changes that eventually redefine an industry. And this is true even in regard to technological development: the frequency of fundamentally 'disruptive technologies' even in the electronic components industry during the period after 1945, for instance,[3] is much rarer than scholars such as Clayton Christenson would have us think.[4] But one particular (mercifully relatively rare) shaping factor, war, can have profound effects on industry dynamics leading to abrupt changes in the composition and structure of the industry while also precipitating longer-term alterations as well.[5]

This chapter uses the case of the development of the industrial gases industry during the rearmament period just before, and during, the Second World War to explore some of the ways in which these dynamics can unfold and to draw some general conclusions from that. We start in section two with an overview of the emergence, initial definition and incremental redefinition of the industrial gases industry through 1940, not least because the industry is much less widely known than many others, but also in order to set the scene for wartime developments. These are examined in section three and resulted in sudden and fundamental changes to the industry in the short term. In section four, we then consider the longer-term, more incremental alterations to the industry that resulted from the war, and in section five we draw some broader conclusions about the implications of this case.

Emergence, Initial Definition and Redefinition of the Industrial Gases Industry Between the Late 19th Century and 1940

Industrial gases, also known as technical gases, comprise purified air gases (i.e. nitrogen, oxygen, argon, xenon etc.) as well as other gases (e.g. carbon dioxide, helium, acetylene, hydrogen etc.) that play a key role in all industrial processes and are also used in a variety of service industries.[6] The industrial gases industry as we know it today, however, is very different from that which emerged in the last decades of the 19th century in the context of the Second Industrial Revolution.[7] Indeed, at the beginning, there were three completely separate industrial gases industries involving entirely different firms, products and markets. The first of these to come into existence was the carbon dioxide industry, with initial markets primarily in the food and drink industry and the hospitality trade. A by-product of distilling and other fermentation processes, carbon dioxide thus involved quite simple technologies of production and also—because the gas is inert and poses no danger of explosion or fire—distribution. The second industrial gases industry that emerged in the late 19th century involved production of acetylene gas from calcium carbide, which in turn was manufactured using energy-intensive processes. Highly flammable and explosive, acetylene in contrast to carbon dioxide required development of special handling and distribution technologies. It was used initially primarily as a source of artificial lighting, competing effectively at first with alternative sources such as kerosene and electricity.

The third industrial gases industry of the late 19th century is the one most scholars would identify as the most important ancestor of the modern industrial gases industry. Oxygen was produced commercially in relatively pure form (95 percent) in Britain in 1886 by Brins Oxygen Company, which eventually became British Oxygen Company, or BOC.[8] In contrast to carbon dioxide and acetylene, purified oxygen was produced using a science-based chemical process. It was remarkable, too, because, unlike the other two gases, there was only a very limited market for oxygen at first: although attempts were made to develop various other applications, the only real market initially was for limelight for stage lighting. It is astonishing in this context that engineer-scientists worked feverishly on discovering alternative means of producing the gas, with Carl Linde's 1895 patent on liquefaction of air (a physical rather than chemical process) an important step towards this.[9] Levels of purity for oxygen produced by this process were, however, significantly lower than those achieved in the chemical process pioneered by Brins, which meant that it posed no challenge at all at first even for the limited stage-lighting market. In other words, this very much represented a solution in search of a problem.

But the problem purified oxygen would solve was not long in coming. Development of oxyacetylene welding technology in the very last years of the 19th century created a vibrant new market not only for purified oxygen, but also for acetylene, which had seen its foothold in artificial lighting eroded and then eliminated by electric lighting. In the meantime, Linde and French inventor Georges Claude developed rectification technologies that allowed for dramatic improvements in air separation, enabling purity levels for oxygen to exceed 99 percent. What is more, purified nitrogen could now be produced (although the market for this initially was very small), as well as, in addition, purified argon, neon and other gases that constitute a fraction of the composition of air in the atmosphere. All of this allowed the air gases industry to service new and growing markets. But welding was by far the most important of them, which would remain the case into the 1930s at least. And the need for both oxygen and acetylene for this burgeoning market led to an amalgamation of two of the initial three industrial gases industries by the outbreak of the First World War.

By that time, too, virtually all of the major companies that would dominate the industrial gases industry internationally for much of the rest of the 20th century had been established, each with dominance in a particular market: BOC in Britain and the British Empire; Linde in Germany; Air Liquide in France and the French Empire; AGA in Scandinavia (and also in much of Latin America); what eventually became Linde Air Products (LAP) (later the Linde Division, which had nothing to do with German Linde even before the outbreak of the First World War) of Union Carbide Corporation and also (by 1915) Air Reduction Company (Airco) in the United States; and Nippon Sanso in Japan. Only one large firm was able to join this oligopoly after 1915, and that was US-based Air Products, established in 1940, which features prominently in the next section, not least because of its profound impact on industry organisation and structure.

The period that followed between 1915 and 1940 witnessed a number of significant changes. Mass motorisation, for instance, which began in the United States, and the rapid rise in small repair shops, provided opportunities for market entry for growing numbers of small-scale producers and distributors of welding gases. This tendency was reinforced in the US and elsewhere by the fact that oxygen in particular could be distributed economically only at a local level. In addition, gases companies entered and then expanded new markets in areas such as medical gases. And new technologies for large-scale production (tonnage plants) and distribution and storage (liquid gas systems) were developed and, to a very limited extent, applied by the 1930s. But in fundamental ways, the industrial gases industry did not change very much in the period between the end of the First and the beginning of the Second World War. A small number of companies dominated the industry commercially and technologically, each of which served a particular geographic area. And, although they were diversifying their product ranges, these companies and the smaller producers and distributors that came into existence beginning in the 1920s continued to rely overwhelmingly on supplying the oxyacetylene welding trade for their sales.

The outbreak of the Second World War in the late 1930s and the globalisation of the conflict that brought the great wing powers, the USSR and the United States, into the war by 1941 provided a shock that altered the international industrial gases industry in fundamental ways in the short term, the aftershocks of which contributed to a reconfiguration of the industry's structure and organisation that took place by the early 1960s. The following sections explore these developments.

The Short-Term Impact of the Second World War on Industry Dynamics

As is well known, industry's role in the preparations for the First World War were minimal, not least because those in politics and the military believed that any conflict must of necessity be short, obviating the necessity of economic and industrial planning. There was no such illusion about the conflict that was looming in the 1930s in the Pacific and Europe. All expected combat—and, more importantly, victory—to be determined in large part by the resources and technology that industry could deliver. Not surprisingly, then, firms and their managers played a significant role in the preparations for war, and companies in the industrial gases industry, which supplied key machinery, materials and technological systems to vital war-related firms in the chemicals, oil refining, shipbuilding and vehicle construction industries, were central to this effort.

Germany was one of the earliest among the highly industrialised countries to embark on these preparations, and, under the National Socialist regime, the country pursued them intensively, especially after 1936 under the auspices of the Four Year Plan Organisation. In this regard, the Nazi government relied heavily on Linde, one of the most technologically advanced firms in the gases industry. The Wiesbaden-based company built several newly developed 'tonnage' air separation units (ASUs) to supply installations for producing gases used in manufacture of synthetic nitrogen (for fertiliser and explosives), synthetic rubber and synthetic oil at plants owned by the giant chemical firm IG Farbenindustrie AG. Linde also exported just six of these tonnage plants, including apparatus sold to Germany's ally, Japan, as well as the Soviet Union (with which Nazi Germany was relatively friendly during the late 1930s until German troops invaded the USSR in June 1941) and Great Britain (which seems to have purchased two such plants by circuitous means in the mid-1930s).[10]

Britain was much slower than Germany to begin war preparations, and such preparations were much less intensive at first. But even if the British government had no equivalent in the run-up to the war to the German Four Year Plan Organisation, with its extensive intervention into and restructuring of the economy, it is clear that Britain pursued rearmament with some determination after 1935/1936 and that there was planning for and movement in this direction even before then.[11] Indeed, the purchase of two tonnage plants from Linde just noted, probably for the production of nitrates for explosives by British chemical firm ICI, formed an indication that there was some considerable movement in this direction. In addition, British industrial gases champion BOC contributed to war preparations through its extensive efforts to secure supplies of acetylene for the UK's welding industry, first through plans to construct a production facility in the Scottish Highlands using hydroelectric power generated there and then, when these plans fell through, through purchase of a Norwegian calcium carbide factory at Odda. Odda's production guaranteed adequate supplies of acetylene until the German invasion and occupation of Norway in 1940, by which time BOC had arranged for supply contracts from Canada that provided sufficient deliveries until the US Americans joined the Allied war effort in late December 1941.[12]

As the relatively late entry of the United States into the war suggests, war preparations there were slower still than those in Britain and, indeed, until 1940, downright leisurely. But in that year, although official entry into the war still lay 18 months or more in the future, industrial mobilisation began in earnest with contracts issued for supply of Great Britain, but also for the US armed forces. One strong indication of this new footing was the establishment in June 1940 of the National Defense Research Committee (NDRC) (the forerunner of the Office of Scientific Research and Development [OSRD], founded a year later) under Vannevar Bush to oversee scientific and technological preparations for the war, a development considered by some to herald the beginning of the US's national security state footing in relation to innovation, science and technology.[13]

Like in Germany and the UK, firms in the American industrial gases industry played a vital role in these war preparations. And the two leading companies in the US industry, Union Carbide Corporation's LAP division and Airco, soon found themselves with a very full order book for supplying ASUs and related apparatus as well as gases for use across the gamut of the armaments industry. Indeed, the two industry leaders were quickly overstretched, so much so that they were forced to concentrate only on filling these orders for existing products and technologies and not on developing new ones. This provided a vital opening for a fledgling company founded by Leonard Pool and his partner Carl Anderson in 1940, Air Products.[14]

Air Products may have been newly founded in 1940, but it did not come out of nowhere. Pool had worked as a salesman at a regional gases supplier in the American Midwest, Burdett Oxygen, during the 1930s, and had founded his own company, Acetylene Gas and Supply, in 1936. When Burdett Oxygen merged with Compressed Industrial Gases in 1938, Pool then left the Midwestern supplier to devote his energies primarily to the company he had founded. For his part, Anderson worked for a small and innovative gases engineering firm, Gas Industries, during much of the 1930s. Gas Industries sent him to the UK in 1936 to oversee deployment of intellectual property (IP) and licences from the American firm at a start-up in the northeast of England, Saturn Industrial Gases. Pool and Anderson, however, left previous commitments behind in 1940 when they joined forces to form Air Products. Not long after Anderson's departure from Gas Industries, which had been rich in ideas but poor in cash flow, his former employer went into receivership. The significance of this will soon become clear.[15]

It is also certainly the case that the firm's activities during the first several years of its existence were not those that its founders intended. We will come to those initial activities, which involved considerable political risk for the new company, shortly, but here it is important to emphasise that Air Products was established in order to realise Pool's vision for a new business model for the industrial gases industry, which he had developed while working at Burdett Oxygen. At that time, in the late 1930s, most large users of gases were companies in other industries (such as chemicals, petroleum refining, metal-working and, to a far lesser degree until after 1945, steelmaking), and these firms purchased ASUs and related equipment from firms in the gases engineering industry (firms which were almost all simultaneously industrial gases producers). These non-gases companies, therefore, almost always owned and often operated their own ASUs, generally focussing on production of one product (usually oxygen, but sometimes nitrogen, and less frequently both). Whatever was not used by the company involved was simply released back into the air. In other words, nearly 80 percent of the expensively produced (ASUs required large amounts of electricity to operate) purified air products of an ASU were wasted in the case of a large-scale oxygen user, while over one-fifth was simply discarded in the case of a nitrogen user. In both cases, moreover, the one percent of air containing the highest-value-added gases (e.g. argon, xenon and neon) was entirely wasted.

Pool's central idea involved his gases company deploying a new model of ownership and distribution for the industry that entailed 'owning the cow and selling the milk'. His company would own and operate the ASU, which would be located 'over the fence' from the main user, a company in another industry. This other company would sign a long-term contract (generally for 12 years, and now called a 'take-or-pay' contract) guaranteeing purchase of a minimum amount of gases per year at a fixed price per unit of volume from Pool's company's ASU. This would not only cost the other company less, involve less organisational effort and provide more security of supply than if it produced its gases from its own ASU; it would also guarantee the amortisation of Pool's investment very rapidly. In the meantime, his company could sell the other air components not used by the large firm with which Pool had the take-or-pay contract to companies in the surrounding area, ensuring healthy profits practically from the start, not least because this model allowed for much more effective capacity utilisation than had previously been the norm.[16] There was another extremely attractive aspect of this arrangement for Pool's company: at the end of the take-or-pay contract, the ASU would still be operational, although long since amortised. The user company could therefore then be offered a very attractive renewal contract that would give them a 'share of the write-offs' of Pool's company's investment in the ASU, ensuring that any potential competitor—which would have to invest in a new ASU—had no chance whatsoever of undercutting the contract.[17]

It was a spectacular and enticing idea, but it was also one that Pool's new company was in no position to realise in the early 1940s. There were three difficulties to begin with. The first was a need for engineering capacity: Pool was an entrepreneur and salesman with limited technical expertise; Anderson had more expertise than Pool, but Anderson was a technical manager rather than an engineer. Neither of them was in a position to design, build and operate an ASU, in particular a large-capacity one that would be required for the purposes that Pool envisaged in his concept. The two partners resolved this bottleneck relatively quickly, however, by hiring a young, newly qualified and highly talented and motivated engineer, Frank Pavliss. The second issue involved potential customers for any new venture. Here, opportunities were limited insofar as the two existing dominant players in the US, LAP and Airco, had practically sewn up the market for ASUs that were purchased by large industrial users, and even the full order books the two firms enjoyed as war approached in the early 1940s did not alter this substantially. What would eventually change the situation entirely, however, were technological developments in relation to steelmaking in the early 1940s that culminated in 'oxygen steel' processes in the early post-war period. These revolutionised not only steel production, but also the market for tonnage ASUs for the gases industry. The latter, not incidentally, provided a crucial opening for realisation of Pool's business model. Finally, regardless of the situation in relation to engineering capacity, which was rapidly solved, and potential customers, which remained problematic, newly formed Air Products faced the perennial problem encountered by all start-ups: limited access to sufficient capital. And that situation was not likely to change anytime soon.

Not in a position technologically or financially to realise Pool's dream immediately, Air Products was therefore required in the short term to improvise in order to survive. Cash flow was a difficult problem, but the firm was kept afloat by income from a very limited number of small contracts and, more importantly, by infusions of cash from Pool, his wife and relatives and acquaintances. Enough money was scraped together by these means to purchase the IP and engineering drawings of Gas Industries from the bankrupt firm's receiver in 1941. Anderson, who had worked for a number of years for Gas Industries, knew the value of the drawings in particular (the patents had for the most part expired), and he and the other members of the small staff of the new company began sifting through them for ideas that could be implemented commercially as quickly as possible.[18]

Gas Industries had developed plans in 1933 for design and construction of mobile oxygen production units, and these in particular appeared to Pool to be just the ticket. There had been no war—the only obvious market for such contraptions—in the offing when Gas Industries had come up with the idea initially, which is why the plans were never pursued through the end of the 1930s. By the early 1940s, however, the situation had changed dramatically, not only in relation to the likelihood of US direct participation in the war soon, but also in relation to aeroplane technology: 'high-flying oxygen', i.e. the oxygen that was essential for pilots and other military personnel operating new aeroplanes that could fly much higher than those produced previously, was going to be in demand soon, and this, coupled with the fact that oxygen could not be transported easily, safely or economically over long distances, meant that mobile ASUs would soon be needed. Pool managed to gain the ear of some officers in the US Army Air Force (USAAF; the US Air Force did not exist as a separate military service until 1947, after the end of the war), who invited him to give a presentation, and he, Anderson and their wives travelled in spring 1941 to the USAAF base at Wright Field in Dayton, Ohio, to deliver it. Air Products won a contract from the USAAF, which then formed the basis for a number of other contracts that extended purchases substantially several times in terms of scale and scope after the US entered the war in December 1941.[19] One of the major outlets here was the US Lend-Lease programme, which supplied US Allies during the war with a range of vital war materials, including mobile ASUs. A number of other small gases engineering firms produced such units, but, crucially, Air Products' mobile ASUs were viewed by the Allies as particularly dependable and well built.[20] As a result, Air Products gained a very positive reputation, especially internationally, by the time the war ended in 1945.

The coming and conduct of the Second World War thus opened up considerable space for market entry into an industrial gases industry that had been dominated by one or two players in each of the major industrialised markets from the immediate pre-1914 period to the early 1940s.

This was particularly true in the United States. Air Products was one of a number of companies that took advantage of this situation, but it was distinguished from the others from the outset by extent of its exposure to political risk by virtue of its almost total reliance on government procurement contracts. More positively, it was distinguished from the others in the breadth of its vision in terms of generating large-scale and long-term future growth, and also by the quality of the engineering products the company produced, which, via Lend-Lease, in turn enabled rapid achievement of international reach and reputation. The war of course did not guarantee either the long-term viability of the new firm nor the realisation of its potential to disrupt the industry—indeed, exclusive reliance on government procurement contracts posed considerable risks for the firm's long-term survival. But in the short term, the war crucially enabled Air Products to survive, and even to thrive, and also to develop significant technological and engineering capabilities that would ensure long-term competitiveness.

Air Products was thus potentially in a very promising competitive position as a result of the war, although it was also extremely vulnerable to cuts in armaments spending. Still, it is important to stress that, in addition to allowing market entry for the American start-up and other firms and the considerable potential for disruption in the longer term that this might entail, the conflict also witnessed a number of other changes to the industry that had long-term consequences, changes that also enabled development of new technologies in other industries as well as scale increases in production that would not have otherwise been possible. For one thing, wartime demand involved massive increases in demand for gases—primarily oxygen and acetylene, but also others—to service traditional areas, including cutting, welding and deseaming (smoothing out cast metal surfaces). Because of the increased use of new alloys for demanding applications in aviation and armour production, among other things, as well as the need for ever greater levels of precision, there was a qualitative as well as a quantitative dimension to this enhanced demand for traditional gases and gas mixtures, a trend that new applications for oxygen, in particular for medical gases and for 'high-flying oxygen', only reinforced.

In addition, some gases that had been relatively limited in terms of demand featured more and more prominently as a result of applications that were either developed for, or increasingly used in, war production. Nitrogen and/or hydrogen, for instance, were used in synthetic fuel and rubber production (especially in Germany, but also in Japan and to some extent Italy), and also (in all of the combatant countries) in oil refining and fertiliser, munitions, radio tube and nylon production and, to some degree, food processing. Indeed, wartime demand for nitrogen in particular for these and other applications entailed the beginning of a quantum leap in demand for the gas, which, not long into the post-war period, eventually outstripped oxygen as the quantitatively most significant product of the industrial gases industry in highly industrialised countries.[21] The war also witnessed increased demand for more specialist gases, including, for instance, helium for a variety of purposes, and argon and krypton for specialist welding and other applications.

Because of vastly increased demand for gases and gas-production equipment in the run-up to and during the conduct of the war, firms in the industrial gases industry were required to change their behaviour and business practices substantially, mainly through rapid adoption of technological systems that had been developed initially in the 1920s and 1930s, but very thinly diffused at that time because of limited applications and demand. Tonnage ASUs have already been mentioned. These had been developed to industrial scale at Linde in Germany in the early 1930s and found their first large-scale application in chemical plants in Germany, mainly in the service of war-related industry. But plants of similar scale were soon being built in all combatant countries. The other revolutionary technological system, liquid gas storage and distribution, was also initially developed in Germany by Heylandt in the 1920s, but found few adopters at first, except in niche markets. However, liquid oxygen (LOX) systems in particular were widely adopted during the war because of the scale of demand, which traditional cylinder-based storage and distribution simply could not handle because of materials shortages for cylinder construction along with sheer volume of demand.[22] Again, the changes at stake were both quantitative and qualitative in nature, heralding a sea change in industry practice and structure that would continue into the post-war period.

All in all, then, the short-term impact of the build-up to and conduct of the Second World War on the industrial gases industry was highly significant. War preparations and production enabled new entrants with new capabilities and ideas—in particular Air Products—to enter an industry that had been characterised by organisational and (to a lesser degree) technological stasis for decades. It also provided an opportunity for the widespread adoption of technologies that had been developed earlier, but also for the development of new technologies and also of new ways of organising the industry. At the same time, it must be underscored that industrial gases, the firms that produced them and the industry that they constituted had a massive impact on production rates, weapons systems and weapon effectiveness that profoundly affected the conduct of the war. Gases, and in particular new means of delivery and distribution for them such as LOX systems, enabled scale increases in other areas of production that would not otherwise have been possible. What is more, gases formed central prerequisites for the production and/or operation of breakthrough technologies that would affect the latter part of the war and especially the post-war period, including new aviation technologies (such as jet aircraft), atomic power and ballistic missiles, among others. In other words, if the industrial gases industry was important to the First World War, it was *essential* to the conduct of the Second World War. The trends that had started or were accelerated by the Second World War culminated by the 1950s and 1960s in a vastly different organisational landscape for the international industrial gases industry.

Longer-Term Effects of the Second World War on the Development of the International Industrial Gases Industry

The shape and, especially, the content of the industrial gases industry that emerged from the Second World War differed from those that characterised the industry in 1940. Vastly expanded demand through wartime production and new technologies gave an opening for new companies not only to enter the industry, but to survive and, indeed, to thrive. They—and especially Air Products, because of its demonstrated innovation capabilities and already established international reputation for quality—now had the potential to pose fundamental challenges to the structure of the industry that had been dominant since before the First World War. In addition, vastly expanded demand, not just for traditional products of the gases industry such as oxygen and acetylene (and, to a lesser extent, nitrogen), but also for more specialised gases and mixtures, gave new opportunities not only to the industry's dominant players, but also to the newcomers. Finally, and related to this, the wartime experience made clear that development of applications, especially in collaboration with business customers, would necessarily form a vital part of the future strategy of industrial gases firms.

But the path these developments would eventually take with regard to the industry's evolution was not entirely clear to actors in, and observers of, the gases sector at the end of the war in spring and summer 1945. The future of companies headquartered in the defeated Axis countries was uncertain, while the dominant players located in the victorious Allied countries experienced a sudden drop in demand from war-related industry with no sense that this demand would be made up fully by peacetime production. Indeed, there was a fear among many that there might eventually be a resumption of the political, economic and business turmoil that characterised most of the two decades following the end of the First World War. For still-young companies such as Air Products, of course, which were heavily exposed to this political risk by virtue of their almost exclusive reliance on war-related procurement, these threats and uncertainties were particularly salient.

Economic historians have identified a range of factors—including US economic and political leadership, reconstruction aid and steadily lowering tariffs—that helped ensure that growth instead of stagnation took place in the capitalist world in the 'Golden Age' that lasted from the late

1940s to the early 1970s. What is more, even as all of these measures were starting to be put into place, it became clear that industry in Germany and Japan (including the gases industry) would not be suppressed, but instead strongly encouraged to rebuild to participate in growing world trade. But these were general structural developments that applied to post-war capitalist economies as a whole, and it is important to recognise that there were also organisational, structural and technological developments that applied specifically to individual industrial sectors, and furthermore that these and other developments can be understood fully only through attention to the role of individuals and groups of individuals who shaped their companies and industries.

For the industrial gases industry, there were a number of specific factors that shaped industry developments after 1945, and especially after the start of the Korean War in 1950, but one stands out: large-scale demand for gases from a number of industries owing to technological change. The first of these technological changes arose out of innovations in steelmaking that had been proceeding incrementally since the 1920s, but which took on revolutionary contours by the immediate post-war period in terms of energy efficiency, quality of raw material inputs and time needed to produce finished product: the increasing deployment of purified oxygen in the steelmaking industry, culminating in the Linz-Donau 'oxygen steel' process developed by 1949, did all of these things.[23] Eventual realisation of oxygen-steel technology in turn would not have been possible had it not been for the development of tonnage ASU technologies in the gases industry because delivery of sufficient volumes of oxygen via cylinders was simply not viable. The market for tonnage ASUs, which had to that point had limited applications, primarily in the chemical industry, suddenly grew exponentially. And, at about the same time, starting in the United States, there was increasing use of nitrogen in the food processing industry, not least for flash freezing technologies, which had been developed earlier but became widely diffused in the post-war period, again leading to substantial new outlets not only for tonnage ASUs, but also for nitrogen gas, demand for which to that point had been relatively limited.

It is possible to imagine a situation in which servicing these new and growing markets might have been achieved by the pre-existing dominant industrial gases and gases engineering companies, largely operating on the longstanding business model of direct sales of ASUs to very large users of gases. Indeed, that is what happened to begin with, and that is also what managers in those companies at the time expected to remain the norm for years to come. But the scale of demand that was emerging, largely as a direct extension of wartime developments, allowed an opening for a new business model, indeed the one that had formed the basis of Pool's vision in founding Air Products in 1940.

Air Products had gone through a very rough patch in the immediate aftermath of the end of the war, as markets for its main product, mobile

ASUs, disappeared completely practically overnight, and the company hovered on the brink of bankruptcy. Its managers recognised the vulnerability that heavy reliance on government contracts entailed and acted on this, for instance in making a key decision in 1946 to relocate its production facilities from Chattanooga, Tennessee, where it had been co-located with other armaments producers, to Allentown, Pennsylvania, where it would be near a large number of producers of civilian goods. Moreover, the firm had developed substantial engineering capability between 1940 and the post-war period, and there were certainly enough potential customers for the gases it could produce if it could build its own large-scale ASUs, although convincing one of these customers to bet on the still relatively new company rather than on established firms such as LAP or Airco was not a trivial task. In the immediate post-war period, Air Products' sales agents courted a range of potential customers for this purpose, primarily in the steel industry. Access to sufficient capital was still a problem for the young firm, but this was speedily overcome once a customer finally came forward. In July 1947, as announced with considerable fanfare in the national press, 'Weirton Steel Company signed a contract with Air Products for the largest oxygen producing plant in the world'.[24]

The contract was a landmark, not just for the firm (because of its realisation for the first time of Pool's new business model in connection with a major steel producer), but also for the industry. The contract pioneered the take-or-pay concept, which guaranteed baseline sales of oxygen for Air Products over a relatively long period of time. It also involved an innovation in financing, one which overcame Air Products' capital shortage. Pool took the contract with Weirton Steel to his bank manager, who was willing to lend the cash to build the ASU to Air Products because of the long-term contract and because of Weirton's ironclad reputation for financial probity. The loan could then be serviced quite easily and repaid in full before the end of the contract with Weirton, not least because sales of nitrogen and other gases from the ASU guaranteed a very high level of capacity utilisation and thus lower costs. Debt financing of this sort became one of the hallmarks of Air Products' *modus operandi* in the United States and, later, abroad.

Indeed, making moves outside the US market was something the firm felt compelled to do by the late 1940s and early 1950s. After all, regardless of the breakthrough that the Weirton Steel contract represented for Air Products and Pool's business model, the company was still somewhat stymied in the US domestic market for industrial gases and equipment, which, although it featured a large number of local and regional distributors and (to a lesser extent) producers, was still dominated by the effective duopoly of LAP and Airco, both at the national level and in the traditionally strong areas of the industrial gases industry at that point in time, i.e. oxygen and acetylene. Air Products responded with a dual strategy. First, it targeted sale of gases that had been in less heavy demand than oxygen and acetylene, which simultaneously avoided for the most part direct product competition with the existing duopoly, involved new users, especially in food processing, and entailed high levels of capacity utilisation for ASUs. Here, nitrogen was a particularly important and attractive product for Air Products, but the firm also focussed on argon and on gases mixtures. The second prong of the strategy involved the company, which by now was based in Allentown, Pennsylvania, deciding that it should internationalise.[25]

Why did this happen? Being stymied in the American market was a large part of the motivation for Air Products' decision to internationalise operations, but three other factors were also important. The first had to do with the medium-term legacy of Lend-Lease, which Air Products had participated in with considerable success, supplying US Allies around the world. As a result, unlike other American gases firms (and indeed most others in the industry, with the exception of Air Liquide, based in France), Air Products had an international reputation for the high-quality and dependability of the equipment it produced. Second, Carl Anderson, one of the founding partners, had substantial overseas experience from the 1930s, when he was seconded to Saturn Industrial Gases from Gases Industries. Thus, through this and Air Products' extensive Lend-Lease experience there during the Second World War, Britain was the logical starting point for the firm's international expansion. This factor combined, in turn, with a third one to determine the initial location of international market entry for Air Products: the American firm, knowledgeable already to some extent about the UK market, seized an opportunity presented in 1951 when the Butterley company, a mixed British concern, was seeking an outlet for funds it had amassed in compensation from the UK government for the nationalisation of its coal holdings. Butterley decided to invest in ASU construction in cooperation with Air Products. The American firm, still capital poor, brought no cash, but instead its considerable capabilities in technology and know-how, to the table in the new venture, which by 1957 had evolved into jointly held Air Products Limited (51 percent Air Products, 49 percent Butterleys). By the late 1950s, the US company bought out Butterleys' share of the joint venture, and Air Products Limited became a wholly owned subsidiary, which had in the meantime already begun to challenge BOC in the UK market.[26] From its British base, Air Products then branched out with subsidiaries into Belgium and then Germany by the mid-1960s.

Air Products' internationalisation strategy, while avoiding competition with the American duopoly in the US market, of course had the drawback of bringing it into direct competition with even more dominant existing players in foreign markets. Indeed, BOC was widely known as the 'Ministry of Oxygen' in the UK,[27] a nod to its 98.5 percent market share in the gas in the British market (BOC also controlled 98.5 percent of the acetylene market).[28] But the American upstart made substantial inroads, first in the UK and then on the continent, by targeting large users for exclusive take-or-pay contracts, using debt financing creatively and focussing on developing and servicing markets for non-traditional gases, which were growing rapidly. Air Products also pioneered in a number of other areas, too, continuing its pursuit of innovations that would give the firm an opportunity to gain a firmer foothold in an industry dominated by established firms. These innovations, which the company initiated in the United States, found their full flowering in overseas markets, first in Britain, and then in continental Europe. They included widespread use of liquid distribution and storage systems, servicing of medium-sized customers with cylinder batteries rather than individual cylinders, high levels of customer service and a focus on applications.

Essentially, then, the full implementation of Pool's concept represented a creative overlay of several modes of distribution—direct supply, LOX delivery and cylinder/battery distribution—that were coordinated and deployed by Air Products to enable maximum capacity utilisation of a capital-intensive plant built on the site of a large user of gases, and all of this was done with a focus on the user/customer. The cost savings over hitherto existing distribution methods were enormous, and it is not surprising that all of these innovations taken together also enabled access to new customers, who eventually purchased all of their gases from Air Products.[29] What is more, Air Products was one of the pioneers in using pipelines to supply multiple customers of varying sizes (and often with differing patterns of demand for various gases) in areas of high industrial concentration, which in many ways represented a logical further extension of Pool's concept: pipelines involved linking several large-scale air separation units into a network, which had multiple positive effects, including even better capacity utilisation of the capital-intensive units, security of supply for customers and, not least, raising the barriers to entry into lucrative areas of industrial concentration to competitors.[30]

All in all, then, as a result of its innovative capabilities in the context of the generalised technological change in industry in the wartime and post-1945 period, Air Products effectively changed the organisational parameters of the industrial gases business. Firms in the industry were eventually forced to become more like Air Products, changing their existing primary focus on supply of a long-established market for oxyacetylene cutting and welding. They instead became companies that had to deliver to multiple markets using diverse logistical capabilities and emphasising development of new applications, which had profound effects on their organisation and on the industry's structure.

It is worth noting here, though, that Air Products' initial competitive strategy did not pose a direct challenge to the gases industry in that the newcomer competed first and foremost at the fringes of the existing industry. But over time, it challenged and then severely disrupted existing arrangements among firms that had essentially carved up the industrial gases markets geographically decades before, forcing those firms to adopt new organisational forms and strategies. BOC, for instance, began to adopt debt financing and other practices pioneered by Air Product by the late 1960s as a direct result of the American firm's successful onslaught in the market it had long dominated. LAP and, to a lesser extent, Airco, followed Air Products' lead in branching out into European markets, while the dominant players in each of those markets began to compete first in other European countries and then, by the 1970s, in the United States, where none of them had been active since the late 1940s, and, for the most part, since long before that. The industrial gases industry that had come into existence by the 1970s, then, was profoundly different from the one that had existed in 1940: continued use of the phrase 'industrial gases industry' thus concealed deep qualitative changes in the content and meaning of the word 'industry'.

Conclusions

In no small part as a result of trends that had started in earnest during the Second World War, but also as a result of the agency of key new players—especially Air Products—that were able to gain or retain footholds in the industry as a result of the war, the international industrial gases industry was transformed by the 1950s and 1960s beyond recognition compared to its situation before the outbreak of the war. Sales volume increased massively, while the industry's product palette (and along with that the range of customers) broadened substantially. Technologies of production and distribution, including tonnage ASUs and liquid gas handling systems, that had been developed in the 1920s and 1930s, but only thinly diffused, were now widely used. Competition, which gentlemen's agreements that had come into existence before the First World War had limited or even eliminated in industrialised countries and in the colonies of the British and French empires, had been stimulated considerably, not least by new entrant Air Products, with its strategy of internationalisation, underpinned by a new business model that involved substantial contractual, financial, logistical and organisational innovations.

In general, then, the history of the international industrial gases industry would seem to confirm the hypothesis that war can serve as a conduit for significant technological and organisational change.[31] The story of the gases industry, however, suggests three caveats. The first has to do with the contrasting effects of the First and Second World Wars on the industry. The former seemed to reinforce existing arrangements (which had just come into existence before the war), while the latter disrupted them. What explains this, especially if war in general tends to usher in significant change to economic, technological and industrial structures? Here, a number of complementary factors seem significant. For one thing, the Great War occurred just after the considerable technological and organisational upheaval that constituted the initial phase of the existence of the modern industrial gases industry, one which resulted by 1913 in oxyacetylene welding as the most important market, the establishment of a relatively small number of major players in the industry and a series of gentlemen's agreements that limited international competition. These remained key and stable features of the industry in the post-1918 period. The trends that the Second World War ushered in for the industry were much more substantial and continued their trajectories well into the post-1945 period. What is more, it is no doubt important in explaining the much more limited effect of the Great War on the industry than that of the Second War that the industry and its products were not all that significant for the former, whereas they were highly significant, even critical, during the latter.

A second caveat concerns the issue of contingency. Much of the story told in this article hinges on the establishment and subsequent behaviour of Air Products, and there is no doubt that Air Products, founded at the beginning of, and surviving and flourishing as a result of, the Second World War was the central player in the technological and organisational disruption of the industry that started in the early 1940s and had been realised by the mid-1960s. But it is crucial to emphasise that Air Products may well not have survived the immediate post-war period. After all, its main customer, the US government, ceased buying its main product, mobile ASUs, in 1945, and the firm's turnover dipped dangerously, a trend reinforced by the company's relocation from Chattanooga, Tennessee, to Allentown, Pennsylvania. As a result, it posted its first loss since 1941 in 1947.[32] In the meantime, of course, the company's managers were busy trying to sell Leonard Pool's new business model to the steel industry, an effort that met with success for the first time in 1947, and this provided a platform for further growth for the firm. But even here it is important to keep in mind the role of contingency. Pool's business model, of course, was not patented or in any other way protected as intellectual property and might be (and eventually was) copied by other companies. Union Carbide's LAP would have been a prime candidate for this, and that firm's reputation and access to capital would have enabled it to see off the potential competitor easily. But LAP had recently invested in a very expensive fleet of rail cars with which to service their large customers, and its managers were reluctant to undercut this in any way, at least initially. As one of Air Products' key managers put it in a 2008 interview, LAP continued using its fleet of rail cars 'long enough for Air Products to become established and to build a reputation as a quality supplier of oxygen and oxygen plants. . . . Had Carbide [LAP] reacted immediately, we probably never would have got started'.[33]

The third caveat has in part to do with the second: Air Products' activities and agency during the war and in the immediate post-war period would have been for nought had it not been for major changes in other industries. In particular, technological change in the steel industry favouring large-scale consumption of purified oxygen, along with the massive growth in outlets for nitrogen provided the opportunity for Air Products—followed not long afterwards by others—to realise Pool's vision of 'owning the cow and selling the milk'. There is no doubt, then, that the Second World War was a key factor in the technological and organisational transformation of the international industrial gases industry and of the firms that comprised it. What is more, both agency and history are essential for understanding these developments.

Notes

1 Banken and Stokes 2015; Stokes and Banken 2016; Kurosawa 2018.
2 See, e.g., Porter 1998.
3 See, for instance, Tushman and O'Reilly 1996.
4 Christensen 1997.
5 Here, the literature on war and technological innovation is particularly relevant. See, e.g., Smith 1985; Ruttan 2006.
6 Stokes and Banken 2016; Almqvist 2003.
7 Landes 2003, esp. ch. 5; Mokyr 1998. For a critical view on the concept of the Second Industrial Revolution, see Homburg 1986.
8 BOC, 'The birth and development of an industry: The history of the British Oxygen Company, 1886–1946' [unpublished manuscript, 1946], in BOC Collection, Linde Unternehmensarchiv (LUM), Munich (BOCM), Box 425.
9 Almqvist 2003, p. 143; Sloane 1920, pp. 307–319.
10 Linde, Abt.-Gasverflüssigung, 'Gelieferte Groß Sauerstoffanlagen nach dem Linde-Fränkl-Verfahren' [n.d., ca. 1962], p. 1, in LUM, location: Fach 39, A 03; 'Bericht über Apparatebau-Anstalt und Lieferungsgeschäft der Abt B für die Aufsichtsratssitzung vom 19.Nov.37', in LUM, location: Fach 41, A 03.
11 Harris 1983, esp. pp 146ff; Miller 2018.
12 BOC, 'The birth and development', pp. 55–57, 65–66. Also: Minutes of the BOC Board, 2 March 1937, BOC Ltd. Minute Book 12, p. 14; and Minutes of the BOC Board, 26 August 1937, BOC Ltd. Minute Book 12, pp. 41–42. Information on the post- 1940 invasion situation is in Minutes of the BOC Board, 8 May 1940, BOC Ltd. Minute Book 13, pp. 91 and 94. All of the board minutes referred to here are in BOC Wales collection (BOCW), Box SEC000459.
13 Mowery and Rosenberg 1989.
14 On the history of Air Products, Butrica 1990; Stokes and Banken 2016, passim.
15 Butrica 1990, pp. 9–47.
16 Interview with Dexter Baker by Ray Stokes, Allentown, PA, 28 October 2008.
17 The point about sharing write-offs comes from an Interview with Aldo Fumagalli, SOL spa, by Ray Stokes, Monza, 10 June 2009.
18 Butrica 1990, pp. 32–36, 41.
19 Butrica 1990, pp. 26–47.
20 Butrica 1990, pp. 32–44.
21 This point is made in BOC 1986, pp. 22–23.
22 Untitled history of BOC during war, 30 August 1944, BOCW, Box 536.
23 Adams and Dirlan 1966; McAdams 1967.
24 Anderson, 'Notes on the early history of APCI', p. 28 [typescript, 31 January 1976], from archival material provided to authors by Hans-Liudger Dienel on

2 April 2008; C. Norman Stabler, 'Huge oxygen production plant to be built for weirton steel', *New York Herald Tribune* (28 July 1947), p. 29; Butrica 1990, pp. 67–70. Quotation from Stabler.

25 Interview with Dexter Baker by Ray Stokes, Allentown, PA, 28 October 2008.

26 The Monopolies and Restrictive Practices Commission, *Report on the Supply of Certain Industrial and Medical Gases* (London: HMSO, 1956), pp. 48–49; 'Butterley and Oxygen [advertisement]', *The Times* (20 May 1954), p. 4; 'Butterley Company Limited', *The Times* (1 July 1954), p. 14; 'The Butterley Company Limited', *The Times* (8 July 1957), p. 15.

27 'International gas man', *Industrial Management & Data Systems* 72, No. 2 (1972), pp. 38–42, here p. 39.

28 The Monopolies and Restrictive Practices Commission, *Report on the Supply of Certain Industrial and Medical Gases* (London: HMSO, 1956).

29 BOC, 'Air Products and Chemicals Incorporated—A Review', 1979, p. 5, in BOCW, Box 20; Stirling, Gadsby & Chown, 'Growth potential set against the background of its markets', August 1968, in BOCM, Box 535, and BOC, 'Report on Air Products for staff college', 1964, pp. 1–6, in BOCW, Box 536.

30 Banken and Stokes 2014.

31 See e.g. Roland 2016; Ruttan 2006.

32 Air Products and Chemicals, Inc., 'Net sales, net income from APCI Annual reports' [n.d., ca. 1988], from archival material kindly provided by Hans-Liudger Dienel on 2 April 2008.

33 Interview with Dexter Baker conducted by Ray Stokes, Allentown, PA, 28 October 2008.

Bibliography

Adams, Walter, and Joel B. Dirlam (1966), 'Big steel, invention and innovation', *The Quarterly Journal of Economics* 80: 167–189.

Almqvist, Ebbe (2003), *History of Industrial Gases* (New York: Kluwer Academic).

Banken, Ralf, and Ray Stokes (2014), 'Die Entstehung der Pipeline-Netze für Industriegase im Ruhrgebiet 1956–1975', *Zeitschrift für Unternehmensgeschichte* 1/2014: 1–26 (with Ralf Banken)

Banken, Ralf, and Ray Stokes (2015), 'Constructing an "industry": The case of industrial gases, 1886–2006', in special issue on 'Re-introducing evolutionary theory to business history', *Business History* 57, No. 5: 688–704.

BOC (1986), *Around the Group in 100 Years The BOC Group Celebrating Our First Century* (London: BOC).

Butrica, Andrew J. (1990), *Out of Thin Air: A History of Air Products and Chemicals, Inc., 1940–1990* (New York: Praeger).

Christensen, Clayton M. (1997), *The Innovator's Dilemma: When New Technologies Cause Great Firms to Fail* (Cambridge, MA: Harvard Business Review Press).

Harris, John Paul (1983), 'The War Office and Rearmament 1935–39' (PhD thesis: Kings College London).

Homburg, Ernst (1986), 'De "Tweete Industriele Revolutie". Een problematisch historisch concept', *Theoretische geschiedenis* 13: 367–385.

Kurosawa, Takafumi (2018), 'Introduction: Industry history: Its concepts and methods', pp. 1–24 in Bouwens, Bram et al., eds., *Industries and Global Competition: A History of Business Beyond Borders* (Abingdon, NY: Routledge).

Landes, David (2003), *The Unbound Prometheus: Technological Change and Industrial Development in Western Europe From 1750 to the Present*, 2nd ed. (Cambridge, NY: Cambridge University Press).

McAdam, Alan K. (1967), 'Big steel, invention and innovation reconsidered', *The Quarterly Journal of Economics* 81: 457–474.

Miller, Christopher (2018), *Planning and Profits: The Military-Industrial Complex and British Naval Arms Manufacture, 1918–1941* (Liverpool: Liverpool University Press).

Mokyr, Joel (1998), 'The Second Industrial Revolution, 1870–1914' (August 1998), available at https://cpb-us-east-1-juc1ugur1qwqqqo4.stackpathdns.com/sites.northwestern.edu/dist/3/1222/files/2016/06/The-Second-Industrial-Revolution-1870-1914-Aug-1998-1ubah7s.pdf <accessed 3 April 2018>.

Mowery, David, and Nathan Rosenberg (1989), *Technology and the Pursuit of Economic Growth* (Cambridge: Cambridge University Press).

Porter, Michael (1998), *The Competitive Advantage of Nations (with a New Introduction)* (Basingstoke: Palgrave).

Roland, Alex (2016), *War and Technology: A Very Short Introduction* (Oxford: Oxford University Press).

Ruttan, Vernon W. (2006). *Is War Necessary for Economic Growth? Military Procurement and Technology Development* (Oxford: Oxford University Press).

Sloane, Thomas O'Conor (1920), *Liquid Air and the Liquefaction of Gases*, 3rd revised and much enlarged edition (London: Constable; first published in London by Sampson, Low, Marston, 1899).

Smith, Merritt Roe (1985), 'Introduction', pp. 1–37, in Merritt Roe Smith, ed., *Military Enterprise and Technological Change: Perspectives on the American Experience* (Cambridge, MA: MIT Press).

Stokes, Raymond G., and Ralf Banken (2016), *Building on Air: The International Industrial Gases Industry, 1886–2006* (Cambridge, NY: Cambridge University Press).

Tushman, Michael L. and Charles A. O'Reilly III, 'Ambidextrous organisations: Managing evolutionary and revolutionary change', *California Management Review* 38, No. 4: 8–30.

Part III

Cold War and Corporate Strategies

8 The Afterlife of a Multinational Enterprise

The Case of Siemens' Subsidiary in Hungary After the Second World War

Judit Klement

Introduction[1]

In the history of Siemens as a multinational enterprise, on several occasions the company was faced with non-market forces or effects. According to W. Feldenkirchen (the 'official' historian of Siemens), for example, the attempt to establish a workshop in Paris in 1878 was a failure because of 'the intensity of anti-German sentiment' after the Franco-Prussian War.[2] Similarly, during the First World War, Britain confiscated the Siemens plants in England,[3] and the new boundaries of the successor states in Central Europe (including Hungary) after the war also compelled the Siemens subsidiaries to adapt to dramatic changes. However, the biggest non-market challenge came after the Second World War. In Germany, the main question was Siemens's participation in the Nazi economy, 'from producing armament to employing concentration camp labour'.[4] The company and its leaders had to cope not only with prosecution for war crimes but also with an appalling reputation.[5] The future of Siemens's assets beyond the German borders, furthermore, was in the hand of the Allies. After the Potsdam Agreement, German wealth was regarded by the Allies, especially the Soviets, as a source for reparations. The Hungarian government signed the armistice in Moscow on 20 January 1945, and the country was occupied by the Soviet army. The Siemens subsidiary in Hungary was a wholly owned German subsidiary, and so it was considered a source for reparations to the Soviets. On the basis of these developments, the history of Hungary's Siemens's subsidiary should have been quite straightforward after 1945, but the reality that emerged was more complex. Both the (ex-)Siemens employees and the Hungarian state tried to change the scenario originally sketched out in Moscow and in Potsdam. These attempts and the events in 1945 and 1946 are the focus of this chapter, in which the fate of Siemens in Hungary after the war will be analysed.

Siemens in Hungary Before 1945

Siemens, established in 1847 and at the time headquartered in Berlin, first appeared on the Hungarian market as a joint venture in 1887. The company played a major role in the construction of the newly formed tramway system of Budapest.[6] In 1894, Siemens set up its own Hungarian subsidiary, initially in a form of a limited partnership and then (from 1900) as a joint-stock company.[7] It is well known that Siemens had been functioning as a multinational company since the 1850s. It had both more and less successful subsidiaries.[8] The subsidiary in Budapest was among Siemens's small but efficient foreign direct investments. The operation of Siemens in Hungary began with the construction and upkeep of Budapest's tramway system. In 1896, Siemens also took part in the construction in Budapest of continental Europe's first underground railway. These functions were at the core of the construction and maintenance of electric plants and, later, the electrification activity of the Hungarian Siemens subsidiary. For over a decade, the Siemens' workshops in Budapest functioned as repair and operating facilities rather than a production plant.[9]

Siemens did not begin production in Hungary until 1904. In that year, the German Siemens and Schuckert firms merged, and so Siemens became a co-owner in Hungarian Schuckert Works and, thereby, a factory owner, because the Schuckert Works already included a machine factory in Pozsony (Pressburg, today Bratislava, Slovakia). The majority of the newly formed Hungarian Siemens enterprise—the precise name of which was Hungarian Siemens-Schuckert Works Electrical Engineering Joint-Stock Company *(Magyar Siemens–Schuckert Művek Villamossági Részvénytársaság)*—belonged to the Austrian Siemens subsidiary (*Österreichische Siemens-Schuckert Werke AG.*—Austrian Siemens-Schuckert Works), and not directly to Berlin (*Siemens & Halske AG.)*.[10] In addition to the machine factory, the company also planned to build a cable factory. The new plant was constructed in Kőbánya, a neighbourhood on the outskirts of Budapest. The purchase of the plot in Kőbánya and the construction on the site of its factory in 1913 was the first production initiative of Hungarian Siemens-Schuckert Works.

After the First World War, the machine factory in Pozsony was lost for the Hungarian Siemens subsidiary when it was annexed to the Czechoslovak Siemens enterprise.[11] So, in 1927, Siemens Hungary started to build a machine workshop in Kőbánya, on which work was completed in 1936. As Siemens's profile expanded worldwide, production in Budapest became more diversified. In the 1930s, the machine factory of Hungarian Siemens-Schuckert Works also began to produce household appliances, in addition to dynamos, switches, engines, etc. Until 1934, another Hungarian Siemens subsidiary handled electrical engineering (low-voltage products), at another plant.[12] But in 1934 this section was merged with Hungarian Siemens-Schuckert, and in 1937 it was moved to Kőbánya.

The main profile of the latter was radio production and the manufacture of mechanical instruments. At the end of the 1930s, three factories were working at Siemens's plant in Kőbánya: a cable factory, machine and an electrical (low voltage) engineering factory.

As a consequence of preparations for war in Hungary—the so-called Győr Project—and the orders placed by the state during the Second World War, the Hungarian Siemens subsidiary expanded rapidly.[13] The plant was extended, and by 1942 it had increased to three and a half times its size in 1913. The number of employees also grew continuously; the three factories together employed more than 1,500 people in 1942.[14] Development was followed by a capital increase. In 1941, the company raised its capital from 4 to 6 million pengős. By this time, 'Schuckert' had disappeared from the official name of the Hungarian firm in alignment with the name of the German parent company.[15] In the 1940s, the Hungarian Siemens subsidiary was called Hungarian Siemens Works Electrical Engineering Joint-Stock Company *(Magyar Siemens Művek Villamossági Részvénytársaság)*, and it functioned under full German ownership in Budapest.

During the Second World War, the cable factory and the machine factory were not seriously damaged, but the low-voltage engineering factory was bombed and destroyed at the beginning of 1945. With the exception of the days of the siege of Budapest, the Siemens plant in Kőbánya continued production until the remaining factory parts were dismantled in March 1945.

Booty and Reparation

As an ally of Nazi Germany, Hungary was defeated in the Second World War, and the Soviet Union occupied the entire country in 1945. The war inflicted immeasurable human casualties and tremendous material losses. According to the secondary literature, the number of people who died as a consequence of the war in Hungary (delineated by the 1941–1944 borders) was somewhere between 830,000 and 950,000, including 340,000–360,000 military casualties and 410,000–460,000 victims of the Holocaust.[16] This puts Hungary in third or fourth place in the ranking of human casualties of the war if the number of casualties is given as a percentage of the country's population. The country was also materially ruined. Budapest suffered in particular at the end of the war. The siege of the capital, which lasted for more than 100 days, was similar to the bloody blockade of Stalingrad, Warsaw and Berlin in terms of loss of life.[17] A few facts serve to give a good impression of the state of affairs in the country after the war.[18] For instance, 40 percent of the national wealth of 1938 was destroyed during the war. Livestock suffered an especially serious loss, as 56 percent of the stock of 1944 perished, which caused immediate difficulties in the post-war food supply and in the resumption of agricultural production. The country struggled with severe problems concerning provisions for the citizenry, partly because the transport system had been incapacitated. The country's obligation to supply provisions for the occupying Soviet army and its allied Romanian, Bulgarian and Yugoslav forces made the situation more difficult, and the situation was made even more intense by the immediate start of Soviet war reparations.

By signing the armistice (20 January), the Hungarian government[19] accepted the Soviet Union's claim for compensation for war damages (a claim which was also made by Yugoslavia and Czechoslovakia). One month later (20 February), Hungary received a detailed catalogue, composed in Moscow, of the goods and products which were to be delivered to the Soviet Union over the course of the next six years. The Hungarian government could not acknowledge this catalogue—as was promptly noted in an official answer. They were unable to assess the situation: the government was only able to move its seat to the capital on 19 April when the front line of the war was no longer in the country. Moreover, most of the industrial plants and mines remained under Soviet military control until summer 1945, which meant that they were in use primarily to meet military needs[20] and were closed to civilians and even government representatives. From April to mid-June, long and exhausting negotiations took place concerning reparations to be paid by Hungary. This process came to an end with the so-called reparation agreement on 15 June. However, the removal of Hungarian valuables, engines, machinery and other assets had begun much earlier, in the spring of 1945, without any mutual consensus, and it continued until summer, independently of the reparation agreement. The Hungarian government, more precisely the Foreign Office, protested several times against what in its eyes was simply plunder, but unsuccessfully. The arbitrary dismantling gradually ceased after the signing of the reparation agreement, but the value of the goods which had been appropriated was not taken into account in Hungary's obligation to make reparations.[21]

The dismantling and removal of the factories of Hungarian Siemens Works Electrical Engineering Joint-Stock Company started on 15 March 1945. By the time it had come to an end, there were only empty buildings left in the cable and machine factory complex.[22] (The low-voltage engineering factory had been destroyed during the siege of the capital.) In one of the many official protests of the Hungarian Foreign Office (dated 25 May), the company was named among the firms which were not mentioned in the reparation list but which had still been totally dismantled.[23] (Before this protest, on 14 May, the Hungarian government received a final list containing the exact names of factories which had to be fully dismantled and removed as part of the reparations to the Soviet Union.) The loss of Hungarian Siemens Works was especially dramatic for the country, because together with the dismantled cable factory of Felten & Guilleaume, it meant the complete disappearance of the Hungarian cable manufacturing industry in spring 1945.[24]

Legally, no change occurred in the management or ownership system of Hungarian Siemens Works in 1945. The directorate which had been elected at the last general assembly in 1944 remained in charge, with two German members among the directors: Ernst Siemens and Dr. Hermann Reyss. However, they did not attend the last assembly, which was held on 21 June 1944, though Wilchelm Mader, a representative of the Berlin firm, did. In these turbulent months, the company was led by the Hungarian directors, with the managing director and director of trade, Miklós Kemper, and the other managing director and technical director, Aladár Szentmártony, playing particularly prominent roles. In summer 1945, as one of the stipulations of the Potsdam Agreement, German properties beyond the borders of Germany were declared objects to be used as reparations for war damage by the Soviet Union. Hungarian Siemens Works operated under full German ownership, so it was only a question of time before the change of ownership would occur.

The legal uncertainty surrounding the Hungarian Siemens subsidiary became obvious at the beginning of 1946. A letter written on 30 January 1946 by Zoltán Tildy, the Hungarian prime minister and president of the Chief Economic Council of Hungary,[25] announced to the leaders of Hungarian Siemens Works that all of the company's shares, which were valued at a total of 6 million pengős, were being given to the Soviet Union as reparations, in accordance with the decisions reached at the Potsdam conference and because the company was in German ownership. Quoting the letter, the government of the Soviet Union would be authorised to exercise the 'shareholders' right'.[26] This meant *en passant* that the form of the business would remain a joint-stock company and the Siemens name would be retained. Consequently, there were general assemblies and the directorate and the board of supervisors elected at the assemblies would continue to work formally according to the constitution. But the members of the management changed as one of the conditions.

The new management of Hungarian Siemens Works was elected only at the extraordinary assembly on 19 October 1946, months after the January decision of the Hungarian state. The assembly removed all members of the leadership who had held positions at the company in or before 1944, and they changed the constitution of the company. The assembly deleted the paragraph from the constitution, which secured a majority for the Hungarian members on the directorate, and it also deleted a paragraph according to which women were not allowed to vote at the assembly. The newly elected board of directors consisted of seven Soviet members and one Hungarian, and the board of supervisors had four members, three Soviet and one Hungarian, and two of the three Soviet members were women. The Soviet participants in the leadership worked as officers at the Soviet Property Holding Office of Hungary.[27] Alongside the Soviet managing director (Ivan Odajnik, who was followed by another Soviet officer, Nyikolaj Romanov, in September 1947), the second most important executive was a Hungarian citizen (Andor Pollák, in some documents Adolf). He was the only Hungarian member of the directorate, and he had not held any position at Hungarian Siemens Works before.

Little is known about the Soviet era of Hungarian Siemens Works Electrical Engineering Joint-Stock Company, apart from the fact that it was under Soviet ownership and control. However, there is evidence to suggest some glitches in its operations. For instance, in a letter written on 15 April 1947, the previous managing director, Miklós Kemper, complained that he had not received any official dismissal notice regarding his employee status. According to the letter, Odajnik had informed him orally, after the general assembly in October 1946, when Kemper was removed from the directorate, that he, Odajnik, would be the managing director from then on. Moreover, Kemper stated that the company continued to use his services.[28] This practice of retaining a looted company and of doing so as if this were a normal manner of operation can be understood only by studying the nature of the firm in the years which followed.

An 'Alternative' Siemens Company

After the factories of Hungarian Siemens Works had been dismantled and removed in the spring of 1945, the leadership of the firm—the original Hungarian-dominated management, decided to give many Siemens employees notice to quit, probably because of the uncertain future of the German-owned company. We do not know how many employees were affected, but 27 people, presumably most of them among the affected, decided to establish a new entity with the name Joint-Stock Company for Electrical Engineering Industry and Trade, or Vikert, the abbreviated form of the Hungarian name *(Villamosipari és Kereskedelmi Részvénytársaság)*.[29] The proposed foundation rules were formulated on 22 May 1945 and signed by 27 (ex-)Siemens officers and chief engineers. On the list of the 27 founders, one finds among the chief engineers and officers Miklós Kemper and Aladár Szentmártony, the two managing directors of the still-existing Hungarian Siemens Works. They each continued to hold positions at Hungarian Siemens Works when they signed the foundation document, so they cannot be seen as ex-Siemens personnel. This fact indicates that Hungarian Siemens Works and Vikert existed in parallel, and it also gives an impression of the significance of the founders group. One could consider the founders a reservoir of crucial knowledge about Siemens's production processes and management in Hungary. Three weeks later, on 12 June 1945, the first assembly (the statutory meeting) of Vikert was held in the Hungarian Siemens headquarter (Budapest, Teréz Boulevard 36); by then, 171 shareholders had invested capital in the firm in the amount of 400,000 pengős (2,000 shares at 200 pengős a share).

The foundation rules and the articles of association of Vikert did not mention Siemens in any way, but the aims and profiles of the new firm were identical word for word with the ones in the last articles of the association of Hungarian Siemens Works from 1943. The seat and the plant of Vikert—registered by the Registry Court Budapest on 3 July—were also the same as those of Hungarian Siemens. Furthermore, Vikert rented the Siemens plant in Kőbánya from Hungarian Siemens Works.[30] Undoubtedly, these 171 persons planned to restart production at the Siemens plant in Kőbánya as their own enterprise, using their newly collected capital.

The modest registered capital of the company (amounted to 400,000 pengős) was provided mostly by minority shareholders. Most of the subscriptions for shares were valid for fewer than ten shares, at a value of less than 2,000 pengős (this was true in the case of 122 shareholders). There were only six shareholders who subscribed for 50 or more shares, at a value of 10,000 pengős. (Electrical engineer László Mayerhuber invested 10,000 pengős; engineer officer István Falusy invested 18,000 pengős; radio engineer Dezső Gregács invested 20,000 pengős; commercial officer József Tóth invested 25,000 pengős; chief engineer Béla Mittelholzer invested 25,000 pengős; and commercial officer Salamon Lichter invested 100,000 pengős.) These six individuals were the biggest shareholders in the new company. The director of trade and still managing director of Hungarian Siemens Works, Miklós Kemper, purchased five shares at a value of 1,000 pengős, and Aladár Szentmártony, the other managing director of Hungarian Siemens Works, bought 25 shares for 5000 pengős.[31]

The directorate of the new company, which was elected by the first assembly, had five members, each of whom had been one of the 27 founders. Four out of the five were also 'big' shareholders (László Mayerhuber, Béla Mittelholzer, József Tóth, and Salamon Lichter).[32] The directorate elected a president from among its members, József Tóth, who also served as managing director. Before holding these positions in Vikert, József Tóth had been working at Hungarian Siemens Works for 21 years.[33]

In the early summer of 1945, inflation was still moderate. The 400,000 pengős capital had some value, but it was nowhere near enough for the resumption of an electrotechnical profile. For the sake of comparison, the last listed capital of Hungarian Siemens Works amounted to 6 million pengős. Securing investment or credit in Hungary or from an international loan in the immediate aftermath of the war was hardly seen as a simple task. The financial sector started to operate again in the spring of 1945, but the banks did not have significant capital for allocation; the only substantial source of money was the central bank (the so-called National Bank). No relevant governmental economic policy was adopted until the summer. Instead, there were only ad hoc provisions. But from mid-1945, when the official delivery of reparations started, one of the main goals became to start and secure industrial production, and for that purpose the state was ready to give loans.[34] The foundation of Vikert closely followed developments at the time. In all likelihood, the new company leadership entered into negotiations to get capital immediately after it had been founded and perhaps even before. Whatever the case, in the summer of 1945, it was given a credit of 2 million pengős from the Ministry of Industry. Together with the credit for starting production, a ministerial commissioner—Károly Thamó—was delegated to the company, and he attended the board meetings.[35]

Over time, the presence of the government grew stronger in this enterprise, which initially had been a kind of bottom-up venture. The source of the idea is not yet known, but the concept appeared already as a fact at a board meeting in September 1945, when the Ministry of Industry expressed its willingness to purchase the shares of Vikert at a value of 3,600,000 pengős, which included the earlier loan of 2 million pengős. Thereby, the listed capital of the company would have increased to 4 million pengős and the Hungarian state would have become the major shareholder, owning 90 percent of the enterprise. For having made such an investment, the Ministry of Industry would delegate nine members to the directorate. The plan required that the company raise the capital by issuing 18,000 shares, on which a decision was made at the extraordinary assembly on 20 September 1945. The minutes noted that the new shares would be offered to the Hungarian Treasury. The Ministry of Industry paid the value of all new shares into the company's current account at Pest Hungarian Commercial Bank on 13 October 1945, so the plan became a reality. It is not possible to detect any significant reduction in the number of old shareholders comparing the share owners and deposits in June, September, or November 1945, so for the most part they clearly held on to their property and continued to believe in Vikert after the state obtained the majority of shares.[36]

The directorate resigned on 16 October 1945. The new board of directors was elected by the extraordinary assembly on 19 November 1945, and it was expanded to 12 members. Out of the 12 members, five came directly from the Ministry of Industry (one undersecretary, one head of department, and three ministerial councillors), and the Ministry of Finance delegated one of its ministerial councillors. The Central Corporation of Banking Companies was represented by a vice-director (Károly Thamó, who had already been delegated to the company as ministerial commissioner of the Ministry of Industry in the summer of 1945), and the Trade Union Council also delegated a member to the board. These eight members were newly elected, and they served as representatives of the state. The ministry nominated an additional member, a worker from Vikert (Ferenc Egyedi), who was intended to represent the workers of Vikert on the directorate. (Ferenc Egyedi had not been one of the founders of the company and had not had any shares before.) Only two members of the original directorate, László Mayerhuber and József Tóth, remained. The explanation for why László Mayerhuber remained on the directorate is interesting. He had been one of the founders of Vikert in May. He had purchased shares (50) in June, but he had also worked as chief engineer at IKART, a company which was in charge of coordinating reparation transfer under the control of Ministry of Industry. Thus, Mayerhuber could also be considered a representative of the Ministry of Industry. His presence clearly indicates the importance of Vikert in Hungary's process of making reparations to the Soviet Union, which offers a plausible explanation for the interest and investment of the Ministry of Industry in the company.

The assembly on 19 November 1945 elected one more member to the directorate, Aladár Szentmártony, who had served as managing director at Hungarian Siemens Works since 1937 and who had purchased 25 shares of Vikert at the time of its foundation. József Tóth remained in his position as managing director and director of trade, but Károly Thamó, the ministerial commissioner and new 'company leader', had more power. According to the original concept of the Ministry of Industry, Tóth should have been in charge of administrative management and Szentmártony of technical management, both of which were under the leadership of Thamó. (Earlier, in the administration of Hungarian Siemens Works, two managing directors had always worked side by side, one as the administrative leader and the other as technical leader. Obviously, Vikert tried to revert to this old, Siemens-type form of management.) However, Szentmártony worked as a technical advisor at Vikert. He refused to accept responsibility as a technical managing director.[37] He may have done this in part because, at the end of 1945, the Hungarian Siemens subsidiary still existed legally in its pre-war structure, so Szentmártony worked there as technical managing director and member of the directorate. This caution on his part is again a sign of parallelism, i.e. for a time the two companies existed side by side.

The membership of the board of supervisors[38] at Vikert was similar to the directorate. The Hungarian Treasury nominated two officers from the Ministry of Industry to this board and one from the Ministry of Finance, as well as a repairman at Vikert. For the fifth position, the assembly could elect a member, and they chose Miklós Kemper, the director of trade and managing director, to work alongside Szentmártony, who had been the second man at Hungarian Siemens Works since 1937.

The resumption of production by Vikert in 1946 brought an array of challenges for the management. Shortage of raw materials was a continuous problem; equipping and making the necessary repairs to the empty factory buildings also posed a serious challenge; the management also needed to handle the problem of low voltage (electrical) engineering and production, because this section of the plant had been destroyed during the war. It was also difficult to evaluate what the company was worth, make an inventory, and assess the value of the raw and semi-raw materials. The assessment was made more difficult by the fact that some of the semi-raw materials had lost their value—temporarily—on account of the shortage of raw materials. Finally, the management had to deal with continuous financing problems.

Moreover, after the summer of 1945, inflation broke loose, which complicated financing and the work of assessment. The value of the pengő started to plummet at the beginning of 1946, which prompted the government to issue currency denominated in almost incomprehensible amounts, for instance one million-million pengős or hundred-million-billion pengős. The Hungarian currency lost its value in practice, and people tried to get ahead without using it. They found other means of payment, like gold, foreign currencies, and any kind of foodstuff or other goods. Even companies adopted the practice of barter rather than the use of currency. The minutes of a Vikert's board meeting mentioned that the firm received tins—for example, rabbit pâté—in exchange for three engines.[39] The hyperinflation of 1945 and 1946 (the worst ever in the country's history) forced the government to replace the pengő with a new currency. The forint was introduced on 1 August 1946.

Despite all the difficulties it faced, Vikert succeeded in restarting the production. Naturally, the main task of the company was to produce goods which the country used to pay its reparations. The manufacturing in the machine and cable factories began as early as 1946, and the new building for the low-voltage engineering factory was under construction at the (Siemens) plant. Meanwhile, Vikert had rented a nearby plot in Kőbánya, where the company had started the production of radios in September 1945. So, Vikert worked, the directorate held regular meetings, and together with the leading operatives, they tried to handle all the problems that arose. According to a memo written by József Tóth,[40] the administration of Vikert was built on the foundation of the hierarchy that had been established in Hungarian Siemens Works, and the system did not change when the state became the major shareholder.

Vikert can be deservedly seen as an 'alternative' Siemens company. The founders (mainly) belonged to the Hungarian Siemens subsidiary, and most of the original shareholders (June 1945) had also been Siemens employees beforehand. The production profile and the management structure were again clearly part of the heritage of the Siemens past. Moreover, the headquarter of Vikert—as announced to the Registry Court—functioned at the same registered address (Budapest, Teréz Boulevard 36) as Hungarian Siemens Works. And finally, the production for Vikert took place at the plant in Kőbánya that Hungarian Siemens Works had used for production before 1945, simply because Vikert rented the plant from Hungarian Siemens Works. The staff of Vikert restarted production successfully, and the Hungarian government was ready to provide support (loans and investments) for the company, because they needed factories that were as productive as possible as quickly as possible in order to help the country meet its reparations' obligations. At the beginning of 1946, when Hungarian Siemens Works became the property of the Soviet

Union, the Hungarian Siemens subsidiary ceased to be under German ownership, but Siemens's business culture lived on at Vikert.

The End of the Story in an East European Version

At the end of 1946, Vikert was also transferred to Soviet ownership. According to a letter of the Hungarian Reparations Office written on 24 December 1946,[41] the shares of Vikert needed to pass into Soviet proprietorship because of the Hungary's reparations obligation. However, Vikert had been established as an independent enterprise in the summer of 1945, and 90 percent of the shares of Vikert belonged to the Hungarian state and 10 percent to Hungarian private shareholders. Nonetheless, in the end, the company was transferred to Soviet ownership because of Germany's reparations obligations. This means that Vikert was declared a successor to Hungarian Siemens Works.

As noted above, Vikert rented the site from Hungarian Siemens Works and started production successfully. The foundation of this success was the knowledge which was brought to the company by the former Siemens employees. At the beginning of 1946, when Hungarian Siemens Works was transferred entirely to Soviet ownership, the Soviet Property Holding Office of Hungary informed Vikert that it would not accept the earlier rental contract, and it was also not willing to sell the property where Vikert operated. Vikert had to assess the possibility of vacating the site or merging into the Siemens Works. The Soviet Office also initiated an investigation to determine whether or not Viker had obtained any Siemens valuables. Although the investigation concluded without finding any proof, the Soviet (Siemens) ownership made the negotiations complex. Formally, the matter was a business disagreement, but the Hungarian Ministry of Industry, as the major shareholder of Vikert, had to take into consideration Soviet interests. During the negotiations, both companies (Soviet Siemens and Vikert) were valued, and according to the assessments, Vikert had a value of 7 million forints, while the Siemens Works was worth only about 1.5 million forints. In spite this, in the end, the Ministry of Industry turned all its Vikert shares over to Soviet ownership. The minority Vikert shareholders got some compensation.[42]

The case of Vikert and Hungarian (Soviet) Siemens Works should be interpreted in a broader context. What happened to Vikert in 1946 was of course influenced by the fact that the Soviet army was present as an occupying power, and the Soviets exerted a profound and continuous influence on the Hungarian political situation, primarily simply by strengthening the position of the Hungarian Communist Party. The first election after the war (4 November 1945) resulted in the victory of the Independent Smallholder's Party (57 percent), although a coalition government was formed, according to the Soviet purpose. For the new government, the economic situation, production and the obtaining of funds to meet reparations obligations remained crucial tasks. In order to coordinate efforts to address these various tasks (reconstruction, reparations and economic policy) the government established an economic institution with oversight powers—the Chief Economic Council—in December 1945. Although the president of this body was the prime minister (Zoltán Tildy) from the Smallholder's Party, the Secretariat of the Council as an initiative and executive body was led by a Communist—Zoltán Vas. Through the Council and its Secretariat, the Communist Party secured a key role in government control of economic issues. The Ministry of Industry remained essentially in the hands of the Social Democrats after the election, but all the ministries lost their importance as they fell under the shadow of the Chief Economic Council.

In parallel with the Council, the state intervened ever more vigorously in the economy and in business life. The first wave of nationalisations at the end of 1945 affected the coal mines in the country. As a next step, at the end of 1946, the five biggest, heavy industry companies were taken into public ownership, but—at the time—only for the period of reparations. Radical nationalisation began only a year later, at the end of 1947, but in 1946 governmental intervention in the economy was more significant than anything directly affecting the private sector. Because of hyperinflation, the state and the National Bank became the only sources for loans and investments. Moreover, together with the new currency, a new price system was introduced, so Hungarian prices broke away from prices on the international market.[43]

These circumstances were in the background when the Ministry of Industry turned its Vikert shares over to Soviet ownership. Hungarian Siemens Works became Soviet property because of the Potsdam agreement, but the firm had been looted. Real production and value were concentrated in Vikert. But the 'alternative' Siemens company could only be appropriated by the use of the power of the occupying army in a country in which the government and the political system were coming increasingly under Soviet influence.

In 1947, Soviet Vikert was given a new name: Directorate of Soviet Enterprises in the Machine Industry, Joint-Stock Company for Electrical Engineering Industry and Trade Vikert *(Gépipari Szovjetvállalatok Igazgatósága, Villamosipari és Kereskedelmi Rt. Vikert)*. None of the previous members of the leadership remained in their positions. The new management had a Soviet majority and a Soviet managing director. The former managing director (József Tóth) was authorised only to joint procuration. Finally, on 29 December 1947, an extraordinary assembly declared that Vikert would be merged with Hungarian (Soviet) Siemens Works without any exchange value. On 18 March 1948, the Registry Court deleted Vikert from the list of Budapest companies.

Because of the new currency, every company had to create an opening balance in forint. Hungarian (Soviet) Siemens Works—including Vikert, still under its old name (Hungarian Siemens Works), but already in Soviet ownership—issued its forint balance sheet in February 1948. According to the opening balance, the company had a net value of 13,470,000 forints. The directorate suggested counting 10 million forints as capital and the rest as reserve funds. The proposal was accepted by the assembly and by the chartered accountant, who controlled the balance. So, the listed capital of (Soviet) Hungarian Siemens Works became 10 million forints, with 10,000 shares with a nominal value of 1,000 forints each.

Until 1951, the company worked in Soviet proprietorship as a joint-stock company with its original name: Hungarian Siemens Works Electrical Engineering Joint-Stock Company (*Magyar Siemens Művek Villamossági Rt.*). The name implied continuity and a Hungarian national identity. Thus, Soviet control was not transparent. In 1951, the name of the firm was changed—Budapest Electrical Company and Cable Factory Co *(Budapesti Villamosgép és Kábelgyár Rt.)*—Siemens was deleted from its name. In September 1952, the ownership was modified. Hungary and the Soviet Union signed an agreement according to which the Hungarian state could buy back all former German possessions (in Hungary) from the Soviet Union. In the case of former Hungarian Siemens Works, this meant that the Hungarian state paid twice: first, it invested money in Vikert in 1945 and then it had to buy back the company which had been launched in large part thanks to its original investment. So, in the end, the Siemens Works was nationalised but still remained a joint-stock company for some years. Thereafter, the firm operated under the Directorate of Power Equipment in the Ministry of Metallurgy and Mining. The last general assembly of the firm was held in August 1955, where a new leadership was elected by the three representatives of the Ministry. Finally, on 12 May 1960, the Registry Court deleted the company from the list of Budapest firms; the plant and factories in Kőbánya became part of a greater heavy industry conglomerate.

Conclusion

During the initial period of reconstruction and the resumption of production after the Second World War, the employees of a Siemens subsidiary in Hungary decided to rebuild the enterprise through their own efforts, but as a new company. This new company was named Vikert. The history of the short-lived firm is an important and interesting subchapter in the events of 1945/1946, the significance of which can be summarised in four main points. First, Hungarian Siemens Works still existed legally when Vikert was established as a new enterprise in June 1945. The initiative of the former Siemens employees was motivated by the fact that Hungarian Siemens Works had been dismantled and removed to the Soviet Union in spring 1945, and they had been dismissed. Secondly, four months after the foundation of the firm Vikert, in the autumn of 1945, the Ministry of

Industry invested in the firm and became the majority shareholder. The ministry was primarily concerned with Hungary's reparations obligations. In all likelihood, the ministry saw a potential for production in Vikert, while the German-owned Siemens would hardly be counted against Hungary's reparations, especially given that it was looted and dismantled by the Soviets. Thirdly, with the state owning most of the firm, the leadership was expected to include a representative of the workers as early as October 1945. This is illustrative of a slight change in state economic policy, though it remained a slight change, since the former directors and managers were able to remain in their management positions even though the company was under state control. This was no longer the case under Soviet leadership neither in Hungarian Siemens Works, nor in Vikert. The pre-war managing director of Hungarian Siemens Works, Aladár Szentmártony, for example, was not permitted to remain in the management or even in the company after Hungarian Siemens Works transferred to Soviet ownership, though he was given a new place in the Research Institute for the Electrical Industry. His technical knowledge was valuable in the new regime as well, later he won a state award—the Kossuth prize—for his work.[44] The staff records of Vikert also prove that for the most part the founding shareholders did not continue to work at Viker after it had come under Soviet control.[45] The Soviet ownership meant a real dividing line in the history of Siemens and Vikert. Fourthly and finally, as a specific characteristic of this interim and unstable period, in 1946, the Soviet Siemens and Vikert operated side by side, indeed on the same site. Hungarian Siemens Works became Soviet property at the end of January 1946 because of the German reparations duty. Vikert was transferred to Soviet ownership at the end of December 1946 for the same reason. However, this parallelism lasted into 1947. The Soviet Siemens and the Soviet Vikert operated side by side. Only in December 1947 was Vikert merged with the Soviet Siemens, which kept the original Siemens name until 1951, surprisingly. Although Vikert was in operation for only one and a half years—between June 1945 and the beginning of 1947—the management performed well. It managed to restart production, which in and of itself was a huge accomplishment. Indeed, the significance of this achievement can be also seen in the fact that the Soviet Siemens—after the merger with Vikert—had assets of more than 10 million forints at the beginning of 1948, and this assessment was made less than three years after the factories had been dismantled.

Notes

1 This paper was supported by the János Bolyai Research Scholarship of the Hungarian Academy of Sciences. I would like to thank Aladár Madarász and György Kövér for their comments on my manuscript, and I owe special thanks to Pál Germuska for his useful advice on sources.

2 Feldenkirchen, *Werner von Siemens*, 91.

3 Wiesen, *West German Industry*, 41.
4 Wiesen, *West German Industry*, 18.
5 Wiesen, *West German Industry*, 17–51.
6 Budapest Főváros Levéltára (BFL) [Budapest Municipal Archive] VII.2.e. Cégbírósági iratok (Cg.) [Registry Court Documents] Cg. 34391; Cg. 32673; *Budapest közúti vasúti közlekedésének fejlődése.*
7 BFL VII.2.e. Cg. 32657; Cg. 2055.
8 Feldenkirchen, *Siemens.*
9 For the whole history of Siemens in Hungary see Frisnyák and Klement, *A Siemens története Magyarországon.*
10 BFL VII.2.e. Cg. 2829 (Okm. 1091).
11 The factory in Pozsony/Bratislava became part of the *Siemens & Co.* limited partnership in Prague, which merged in 1926 with Elektrizitäts- und Maschinenbau AG. Mohelnice (Müglitz). They were eventually made part of *Siemens Elektrizität AG.* (in Czechoslovak *Elektrotechna*). *Compass Leonhardt* (Vienna, 1929), 1081. On the history of *Elektrotechna* see Boyer, 'Economic efficiency and nationality', 307–324.
12 The Hungarian Siemens's subsidiaries worked in the same organisational structure as the company did in Berlin and Vienna. The Siemens & Halske JSC (Budapest)—established in 1900—functioned as the headquarters for the Hungarian market and, later, also as a centre for radio production and reparation. However, the main manufacturing activity—cables and machines—was done by Hungarian Siemens-Schuckert Works. Because of the Great Depression, cuts had to be made to the Budapest subsidiaries, and the Siemens & Halske JSC (Budapest) was liquidated. Its functions were taken over by Hungarian Siemens-Schuckert Works. (BFL VII.2.e. Cg. 32657); Cg. 2055. Since 1925, the medical device technology profile had belonged to another Hungarian Siemens company, and this production field remained separate. (BFL VII.2.e. Cg. 7368.).
13 The Hungarian air force ordered e.g. radio and piece parts mainly from the Hungarian Siemens's subsidiary. Kováts, 'A Magyar Repülőgépszerelvénygyár Rt. története 1941–1950', 160. Trends which were brought about by the war can generally be assessed according to hourly wages in the iron and machine industry. During the war (1941–1944), nominal wages in this sector increased yearly by 21.72 percent on average. Pogány, 'Munkabérek a két világháború közötti Magyarországon', 86.
14 In 1917 the company had 1,250 employees together in the machine factory (Pozsony) and the cable factory (Budapest). (BFL VII.2.e. Cg. 2829. 58. d.) According to some suggestions, during the Great Depression the number of employees decreased significantly. The regeneration began in 1937 when the number of employees rose by 15 percent. The annual reports of the directorates mentioned further increases in employment in 1938 and 1939. (BFL VII.2.e. Cg. 2829 (Okm. 1091) 1610 kd.).
15 After the Anschluß, the German-Austrian Siemens-Schuckert property in Vienna became German. Feldenkirchen, *Siemens. 1918–1945.*
16 Gyarmati, Püski, and Barta, *Magyarország a XX. században. I–V.* Vol I., 397–398. For details in English see Stark, 'War casualties'.
17 Tamási and Ungváry, *Budapest, 1945*, 5–20.
18 Honvári, *A XX. századi magyar gazdaságtörténet*, 85–94.
19 The Temporary National Government—formed according to a four-party coalition—was established in December 1944 and remained in power until November 1945. The prime minister was Colonel General Béla Dálnoki Miklós, who was independent of any political party. Romsics, *Magyarország története a XX. században*, 277–278.
20 Pető and Szakács, *A hazai gazdaság*, 51.

21 Vass G., 'Dokumentumok'.
22 *A Villamosgép és Kábelgyár 50 éve*, 21, 24.
23 Magyar Nemzeti Levéltár Országos Levéltára (MNL OL) XIX-A-58., 116/F. B. irat, A külügyminiszter tiltakozása a Szövetséges Ellenőrző Bizottságnál [Protest of the Minister of Foreign Affairs against the Allied Control Commission]. Quoted in Vass G., 'Dokumentumok' 3.a) document.
24 In Berlin, the situation was similar. 40 percent of the plant had been destroyed. The Soviet troops arrived in Siemensstadt (Siemens City) on 26 April and left it mid-July. They confiscated 22,700 out of a total of 23,100 machine tools (98 percent). Wiesen, *West German Industry*, 20–21.
25 The election on 4 November 1945 ended in a victory for the Independent Smallholder's Party (57 percent), but because of Soviet pressure (through Kliment Yefremovich Voroshilov), a coalition government was formed. Zoltán Tildy was the president of the winning party and became prime minister. Romsics, *Magyarország története*, 284–285. The Chief Economic Council was established in December 1945 with the aim of coordinating reconstruction and economic policy. Pető and Szakács, *A hazai gazdaság*, 65–66.
26 BFL VII.2.e. Cg. 2829 Documents of Hungarian Siemens-Schuckert Works Electrical Engineering Joint-Stock Company, 6033 kd. 30 January 1946. Letter of Zoltán Tildy to Marshal Voroshilov (president of the Allied Control Commission in Hungary).
27 The member of this office represented Soviet interests on directorates of the firms given to the Soviet Union as reparations. One finds the same names on the board of directors of Hungarian Aircraft Assembly Plant JSC as on the board of directors of the Siemens Works, e.g. Georgi Popov, Vladimir Bezugli, and Boris Romanov. (Kováts, 'A Magyar Repülőgépszerelvénygyár Rt. története 1941–1950', 176.) Hungarian Aircraft Assembly Plant JSC came under Hungarian–Soviet ownership in 1946, because the German share of ownership was only about 50 percent. However, this process took less than a year, and the leadership of the firm was controlled by the Soviet members of the directorates.
28 MNL OL Z 1190 1. cs. 1. t. Letter of Miklós Kemper to Hungarian Siemens Works JSC., 15 April, 1947.
29 The narrative of the history of Vikert presented here is based on the following sources: BFL VII.2.e. Cg. 47950; MNL OL Z 1183; Z 1190; *A Villamosgép és Kábelgyár 50 éve*, 13–45.
30 MNL OL Z 1183 Vikert, Documents of managing directorship, record of 20 November 1945.
31 BFL VII.2.e. Cg. 47950, Shares bought and paid in Pest Hungarian Commercial Bank, 5–12 June 1945.
32 The fifth member of directorate was commercial officer Béla Raschovszky, who had 10 shares at a value of 2,000 pengős. BFL VII.2.e. Cg. 47950, statutory meeting on 12 June 1945.
33 MNL Z 1190 Vikert, Department of Staff and Labour, records about József Tóth.
34 Pető and Szakács, *A hazai gazdaság*, 52, 59.
35 The representation of the state in manufacturing was not unusual, in this instance. In order to ensure continuous production, the Ministry of Industry sent a ministerial commissioner to the municipal authorities in May 1945. Pető and Szakács, *A hazai gazdaság*, 52.
36 My analysis of the shareholders is based on the share subscriptions in June and the share deposits before the general assemblies (12 June 20 September, 19 November 1945). BFL VII.2.e. Cg. 47950.

37 MNL OL Z 1190 Vikert, Department of Staff and Labour, Memo about the job of József Tóth, 7 January 1947, written by Tóth.
38 The Hungarian joint-stock companies operated with a dual board system. The directorate worked as strategic leadership; its members were elected by the shareholders and they reported annually about their work to the shareholders. The directorate appointed the director(s) for operative leadership. The board of supervisors (also elected by the shareholders) controlled the operation of the directorate and guaranteed each year that the company worked according to the law and to the interests of the shareholders. The two boards had completely separate memberships.
39 BFL VII.2.e. Cg. 47950, minutes of meeting of directorate on 17 September 1945.
40 MNL OL Z 1190 Vikert, Department of Staff and Labour, Memo about the job of József Tóth, 7 January 1947, written by Tóth.
41 BFL VII.2.e. Cg. 47950, a document attached to the extraordinary assembly on 28 April 1947.
42 MNL OL XIX-F-1-b. 44. d. 77.933/V.-1946.IP.M.; MNL OL XIX-F-1-kk. 8.d. The history of the negotiation is presented in Gábor, *Jóvátétel és külkereskedelmi orientációváltás Magyarországon, 1945–1949/51*, 129–130, accessed 28 December 2017, http://pea.lib.pte.hu/handle/pea/16125
43 Pető and Szakács, *A hazai gazdaság*, 62–82.
44 'Herr Tuppel csodálkozik'. *Népszabadság*, 24 October 1958, 2–3.
45 Of the 171 founding shareholders, 99 had an employee registry sheet in the archive. Only 17 of them were still working at Soviet Vikert in 1947. MNL OL Z 1190 Vikert, Department of Staff and Labour, 2. and 3. cs.

Primarily Sources

Budapest Főváros Levéltára (BFL) [Budapest Municipal Archive]
VII.2.e. Cégbírósági iratok (Cg.) [Registry Court Documents]
Cg. 2055 Siemens & Halske Rt. [Siemens & Halske JSC].
Cg. 2829 (Okm. 1091) Magyar Siemens–Schuckert Művek Villamossági Rt. iratai [Documents of Hungarian Siemens–Schuckert Works Electrical Engineering Joint-Stock Company].
Cg. 7368 Magyar Siemens–Reinigen Művek Rt. iratai [Dokuments of the Siemens–Reinigen Works JSC].
Cg. 32673 Budapest Városi Vasút Vállalat Siemens & Halske [Budapest City Rail Company Siemens & Halske].
Cg. 32657 Siemens & Halske Bt. [Siemens & Halske LP].
Cg. 34391 Körúti Villamos Vasút Vállalat Siemens & Halske [Boulevard Tramway Company Siemens & Halske].
Cg. 47950 Villamosipari és Kereskedelmi Rt. [Joint-Stock Company for Electrical Industry and Trade].
Magyar Nemzeti Levéltár Országos Levéltára (MNL OL) [Hungarian National Archives]
XIX-A-58. Fegyverszüneti Tárcaközi Bizottság iratai [Documents of the Interdepartmental Committee for Truce].
XIX-F-1-b. Iparügyi Minisztérium, általános iratok [Ministry of Industry, general documents].
XIX-F-1-kk. Bán Antal miniszter iratai [Documents of Minister Antal Bán]
Z 1183 Villamosipari és Kereskedelmi Rt., Ügyvezető igazgatóság [Joint-Stock Company for Electrical Industry and Trade, Managing Directorship].

Z 1190 Villamosipari és Kereskedelmi Rt., Személyzeti és munkaügyi osztály [Joint-Stock Company for Electrical Industry and Trade, Department of Staff and Labour].

Compass Leonhardt. Vienna, 1929.

Népszabadság, 24 October 1958, 2–3.

Bibliography

Boyer, Christoph. 'Economic Efficiency and Nationality: The Siemens Subsidiary Elektrotechna in the First Czechoslovakian Republic', in *Business and Politics in Europe, 1900–1970: Essays in Honour of Alice Teichova*. Edited by Terry Gourvish, 307–324. Cambridge: Cambridge University Press, 2003.

Budapest közúti vasúti közlekedésének fejlődése 1865–1922 és a BSZKRT tíz évi működése, 1923–1933 [The Development of City Rail System in Budapest 1865–1922 and Ten Years of BSZKRT, 1923–1933] Budapest: BSZKRT Directorate, 1934.

Feldenkirchen, Wilfried. *Siemens. 1918–1945*. Munich and Zurich: Piper, 1995.

Feldenkirchen, Wilfried. *Siemens. From Workshop to Global Player*. Munich and Zurich: Piper, 2000.

Feldenkirchen, Wilfried. *Werner von Siemens: Inventor and International Entrepreneur*. Columbus: Ohio State University Press, 1994.

Frisnyák, Zsuzsanna and Judit Klement. *A Siemens története Magyarországon, 1887–2017* [The History of Siemens in Hungary 1887–2017]. Edited by Orsolya Sebők. Budapest: Siemens Zrt., 2017.

Gábor, Péter. *Jóvátétel és külkereskedelmi orientációváltás Magyarországon, 1945–1949/51* [Reparations and Orientation Change in Foreign Trade in Hungary, 1945–1949/51] PhD diss., Pécs: University of Pécs, 2013. Accessed 28 December 2017, http://pea.lib.pte.hu/handle/pea/16125.

Gyarmati, György, Levente Püski, and Róbert Barta. *Magyarország a XX. században. I–V.* [Hungary in the Twentieth Century] Vol I. Politika, társadalom, hadtörténet, jogalkotás [Politics, Society, Military History, Legislation]. Szekszárd: Babits, 1996.

Honvári, János. *A XX. századi magyar gazdaságtörténet* [The Economic History of Hungary in the Twentieth Century]. Budapest: Aula, 2006.

Kováts, Lajos. 'A Magyar Repülőgépszerelvénygyár Rt. története 1941–1950' [The History of the Hungarian Aircraft Assembly Plant JSC, 1941–1950], in *Tanulmányok Budapest múltjából* 26 [Essays on the Past of Budapest, vol. 26.], 153–183. Budapest: BTM, 1997.

Pető, Iván and Sándor Szakács. *A hazai gazdaság négy évtizedének története, 1945–1985* [The History of Four Decades of Hungarian Economy, 1945–1985]. Vol 1. Az újjáépítés és a tervutasításos irányítás időszaka, 1945–1968 [The Period of Reconstruction and the Planned Economy, 1945–1968]. Budapest: Közgazdasági és Jogi Kiadó, 1985.

Pogány, Ágnes. 'Munkabérek a két világháború közötti Magyarországon' [Wages in the Interwar Period in Hungary], *Történelmi Szemle* [Historical Review] 31, no. 1–2 (1989): 70–95.

Romsics, Ignác. *Magyarország története a XX. században* [The History of Hungary in the Twentieth Century]. Budapest: Osiris, 1999.

Stark, Tamás. 'War Casualties', in *Hungarian Economy and Society During World War II*. Edited by György Lengyel, 171–260. New York: Atlantic Research Publication, 1993.

Tamási, Miklós and Krisztián Ungváry. *Budapest, 1945*. Budapest: Corvina, 2006.

Vass G., István. 'Dokumentumok a magyar–szovjet jóvátételi egyezmény létrejöttéhez' [Documents Related to the Formation of the Hungarian–Soviet Reparation Agreement], *archívNET* 11, no. 2 (2011). Accessed 28 December 2017, www.archivnet.hu/diplomacia/dokumentumok_a_magyarszovjet_jovateteli_egyezmeny_letrejottehez.html.

A Villamosgép és Kábelgyár 50 éve és szerepe a magyar villamosipar fejlődésében, 1913–1963 [50 Years of the Electric Machine and Cable Factory and the Development of the Hungarian Electrical Industry]. Edited by Ferenc Keller. Budapest: KJK, 1963.

Wiesen, S. Jonathan. *West German Industry and the Challenge of the Nazi Past, 1945–1955*. Chapel Hill and London: University of North Carolina Press, 2001.

9 International Business and the Cold War

The Case of the Trans-European Pipeline, 1956–1960

Marten Boon

Introduction

The Cold War was a total war by intention rather than in practice.[1] Nonetheless, the bipolar world that emerged from World War II changed international business and international relations fundamentally. Western Europe, squeezed between two nuclear superpowers, lost their empires and depended for its military and energy security on American stewardship. Relying on abundant domestic reserves of coal before the war, West European countries became increasingly dependent on imported oil after the war.[2] Most of the oil came from the Middle East. Previously under French and British mandate, the region became a hotbed of Cold War contestation after 1945. Oil supply depended on eight multinational oil companies.[3] They jointly controlled the oil reserves in the Middle East based on the interlocking ownership of concessions that were granted under British imperial influence before the war.[4] Post-war decolonisation and Soviet support for Arab nationalism threatened this edifice of oligopolistic control over oil production. Moreover, growing oil exports from countries outside the Middle East threatened the majors' control over West European markets in the late 1950s. Such threats came most pertinently from rising Soviet exports but also from France's policy of pursuing oil independence through its state-controlled oil production in Algeria. As such, the first decades of the Cold War challenged the market power of the major oil companies. The companies responded with new legal and organisational measures to harness their power and protect their interests from the threat of sequestration in the Middle East and emerging competition in Western Europe. One important, although largely overlooked, part of their efforts was the construction of oil pipelines in Western Europe.

As post-war economic growth took-off, pipelines were the most economically efficient means to carry growing volumes of crude oil to the inland markets of Western Europe. In 1956, Royal Dutch Shell (RDS), British Petroleum (BP) and Standard Oil of New Jersey (Jersey Standard) considered the possibility of constructing a Trans-European Pipeline (TEP) from the French port of Marseille.[5] The companies had already cooperated on building export pipelines in the Middle East, but large-scale importing pipelines in Europe were a novelty at the time. The outward rationale of the plan was to devise a pan-European import pipeline as a more efficient alternative to plans for national pipelines that had emerged in France and West Germany a year before. The underlying agenda was to raise a barrier to entry. A fully integrated importing pipeline for Western Europe would make it exceedingly difficult for new competitors to enter the West European oil market, protecting the market share of the oligopoly. As such, TEP was a direct response to new competitors clamouring at the gates to the West European market. In 1955, the Soviet Union launched its Druzhba pipeline system that would carry oil to the western borders of the Eastern bloc. In addition, the Italian state-owned company Ente Nazionale Idrocarburi (ENI) threatened to break into the majors' markets with a pipeline from Genoa to Southern Germany. By establishing and controlling an integrated pipeline for the whole of Western Europe, the companies hoped to outcompete these rival pipelines. The plan failed, however, and in subsequent years, five separate crude oil pipelines were constructed (Figure 9.1).

This chapter considers the question of why the TEP failed while other cross-border pipelines were realised. The TEP was economically and technically feasible but legal and organisational issues delayed the decision-making to the extent that the economic window of opportunity closed. While part of the delay derived from the consortium's internal problems, the most interesting and important part of the story is how the major oil companies attempted to devise a legal and organisational structure that would protect the pipeline from state interference. In this respect, the TEP served a dual purpose. It sought primarily to protect the pipeline against French state interference, but, if successful, it would also set a legal precedent for the protection of foreign-owned assets in the Middle East. In addition, such a legal and organisational structure would allow the pipeline to function fully as a barrier to entry in European markets. Essentially, TEP was an attempt by the majors to harness their oligopolistic control over the oil market in the face of challenges to their position. The case provides a unique insight into how multinational enterprises adjusted to conducting international business and foreign direct investment during the early stages of the Cold War.

The first section of the paper discusses economics and institutional aspects of oil pipelines in the context of the Cold War. The second section discusses the TEP during its planning stage between 1956 and 1958. The third section considers the continued efforts of the consortium to influence pipeline planning after the failure of the TEP. The chapter closes with a conclusion on the implications and legacies of the TEP case for international business organisation.

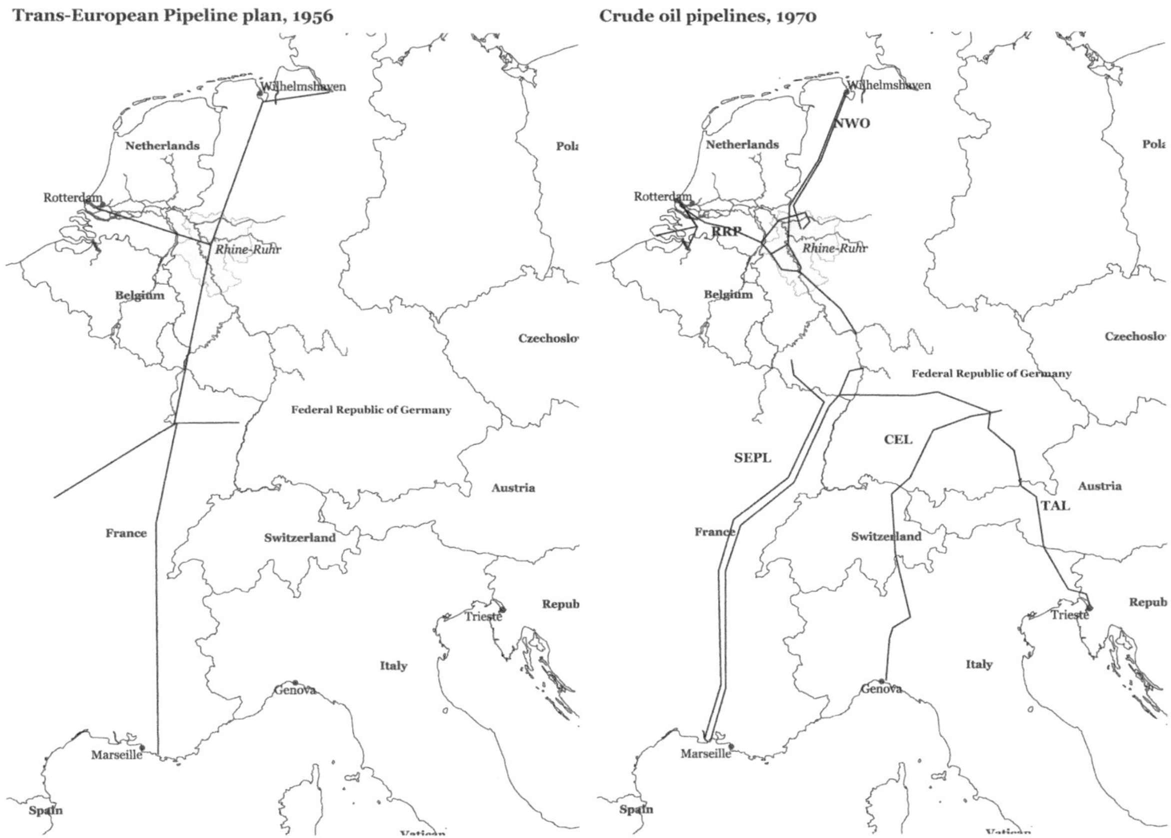

Figure 9.1 Crude oil pipelines in Western Europe

Source: British Petroleum Archive 43379, Sappeur NV minutes of meetings, 'SAPPEUR NV. Aide memoire to a General Meeting of Shareholders' Experts held in the Hague on the 31st January 1957', undated, Attachment 2a ('Trans-European pipeline flow rates and refining demands'); W. Molle and E. Wever, *Oil refineries and petrochemical industries in Western Europe: buoyant past, uncertain future* (Aldershot 1984) 53, 164–168. Maps created by the author.

Pipelines in the Cold War: Asset Specificity and Political Risk

The TEP was economically and technically feasible. By the mid-1950s, Western Europe relied on the Middle East for 80 percent of its oil supply, and most of that oil came through the Mediterranean, either via the Suez Canal or by pipeline from Saudi Arabia and Iraq.[6] Transhipping it via Marseille was logical. Given concentrated flows of oil, pipelines are by far the cheapest mode of transportation; only maritime oil tankers can be cheaper. Although the initial capital investment for pipelines and tankers is high, their running costs at sufficient scale are lower than any other mode of transportation. Therefore, the structure of the supply chain of Middle Eastern crude oil to Western European inland markets depended economically on the relative transport costs of pipelines and tankers.[7]

As long as tankers remained relatively small, which they did up to the mid-1950s, pipelines presented the largest relative transport cost reduction in the supply chain. Short sea routes between the Middle East and Western Europe and long pipelines across the European continent were therefore economically favourable. When tankers became bigger and therefore more economical, which they did after 1956, long sea routes no longer mattered and could even offer an advantage in combination with short pipelines. This trade-off between the relative economies of scale of pipelines and tankers was an important economic factor in reshaping the crude oil transport infrastructure to and within Western Europe. The companies studying the TEP were well aware of this trade-off between tankers and pipelines and that therefore the economic window of opportunity for a large, transnational pipeline system depended on the speed of their decision-making and the development of the international tanker fleet.[8]

Speedy decision-making also mattered because of differences among the 14 consortium members: those planning and constructing refineries in the German Rhine-Ruhr area were much more pressed for time than companies planning refineries in Southern Germany or Northeastern France. With its urban and industrial agglomerations, the Rhine-Ruhr area was the centre of gravity of oil demand in Western Europe in the 1950s. Demand in the other areas served by the pipeline was expected to take off later. The German subsidiaries of the three major oil companies, Deutsche Shell, Deutsche BP and Esso AG, as well as several smaller German refiners, needed an operational pipeline by 1959, while companies planning refineries in other areas could wait for a few more years. Time was therefore an essential aspect of the deliberations of the consortium if the pipeline was to be built as planned.

Pure pipeline economics were not the only determining factor of pipeline planning because institutional issues are just as important in the decision to invest or not.[9] Pipelines have a high degree of asset specificity, meaning that they are geographically fixed and dedicated to serve a limited number of users in a limited space. Beyond transporting oil from A to B they are useless. Because the capital invested in pipelines is sunk, the routing, operation, transport tariffs and fiscal and regulatory issues of the pipeline need to be concluded and fixed before construction commences. Another source of uncertainty is government legislation and regulation. Jeffrey Makholm's recent study of the history of the political economy of pipelines shows that, although oil and gas pipelines are technically similar the world over, their operations, governance and regulation differ from country to country.[10]

In contrast to the US, where pipeline legislation and regulation was already in place—an inheritance from the Standard Oil Trust era—in Western Europe, no pipeline legislation existed in the 1950s. Although European economic integration had been launched in 1957, and the member states of the European Economic Community (EEC) recognised a common transport and energy policy as an important future task, harmonisation of laws and regulations, and coordination between member states was yet to come about.[11] The oil companies considering pipelines in Western Europe in the 1950s were, therefore, undertaking planning in a regulatory void. The main sources of institutional uncertainty for the consortium, however, were political risks associated with the Cold War and decolonisation, specifically the rise of (economic) nationalism in (former) colonial territories in North Africa and the Middle East and the precarious oil supply position of France—the pipeline's principle transit country.

The oil companies were experienced with building coalitions and consortia to mitigate risks. In that regard, the TEP was not very different from comparable pipeline projects in the Middle East or other joint ventures in production or refining. Moreover, from the interwar period, the major oil companies had emerged as an oligopoly, skilled at informal collusion and cooperation through the cross-ownership of oil concessions and long-term supply contracts that observed and protected the market shares of the oligopoly.[12] However, the post-war world was rapidly changing as the Cold War and decolonisation brought new political risks to bear on the companies' international investments. Following the renegotiation of oil concessions in Venezuela and the Middle East in the 1940s and early 1950s, pipeline transit countries—in particular Syria and Lebanon—began demanding higher transit fees and sabotaging pipelines in support of their demands.[13] In line with the obsolescing bargain model—which posits that the bargaining position of foreign companies vis-à-vis the host government deteriorates once investments are sunk—the companies were forced to concede better terms to the transit countries.[14] As such, oil companies were preoccupied with protecting their foreign assets from host nations' asymmetrical bargaining power.

The TEP differed from the Middle Eastern joint ventures because it had a different objective—oil imports rather than exports—and was far bigger, with a heterogeneous group of 14 oil companies who competed in the same West European markets. Moreover, if the pipeline were to be the only import trunk line into Western Europe, inland refineries would have no alternatives for receiving their crude oil. In the case of the Middle Eastern export lines, tanker shipping could circumvent a temporary pipeline blockade. In the case of TEP, closure of the pipeline would leave inland refiners without ready alternative supply options. Without a common European institutional framework regulating cross-border oil pipelines—as was still the case in the late 1950s—the question of how to organise the governance of the planned pipeline was therefore a very urgent and important question. The question centred on the position of France as the pipeline's principle transit country.

Occupied during World War II, France emerged from the war as the weakest of the Allied powers, which affected its security of oil supply after the war. In the perception of the French state, its security of supply had been seriously impaired by US foreign policy after 1945. With the discovery of major new reserves in the Middle East and the rising threat of Soviet interference in the region after 1945, the US State Department spurred the US major oil companies to increase their stake in the region.[15] Middle Eastern oil exploration was cartelised in what was known as the 1928 Red Line Agreement between the companies participating in the Iraq Petroleum Company (IPC).[16] The Agreement obliged the shareholders to jointly develop Middle Eastern oil reserves, excluding Kuwait and Iran, which were both under British influence. After World War II, Jersey Standard and Socony upended the agreement to acquire a 40 percent stake in the Arabian American Oil Company (Aramco), which held the Saudi Arabian concession. The end of the Agreement diluted France's share in Middle Eastern oil, increasing its already high dependence on the US for its oil supply security.[17] France initially protested the abrogation of the Red Line Agreement but consented in 1948.[18]

A second threat to French interests was rising Arab nationalism, which fuelled anticolonial movements in France's colonial dependencies in North Africa, in particular in Algeria. After its marginalisation in Middle Eastern oil production, France turned to its North African territories in the hope of striking oil and reducing its dependence on American-controlled oil supplies. Independence movements threatened these objectives, which was a major reason for the French to join Britain and Israel in the invasion of Egypt after the nationalisation of the Suez Canal in 1956.[19] US president Eisenhower was infuriated by the imperialistic invasion of Egypt and threatened to withhold US oil supplies to offset the blockage of the Suez Canal until Britain, France and Israel retreated.[20]

The French perception in 1956–1957, following Suez, was that the US had colluded with the Arab nationalists and that France could not entrust its oil security to the Americans.[21] In search of more French-controlled oil sources, the state had promoted oil exploration in overseas territories through state-owned enterprises grouped in the *Bureau de Recherches Pétroliers* (BRP) and the *Régie Autonome des Pétroles* (RAP).[22] In 1956, RAP made a discovery in Algeria. The substantial find sparked dreams of French oil independence, which were only strengthened by the events of the Suez Crisis.[23] The prospect of France rapidly developing an alternative source of oil in an already oversupplied market was not particularly welcomed by the multinational oil companies.[24]

From 1928, French petroleum laws subjected the French oil market to tight government regulation, with a cartelised market, regulated prices and clauses that could force private companies to purchase and hold oil in the interest of national security.[25] As such, the law allowed the French state to force refiners to absorb Algerian crude oil and achieve France's goal of oil independence.[26] Although the actual decrees were declared in 1958, it was clear by 1957 that France would take this road.[27] Algerian oil, therefore, not only promised to fulfil the French dream of independence from Anglo-American oil interests, but the French state also had the legal instruments to enforce it in practice. Although Algerian oil did not fulfil its promise in the long run, the TEP consortium feared the political motivation and legal instruments of the French government because they could be used to interfere with the policies and operations of the pipeline.[28] Moreover, since Algeria was a *département* of France and as such an integral part of the Europe of the Six, Algerian oil could potentially gain a privileged position on the European market vis-à-vis Middle Eastern oil.[29]

Planning the Trans-European Pipeline

The institutional framework is an essential aspect of pipeline planning, and the TEP faced multiple challenges in this regard. The pipeline disputes in the Middle East had heightened the consortium's concern over state interference, while French oil policies and uncertainty over European pipeline regulations did nothing to ease their concerns. States could take four basic approaches to regulating oil pipelines. The first was to opt for no regulation beyond safety and rights of way.[30] Rights of way are often arranged through a legal arrangement whereby a state has the power to declare the expropriation of privately owned land in the interest of the common good. The right to expropriate can be assigned to corporations, in the present case for the purpose of constructing pipelines, which can either take the form of a full transfer of ownership or as a right of way.

The second approach was to regulate access and tariffs, such as in the United States, where pipeline companies were compelled to allow third-party shippers without tariff discrimination. The third approach was to subject pipelines to taxation—in addition to normal business taxes—in the form of import and export duties or transit fees, such as in the case of the Middle Eastern export pipelines. The fourth was to take an active role in pipeline operations, such as the French state had done by becoming a shareholder in the Le Havre-Paris pipeline in the 1940s. Both at the national and at the European level, governments debated these options at length during the late 1950s and early 1960s.[31] For the TEP consortium, these discussions had no predictable outcomes and a strong role for the state was perceived as a distinct possibility.

Facing uncertainty about state interference, the consortium focussed heavily on the legal and organisational aspects of the pipeline. The consortium's main objective was to achieve an organisation and legal structure for the pipeline company that could, in the words of the consortium's legal committee, 'ensure the permanent stability not only of the legal but also of the economic and fiscal conditions regulating its activities in the various territories concerned'.[32] The legal committee was headed by the Dutch lawyer C.R.C. Wijckerheld Bisdom, whose leading role in the *Consortium for Iran* in 1954 made him an expert in oil-related international law.[33] Although the consortium acknowledged that the contours of a unified Europe were emerging, it instructed the legal committee to find an organisational structure with an appropriate international legal status that could protect the pipeline from any state interference.[34]

The legal conditions required for the consortium consisted of the freedom of transport and transit and a legal status permitting the company to arrange rights of way, taxes and currency issues in the various jurisdictions the pipeline was to operate. The central question was whether to opt for separate national operating companies or a single international company with an international legal status. No particular international legal agreements were required where a number of national operating firms were involved, as each firm operated under national law, but such a setup could lead to potential problems in the case of disagreements between these national companies or the respective states. The alternative, namely a single company responsible for the construction and operation of the entire pipeline system, seemed to be the best solution. However, to enable such a company to operate satisfactorily, an international legal status was required to manage the international legal issues that the national legislation of the company's country of domicile would not be able to resolve. The pipeline's legal status would thus need to be laid down in international agreements between the respective national governments and the company operating the pipeline, with the inclusion of an international arbitration arrangement in case of disagreements between the signatories.[35] Such an agreement would offset the danger of individual countries asserting their national interest over the pipeline and its parent companies.[36] Not only could the arrangement neutralise French interference and solve the cumbersome process of obtaining individual concessions for each country involved in the TEP, it could also serve as a useful precedent for the Middle East.

Rather than an isolated case, TEP exemplified how the multinational oil companies were trying to deal with a changing global business environment. Up to World War II, these companies had enjoyed the protection of the European empires, which had been instrumental in arranging the Middle Eastern concessions that gave the majors full control over oil production in the region. Their cross-ownership of these concessions and the long-term crude oil supply contracts between the majors made for a strong informal cartel capable of controlling production rates, prices and market shares.[37] Decolonisation and the Cold War gradually disassembled the imperial system, emboldening post-colonial countries to claim a bigger share of and ultimately sovereignty over oil rents. As such, the institutional aspects of the TEP project were part of a wider effort by capital-exporting countries to secure their investments in post-colonial countries.[38] Global trade and investment governance had been conceived in the 1947 Havana Charter but when it was not ratified by the US, only trade, and not investments, became regulated by the General Agreement on Tariffs and Trade.[39] The late 1950s and early 1960s marked a high point in the drafting of various solutions to the question of the international regulation and protection of foreign-owned assets.[40]

In response to the costly renegotiations of the transit agreements for the Middle Eastern pipelines and their sabotaging during the Suez Crisis, the oil companies attempted to secure their investments in the region and protect them from government interference through an international agreement under international law.[41] The agreement reflected the changed relationships of the Middle East with the West. For Western Europe, the Middle East was rapidly becoming its most important supplier of oil but its security of supply depended mostly on the Anglo-American companies that dominated production in the Middle East. As such, US investments in the Middle East underpinned the oil power of the Western bloc. However, with waning British influence in the region substituted by the Truman and Eisenhower Doctrines, power in the relationship was shifting to the Middle Eastern states.[42] Finding a new international arrangement between the emboldened regimes of the Middle East and Western oil companies therefore had the highest priority.[43] The proposed agreement contained guarantees with respect to the free flow of oil, the restitution of damages, the prohibition of nationalisation and the option of bringing disputes to the International Court of Justice in the case of violations.

The French government, seeing an opportunity to carve out its own space in the Middle East, drafted a counter proposal with more emphasis on the sovereign position of the Middle Eastern countries to achieve a more balanced agreement.[44] The French position in these efforts strengthened the perception of the TEP consortium that France posed a considerable risk as a transit country. Facing the legal and regulatory void in Western Europe and the oil policies of France, the TEP consortium applied its experience in the Middle East to Europe. Moreover, when RDS decided to construct a pipeline to the Rhine-Ruhr area separately from TEP in 1957, it also pressed for an international agreement between the Netherlands and West Germany. In West Germany, however, the federal government had adopted a liberal approach to oil pipelines following a heated debate in the Cabinet in 1956.[45] Because the Dutch government used a similarly liberal approach, arranging all the legal, fiscal and financial issues had been concluded without difficulty, both in the Netherlands and in West Germany. An international agreement in this case served no other purpose than to set a precedent for the TEP and the Middle Eastern pipelines.[46] As such, the TEP consortium was part of a wider strategy of the oligopoly to protect its market power.

That the international agreements pursued by the major oil companies were essentially a ploy to secure their powerful position in a changing environment, both in the Middle East and in Europe, did not go unnoticed at the time. The legal section of the Dutch Foreign Ministry commented internally on how skewed the agreements were.[47] The companies demanded special concessions and full protection from state interference but categorically denied any state oversight or regulation of their industry. Already possessing formidable control over the oil market, RDS and the other majors appeared to want to fortify that position in international law.

Pipeline Competition

The preoccupation with legal issues slowed down decision-making in the consortium and diverted attention away from the economics of the pipeline, which ultimately rendered the pipeline's business case unviable. Facing delays, some of the companies in the consortium decided to build separate pipelines from North Sea ports (see Figure 9.1) to the German Rhine-Ruhr area, where refineries needed operational pipelines from 1959 onwards. The TEP, however, depended for its initial payload on demand in the Rhine-Ruhr region. When that demand was captured entirely by the two North Sea pipelines, a smaller diameter pipeline from Marseille to Karlsruhe was substituted for the TEP. Although the major companies were adamant that the separate pipelines would be integrated at a later stage, the rapidly increasing size of tankers reduced the potential cost savings from an integrated pipeline to the extent that the Marseille pipeline could not deliver competitive transport to markets north of Karlsruhe, while the Rotterdam and Wilhelmshaven pipelines could not compete in markets south of Frankfurt.[48]

Why were the major oil companies determined to realise an integrated European pipeline even after the failure of the TEP project? The answer lies in the majors' attempts to ward off rising competition in Western Europe. Apart from Algerian oil, the resurgence of Soviet oil exports in the late 1950s provided opportunities for newcomers to break into the markets of the majors.[49] The most potent threat came from the Italian state-owned oil company Ente Nazionale Idrocarburi (ENI), led by its charismatic first president Enrico Mattei. Mattei was determined to break the majors' market power by securing access to crude oil from sources outside of their control, including the Soviet Union.[50] Pipelines played a crucial role in both the Soviet and the ENI offensives on the Western European market. The Soviet Druzhba pipeline system—plans for which emerged in 1957—threatened to carry Red oil into Western Europe, while ENI's Central European Pipeline (CEL) from Genoa to Bavaria, announced in 1957, stood to compete with the majors in the German market.[51] When the construction of CEL started in June 1961, Mattei celebrated it as the only pipeline project of its sort that had no involvement of any of the majors.[52]

In light of the Soviet and ENI offensives, TEP was essentially an attempt to build a barrier to entry against competitors by establishing a pipeline oligopoly that jointly owned Western Europe's crude oil pipeline system. The strategic and commercial value of an integrated pipeline system, therefore, prompted RDS, BP and Jersey Standard to continue pursuing the integration of the northern and southern pipeline sections (see Figure 9.1) even after TEP had failed in its intended form in 1958. When the French companies CFP and Pechelbronn-ANTAR proceeded with a pipeline from Marseille to Karlsruhe in 1958, RDS, BP and Jersey Standard participated in the pipeline to make sure that it's technical and organisational setup allowed for future integration with the northern pipelines.[53] The majors used TEP as a platform to coordinate pipeline development in Western Europe and to make sure that new pipelines would adhere to its principles—owned and operated by private enterprises and free from any state influence.[54] As such, the TEP consortium was designed to function in a similar fashion as the production concessions in the Middle East; the obvious subtext was to retain control over pipelines and markets. As such, TEP was a means to defend the oligopoly against states and companies that were not inclined to align with the majors' market interests.

Finally, the apparent close cooperation between the majors and the CFP/Pechelbronn group warrants a closer inspection. Despite being state-owned, CFP seemed more aligned with the majors than with the French state or its Italian counterpart ENI. CFP had been created in 1924 to manage the German shareholding in the Turkish, later Iraq, Petroleum Company that France was mandated after the Great War. CFP remained chiefly dependent on this share in the Iraq concession and it had little dealings in other French exploration and production efforts outside of Iraq.[55] When the French government contemplated setting up a new, fully integrated state-owned oil company to market Algerian oil in France, CFP and the other majors feared dilution of their market shares.[56] The Pechelbronn-ANTAR group was in a similar position.[57] Facing the same threats to their markets, both the CFP/Pechelbronn group and the majors had aligned interests when it came to the defence of their markets. Hence, when CFP/Pechelbronn initiated the Southern European Pipeline (SEPL) between Marseille and Karlsruhe in 1958, RDS, BP and Jersey Standard immediately joined the venture as shareholders.[58] SEPL subsequently became the vehicle for defending their markets in the spirit of the TEP consortium. When ENI's plans for the CEL from Genoa to Bavaria took shape, SEPL immediately responded with a branch pipeline from Karlsruhe to Bavaria, the Rhein-Donau Pipeline (RDO).[59] Even though the idea of an integrated trans-European pipeline had come to nothing, the tacit collusion between the majors—including CFP—that underpinned the TEP consortium remained influential in oil pipeline planning in Western Europe.

In retrospect, the institutional preoccupations of the TEP consortium appear somewhat over the top. The Treaty of Rome was a major step toward a more secure and harmonised legal and regulatory environment for cross-border pipelines. After the ratification of the Treaty, the Strasbourg Common Assembly had set up a Transport Committee discussing common transport policies in the EEC. These provided for a European platform to discuss the legal framework regarding international oil pipelines, as well as (the promise of) curbing the market-intervening powers of individual member states, including France.[60] Moreover, the French state proved to be much more lenient toward international transit pipelines, as became apparent with the launch of the SEPL plan. In fact, the TEP consortium had never established direct contact with the French government, fearing to attract government attention before its legal and organisational plans were fully developed. This apprehension further underlines that the TEP plan was first and foremost designed to protect the position of the oligopoly rather than serve the interests of the European states that were to receive their oil supply through the pipeline.

Conclusion

This chapter has sought to explain why the major oil companies in the Trans-European pipeline consortium perceived the need for elaborate legal and organisational measures to secure the operations of the pipeline. Oil consumption in Western Europe was growing rapidly in the 1950s and pipeline infrastructure was needed to supply inland markets. As such, the TEP plan was a genuine, and economically and technically feasible, solution. However, the Cold War brought political risks to bear on the pipeline, which prompted the companies to focus on the project's institutional issues. These risks threatened the strong position that the oligopoly of eight major oil companies had established before the Second World War. Their market power rested on the cross-ownership of Middle Eastern concessions, giving the companies control over production as well as the means to maintain stable market shares, profit margins and prices. The changing political structure and international relations during the first 15 years of the Cold War threatened to upend that structure.

The consortium faced two sets of political risks: one pertaining to its oil production interests in the Middle East, another threatening its markets in Western Europe. Decolonisation and Soviet support for Arab nationalism emboldened regimes in the Middle East and North Africa to demand more revenues and control over natural resources and foreign-owned assets, prompting the majors to seek protection for their interests in the region. The Cold War stimulated new sources of supply, from the Soviet Union and Algeria, for instance, which enabled new competitors to enter the market. Both sets of risks converged on France, the principle transit country of the TEP. France felt its oil interests in the Middle East marginalised by the US and turned to Algerian oil to reduce its dependence on the US and the Anglo-American companies. The French government also had the legal means to force the oil companies to accept competition from Algerian oil. Moreover, the consortium faced uncertainty over the amount of pipeline regulation in other Western European countries. In the eyes of the TEP consortium, therefore, the risk of state interference in Western Europe and the Middle East were of a similar kind. Indeed, in the consortium's legal and organisational efforts, the two were clearly linked; the international agreement that was envisioned would, therefore, safeguard the TEP from state interference in Europe and set a precedent for the Middle East.

The legal and organisational structure for TEP served a second objective. Protecting the pipeline from state interference would also allow the consortium to establish the TEP as a pipeline oligopoly in Western Europe, posing a formidable barrier to entry for competing pipelines, such as the Soviet Druzhba pipeline and ENI's Central European Line. As such, the consortium was more than just a pipeline venture. It was a platform devised by the three biggest oil companies, RDS, Jersey Standard and BP, to coordinate pipeline planning and investment in Western Europe along the interests and principles of the oligopoly. This became exceedingly clear when the consortium remained active in other pipeline ventures after the TEP plan had failed in 1958. Essentially, the three majors attempted to create the TEP consortium in the image of the Middle Eastern concessions. At first by attempting to establish an integrated pipeline system, and when that failed by trying to establish control through coordinated planning and cross-ownership of other pipeline ventures.

Although the case of the Trans-European pipeline did not result in lasting organisational innovations, it provides a unique insight into how multinational enterprises responded to the vagaries and risks of the early Cold War. The international agreement proposed by the consortium served to deal with short-term uncertainty over the legal and regulatory environment in which the oil companies were planning substantial investments. After 1958, the EEC slowly but surely addressed the uncertainties that the consortium had faced. The liberalisation of the internal market and legal and regulatory harmonisation created the liberal business environment that the TEP consortium had sought to create with an international agreement between the pipeline countries and the consortium. On the one hand, it could be argued that the TEP was a precursor to European integration. On the other hand, the EEC ran counter to the barrier-to-entry objective of the TEP plan because it created a level playing field that made it increasingly difficult to establish a pipeline oligopoly. As such, the consortium's attempt to carve out an international legal space for its objectives was contradictory. It aimed to establish and protect a pipeline oligopoly, but in effect it created the level playing field that engendered rather than restricted pipeline competition in Western Europe. As such, the TEP case is a fascinating example of how multinational oil companies struggled to adjust to a rapidly changing world in which the contours of trade liberalisation and multilateralism were taking shape but where decolonisation and the Cold War gave rise to major uncertainties and risks in the short term. In the absence of regional or global institutions, the TEP consortium attempted to devise such institutions through international law.

Notes

1 M. Sheehan, 'The Evolution of Modern Warfare'. In *Strategy in the Contemporary World: An Introduction to Strategic Studies*, edited by J. Baylis, J. J. Wirtz, and C. S. Gray (Oxford: Oxford University Press, 2010), 61; L. Freedman, *The Evolution of Nuclear Strategy* (Basingstoke: Palgrave Macmillan, 2003), 232–236.
2 P. R. Odell, *Oil and World Power* (Harmondsworth: Penguin Books, 1983), 119.
3 They consisted of the so-called Seven Sisters: Royal Dutch Shell, Standard Oil of New Jersey (Exxon), British Petroleum, Standard Oil of New York (Mobil, presently part of Exxon-Mobil), Gulf Oil (now part of Chevron), Standard Oil of California (Chevron) and Texaco (now part Chevron). The eighth company was the French state-owned Compagnie Française des Pétroles.
4 J. E. Hartshorn, *Oil Companies and Governments: An Account of the International Oil Industry in Its Political Environment* (London: Faber and Faber, 1962), 391–392.
5 Other members of the consortium were Caltex, Socony, Deutsche Erdöl AG, Gelsenberg Benzin, Scholven Chemie, Union Kraftstoff, Ruhrchemie, CFP, Pechelbronn SA, Petrofina and Wintershall.
6 W. Levy, 'Issues in International Oil Policy'. *Foreign Affairs* 35, no. April (1957): 457–459.
7 G. Manners, 'The Pipeline Revolution'. *Geography* 47 (1962): 157–159.
8 BPA 43379, Sappeur NV minutes of meetings, 'SAPPEUR NV. Aide memoire to a General Meeting of Shareholders' Experts held in the Hague on the 31st January 1957', undated, 2.
9 J. D. Makholm, *The Political Economy of Pipelines* (Chicago: University of Chicago Press, 2012), 30.
10 Ibid., 1–3.
11 T. G. Weyman-Jones, *Energy in Europe: Issues and Policies* (London: Methuen, 1986), 17–18; V. L. Birchfield et al., 'Taking Stock of EU Energy Policy: Problems, Progress, and Prospects'. In *Toward a Common European*

Union Energy Policy, edited by V. L. Birchfield and J. S. Duffield (New York: Palgrave Macmillan, 2011), 263–276; J. S. Duffield, *Fuels Paradise: Seeking Energy Security in Europe, Japan, and the United States* (Baltimore: Johns Hopkins University Press, 2015).

12 M. A. Adelman, *The Genie Out of the Bottle: World Oil Since 1970* (Cambridge, MA: MIT Press, 1995), 48; C.v.d. Linde, *Dynamic International Oil Markets: Oil Market Developments and Structure, 1860–1990* (Dordrecht: Kluwer Academic Publishers, 1991), 60.

13 J. H. Bamberg, *British Petroleum and Global Oil, 1950–1975: The Challenge of Nationalism* (Cambridge: Cambridge University Press, 2000), 76–79.

14 P. Stevens. 'Pipelines or Pipe Dreams? Lessons From the History of Arab Transit Pipelines'. *Middle East Journal* 54, no. 2 (2000): 236.

15 A. Toprani. 'The French Connection: A New Perspective on the End of the Red Line Agreement, 1945–1948'. *Diplomatic History* 36, no. 2 (2012): 262; D. Painter, 'Oil, Resources, and the Cold War, 1945–1962'. In *The Cambridge History of the Cold War: Volume 1 Origins*, edited by M. P. Leffler and O. A. Westad (Cambridge: Cambridge University Press, 2010), 496–497.

16 Shareholders in IPC were: Anglo-Persian Oil Company (today BP), 23.75 percent; Compagnie Française des Pétroles (today Total), 23.75; Royal Dutch/Shell, 23.75; Near East Development Company, consisting of Jersey Standard, Standard Oil of New York (Socony, today Mobil, part of Exxon-Mobil), Gulf Oil, Pan-American Petroleum & Transportation Co., and Atlantic Refining Co., 23.75. The latter three sold their stake to Jersey Standard and Socony in 1931 and 1934. Toprani, 'The French Connection', 261.

17 Ibid., 273; A. Williams, *Britain and France in the Middle East and North Africa: 1914–1967* (London: Macmillan, 1968), 77–80.

18 Toprani, 'The French Connection', 263–264; D. Yergin, *The Prize: The Epic Quest for Oil, Money and Power* (London: Pocket Books, 1993), 413–416.

19 M. Connelly, *A Diplomatic Revolution: Algeria's Fight For Independence and the Origins of the Post-cold War Era* (Oxford: Oxford University Press, 2002), 107–108.

20 Yergin, *The Prize*, 489–493.

21 I. M. Wall, *France, the United States, and the Algerian War* (Berkeley: University of California Press, 2001), 59, 95, 135.

22 H. B. Feigenbaum, *The Politics of Public Enterprise: Oil and the French State* (Princeton: Princeton University Press, 1985), 60–61.

23 Connelly, *A Diplomatic Revolution*, 43, 99, 203–204; Yergin, *The Prize*, 526–527.

24 Connelly, *A Diplomatic Revolution*, 204; Adelman, *The Genie Out of the Bottle*, 49–50; R. Cantoni, *Oil Exploration, Diplomacy, and Security in the Early Cold War: The Enemy Underground* (New York: Routledge, 2017), 196–197.

25 Feigenbaum, *The Politics of Public Enterprise*, 37–39.

26 Ibid., 50.

27 F. W. Saad, 'France and Oil: A Contemporary Economic Study' (PhD diss., Massachusetts Institute of Technology, 1969), 33, 39.

28 S. Saul, 'SN REPAL, CFP and "Oil-Paid-in-Francs"'. In *A Comparative History of National Oil Companies*, edited by A. Beltran (Bruxelles: Peter Lang, 2010), 105–106.

29 I. W. Zartman, 'North Africa and the EEC Negotiations'. *Middle East Journal* 22, no. 1 (1968): 1–2; Cantoni, *Oil Exploration*, 215–217.

30 Different terms are in use to describe the state's prerogative to expropriate land. Most frequently used are *eminent domain* (US), *compulsory purchase* or *expropriation* (Europe).

31 See, for instance: BAK, B102/59230, Rechtsfragen zum Bau und Betrieb von Rohrleitungen, 1960–1965; BAK, B102/59212, Regelung im Ausland; M. Bader-Gassner, *Pipelineboom, Internationale Ölkonzerne im westdeutschen Wirtschaftswunder* (Baden-Baden: Nomos, 2014), 90 ff.

32 BPA 43379, Sappeur NV minutes of meetings, 'SAPPEUR NV. Aide memoire to a Board Meeting held on Thursday, 14th March 1957 at the Company's office, the Hague', 22nd March 1957, Attached 'Note on some legal aspects of the proposed Trans-European Pipeline', 1.

33 BPA 43379, Sappeur NV minutes of meetings, 'SAPPEUR NV. Aide memoire to a Board Meeting held on Thursday, 14th March 1957 at the Company's office, the Hague', 22nd March 1957, 3. The *Consortium for Iran* consisted of the *Seven Sisters* and several smaller American oil companies that succeeded in 1954 in obtaining a licence to operate in Iran after it had nationalised the oil industry in 1951.

34 BPA 43379, Sappeur NV minutes of meetings, 'SAPPEUR NV. Aide memoire to a Board Meeting held on Thursday, 14th March 1957 at the Company's office, the Hague', 22nd March 1957, Attached 'Note on some legal aspects of the proposed Trans-European Pipeline', 1.

35 BPA 43379, Sappeur NV minutes of meetings, 'Recommendations on the legal aspects of the Trans-European pipeline project, submitted by Mr. C.R.C. Wijckerheld Bisdom', 5 June 1957.

36 Ibid.

37 T. H. Moran, 'Managing an Oligopoly of Would-Be Sovereigns: The Dynamics of Joint Control and Self-Control in the International Oil Industry Past, Present, and Future'. *International Organization* 41, no. 4 (1987): 578–592.

38 K. J. Vandevelde, 'A Brief History of International Investment Agreements'. *U.C. Davis Journal of International Law & Policy* 12, no. 1 (2005): 162, 166.

39 P. Demaret, 'Metamorphoses of the GATT: From the Havana Charter to the World Trade Organization'. *Columbia Journal of Transnational Law* 34, no. 1 (1996): 126–127.

40 A. A. Fatouros, 'An International Code to Protect Private Investment-Proposals and Perspectives'. *The University of Toronto Law Journal* 14, no. 1 (1961): 77–102.

41 NL-HaNA, Ministerie van Buitenlandse Zaken: Code-archief 1955–1964, nummer toegang 2.05.118, inventarisnummer 12024, memo of the legal advisor to the Ministry of Foreign Affairs to the Minister of Foreign Affairs, 19 June 1957.

42 Levy, 'Issues in International Oil Policy', 457–459.

43 Ibid., 460.

44 NL-HaNA, Buitenlandse Zaken/Code-Archief 55–64, 2.05.118, inv.nr. 12024, memo of the legal advisor to the Ministry of Foreign Affairs to the Minister of Foreign Affairs, 20 May 1957.

45 M. Boon, 'Oil Pipelines, Politics and International Business. The Rotterdam Oil Port, Royal Dutch Shell and the German Hinterland, 1945–1975' (PhD diss., Erasmus University, 2014), 131–134; Bader-Gassner, *Pipelineboom*, 112–124.

46 NL-HaNA, Buitenlandse Zaken/Code-Archief 55–64, 2.05.118, 12024, memo of the legal advisor to the Dutch Ministry of Foreign Affairs to the Dutch Minister of Foreign Affairs, 19 June 1957.

47 Ibid.

48 Boon, 'Oil Pipelines', 161–163.

49 N. Jensen-Eriksen. 'The First Wave of the Soviet Oil Offensive: The Anglo-American Alliance and the Flow of "Red Oil" to Finland During the 1950s'. *Business History* 49, no. 3 (2007): 348–366.

50 Bader-Gassner, *Pipelineboom*, 53, 59; Cantoni, *Oil Exploration*, 181–182.
51 Bader-Gassner, *Pipelineboom*, 158, 160.
52 Paraphrased from quotation in ibid., 166.
53 BPA, 130129, note on meeting between BP, Shell and SO, JEH Davies (BP), 19th December 1957.
54 BPA, 130129, anonymous note 'Memorandum re: Sappeur', 13th December 1957.
55 Saul, 'SN REPAL', 97–98.
56 Ibid., 106.
57 Ibid., 113–114.
58 BPA, 130129, record of Sappeur Board meeting, 2nd April 1958.
59 Bader-Gassner, *Pipelineboom*, 167.
60 A. Demagny, 'France and the Project for a Community Oil Policy, From the Signature of the Treaty of Rome to the First Oil Shock'. In *Comparative History of National Oil Companies*, edited by A. Beltran (Bruxelles: Peter Lang AG, 2010), 306.

Bibliography

Adelman, M. A. *The Genie Out of the Bottle: World Oil Since 1970*. Cambridge, MA: MIT Press, 1995.

Bader-Gassner, M. *Pipelineboom, Internationale Ölkonzerne im westdeutschen Wirtschaftswunder*. Baden-Baden: Nomos, 2014.

Bamberg, J. H. *British Petroleum and Global Oil, 1950–1975: The Challenge of Nationalism*. Cambridge: Cambridge University Press, 2000.

Birchfield, V. L., and J. S. Duffield. 'Taking Stock of EU Energy Policy: Problems, Progress, and Prospects'. In *Toward a Common European Union Energy Policy*, edited by Vicki L. Birchfield and John S. Duffield, 263–276. New York: Palgrave Macmillan, 2011.

Boon, M. 'Oil Pipelines, Politics and International Business. The Rotterdam Oil Port, Royal Dutch Shell and the German Hinterland, 1945–1975'. Ph.D. diss., Erasmus University, 2014.

Cantoni, R. *Oil Exploration, Diplomacy, and Security in the Early Cold War: The Enemy Underground*. New York: Routledge, 2017.

Connelly, M. *A Diplomatic Revolution: Algeria's Fight for Independence and the Origins of the Post-cold War Era*. Oxford: Oxford University Press, 2002.

Demagny, A. 'France and the Project for a Community Oil Policy, From the Signature of the Treaty of Rome to the First Oil Shock'. In *Comparative History of National Oil Companies*, edited by Alain Beltran, 305–322. Bruxelles: Peter Lang AG, 2010.

Demaret, P. 'Metamorphoses of the GATT: From the Havana Charter to the World Trade Organization'. *Columbia Journal of Transnational Law* 34, no. 1 (1996): 123–171.

Duffield, J. S. *Fuels Paradise: Seeking Energy Security in Europe, Japan, and the United States*. Baltimore: Johns Hopkins University Press, 2015.

Fatouros, A. A. 'An International Code to Protect Private Investment-Proposals and Perspectives'. *The University of Toronto Law Journal* 14, no. 1 (1961): 77–102.

Feigenbaum, H. B. *The Politics of Public Enterprise: Oil and the French State*. Princeton: Princeton University Press, 1985.

Freedman, L. *The Evolution of Nuclear Strategy*. Basingstoke: Palgrave Macmillan, 2003.

Hartshorn, J. E. *Oil Companies and Governments: An Account of the International Oil Industry in Its Political Environment*. London: Faber and Faber, 1962.

Jensen-Eriksen, N. 'The First Wave of the Soviet Oil Offensive: The Anglo-American Alliance and the Flow of "Red Oil" to Finland During the 1950s'. *Business History* 49, no. 3 (2007): 348–366.

Levy, W. 'Issues in International Oil Policy'. *Foreign Affairs* 35, no. April (1957): 454–469.

Makholm, J. D. *The Political Economy of Pipelines*. Chicago: University of Chicago Press, 2012.

Manners, G. 'The Pipeline Revolution'. *Geography* 47 (1962): 154–163.

Moran, T. H. 'Managing an Oligopoly of Would-Be Sovereigns: The Dynamics of Joint Control and Self-Control in the International Oil Industry Past, Present, and Future'. *International Organization* 41, no. 4 (1987): 575–607.

Odell, P. R. *Oil and World Power*. Harmondsworth: Penguin Books, 1983.

Painter, D. 'Oil, Resources, and the Cold War, 1945–1962'. In *The Cambridge History of the Cold War: Volume 1 Origins*, edited by M. P. Leffler and O. A. Westad, 486–507. Cambridge: Cambridge University Press, 2010.

Saad, F. W. 'France and Oil: A Contemporary Economic Study'. Ph.D. diss., Massachusetts Institute of Technology, 1969.

Saul, S. 'SN REPAL, CFP and "Oil-Paid-in-Francs"'. In *A Comparative History of National Oil Companies*, edited by Alain Beltran, 93–123. Bruxelles: Peter Lang, 2010.

Sheehan, M. 'The Evolution of Modern Warfare'. In *Strategy in the Contemporary World: An Introduction to Strategic Studies*, edited by John Baylis, James J. Wirtz and Colin S. Gray, 43–66. Oxford: Oxford University Press, 2010.

Stevens, P. 'Pipelines or Pipe Dreams? Lessons From the History of Arab Transit Pipelines'. *Middle East Journal* 54, no. 2 (2000): 224–239.

Toprani, A. 'The French Connection: A New Perspective on the End of the Red Line Agreement, 1945–1948'. *Diplomatic History* 36, no. 2 (2012): 261–299.

van der Linde, C. *Dynamic International Oil Markets: Oil Market Developments and Structure, 1860–1990*. Dordrecht: Kluwer Academic Publishers, 1991.

Vandevelde, K. J. 'A Brief History of International Investment Agreements'. *U.C. Davis Journal of International Law & Policy* 12, no. 1 (2005): 157–194.

Wall, I. M. *France, the United States, and the Algerian War*. Berkeley: University of California Press, 2001.

Weyman-Jones, T. G. *Energy in Europe: Issues and Policies*. London: Methuen, 1986.

Williams, A. *Britain and France in the Middle East and North Africa: 1914–1967*. London: Macmillan, 1968.

Yergin, D. *The Prize: The Epic Quest for Oil, Money and Power*. London: Pocket Books, 1993.

Zartman, I. W. 'North Africa and the EEC Negotiations'. *Middle East Journal* 22, no. 1 (1968): 1–16.

10 From Cold War to the Washington Consensus

Evolution of the Multinational Corporations' Strategies in Chile

Marcelo Bucheli

Introduction[1]

In 1975, the documentary film *La batalla de Chile* ('The battle of Chile'),[2] directed by Chilean filmmaker Patricio Guzmán, premiered at the Cannes film festival; great international success followed.[3] This three-part documentary chronicles the fierce polarisation between the Chilean political left and right during the months preceding the election of Marxist president Salvador Allende in 1970, the deepening of those tensions during Allende's administration, and the coup that ended the Allende government in 1973 and started the military dictatorship of Augusto Pinochet that lasted until 1989. The title of the film is consistent with the global perception of the events in Chile as a major Cold War battle between capitalism and Communism. On one side, the United States Central Intelligence Agency (CIA) spent resources (unsuccessfully) to prevent Allende's election and later conspired successfully with different Chilean political actors to overthrow him.[4] On the other side, the Latin American left led by Cuba's Fidel Castro considered Allende's accession to power as the continent's most important revolutionary triumph after the Cuban Revolution.[5] The policies developed by Pinochet's dictatorship after the coup have also been considered paradigmatic in terms of representing changes that eventually took place at the global level. Shortly after taking power, Pinochet embarked on a series of economic reforms consisting of mass privatisations (including most utilities and social security) and opening of the economy to foreign markets. In this way, in the early 1980s Chile was following a recipe that was eventually adopted in most countries in the 1990s (although not equally everywhere). In fact, in his history of neo-liberalism, David Harvey puts Pinochet at the same level of Ronald Reagan, Deng Xiao Ping and Margaret Thatcher in terms of his importance in pushing the new economic agenda that dominated the post-1990s world.[6] In this way, Chile constitutes a textbook-case example of a country that experimented with the different economic models debated during the Cold War and the following period of open markets (or neo-liberalism).

Multinational corporations have been at the centre of the political and academic debate during the Cold War and the subsequent neo-liberal period. At the height of the Cold War, they were one of the preferred targets of the left who considered them an arm of imperialistic exploitation that acted with the complicity of a segment of the domestic bourgeoisie.[7] Another group of economists and sociologists working for the Economic Commission for Latin America (ECLA) considered multinationals potential partners in state-led programmes of industrialisation.[8] Even though both groups had a different view of what types of policies governments should follow with respect to multinational corporations, they both agreed with the idea that the economic structure of their countries needed to change from being one based on exports of raw materials into an industrial one. These views partially explain policies towards multinationals in less developed countries during the 1960s and 1970s. They ranged from expropriation of assets owned by foreign multinationals for the creation of domestic state-owned enterprises, renegotiation of contracts with foreign firms, or incentives to foreign firms to invest in nascent industries.[9] These views lost steam and popularity in Latin America during the 1980s and 1990s when, after a series of economic crises, governments abandoned import substitution in favour of open market policies that returned to the idea of exploiting the continent's rich natural resources as a way to achieve economic prosperity.[10] The multinational corporations played a new role in this environment by investing heavily in buying privatised government property, including state property resulting from previous expropriations. Multinationals participating in this process included firms originating from countries such as Spain, China or Russia—rather than from the traditional post-World War II capital-exporting countries (namely, the United States, United Kingdom, Germany, France, Switzerland, Holland and Japan).[11]

This chapter studies how multinational firms adapt to a changing political and economic environment through the political composition of their boards of directors. These boards play a crucial role in any organisation at creating links between the firm and other firms, industries, or political actors. Although a changing composition of a board of directors is not reflected in the general organisational structure of a firm, this chapter shows how the way a firm determines the political composition of this board has serious implications for the way the firm relates to other companies or the government. The chapter shows how the political composition of the board of directors was an asset or a liability depending on how the board members provided the firm with connections to the most relevant decision makers in the changing political context.[12]

The role of foreign multinationals in the Chilean telecommunications sector evolved in the following manner. Between 1927 and 1964 the sector was completely dominated by one firm: the US-based multinational International Telephone and Telegraph Company (ITT), which owned the

Compañía de Teléfonos de Chile (hereafter CTC). After 1964, ITT shared a small fraction of the market with the state-owned firm Entel. This situation remained until 1972, when Allende expropriated ITT. In 1987, the Pinochet regime started gradually selling the CTC shares of the firm and by 1989 the Australian firm Bond Corporation became the new owner. Later, in 1990, the Spanish multinational Telefónica acquired Bond's shares and renamed the firm as Telefónica Chile CTC. During the Pinochet regime, Entel had a similar fate. The government sold its participation between 1986 and 1992. In its early years, the main investors were from Italy and Chile, but, eventually, the Chilean investors took over the totality of the firm's ownership.[13] The decision-making process in each of the two multinationals was not the same, although there were some elements in common. ITT's subsidiaries enjoyed a great degree of independence. Since its early years, the firm was organised as a federation in which the headquarters allowed the subsidiaries to develop their own strategy independently from other places.[14] This made sense given the differences in the regulatory environment of the countries in which ITT operated. In the case of Telefónica, the firm also gave its subsidiaries a great degree of independence, but a general strategy was laid out from the headquarters.[15]

ITT and Cold War Debates on Foreign Direct Investment

Few firms have been closer to the centre of the debates about the role of multinationals than ITT and part of it is due to the firm's operations in Chile. In 1972, the firm made headlines after the *Washington Post* leaked a series of cables between ITT and the US Department of State in which the firm volunteered to aid Washington in overthrowing the Allende government.[16] ITT could do little to argue against the accusations and its reputation was tainted by this event for a long time. In fact, an informal poll among historians conducted by the American publication *The Daily Beast* put ITT among the 13 world's most-hated companies.[17]

ITT arrived in Chile in 1927 and controlled the totality of Chile's telecommunications until the 1960s, but was required to have two members of the government on the board of directors. The timing of ITT's arrival was particularly favourable for the firm, because an authoritarian regime was at that moment creating incentives for foreign investors, particularly in the utilities sector.[18] The regime fell partially as a result of the Great Depression and by 1932 was replaced by a democratic one that started the adoption of the state-led, protectionist import substitution industrialisation model (hereafter ISI). This year started a period in which the Chilean political landscape was defined by two traditional right-wing parties—the Liberals and Conservatives (representing the secular, urban and pro-industrialisation and Catholic, landed and rural elites, respectively)—the centre middle class-oriented Radical Party and the rising labour-oriented Socialist and Communist parties.[19]

Fighting Communism through Industrialisation: The Adoption of ECLA's Ideas and Policies Towards ITT in Chile

The ISI model has long been attributed to the ideas of Argentine economist Raúl Prebisch and the economists and sociologists working at the United Nations Economic Commission for Latin America (ECLA) in Santiago. The influence of ECLA in economic policy in Latin America cannot be overstated. ECLA did not limit itself to writing technical economic reports on the region, but also adopted a historically informed view to analyse the roots of Latin American underdevelopment.[20] Additionally, ECLA trained hundreds of Latin American central bank and ministry of finance officials through courses taught in Chile and in other countries.[21] Partially inspired by the writings of Nobel Prize economist Arthur Lewis (particularly his work 'Economic development with unlimited supplies of labour'), many ECLA economists believed that in order to jump start a process of economic development the government and foreign multinationals needed to provide investment in strategic and other crucial areas of the economy.[22]

Chile was a serious follower of ECLA's recipe and the country's political development was closely linked to its economic transformations. The adoption of the ISI model led to dramatic changes in Chilean society. First, the percentage of urban population increased from 49.4 percent in 1930 to 75 percent in 1970. As Table 10.1 shows, the growth was constant, but dramatic. Second, spending on social welfare led Chile to rank fourth in terms of levels of literacy, while public spending on infrastructure funded from taxes levied on the foreign companies in the copper sector allowed the government to set the basis for industrialisation.[23] These social changes were reflected in the political landscape of the country. A larger urban industrial sector meant also a larger industrial

Table 10.1 Percentage of urban population in Chile between 1930 and 1982

Urban Population (as recorded in National Census Data)				
	Urban	*Total*	*Percent*	*%Change*
1930	2119221	4287445	49.4%	
1940	2638311	5023559	52.5%	6.2%
1952	3573122	5932995	60.2%	14.6%
1960	5028060	7374115	68.2%	13.2%
1970	6675137	8884768	75.1%	10.2%
1982	9316120	11329736	82.2%	9.4%

Source: Chile, Instituto Nacional de Estadísticas (1930, 1940), *Censo de población*. Santiago: Imprenta Nacional; Chile, Instituto Nacional de Estadísticas (1952, 1960, 1970, 1982), *Censo de población y vivienda*. Santiago: Imprenta Nacional.

proletariat that organised itself around labour unions, whose membership quadrupled between 1932 and 1940.[24] The middle class-oriented Radical Party and the Socialist and Communist parties increased their share of the electorate, while the traditional Liberals and Conservatives gradually dwindled.[25]

As long as ISI was consolidated in Chile, the political parties aligned with urban sectors became increasingly popular. This led to the creation of a coalition between the Radicals and the left-wing parties known as the Popular Front, which ruled Chile between 1938 and 1941. This coalition reinforced ISI and created a series of government agencies to channel resources towards the industrialisation effort, the most important one being the Corporación de Fomento (CORFO), established in 1939. CORFO's leadership strongly believed in the role of the state in creating the foundations or inputs for a powerful privately owned industrial private sector.[26] Around the same period, the Chilean corporate sector consolidated a process of organising itself around large diversified conglomerates (or business groups), which gave them even stronger capacity to coordinate their activities with each other and with the government.[27] As Schneider summarised it, 'after 1939, most of the crucial economic decisions in Chile were made, not by the Senate but by CORFO in closed-door meetings'.[28]

As part of the government's efforts to have a stronger power to coordinate the economy, soon after its creation CORFO purchased 12.5 percent of ITT's shares, and the government remained with its two representatives on the board.[29]

Societal change directly affected the telecommunications sector. The number of telephones went from 33,285 in 1927 (or 8 per thousand people) to 127,344 in 1950 (or 20.9 per thousand of people).[30] In fact, by 1947, Chile was ITT's largest consumer of telephones in the world.[31]

ITT, Board Composition and New Ideas of Development

The rise of centre and left-wing parties translated into challenges to the existing economic model. In 1952, former president Carlos Ibáñez was elected with strong support of the political left. Ibáñez, however, found the country going through a seemingly uncontrollable inflation of 71 percent in 1954 and 83 percent in 1955, which he fought by cutting down on social spending and subsidies and increasing utilities rates (including telephone). As a result, the left broke its alliance with the president forcing him to re-approach them at the end of his administration to obtain support for a constitutional reform that would increase mass participation in politics and reduce the power the right had in the countryside.[32] In spite of this re-approach, Ibáñez also revised ITT-CTC's concession, awarding the firm a new contract under which the multinational committed to increase coverage, while the government ensured a 10 percent profit rate to the firm—a promise that enraged the left and the centre.[33]

During the 1950s, the inflation-generated economic crisis changed the political landscape in Chile in a way that resembled wider debates worldwide. A new centre political party oriented towards the urban middle class was created, in 1957, under the name of Christian Democratic Party. This party followed the general beliefs of Christian Democratic parties in other countries, including the Catholic moral obligation to relieve poverty (even if this meant income redistribution), whilst opposing the Communist option. The Chilean Christian Democratic political platform strongly resembled the ideas developed by ECLA and was supported by the World Bank.[34] The left also reorganised itself around the Frente de Acción Popular (FRAP), created by the Communist and Socialist parties in 1956, which adopted the world view developed by the Dependency scholars, who interpreted Latin America's underdevelopment as a result of economic imperialism (of which the multinationals were accomplices—a view later summarised in the highly popular work of André Gunder Frank).[35] The rise of these two parties came at the expense of the popularity of the traditional right-wing Liberal and Conservative parties.[36]

The new political forces, which came to dominate the political debate in the 1960s, challenged the way the ISI model was operating at that time. The Christian Democrats argued that the model had been too oriented towards big business and had not had major redistributive effects. These criticisms coincided with some self-criticisms at the ECLA level and by Prebisch himself, who stated that ISI had not had the expected results and claimed that lack of economic integration impeded development.[37] Additionally, the US government, concerned about the popularity of the Cuban Revolution and supported partially by the writings of Lewis, started advocating land redistribution programmes in Latin America as a way to overcome some of the industrialisation bottlenecks (mainly a lack of a large enough domestic market).[38] The left-wing FRAP agreed that ISI had not benefitted the lower classes but maintained that as long as big businesses (either domestic or foreign) dominated the programme it was always going to benefit the oligarchy. Their solution was expropriation of foreign property and state control of monopolies, the financial sector, foreign trade, and strategic sectors. Finally, the Conservatives and Liberals also questioned some aspects of ISI. From their viewpoint, the strong state-interventionism in the economy was to blame for the inflation and they proposed as the solution privatisation and opening of the economy.[39] In this way, the right was preceding the arguments eventually used in the 1970s to dismantle ISI.[40] The Chilean right formed a coalition for the 1958 elections and narrowly won with 31.6 of the votes against 28.5 percent for FRAP, and 20.5 for the Christian Democrats.[41] The polarisation of ideas was apparent.

The ideas around how the economy should be managed were reflected in debates around the telecommunications industry. By the late 1950s and early 1960s, ITT was repeatedly attacked by the media and politicians for its poor and expensive service. Interestingly, all political parties agreed that the firm enjoyed a very generous concession, opposed the guaranteed ten percent profit rate, and believed that coverage was poor, narrow and expensive. However, they differed on the solutions. The Christian Democrats were divided among those advocating expropriation and those calling for more regulation, the left proposed expropriation and a national state-owned monopoly, while the right proposed deregulation and opening of the market to other firms. In congressional debates, the left justified its calls for expropriation as a defence for national sovereignty and anti-imperialism. Members of the centre and the right maintained that even though they did not like the contract ITT operated under, as a country with the rule of law they could not simply change it overnight.[42]

The debate took another turn after an earthquake in the year of 1960. The earthquake destroyed a significant part of the telecommunications infrastructure, leading politicians of the centre and those affiliated to CORFO to call for the creation of a parallel state-owned firm. Fearing that this was a first step towards state control of the economy, both ITT and the US embassy opposed the initiative increasing tensions with the rising centre and left political parties.[43]

The political composition of ITT's board of directors worked to the firm's disadvantage at moments when it was under attack. Out of 36 directors sitting on the firm's board between 1950 and 1970, 16 belonged to the Conservative or Liberal parties and just four where affiliated to the Christian Democrats. Among the directors and executives who worked for more than four years for the firm during the same period, there was only one Christian Democrat and ten Liberals and Conservatives Congressmen from the Christian Democratic party and the left explicitly used this information to accuse the firm of being a relic of the past that reflected less democratic periods.[44]

ITT and the Battle of Chile

The 1964 presidential elections pushed Chile even further towards a Cold War battlefield. Christian Democrat candidate Eduardo Frei won with 56 percent of the vote, followed by Marxist Salvador Allende (FRAP) with 38.9 percent, and the Radical candidate with a mere 5 percent.[45] With these elections, the Liberals and Conservatives had lost relevance, while those representing the harshest critics of ITT dominated the political arena.

The Chilean elections were being watched closely from Washington. Some analysts considered Frei a good alternative to the lure of the Cuban Revolution. Some of his seemingly radical proposals such as the nationalisation of the copper industry or the redistribution of land among poor peasants were not inconsistent with plans proposed by the Alliance for Progress (an initiative from US President John F. Kennedy to channel development funds to Latin America as a counterweight to the Communist offensive).[46] An analysis of Frei and Chile published in the United States called him the 'last best hope' for the West to show a credible and viable alternative to Communism.[47]

The idea that Frei acted as a bulwark against Communism went beyond approving publications in the United States. After Frei's triumph, the CIA channelled funds to the Christian Democratic candidates for the 1965 congressional elections, while ITT itself volunteered to support these efforts financially (a proposal rejected by the CIA).[48] The Christian Democratic candidates handsomely won 43.6 percent of the votes in those elections, but, to the concern of Washington and the Chilean elite, Allende's FRAP came second with 26.3 percent and the Liberals and Conservatives obtained 3.1 and 1.9 percent of the votes respectively.[49]

Washington's support to Frei did not mean the Chilean right agreed that he was the best alternative to Communism. In fact, the constituency of the Conservative party (mainly the landed oligarchy) strongly opposed agrarian reform and the government empowerment of labour unions in the countryside and the urban areas. For this segment of the population, Frei was simply 'paving the road to Communism in Chile'.[50] At the same time, Frei was also attacked by the left who accused him of being the 'candidate of imperialism'.[51]

Shortly after taking power, Frei created the state-owned telecommunications firm ENTEL to serve areas neglected by ITT, increased government oversight of ITT's operations, and authorised CORFO to buy 49 percent of ITT-CTC shares.[52] Even though CORFO did not actually conduct the purchase of those shares, the fact that the legislation to do so was there indicated increasing interest by government to intervene in the sector.[53]

Despite the heated political environment, ITT did not change the political composition of its board of directors. One reason the company might have been reluctant to do this was because its board provided the firm with important links with corporate Chile. According to an article written by investigative journalists of *Vistazo*, Chile's weekly magazine, the presence on the board of an individual who was also sitting on the board of the powerful Banco de Crédito e Inversiones made it possible for the firm to obtain cheap loans, while having shared directors with Chile's private oil company, COPEC, allowed ITT indirectly to have relations with the government.[54] At least 38 percent of ITT's directors sat on the board of another firm giving ITT connections with 22 firms in 14 industries. Two of the firms ITT had strongest connections with were the country's major cement firm, Cementos Bío Bío (a firm highly involved in most ISI projects), and the state-owned national electricity firm (Empresa Nacional de Energía).[55]

Another possible reason as to why ITT remained so stubbornly with a board composed of discredited political parties is that the firm was simply doing what it had done in other countries. Since its early years one strategy the firm followed in most countries was to have boards composed of members of the domestic elite as a way to have access to information and resources.[56] The firm started with this practice in Spain and later continued using it in other countries.[57] The fact that the Liberal and Conservative parties were not popular anymore did not mean their constituency had stopped being members of the Chilean economic elite, so even though the board composition did not provide political benefits, it could provide economic ones. In the remaining years of the 1960s, however, events were to prove that political considerations should have taken greater importance than economic ones when choosing board members.

In the run-up to the 1970 elections, the Chilean political environment became increasingly polarised. In 1967, the weakened Liberal and Conservatives reinvented themselves under a new party known as the National Party and immediately started opposing Frei. That same year, the Socialist party openly declared the legitimacy of armed struggle and the following year a new clandestine left-wing Cuba-inspired group was created (the Movimiento de Izquierda Revolucionaria, or Revolutionary Left Movement, MIR).[58] As early as 1969, radical left groups put bombs in the American Cultural Institute and the *El Mercurio* newspaper building, while a group of right-wing army officers unsuccessfully rebelled against the government. The National Party added fuel to the fire by declaring the army rebellion a justifiable act and the inevitable outcome of what they considered Frei's failed policies. Frei even faced challenges within his own Christian Democratic party, when its left-wing faction created its own movement known as MAPU and joined the Allende coalition. Voters rewarded the boldness the new National Party showed when criticising increasing chaos by giving them an outstanding 20 percent of the votes in the parliamentary 1969 elections.[59]

In this environment, for the presidential 1970 elections the National Party nominated former president, Jorge Alessandri, the Christian Democrats nominated Radomiro Tomic (from the Christian Democratic left-wing faction), and the left (now under an umbrella known as Popular Unity, UP) re-nominated Allende. The stakes of this election were too high for the US government, and it did not wait passively for the election results. A plan was envisioned by the CIA by which it would provide funding for both the Christian Democrats and the National Party in addition to media outlets in Chile and worldwide, instigate a coup after the elections in case Allende won, and encourage congressmen to frustrate his accession to power due to constitutional technicalities.[60] Neither one of these plans worked, so after Allende's election the CIA sought to undermine the Chilean economy to generate discontent among the population.[61]

In 1972, Allende was facing fierce opposition from the right, centre, the United States, and other Latin American governments.[62] US Secretary of State Henry Kissinger was already justifying a coup in a leaked cable when he said, 'I don't see why we need to stand by and watch a country go Communist due to the irresponsibility of its own people'.[63] That year, Jack Anderson, a *Washington Post* journalist, made public some cables that showed ITT enthusiastically offering to fund the CIA operations in Chile to overthrow Allende.[64] This was a global scandal that put Chile and ITT in the world's headlines and Allende soon decreed the expropriation of ITT-CTC. Despite the strong opposition to Allende's policies, ITT-CTC counted with little support in the Chilean parliament.[65] The bad reputation ITT had earned for years due to its bad and expensive service and the type of political composition of its board had left it with little chance of earning political support. Even though Allende was eventually overthrown, the new military government of Pinochet did not return ITT's assets, and the firm never returned to Chile.

After the Cold War: Building the Neo-Liberal Project With New Actors

General Augusto Pinochet is considered the quintessential Western Cold War proxy.[66] After taking power, he started a harsh counter-offensive to 'extirpate' what one of the members of his military junta called 'the Marxist cancer'.[67] As a result, around 3,000 were killed by government forces and another 200,000 went into exile (out of a population of fewer than 9 million).[68] Members of the traditional political parties that opposed Allende and celebrated the coup were quickly disappointed when it became increasingly clear that Pinochet was not going to return power to the civilians soon. Pinochet rapidly amassed power around himself, decreased the importance of the other members of the military junta and closely aligned himself with the United States.[69] In 1980, Pinochet called for a referendum to approve a new constitution written by his inner circle, by which he would remain in power until a new referendum in 1989, and after which he would remain senator for life. The new constitution also gave important economic and political benefits to the military. During the campaign for the 1980 plebiscite the government gave almost no space to the opposition (led by Frei and the Christian Democrats) to campaign and eventually the new constitution was approved.[70]

Pinochet's break with the past also included the economic arena. Pioneering open market policies, starting in 1973 the regime went through an aggressive process of opening the economy to external markets and radically reducing the size of the state through privatisations of state-owned firms. Between 1973 and 1982, Chile experimented with a radical version of laissez faire economics. Pinochet shunned the traditional industrial and agricultural business groups (who had a strong say in economic policy before Allende), and put unprecedented power in economic policy planning into the hands of a narrow group of young technocrats popularly known as the 'Chicago Boys'—Chilean former students of Milton Friedman at the University of Chicago.[71] The Chicago Boys applied an extreme version of Friedman's free market ideology, carrying out one of the world's most aggressive processes of privatisation of state-owned companies and eliminating subsidies and protection to the private sector.[72] Between 1973 and 1980, the number of state-owned enterprises went from 596 to 48 (by the time Allende took power in 1970 the Chilean state-owned 68 enterprises).[73] The new model discouraged investment in manufacturing and Chile rapidly de-industrialised.[74]

The policies developed by Pinochet and the Chicago Boys reflected the wider fight of ideas. Following its technical approach, ECLA had started a series of self-criticisms that were later used by those to criticise the institution itself.[75] Additionally, the popularity of American graduate programmes in economics among the Latin American elite delegitimised approaches developed within Latin America (mainly historically informed analyses not completely based on quantitative methods).[76]

The Chicago Boys' model crumbled in 1982 when global credit tightening led Chile to a severe economic crisis.[77] In 1983, Pinochet faced mass demonstrations from the unemployed and subtle messages from a private sector threatening to join the growing opposition. In order to assure a loyal coalition, Pinochet replaced the Chicago Boys with individuals connected to Chile's traditional business elite and, starting in 1984, followed a new economic policy that respected free markets but acknowledged the need of government intervention to stabilise prices and promote production.[78]

In 1989, Pinochet lost a new plebiscite in which Chile would decide whether he would remain in power or not, but his defeat did not mean a defeat for his project. The civilian government that followed respected the 1980 constitution, Pinochet remained senator for life until his death in 2006, when he was buried with the honours reserved for former heads of state, and the new centre and centre-left governments did not challenge the basics of the economic model.[79]

The economic policies developed by the Pinochet regime made Chile the darling of multinational corporations. Between 1978 and 1990, foreign direct investment in Chile went from US$168 million to US$1,194.3 million. While the amount of foreign investment in 1978 represented 6.1 percent of the country's gross investment, it went up to 41.9 percent in 1989.[80]

Between 1990 and 2010 Chile was uninterruptedly ruled by a centre-left coalition known as the Concertación. The Concertación did not challenge Pinochet's economic system, but developed some redistributive policies arguing that the years of economic growth of the dictatorship had benefitted mostly a small segment of the population.[81]

The next section shows how the composition of the Concertación's coalition, the changing landscape in the global economy, and Chilean government policies determined the type of policies towards the telecommunications sector as well as the way the new investors organised the composition of their board of directors.

Importing the Spanish Legacy: Telefónica's Approach to the Political Elite

Developments in Spain resembled in some aspects those that took place in Chile. Spain entered the 20th century ruled by a weak constitutional monarchy that could not control the increasing tensions between the right and the left.[82] The right took power with a dictatorship (1923–1929), followed by a brief democratic experiment, which collapsed with the bloody Civil War (1936–1939) in which the right triumphed and installed dictator Francisco Franco. Franco remained in power until his death in 1975.

Despite political instability, there was some continuity in Spanish economic policy. Protectionism dominated before and during Franco, with the dictator aggressively pushing for a faster industrialisation process. This process increased Spain's per-capita income, but the country remained behind comparable countries like Italy. Due to the fascist nature of Franco's regime, the Allies did not include Spain in the Marshall Plan after World War II, so Spain remained isolated from the rest of Western Europe with an outdated political and economic regime.[83]

In the 1960s, Franco created incentives for foreign direct investment in manufacturing, attracting many multinationals, and setting the basis for a rapid economic growth period (6.9 percent in real terms between 1960 and 1975), known as the 'Spanish Miracle'.[84] The main beneficiaries of this economic growth were the so-called 'business groups' who were a collection of firms with diversified investments and a relatively unified entrepreneurial guidance, and who had a very close relationship with key government officials.[85]

Franco's death in 1975 led to rapid and dramatic changes in Spain. The country became a democracy, gradually abandoned its traditional protectionist policy, and was accepted in the European Economic Community in 1986. The latter process led to unprecedented inflows of foreign direct investment and the beginning of the expansion of Spanish firms outside their national borders, with some business groups modernising and re-orienting themselves to global markets, while others failed and were bankrupted.[86] Between 1996 and 2001, the Spanish government received around 30 billion Euros resulting from massive privatisations of state-owned firms including the country's flagship airline Iberia, the electricity firm Endesa, and Telefónica, with Telefónica being one of the first firms moving abroad.[87] As a result, Spanish investments in Chile increased from US$ 313 million in 1990 to $12.9 billion in 2006. By 2008, 51.7 percent of these investments went to the utilities sector (gas, water, electricity), 17.5 percent to telecommunications, and 15.8 percent to finance.[88]

Pinochet's closest advisers watched closely the events taking place in Spain and some of them strongly admired Franco.[89] Even Pinochet considered himself the heir of Franco in the sense that he thought of himself and Franco as leaders that intervened at crucial moments to save their countries from Communism.[90] In fact, one of the few trips Pinochet made abroad during his regime was to Spain to attend Franco's funeral.[91]

The relevance of taking into consideration the political and economic development of Spain is that it allows us to understand how Telefónica organised itself when operating in Chile. Joining the group of Spanish firms that were expanding to Latin America and taking advantage of the wave of privatisations in those countries, Telefónica arrived to Chile in 1990 after acquiring the shares of the Australian firm Bond Corporation and changed the name of the firm to Telefónica CTC, starting a period in which the firm controlled Chile's domestic and foreign communications.[92]

One practice that Telefónica followed after its privatisation in Spain was to appoint politically connected individuals as members of its board of directors.[93] This practice was inherited from the time of the dictatorship and was followed by many other firms in Spain.[94]

When Telefónica arrived in Chile, it followed the same strategy it had followed in Spain (and that it followed elsewhere)—building links with the host country's political elite. When doing so, Telefónica went against the Chilean firms' practices and approached people linked to the centre-left of the political spectrum. At that time, Chilean firms were still strongly aligned with the right-wing political parties that promised to continue the Pinochet agenda and distrusted parties they considered aligned to the long gone but still remembered Allende administration.[95] Telefónica went as far as appointing, in 1991, Mr. Oscar Garretón to its board of directors. Garretón's resumé was certainly very different from what was expected to be found in Chile's corporate boards at that time. During the Allende administration, Garretón was the person in charge of expropriation of private property and was one of the founders of the left-wing political movement MAPU.[96] Garretón tried unsuccessfully to prevent Pinochet taking power by trying to convince some sailors to mutiny against their commanders, should a coup take place.[97] Right after the coup, Garretón appeared in the newspaper pages as one of the top ten 'most wanted' individuals in Chile, so he rapidly smuggled himself out of the country and into exile in Cuba, only to return to Chile in 1989 after living some time in Argentina.[98] In addition to Garretón, Telefónica also appointed members of the centre Christian Democratic Party that had participated in the (also hated by the Chilean right) Frei government that preceded Allende.[99]

Telefónica's decision to appoint a left-wing director was not isolated from events taking place in Spain. This appointment took place when Spain was ruled by the Socialist Party (PSOE), which had strong links with the Concertación and enthusiastically supported Chile's transition to democracy. In Spain, Telefónica also had links with members of PSOE.[100] By 1994, 40 percent of Telefónica's directors in Chile were from the centre-left, a percentage that decreased only between 1998 and 2000, when the right-wing Popular Party was in power in Spain.[101] A re-appointment of left-wing individuals came after 2000, when Telefónica's leadership realised they needed close relations to the Concertación if they wanted to negotiate successfully with the government. In 2001, the firm appointed Fernando Bustamante, a former union leader and member of the Socialist Party, who was the manager of Chile's oil state-owned firm during the Allende administration and who was later jailed and tortured during the Pinochet regime.[102] Both Bustamante and Garretón were crucial negotiators at different moments with the government and the labour unions, when Telefónia considered some layoffs.[103]

Conclusion

This chapter explores how multinational corporations operating in the Chilean telecommunications sector organised the political composition of their board of directors in the context of the battle of ideas around economic development during the Cold War and the years afterwards. The chapter focuses on two firms, the US-based ITT and Spain's Telefónica between 1958 and 2001. This period covers dramatic changes taking place both in Chile and at the global level. As the chapter shows, Chile's political and economic development provides extreme examples of the type of transitions taking place internationally. When deciding the composition of its board of directors, ITT chose members of the Chilean economic elite that gave the firm links with major domestic firms. In the 1960s, however, Chile became a major Cold War battlefield in which clearly defined right, centre and left-wing parties competed for power. The centre and left-wing parties used ITT's board composition—consisting of members of the discredited right—to call for expropriation or for an increase of government oversight of the industry. The political events in Chile were closely watched by Washington and other Latin American governments, who did their best to avoid Allende succeeding in his political agenda. As a firm coming from a Western power, ITT joined the fight and this cost it all its Chilean assets when the firm's collusion with the CIA was made public. The right-wing military dictatorship that followed the Allende government turned Chile into a model of free market economics that was later adopted in most of the world. The reduction of the size of the state in other countries led to an expansion of a new breed of multinationals that went into other countries using other organisational practices. One of them was Spain's Telefónica that followed in other countries the practice of appointing to its subsidiaries' boards individuals closely connected to the host country's political power. This practice is more common among emerging markets multinationals than among those originating in the United States. As a result, Telefónica was the first major firm in Chile appointing members of the centre-left to its board, which gave the firm good access to policy-makers. By this time, the Cold War was over, but global neo-liberal reforms pushed for the expansion of new firms that did not copy the Western model, but expanded using practices that were a better fit for emerging market environments. In this respect, the difference in practices between the American and Spanish investors is apparent and this chapter shows how approaching the government, even if this meant bringing in former Communists, was beneficial for the Spanish investors, while aligning to the right proved counter-productive for the American investors.

The chapter shows that corporate decisions such as those that relate to the political composition of a multinational's board of directors cannot be analysed in isolation from (a) changes in political economy and, (b) the wider shifting ideological context. Following Wadhwani and Bucheli, the chapter points to the need for a type of analysis that focuses on decisions made at the corporate level in the context of wider social, political and economic changes preceding and succeeding such decisions.[104]

Notes

1 The author wishes to thank the feedback by seminar participants at Kyoto University (2017), especially Asli Colpan and Takashi Hikino. He also thanks Thomas DeBerge for valuable research assistantship.

2 'The Battle of Chile', Icarus Films, accessed October 25, 2017, http://icarusfilms.com/if-boc. *La batalla de Chile* was previously released in Havana (Cuba). The film won eight film awards worldwide and was widely acclaimed by film critics. After its American release in 1978, the *Village Voice* classified *La batalla de Chile* as 'the major political film of our time'.

3 Ana M. Lopez, 'The Battle of Chile: Documentary, Political Process, and Representation', in *The Social Documentary in Latin America*, ed. Julianne Burton (Pittsburgh: Pittsburgh University Press, 1990), 267–287. In a very risky move, shortly after the coup Guzmán smuggled the film reels, with which he created the documentary, outside of the country while he exiled himself in Sweden.

4 Lubna Qureshi, *Nixon, Kissinger, and Allende: US Involvement in the 1973 Coup in Chile* (New York: Lexington Books, 2009); United States Senate. Select Committee to Study Governmental Operations with Respect to Intelligence Activities, *Covert Action in Chile, 1963–1973* (Washington, DC: US Government Printing Office, 1975).

5 Tanya Harmer, *Allende's Chile and the Inter-American Cold War* (Chapel Hill: University of North Carolina Press, 2011).

6 David Harvey, *A Brief History of Neo-Liberalism* (Oxford: Oxford University Press, 2005).

7 Theotonio Dos Santos, 'The structure of Dependence', *American Economic Review* 60, no. 2 (1970): 231–236; Peter Evans, *Dependent Development: The Alliance of Multinational State and Local Capital in Brazil* (Princeton: Princeton University Press, 1979).

8 Eduardo Devés Valdés, *El pensamiento latinoamericano en el siglo XX*. Vol. 2 (Buenos Aires: Biblos, 2003).

9 David A. Jodice, 'Sources of Change in Third World Regimes for Foreign Direct Investment', *International Organization* 34, no. 2 (1980): 177–206.

10 Joseph Love, 'The Rise and Decline of Economic Structuralism in Latin America: New Dimensions', *Latin American Research Review* 40, no. 3 (2005): 100–125.

11 Alvaro Cuervo-Cazurra, William Newberry, and Seung Ho Park, *Emerging Market Multinationals: Managing Operational Challenges for Sustained Economic Growth* (Cambridge: Cambridge University Press, 2016); Geoffrey Jones, *Multinationals and Global Capitalism: From the Nineteenth to the Twenty-First Century* (Oxford: Oxford University Press, 2005).

12 Some results of this research were previously published in Bucheli and Salvaj (2013, 2014, 2018) and Bucheli, Salvaj, and Kim (2019). This paper frames those findings within the context of the challenges faced by multinationals in the transition from the Cold War to the Neo-Liberal period.

13 Marcelo Bucheli and Erica Salvaj, 'Reputation and Political Legitimacy: ITT in Chile, 1927–1972', *Business History Review* 87, no. 4 (2013): 729–755; Marcelo Bucheli and Erica Salvaj, 'Adaptation Strategies of Multinational Corporations, State-Owned Enterprises, and Domestic Business Groups to Economic and Political Transitions: A Network Analysis of the Chilean Telecommunications Sector, 1958–2005', *Enterprise and Society* 15, no. 3 (2014): 534–576.

14 Robert Sobel, *ITT: The management of opportunity* (New York: Beard Books, 1982).

15 Gabriela Martínez, *Latin American Telecommunications: Telefónica's Conquest* (Lanham: Lexington Books, 2008).

16 Jack Anderson, *The Anderson Papers* (New York: Ballantine Books, 1974); United States Senate. Select Committee on Foreign Relations, *The International Telephone and Telegraph in Chile, 1970–71* (Washington, DC: US Government Printing Office, 1973).

17 Daily Beast, 'Most Hated Companies', *The Daily Beast*, June 21, 2010. www.thedailybeast.com/most-hated-companies. A simple Google search of 'ITT+Chile' shows that most entries are about the conspiracy against Allende more than anything else (search conducted in December 1, 2017).

18 Harold Blakemore, 'From the War of the Pacific to 1930', in *Chile since Independence*, ed. Leslie Bethell (Cambridge: Cambridge University Press, 1993), 33–86.

19 Michael Monteón, *Chile and the Great Depression: The Politics of Underdevelopment, 1927–1948* (Tempe: University of Arizona Press, 1998).

20 Love, 'The Rise and Decline of Economic Structuralism', 100–125.

21 Ibid.

22 Arthur Lewis, 'Economic Development With Unlimited Supplies of Labor', *The Manchester School* 22, no. 2 (1954): 139–191; Devés Valdés, *El pensamiento latinoamericano*.

23 Patricio Meller, 'Una perspectiva de largo plazo del desarrollo económico chileno, 1880–1990', in *Trayectorias divergentes: comparación de un siglo de desarrollo económico latinoamericano y escandinavo*, ed. Patricio Meller and Magnus Blomström (Santiago: CIEPLAN, 1990).

24 Ibid.

25 Lois Oppenheim, *Politics in Chile: Socialism, Authoritarianism, and Market Democracy* (Boulder: Westview, 2007).

26 Adolfo Ibáñez, *Herido en el ala: Estado, oligarquías y subdesarrollo* (Santiago: Editorial Biblioteca Americana, 2003).

27 Fernando Dahse, *Mapa de la extrema riqueza: los grupos económicos y el proceso de concentración de capitales* (Santiago: Aconcagua, 1979).

28 Ben Ross Schneider, *Business, Politics, and the State In Twentieth-Century Latin America* (Cambridge: Cambridge University Press, 2004), 155.

29 ITT-CTC, *Memoria Anual* (Santiago: ITT-CTC, various years).

30 Oxford-Montevideo Economic History Database, 'MOxLaD Database', accessed December 1 2017. www.lac.ox.ac.uk/moxlad-database.

31 ITT-CTC, *Memoria Annual.*

32 Tomás Moulian, *Fracturas: De Pedro Aguirre Cerda a Salvador Allende, 1938–1973* (Santiago: LOM, 2006).
33 Bucheli and Salvaj, 'Reputation and Political Legitimacy', 729–755.
34 Devés Valdés, *El pensamiento latinoamericano*; Love, 'The Rise and Decline of Economic Structuralism', 100–125.
35 André Gunder Frank, *Capitalism and Underdevelopment in Latin America* (New York: Monthly Review Press, 1967).
36 Alberto Cardemil, *El camino de la utopía: Alessandri, Frei y Allende. Pensamiento y obra* (Santiago: Andrés Bell, 1997).
37 Love, 'The Rise and Decline of Economic Structuralism', 100–125.
38 Devés Valdés, *El pensamiento latinoamericano*; Lewis, 'Economic development', 131–191.
39 Luis Corvalán, *Del anticapitalismo al neoliberalismo en Chile: Izquierda, centro y derecha en la lucha entre los proyectos globales, 1950–2000* (Santiago: Sudamericana, 2002).
40 Devés Valdés, *El pensamiento latinoamericano*.
41 Paul Drake, 'Chile: 1930–1958', in *Chile Since Independence*, ed. Leslie Bethell (Cambridge: Cambridge University Press, 1993), 87–128.
42 Bucheli and Salvaj, 'Reputation and Political Legitimacy', 729–755.
43 Julio Covarrubias, *Un cable al cielo: Telefónica CTC Chile, 1880–2005* (Santiago: Quebecor World, 2005).
44 Bucheli and Salvaj, 'Reputation and Political Legitimacy', 729–755.
45 Mariana Aylwin et al., *Chile en el siglo XX* (Santiago: Planeta, 1990).
46 Kate Willis, *Theories and Practices of Development* (New York: Routledge, 2005).
47 Leonard Gross, *The Last, Best Hope: Eduardo Frei and Chilean Democracy* (New York: Random House, 1967).
48 United States Senate, *Covert Action*.
49 Aylwin et al., *Chile en el siglo XX*.
50 Corvalán, *Del anticapitalismo*, 103.
51 Patricio Dooner, *Cambios sociales y conflicto político: El conflicto político nacional durante el gobierno de Eduardo Frei (1964–1970)* (Santiago: Corporación de Promoción Universitaria, 1983).
52 Ahmed Galal, 'Chile: Regulatory Specificity, Credibility of Commitment, and Distributional Demands', in *Regulations, Institutions and Commitment: Comparative Studies on Telecommunications*, ed. Brian Levy and Pablo Spiller (Cambridge: Cambridge University Press, 1996), 121–144.
53 Guillermo Guajardo, 'Nacionalismo económico y tecnología internacional: Estados Unidos y la industrialización de México y Chile', in *Ni éxito, ni fracaso: ideas, recursos y actores en las políticas económicas latinoamericanas del siglo XX*, ed. Guillermo Guajardo (Mexico City: UNAM, 2005).
54 Vistazo, 'Ocho sociedades con cuñas en diez poderosos bancos', *Vistazo* 596 (1963): 11.
55 Bucheli and Salvaj, 'Adaptation Strategies', 534–575.
56 Sobel, *ITT*.
57 Martínez, *Latin American Telecommunications*.
58 Corvalán, *Del anticapitalismo*.
59 Aylwin et al., *Chile en el siglo XX*; Corvalán, *Del anticapitalismo*.
60 Anderson, *Anderson Papers*; United States Senate, *International Telephone and Telegraph*.
61 United States Senate, *Covert Action*.
62 Harmer, *Allende's Chile*.
63 Alistair Home, *Kissinger: 1973, the Crucial Year* (New York: Simon and Schuster, 2009), 197.

64 Anderson, *Anderson Papers*; Chile, Secretary of the President, *Los documentos secretos de la ITT* (Santiago: Empresa Editoria Nacional Quimantu, 1972).
65 Bucheli and Salvaj, 'Reputation and Political Legitimacy', 729–755.
66 Doug Rossinow, *The Reagan Era: A History of the 1980s* (New York: Columbia University Press, 2017).
67 Pablo Heneeus, *Chile un país dividido: La actualidad del pasado* (Santiago: Catalonia, 2003), 41.
68 Chilean National Commission on Truth and Reconciliation, *Rettig Report of the Chilean National Commission on Truth and Reconciliation* (Notre Dame: University of Notre Dame Press, 1993); Thomas C. Wright and Rody Onate Zúñiga, 'Chilean Political Exile', *Latin American Perspectives* 4, no. 31 (2007): 31–49.
69 Verónica Valdivia, *El golpe después del golpe: Leigh vs. Pinochet, 1960–1980* (Santiago: LOM, 2005).
70 Pablo Heneeus, *El régimen de Pinochet* (Santiago: Taurus, 2016).
71 Patrcio Silva, 'Technocrats and Politics in Chile: From the Chicago Boys to the CIEPLAN Monks', *Journal of Latin American Studies* 23, no. 2 (1991): 385–410.
72 Marion Fourcade-Gourinchas and Sarah Babb, 'The Rebirth of the Liberal Creed: Paths to Neo-liberalism in Four Countries', *American Journal of Sociology* 108, no. 3 (2002): 533–579; Eduardo Silva, 'Business Elites, the State, and Economic Change in Chile', in *Business and the State in Developing Countries*, ed. Sylvia Maxfield and Ben Ross Schneider (Ithaca: Cornell University Press, 1997), 152–191.
73 Dominique Hachette and Rolf Luders, *Privatization in Chile: An Economic Appraisal* (San Francisco: International Center for Economic Growth, 1993).
74 Silva, 'Business Elites', 152–191.
75 Love, 'The Rise and Decline of Economic Structuralism', 100–125.
76 Jairo Estrada Alvarez, *Intelectuales, tecnócratas y reformas neoliberales en América Latina* (Bogotá: Universidad Nacional de Colombia, 2005).
77 Silva, 'Business Elites', 152–191.
78 Silva, 'Business Elites', 152–191; Schneider, *Business, Politics, and the State.*
79 Corvalán, *Del anticapitalismo.*
80 Manuel R. Agosin, *Foreign Direct Investment in Latin America* (Washington, D.C.: Inter-American Development Bank, 1995).
81 Andrés Solimano, 'Three Decades of Neoliberal Economics in Chile: Achievements, Failures, and Dilemmas', in *Achieving Development Success: Strategies and Lessons From the Developing World*, ed. Agustín Fosu (Oxford: Oxford University Press, 2013), 321–359.
82 Jaume Vives, *An Economic History of Spain* (Princeton: Princeton University Press, 1969).
83 Gabriel Tortella, *The Development of Modern Spain* (Cambridge, MA: Harvard University Press, 2000).
84 Jose Campa and Mauro Guillén, 'Spain: A Boom From Economic Integration', in *Foreign Direct Investment and Governments*, ed. John H. Dunning and Rajneesh Narula (New York: Routledge, 1996), 207–239; Alison Wright, *The Spanish Economy, 1959–1976* (New York: Holmes and Meier, 1977).
85 Mauro Guillén, *The Limits of Convergence: Globalization and Organizational Change in Argentina, South Korea, and Spain* (Princeton: Princeton University Press, 2001); Jesús María Valdaliso, 'Grupos empresariales, marco institucional y desarrollo económico en España en el siglo XX: los negocios de la familia Aznar (c. 1937–c. 1983)', *Revista de Historia Económica* 20, no. 3 (2002): 577–624.

86 Campa and Guillén, 'Spain: A Boom'; Guillén, *The Limits of Convergence.*

87 Roberto García-Castro and Ruth Aguilera, 'A Decade of Corporate Governance Reforms in Spain, 2000–2010', in *The Convergence of Corporate Governance: Promise and Prospects*, ed. Abdul Rasheed and Toru Yoshikawa (Houndmills: Palgrave Macmillan, 2012), 187–211; Mauro Guillén and Adrian Tschoegl, 'The Internationalization of Retail Banking: The Case of the Spanish Banks in Latin America', *Transnational Corporations* 9, no. 3 (2000): 63–97; Keith Salmon, 'Spanish Foreign Direct Investment, Transnationals and the Redefinition of the Spanish Business Realm', *International Journal of Iberian Studies* 14, no. 2 (2001): 95–110.

88 Spain, Spanish Embassy in Chile, *Inversiones españolas en Chile* (Santiago: Spanish Embassy, 2008).

89 Jerry Dávila, *Dictatorship in Latin America* (Chichester: Wiley-Blackwell, 2013).

90 Ariel Dorfman, *Exorcising Terror: The Incredible Unending Trial of Augusto Pinochet* (New York: Seven Stories Press, 2002).

91 Heraldo Muñoz, *The Dictator's Shadow* (Philadelphia: Basic Books, 2008). Pinochet avoided travelling abroad because of the international condemnation of his regime by many governments or political parties and to avoid being embarrassed by his hosts. One case of embarrassment that discouraged even more travelling outside Chile was his trip to the Philippines in 1980. Considering Filipino president Ferdinand Marcos as another authoritarian ally against Communism Pinochet accepted an invitation to visit the Philippines. Marcos, however, cancelled the invitation when Pinochet's plane was flying over the Pacific. Pinochet landed an empty Manila airport that had all its lights off, there were no employees, or official delegations to receive him. Pinochet's plane had to return to Chile without setting a foot in the Filipino soil and completely humiliated. After Chile's return to democracy, Pinochet made another foreign trip to the 'safe' territory of Great Britain, where he was arrested following a warrant from Spanish judge Baltazar Garzón. The British government intervened allowing Pinochet to return safely to Chile. After the latter experience, Pinochet never travelled out of Chile again.

92 Martínez, *Latin American Telecommunications.*

93 Ibid.

94 Juan Pedro Velázquez-Gaztelu, *Capitalismo a la española* (Madrid: La esfera de los libros, 2015).

95 Bucheli and Salvaj, 'Adaptation Strategies', 534–575.

96 Simon Collier and William Sater, *A History of Chile* (Cambridge: Cambridge University Press, 2004).

97 Edward Boornstein, *Allende's Chile: An Inside View* (New York: International Publishers, 1977).

98 Katherine Hite, *When the Romance Ended: Leaders of the Chilean Left, 1968–1998* (New York: Columbia University Press, 2000).

99 Bucheli and Salvaj, 'Adaptation Strategies', 534–575.

100 Velázquez-Gaztelu, *Capitalismo.*

101 Bucheli and Salvaj, 'Adaptation Strategies', 534–575.

102 Ibid.

103 Marcelo Bucheli and Erica Salvaj, 'Embrace Your Enemy', *Harvard Business Review* 87, no. 5 (2009): 22–23.

104 Daniel R. Wadhwani and Marcelo Bucheli, 'The Future of the Past in Management and Organization Studies', in *Organizations in Time: History, Theory, Methods*, ed. Marcelo Bucheli and R. Daniel Wadhwani (Oxford: Oxford University Press, 2014), 1–36.

Bibliography

Agosin, Manuel R. *Foreign Direct Investment in Latin America*. Washington, DC: Inter-American Development Bank, 1995.

Anderson, Jack. *The Anderson Papers*. New York: Ballantine Books, 1974.

Aylwin, Mariana, Carlos Bascuñán, Sofía Correa, Cristián Gazmuri, Sol Serrano, and Matías Tagle. *Chile en el siglo XX*. Santiago: Planeta, 1990.

Blakemore, Harold. 'From the War of the Pacific to 1930'. In *Chile Since Independence*, edited by Leslie Bethell, 33–86. Cambridge: Cambridge University Press, 1993.

Boornstein, Edward. *Allende's Chile: An Inside View*. New York: International Publishers, 1977.

Bucheli, Marcelo and Erica Salvaj. 'Embrace Your Enemy'. *Harvard Business Review* 87, no. 5 (2009): 22–23.

Bucheli, Marcelo and Erica Salvaj. 'Reputation and Political Legitimacy: ITT in Chile, 1927–1972'. *Business History Review* 87, no. 4 (2013): 729–755.

Bucheli, Marcelo and Erica Salvaj. 'Adaptation Strategies of Multinational Corporations, State-Owned Enterprises, and Domestic Business Groups to Economic and Political Transitions: A Network Analysis of the Chilean Telecommunications Sector, 1958–2005'. *Enterprise and Society* 15, no. 3 (2014): 534–576.

Bucheli, Marcelo and Erica Salvaj. 'Political Connections, the Liability of Foreignness, and Legitimacy: A Business Historical Analysis of Multinationals' Strategies in Chile'. *Global Strategy Journal* 8, no. 3 (2018): 399–420.

Bucheli, Marcelo, Erica Salvaj, and Minyoung Kim. 'Better Together: How Multinationals Come Together with Business Groups in Times of Economic and Political Transitions'. *Global Strategy Journal*. DOI: https://doi.org/10.1002/gsj.1326.

Campa, José and Mauro Guillén. 'Spain: A Boom From Economic Integration'. In *Foreign Direct Investment and Governments*, edited by John H. Dunning and Rajneesh Narula, 207–239. New York: Routledge, 1996.

Cardemil, Alberto. *El camino de la utopía: Alessandri, Frei y Allende. Pensamiento y obra*. Santiago: Andrés Bell, 1997.

Chilean National Commission on Truth and Reconciliation. *Rettig Report of the Chilean National Commission on Truth and Reconciliation*. Notre Dame: University of Notre Dame Press, 1993.

Chile Secretary General of the President. *Los documentos secretos de la ITT*. Santiago: Empresa Editora Nacional Quimantu, 1972.

Collier, Simon and William Sater. *A History of Chile*. Cambridge: Cambridge University Press, 2004.

Corvalán, Luis. *Del anticapitalismo al neoliberalismo en Chile: Izquierda, centro y derecha en la lucha entre los proyectos globales, 1950–2000*. Santiago: Sudamericana, 2002.

Covarrubias, Julio. *Un cable al cielo: Telefónica CTC Chile, 1880–2005*. Santiago: Quebecor World, 2005.

Cuervo-Cazurra, Alvaro, William Newberry, and Seung Ho Park. *Emerging Market Multinationals: Managing Operational Challenges for Sustained Economic Growth*. Cambridge: Cambridge University Press, 2016.

Dahse, Fernando. *Mapa de la extrema riqueza: los grupos económicos y el proceso de concentración de capitales*. Santiago: Aconcagua, 1979.

Daily Beast. 'Most Hated Companies'. *The Daily Beast*, June 21, 2010. www.thedailybeast.com/most-hated-companies.

Dávila, Jerry. *Dictatorship in Latin America*. Chichester: Wiley-Blackwell, 2013.

Devés Valdés, Eduardo. *El pensamiento latinoamericano en el siglo XX*. Vol. 2. Buenos Aires: Biblos, 2003.

Dooner, Patricio. *Cambios sociales y conflicto político: El conflicto político nacional durante el gobierno de Eduardo Frei (1964–1970)*. Santiago: Corporación de Promoción Universitaria, 1983.

Dorfman, Ariel. *Exorcising Terror: The Incredible Unending Trial of Augusto Pinochet*. New York: Seven Stories Press, 2002.

Dos Santos, Theotonio. 'The Structure of Dependence'. *American Economic Review* 60, no. 2 (1970): 231–236.

Drake, Paul. 'Chile: 1930–1958'. In *Chile Since Independence*, edited by Leslie Bethell, 87–128. Cambridge: Cambridge University Press, 1993.

Estrada Alvarez, Jairo. *Intelectuales, tecnócratas y reformas neoliberales en América Latina*. Bogotá: Universidad Nacional de Colombia, 2005.

Evans, Peter. *Dependent Development: The Alliance of Multinational State and Local Capital in Brazil*. Princeton: Princeton University Press, 1979.

Fourcade-Gourinchas, Marion and Sarah Babb. 'The Rebirth of the Liberal Creed: Paths to Neo-liberalism in Four Countries'. *American Journal of Sociology* 108, no. 3 (2002): 533–579.

Frank, André Gunder. *Capitalism and Underdevelopment in Latin America*. New York: Monthly Review Press, 1967.

Galal, Ahmed. 'Chile: Regulatory Specificity, Credibility of Commitment, and Distributional Demands'. In *Regulations, Institutions and Commitment: Comparative Studies on Telecommunications*, edited by Brian Levy and Pablo Spiller, 121–144. Cambridge: Cambridge University Press, 1996.

García-Castro, Roberto and Ruth Aguilera. 'A Decade of Corporate Governance Reforms in Spain, 2000–2010'. In *The Convergence of Corporate Governance: Promise and Prospects*, edited by Abdul Rasheed and Toru Yoshikawa, 187–211. Houndmills: Palgrave Macmillan, 2012.

Gross, Leonard. *The Last, Best Hope: Eduardo Frei and Chilean Democracy*. New York: Random House, 1967.

Guajardo, Guillermo. 'Nacionalismo económico y tecnología internacional: Estados Unidos y la industrialización de México y Chile'. In *Ni éxito, ni fracaso: ideas, recursos y actores en las políticas económicas latinoamericanas del siglo XX*, edited by Guillermo Guajardo. Mexico City: UNAM, 2005.

Guillén, Mauro. *The Limits of Convergence: Globalization and Organizational Change in Argentina, South Korea, and Spain*. Princeton: Princeton University Press, 2001.

Guillén, Mauro. *The Rise of Spanish Multinationals: European Business in the Global Economy*. Cambridge: Cambridge University Press, 2005.

Guillén, Mauro and Adrian Tschoegl. 'The Internationalization of Retail Banking: The Case of the Spanish Banks in Latin America'. *Transnational Corporations* 9, no. 3 (2000): 63–97.

Hachette, Dominique and Rolf Luders. *Privatization in Chile: An Economic Appraisal*. San Francisco: International Center for Economic Growth, 1993.

Harmer, Tanya. *Allende's Chile and the Inter-American Cold War*. Chapel Hill: University of North Carolina Press, 2011.

Harvey, David. *A Brief History of Neo-Liberalism*. Oxford: Oxford University Press, 2005.

Heneeus, Pablo. *Chile un país dividido: La actualidad del pasado*. Santiago: Catalonia, 2003.

Heneeus, Pablo. *El régimen de Pinochet*. Santiago: Taurus, 2016.

Hite, Katherine. *When the Romance Ended: Leaders of the Chilean Left, 1968–1998*. New York: Columbia University Press, 2000.

Home, Alistair. *Kissinger: 1973, the Crucial Year*. New York: Simon and Schuster, 2009.

Ibáñez, Adolfo. *Herido en el ala: Estado, oligarquías y subdesarrollo*. Santiago: Editorial Biblioteca Americana, 2003.

Icarus Films. 'The Battle of Chile'. Accessed on October 25, 2017. http://icarusfilms.com/if-boc.

ITT-CTC. *Memoria Anual*. Santiago: ITT-CTC, various years.

Jodice, David A. 'Sources of Change in Third World Regimes for Foreign Direct Investment'. *International Organization* 34, no. 2 (1980): 177–206.

Jones, Geoffrey. *Multinationals and Global Capitalism: From the Nineteenth to the Twenty-First Century*. Oxford: Oxford University Press, 2005.

Lewis, Arthur. 'Economic Development With Unlimited Supplies of Labor'. *The Manchester School* 22, no. 2 (1954): 139–191.

López, Ana M. 'The Battle of Chile: Documentary, Political Process, and Representation'. In *The Social Documentary in Latin America*, edited by Julianne Burton, 267–287. Pittsburgh: Pittsburgh University Press, 1990.

Love, Joseph. 'The Rise and Decline of Economic Structuralism in Latin America: New Dimensions'. *Latin American Research Review* 40, no. 3 (2005): 100–125.

Martínez, Gabriela. *Latin American Telecommunications: Telefónica's Conquest*. Lanham: Lexington Books, 2008.

Meller, Patricio. 'Una perspectiva de largo plazo del desarrollo económico chileno, 1880–1990'. In *Trayectorias divergentes: comparación de un siglo de desarrollo económico latinoamericano y escandinavo*, edited by Patricio Meller and Magnus Blomström. Santiago: CIEPLAN, 1990.

Monteón, Michael. *Chile and the Great Depression: The Politics of Underdevelopment, 1927–1948*. Tempe: University of Arizona Press, 1998.

Moulian, Tomás. *Fracturas: De Pedro Aguirre Cerda a Salvador Allende, 1938–1973*. Santiago: LOM, 2006.

Muñoz, Heraldo. *The Dictator's Shadow*. Philadelphia: Basic Books, 2008.

Oppenheim, Lois. *Politics in Chile: Socialism, Authoritarianism, and Market Democracy*. Boulder: Westview, 2007.

Oxford-Montevideo Economic History Database. 'MOxLaD Database'. Accessed December 1, 2017. www.lac.ox.ac.uk/moxlad-database.

Qureshi, Lubna. *Nixon, Kissinger, and Allende: US Involvement in the 1973 Coup in Chile*. New York: Lexington Books, 2009.

Rossinow, Doug. *The Reagan Era: A History of the 1980s*. New York: Columbia University Press, 2017.

Salmon, Keith. 'Spanish Foreign Direct Investment, Transnationals and the Redefinition of the Spanish Business Realm'. *International Journal of Iberian Studies* 14, no. 2 (2001): 95–110.

Schneider, Ben Ross. *Business, Politics, and the State in Twentieth-Century Latin America*. Cambridge: Cambridge University Press, 2004.

Silva, Eduardo. 'Business Elites, the State, and Economic Change in Chile'. In *Business and the State in Developing Countries*, edited by Sylvia Maxfield and Ben Ross Schneider, 152–191. Ithaca: Cornell University Press, 1997.
Silva, Patricio. 'Technocrats and Politics in Chile: From the Chicago Boys to the CIEPLAN Monks'. *Journal of Latin American Studies* 23, no. 2 (1991): 385–410.
Sobel, Robert. *ITT: The Management of Opportunity*. New York: Beard Books, 1982.
Solimano, Andrés. 'Three Decades of Neoliberal Economics in Chile: Achievements, Failures, and Dilemmas'. In *Achieving Development Success: Strategies and Lessons From the Developing World*, edited by Agustín Fosu, 321–359. Oxford: Oxford University Press, 2013.
Spain, Spanish Embassy in Chile. *Inversiones españolas en Chile*. Santiago: Spanish Embassy in Chile, 2008.
Tortella, Gabriel. *The Development of Modern Spain*. Cambridge, MA: Harvard University Press, 2000.
United States Senate. Select Committee on Foreign Relations. *The International Telephone and Telegraph in Chile, 1970–71*. Washington, DC: U.S. Government Printing Office, 1973.
United States Senate. Select Committee to Study Governmental Operations with Respect to Intelligence Activities. *Covert Action in Chile, 1963–1973*. Washington, DC: U.S. Government Printing Office, 1975.
Valdaliso, Jesús María. 'Grupos empresariales, marco institucional y desarrollo económico en España en el siglo XX: los negocios de la familia Aznar (c. 1937–c. 1983)'. *Revista de Historia Económica* 20, no. 3 (2002): 577–624.
Valdivia, Verónica. *El golpe después del golpe: Leigh vs. Pinochet, 1960–1980*. Santiago: LOM, 2005.
Velázquez-Gaztelu, Juan Pedro. *Capitalismo a la española*. Madrid: La esfera de los libros, 2015.
Vistazo. 'Ocho sociedades con cuñas en diez poderosos bancos'. *Vistazo* 596 (1963): 11.
Vives, Jaume. *An Economic History of Spain*. Princeton: Princeton University Press, 1969.
Wadhwani, R. Daniel and Marcelo Bucheli. 'The Future of the Past in Management and Organization Studies'. In *Organizations in Time: History, Theory, Methods*, edited by Marcelo Bucheli and R. Daniel Wadhwani, 1–36. Oxford: Oxford University Press, 2014.
Willis, Kate. *Theories and Practices of Development*. New York: Routledge, 2005.
Wright, Alison. *The Spanish Economy, 1959–1976*. New York: Holmes and Meier, 1977.
Wright, Thomas C. and Rody Onate Zúñiga. 'Chilean Political Exile'. *Latin American Perspectives* 4, no. 31 (2007): 31–49.

Index